Corner House Publishers

LITERATURE REPRINT SERIES

❀ ❀ ❀

General Editor MAURICE FILLER

PLATE I

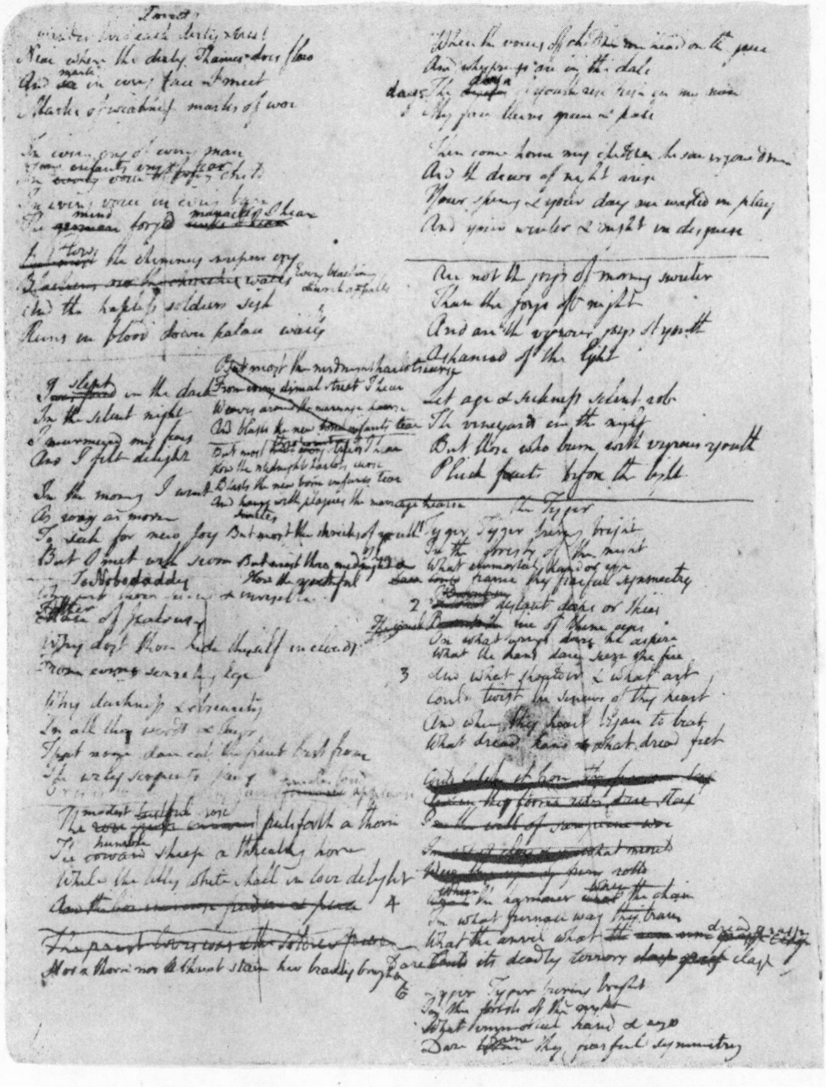

ROSSETTI MS., p. 109 (reversed), showing early draft of some of the *Songs of Experience* and other poems, written circa 1793. See p. 149, Index to Rossetti MS.

THE POETICAL WORKS

OF

WILLIAM BLAKE

A NEW AND VERBATIM TEXT FROM THE MANUSCRIPT ENGRAVED AND LETTERPRESS ORIGINALS

WITH

VARIORUM READINGS AND BIBLIOGRAPHICAL NOTES AND PREFACES

BY

JOHN SAMPSON

LIBRARIAN IN THE UNIVERSITY OF LIVERPOOL

CORNER HOUSE PUBLISHERS

WILLIAMSTOWN, MASSACHUSETTS 01267

1978

HENRY FROWDE, M.A.
PUBLISHER TO THE UNIVERSITY OF OXFORD
LONDON, EDINBURGH
NEW YORK AND TORONTO

THIS EDITION WAS
FIRST PUBLISHED IN 1905

REPRINTED 1978

BY

CORNER HOUSE PUBLISHERS

In Memoriam

FREDERICK YORK POWELL

GENERAL PREFACE

I. TEXT

THE literary remains of William Blake fall into three broad and generally recognized divisions, poetry, prose, and the prophetic books. The present work is a complete collection of Blake's poems, including all lyrical and metrical pieces scattered throughout his prose works and visionary writings.

This edition furnishes readers with a new text, literally reproduced from the original manuscript, engraved, and printed sources. The primary object has been to recover and present Blake's own version of his poetry without the customary attempts at emendation. Apart from the natural question whether most editors of Blake are competent to effect improvement in the works of a man of singular and individual genius, it may perhaps be pertinent to recall that no writer would have more strongly resented interference with his own mode of expression than he who held that 'every minute particular is holy' and that 'no one can finish so high as the original inventor.' Even if we assume, with one of these critics, that what he styles a 'disservice' is done to the poet by reprinting his works without correction, there may still be some so curious as to desire to refer to his poems in the form which commended itself to their author.

That such a restoration of text should be necessary at all in the case of a modern writer whose works have passed through many editions may seem to require explanation. The reasons, however, lie on the surface.

First should be specified the difficulties encountered in referring to the originals. It should be remembered that during Blake's lifetime few of his poems were either printed or published in the usual manner. His first work, the *Poetical Sketches*, was indeed produced in ordinary typography, but only a few copies were issued to friends, and the little volume remained so rare, that until its recent acquisition by the British Museum it might be regarded as generally inaccessible. Our great national libraries are still very deficient in first editions of Blake. Most examples of the engraved works are widely scattered in the libraries of private collectors in this country and in America, and since the various impressions of the same book often differ from one another in contents and arrangement, the collation of several copies is necessary if incorrect conclusions are to be avoided. Still greater difficulties exist in the case of poems which Blake himself never engraved or published. The MSS. in which these are found have always been private possessions, and even when the courtesy of owners has permitted them to be made use of, the work of transcription is full of pitfalls for the copyist. Many of the poems are hastily or not over legibly written, and unfamiliarity with Blake's hand accounts for a number of errors which have crept into the published texts. Again several pieces are left by their author in rough draft, and Blake's various changes, additions, and mode of indicating his successive rearrangements of lines and stanzas, exact careful study before his final intention can be accurately determined. A few misreadings must also be attributed to the inability of editors to decipher their own transcripts, originating in this way errors which tend to become fixed. Thus we find Gilchrist, followed by all later editors, misreading ' icy dungeons ' for ' my dungeons,' though the latter is clearly engraved in the original impressions of ' The Keys of the Gates.'

A further and more important source of error is to be found in the changes which some of Blake's editors have deliberately introduced. It is comprehensible that Dante Gabriel Rossetti, in his desire to present an almost unknown poet to the public in as favourable a light as possible, should have considered himself justified in making grammatical and other changes in the endeavour to remove what he regarded as blemishes. Yet, even in this case, every lover of Blake must feel that the intended emendations not only are made on no consistent principle, but are often destructive of the happy grace and artless simplicity of the original. No equally valid defence can be made for the perversions of more recent editors, especially if new readings, which can hardly be regarded as improvements, are found in conjunction with professions of scrupulous regard for textual fidelity. Reference to the variorum readings given in the footnotes to the present edition will show the extent to which this passion for emendation has been carried. It will be seen that scarcely a single poem or even epigram has been suffered to remain as Blake wrote it. Words and phrases are changed, stanzas are transposed or omitted, and readings destructive of sense, syntax, and prosody are introduced without obvious reason. Unauthorized titles are added which, as in the case of 'Broken Love,' impart to the poem a meaning undreamt of by its author. Two or more lyrics are printed as one, and vice versa. In one instance a new piece has been created out of three shorter poems welded together by a line which is apparently the composition of the ingenious and modest editor. Blake's text has, in short, become a sort of poor palimpsest where each new owner has overwritten his own poetry. Liberties such as no one would venture on with Burns or Shelley, are everywhere taken with Blake by those who still profess their admiration for his 'exquisite metrical gift and rightness of form.' It is not a little bewildering to find one great poet and critic extolling Blake for the 'glory of metre' and 'sonorous beauty of lyrical work' in the two opening lyrics of the *Songs of Experience*, while he introduces into the five short stanzas quoted no less than seven emendations of his own, involving additions of syllables and important changes of meaning.

In the present edition Blake's final version is uniformly adopted as the text, while all earlier or cancelled readings are supplied in footnotes. The spelling and capitalization of the original are adhered to throughout. That Blake himself attached some importance to the use of capitals for the sake of emphasis or artistic effect, is apparent from the careful manner in which he has added them as corrections in the revised versions of several of his MS. poems, or in the engraved form of songs found also in rough draft. In my retention of Blake's orthography I have been influenced not only by the desire to preserve as far as possible the colour of the original in such pleasant archaisms as ' desart,' ' tyger,' and ' lilly,' but also by the fact that in some instances his own spelling is a valuable aid to the just reading of lines or stanzas. In all existing editions the melody of many of the songs has been marred by ignoring the fact that Blake's use of ''d' or ' ed,' in the participle or preterite, was never arbitrary, but based on system. Both in his manuscript and engraved books he followed the contemporary practice of using the latter only when he intended the final syllable to be separately pronounced. I have thought it better to prevent any misconception on this point by retaining the 'd in the former case, and, in the latter, by supplying an accent which is not in the original.

In the matter of punctuation the poet has left his editors almost entirely to their own resources. Blake's autograph MSS. are, as a rule, without points of any kind, while those in the engraved books are inserted in such a haphazard manner that, if reproduced, they would only serve to confuse the reader. I have accordingly supplied my own punctuation; though Blake's pointing, where it occurs, has been taken into consideration, and occasionally, as in the third stanza of ' The Tyger,' is an indication of the way in which a particular passage was intended to be read. Blake omitted apostrophes and inverted commas in his engraved as well as in his manuscript writings, and it should be understood that when these are found in the text they have been added at the discretion of the editor. The detail is not a purely trivial one, since Blake's omission of quotation marks contributes to the difficulty of obscure poems by leaving it questionable to whom particular speeches should be assigned. Instances of possible confusion arising from this cause may be noted in 'The Everlasting Gospel,' in which it is sometimes not apparent where quoted speeches end and Blake resumes the discourse in his own person; or in the poem beginning 'My spectre around me night and day,' where the untabulated persons of the drama are the narrator, his 'spectre,' and his 'emanation,'—characters whose respective parts are not immediately obvious to those who will have no dealings with the visionary writings.

II. NOTES

The notes to the poems are of several kinds.

1. In the first place, the source of every poem is stated, with precise reference to the page or folio of the printed, engraved, or manuscript book from which each is taken. I add also, where necessary, the names of the editors or commentators by whom the poem has been printed. The phrase 'all editors' must of course be understood to refer to those only who print some version of a particular poem. In the case of the Rossetti MS., for example, it necessarily excludes Wilkinson and Shepherd, who print no part of this MS.

2. All Blake's earlier or cancelled readings are given in footnotes in the order of composition.

3. These are followed by the variant readings of all editors who have not merely reprinted some existing text. Differences are noted in all cases except where they consist only of trivial variations of spelling, capitals, or punctuation.

4. In every case where a poem has been left in rough draft, or has been subjected to repeated alterations, I have

endeavoured to explain the author's mode of composition by longer prefatory or appended notes, indicating the successive changes by which he arrived at his final version. Interesting examples of the pains taken by Blake in perfecting his verses will be found in the notes to ' The Tyger,' ' Fayette,' and ' The Everlasting Gospel.' These not only supply the student with data which, were the actual MS. before him, could only be ascertained after considerable study, but enable him to follow for himself the reasons that have led the editor to arrange lines or stanzas in the order in which they appear in the text.

5. Many poems would prove unintelligible were it not for the light thrown upon them by the Prophetic Books, where the key to obscure mystical allusions is generally to be found. Readers of Blake's simpler poetry only who, with Mr. W. M. Rossetti, turn from the visionary writings after a ' hasty and half-shuddering glance,' will be ignorant of the consistency with which his self-invented system of mythology is expounded, and the absolute uniformity with which definite symbolical figures are used to express definite conceptions. While Blake has been at little pains to supply the world with a chart of his mental voyagings, it is impossible to study the prophetical writings without becoming aware of the extreme precision of his mystical terminology. In the books of Euclid such terms as ' radius,' ' pentagon,' ' equal,' or ' parallel ' are not more absolutely descriptive of certain mathematical figures or relations, than are such locutions as ' Jerusalem,' ' spectre,' ' emanation,' ' hermaphrodite,' or ' natural religion ' of symbolic meanings in the writings of Blake. I have therefore endeavoured to make the poet his own interpreter by appending to these poems elucidatory passages from the Prophetic Books, coupled occasionally with brief explanations of what I conceive to have been his meaning. The value of these references in the interpretation of difficult poems like ' My spectre around me ' in the Rossetti MS. or ' The Mental Traveller ' in the Pickering MS. will not

pass unnoticed. And even in such comparatively simple
lines as the verses to Butts beginning 'With happiness
stretch'd across the hills,' the allusion to the 'rock' and
'cave' in l. 40 may only be understood through the associa-
tions of the same figures in *The Four Zoas* and *Jerusalem*.
While interpretation is here restricted to passages in the
lyrical poems which seem to require explanation, the editor
may claim that the parallelisms from the Prophetic Books
have been selected after many readings of the visionary
writings, and with some knowledge of the chief literature
written around them.

6. I have similarly illustrated Blake's epigrams on art
and artists by quotations from prose writings where his
opinions or prejudices are expressed with his customary
energy and conviction.

7. I give also occasional indications of the date or place at
which particular poems were written, as well as cross references to lines or passages repeated in different pieces. As
these repetitions have been adduced as evidence of Blake's
poverty of thought and language in Mr. Henry Gay Hewlett's
ingenious article in the *Contemporary Review*, it may be
proper to point out that the writings from which identical expressions are borrowed were not published by their author,
nor was it probably contemplated by him that they would
ever see the light. In only a single instance, that of the
'Mad Song' (*Poetical Sketches*) and 'Infant Sorrow' (*Songs
of Experience*), has a line been transferred from one printed
work to another, and as I have elsewhere explained, Blake
never seems to have regarded the privately printed *Poetical
Sketches* as one of his actual publications.

III. ARRANGEMENT

There is some reason to suppose that most of the existing
groupings of Blake's poems would have fallen under the
poet's lash for those whose 'chiefest arts' are to 'blend and
not define the parts.' If 'to make out the parts,' as he assures

us, ' is the wise man's aim,' it becomes a task of no little difficulty when such editorial titles as ' Ideas of Good and Evil,'
'Miscellaneous Poems,' or 'Later Poems,' are arbitrarily used
to comprehend pieces collected from a number of undefined
sources belonging to widely different periods. In one case
at least the heading ' Later Poems ' is made to include a
song written in Blake's early youth.

The present arrangement conserves the integrity of the
various books, whether letterpress, engraved, or in manuscript, ' every one in its own identity.' In each of these
groups the poetical contents are printed in the order in
which they occur in the original, a plan which has the
advantage of illustrating how poems found in juxtaposition
have often been suggested by or grown out of one another.
It is also in many cases a valuable aid to the dating of
particular pieces.

This arrangement is of course a bibliographical, rather
than a purely historical one. While the contents of the
Pickering MS. are obviously all of a kind and written about
the same time, those of the larger Rossetti MS. extend over
a period of more than twenty years and are of the most
diverse character. The latter is indeed of the nature of a
notebook, the earliest poetic entries in which antedate the
publication of the *Songs of Experience* and the latest
postdate most of the Prophetic Books. The three broad
sections into which its contents fall are however clearly
marked and occasion no confusion. The first of these,
written about 1793, consists chiefly of lyrical poems,
including the original drafts of many of the *Songs of
Experience*. Between the first and second section inter-
vened a period of about seven years, during which Blake
wrote and engraved the shorter Prophetic Books. The
earlier pieces in the second section include a few poems
written in a strain of more highly developed mysticism,
among them first drafts of certain lyrics afterwards transcribed into the Pickering MS., or engraved as part of
Jerusalem. Before we reach the epigrams, which were

an overflow from Blake's marginalia to Reynolds' '*Dis-courses*,' the Pickering MS., the letters to Butts, and some portion at least of *Jerusalem* and *Milton* had been written. Lastly, as the third section, we have the fragments of 'The Everlasting Gospel'—the latest of Blake's surviving poems with the possible exception of 'The Keys of the Gates.'

In the bibliographical prefaces to the various sections I have tried to give fairly full and accurate accounts of printed books or manuscripts which have hitherto been somewhat slightly or incorrectly described. All accessible copies of the *Songs of Innocence and of Experience* have been collated, and Blake's successive arrangements tabulated and classified. A complete index of the contents of the Rossetti MS. is given; and the Pickering MS., or 'smaller autograph collection,' is described for the first time. I have also supplied brief bibliographical descriptions of the manuscript and engraved Prophetic Books, and have made some corrections in the dates of their composition or publication. Comparison of a number of copies has established the fact that there were three several editions of *The Gates of Paradise*, the two later only including the verses which distinguish the issue 'For the Sexes.' In my notes to this book I have drawn attention to a hitherto ignored publication of Blake, his *History of England for Children*, a companion volume to *The Gates of Paradise*; and possibly the list of its contents recovered from the MS. Book may be the means of bringing this lost work to light. The attention of the curious bibliophile may also be directed to the entry in the Rossetti MS. (p. 56) that 'This day is Publish'd Advertizements to Blake's Canterbury Pilgrims from Chaucer, containing anecdotes of Artists.' This may of course have been merely an experimental draft of a notice for insertion in the newspapers in case he thought fit to publish as a pamphlet with this title the paragraphs jotted down in his notebook. On the other hand, it is not improbable that it may have been printed for him in the same manner as the *Descriptive Catalogue*, possibly by the same printer, D. N. Shury, and that a copy may still be discovered, preserved perhaps, as is so often the case, by being bound up with contemporary tracts. Among other lost works of Blake may be mentioned the first book of the *French Revolution*, said to have been published by Johnson in 1791, and the engraved *Book of Outhoon*. Works referred to by Blake himself, but of which no trace is known, are *The Book of Moonlight*, and *Barry: a Poem*.

IV. BLAKE'S ILLUMINATED PRINTING

It is to Blake's singular mode of publication that we must attribute the scanty recognition accorded to his poetic genius during his own lifetime, as his public was necessarily restricted to the few friends or patrons who had obtained copies of his works from ' the Author and Printer.' The circumstances under which he first conceived the idea of producing his books by his invention of relief engraving possess therefore much more than the merely technical interest attaching to a new and curious art process.

According to the commonly received account it was in consequence of his failure to secure a publisher for the *Songs of Innocence* in the ordinary way, and of his extreme indigence which prohibited him from bringing out the book in letterpress at his own cost, that Blake was driven to resort to the laborious expedient of engraving and printing the *Songs* by his own hand. Verisimilitude is added by the picture of the poet's wife ' going out with their last half-crown to buy the necessary materials,' a detail of but little relevance when it is remembered that the engraving, printing, and colouring of the first issue occupied an entire year. I believe this story, which may be traced to a loose statement of Gilchrist's, to be without foundation.

In the first place it may be observed that the supposition

that Blake desired to put his Songs into circulation through
the medium of a publisher is altogether at variance with
that characteristic independence which led him throughout
his life to do most things for himself in his own way,
regardless of toil which he loved, and disdainful of external
assistance. In the case of Blake's earlier work, the *Poetical
Sketches*, the sheets of which, printed in letterpress at the
expense of Mathew and Flaxman, were, as Smith tells us,
handed to the author to publish or sell privately as he saw
fit, he seems to have made no attempt to dispose of the
copies through a bookseller or even to sell them personally.
While there is no positive evidence that such was the case
it is not improbable that he himself may have destroyed
the greater part of this small edition. Blake, it must be
remembered, was an artist as well as a poet, and the same
attitude of mind which caused him on being shown
a number of the *Mechanic's Magazine* to exclaim 'these
things we artists HATE!' doubtless led him to regard as
unworthy of him a book in which his conceptions were
inadequately presented by a merely mechanical and somewhat unlovely process. His deliberate exclusion of the
Poetical Sketches from the catalogue of his works offered
for sale in 1793—a list which includes books produced by
ordinary engraving as well as by 'illuminated printing'—
seems to me to support this view.

It is more reasonable to conclude that Blake brought
out his books himself by his own process, because no
publisher or printer could have produced for him the new
kind of illustrated work which he had in his mind. The
method then in vogue admitted of artistic embellishments
only in the shape of steel or wood engravings, stiffly
surrounding or clumsily placed in juxtaposition to the
type of the text, while that of Blake interwove text, design,
and colouring into one harmonious whole with the happiest
and most exquisite effect.

Relating the story of the invention of this process,
Blake's biographers have represented it rather in the

light of a happy accident than as a deliberate attempt to deal with a clearly realized artistic difficulty. According to the account derived from Smith, this mode of engraving was revealed to him in a vision by the spirit of his favourite brother Robert, and there is no particular reason to doubt that, in a dream or daydream, Blake may have solved a problem which had long occupied his thoughts. Striking confirmation of the fact that at least five years before the publication of the *Songs of Innocence* he had contemplated—and not entirely, it may be noted, without a view to the superior profits of such a work— some new kind of illuminated printing is found in the early MS. known as *An Island in the Moon*. This passage begins, imperfectly, at the head of the recto of the ninth leaf : '. . . " Illuminating the Manuscript"—" Ay," said she, " that would be excellent." " Then," said he, " I would have all the writing Engraved instead of Printed, & at every other leaf a high finished print, all in three Volumes folio, and sell them a hundred pounds a piece. They would Print off two thousand." " Then," said she, " whoever will not have them, will be ignorant fools & will not deserve to live." . . . " I was at Mrs. Sicknakers, & I was speaking of my abilities, but their nasty hearts, poor devils, are eat up with envy—they envy me my abilities, & all the Women envy your abilities, my dear ; they hate people who are of higher abilities than their nasty filthy Selves." '

The unfortunate loss of one or more leaves preceding the last page may have deprived us of a description of the literary contents of the book which the speaker Quid the Cynic (or Blake) designed to bring out in this manner. But since three of the most characteristic of the *Songs of Innocence* appear in rough draft in this MS., it seems not unlikely that Blake may have had already in view the completion of a series of songs for children ; perhaps suggested by Dr. Watts' *Divine and Moral Songs for Children*. In the preface to that popular book Watts

modestly refers to his songs as 'a slight specimen, such as
I could wish some happy and condescending genius would
undertake for the use of children, and perform much
better,' and it is likely enough that Blake may have rightly
felt himself to be this destined genius. It has been pointed
out by Mr. Hewlett, who, as I find, anticipated me in this
conjecture, that 'the subjects of several of Blake's songs
are identical with those of Watts,' while it may also be
noted that the moral tags with which the 'Chimney
Sweeper,' 'Holy Thursday,' and other songs somewhat
abruptly conclude, recall the manner of Blake's didactic
prototype.

Though nowhere definitely stated by the poet himself,
we have no grounds for questioning Smith's statement
that the *Songs of Innocence* was the first of his works
engraved in this manner. A colophon to the *Ghost of
Abel*, 1822, the last of Blake's Prophetic Books, informs
us that 'W. Blake's Original Stereotype was 1788'; but
since this statement cannot possibly refer to an earlier
issue of the same sibylline leaflet, it probably means that
the first plate of the *Songs* was engraved in the year
preceding the publication of the completed book.

In Blake's prospectus 'To the Public' of October, 1793,
he styles this process 'illuminated printing,' a phrase
evidently suggested by the passage quoted above from
the *Island in the Moon*. 'The Author,' says Blake, 'has
invented a method of Printing both Letter-press and
Engraving in a style, more ornamental, uniform, and
grand, than any before discovered, while it produces works
at less than one-fourth of the expense. If a method of
Printing which combines the Painter and the Poet is
a phenomenon worthy of public attention, provided that
it exceeds in elegance all former methods, the Author
is sure of his reward.' Blake's observation as to the com-
parative cheapness of this mode of printing seems to
require some explanation, as it cannot be intended to
suggest that this illuminated printing was cheaper than

ordinary typography. Probably what he meant was that the engraving and printing of lettering and design simultaneously was less expensive than intaglio engraving and letterpress, printed separately by two different processes. The qualification should, of course, be understood, that to produce books in Blake's manner the author must be, as he was, his own artist, engraver, and printer.

V. LIFE

Little is known of the life of William Blake, though our ignorance is comfortably veiled from us in several existing biographies. It may be confessed at once that with regard to what Blake called his 'vegetative existence' we are almost wholly in the dark. The slightness of our knowledge of the events of his material career is, however, of little consequence. Blake's real life was a mental and spiritual one. And the only true biography must be that in which his own writings, rather than petty contemporary gossip, are made the foundation of an endeavour to trace this mental and spiritual development. To understand him, some degree of intellectual sympathy with an uncommon mind and temper is desirable, and a larger visionary endowment than that which he esteemed the merely deceptive faculty of 'seeing with, and not *through*, the eye.' We need too some deeper study than has yet been attempted of the sources from which he received and absorbed his ideas— notably the influence of the Wesleyan revival, his precise debt to Swedenborg, and later, the manner in which the doctrines of the French Revolution affected one who, although the very opposite of reactionary, was antagonistic to the scientific spirit in all its works and ways. Such a task should not be undertaken with slight equipment, or in a spirit of condescension towards 'our good Blake,' the somewhat illiterate, but amiable enthusiast, who, though 'slightly touched,' was capable now and then of happy flights of fancy which are to be sought for as oases in the Sahara of his writings. To some of those who have essayed to follow with more or less success Blake's almost untrodden path, the converse is rather the case,

> 'And every sand becomes a Gem
> Reflected in the beams Divine,
> Blown back they blind the mocking eye
> But still in Israel's paths they shine.'

That Blake's life was to himself a harmony is undoubted, nor is it less clear that it was also in the fullest sense, borrowing the phrase which Shelley applied to his own, an 'impassioned pursuit of virtue.' To represent this mental, moral, and artistic harmony is the difficult work awaiting him who would present Blake aright, grasping at such pieces of self-revelation as the writings afford, studying the influences which touched him and the degree in which they were modified by a naturally heretical mind ; and tracing step by step through the surviving Prophetic Books the evolution of the extraordinary system of mythology created by him for the expression of his philosophical and religious views.

This true line of investigation first apprehended by Wilkinson, and finely expressed with entire insight and sympathy by the author of *The City of Dreadful Night*, has been carried further by Swinburne in that *Essay* which, were Blake's remaining works destroyed by a new Tatham, would still remain a sufficing monument to his genius.

The chief sources of our knowledge of Blake's life are particularized below.

1. *Autobiographical.* Despite the destruction of the greater part of the MSS. much autobiographical material survives in his pictures, MS. Book, letters, marginalia, and published and unpublished writings, delineating Blake in his 'threefold' character of artist, poet, and mystic.

Blake's pictorial art may be studied at first hand from examples preserved in the British Museum or in private collections, as also in his engraved works or in various facsimiles. His views on the province of art, and criticisms of schools of painters, are expounded at length in his *Descriptive Catalogue* of his exhibition of 1809, in his *Advertisement* or ' Public Address,' of 1810, in the jottings in his copy of Reynolds' *Discourses*, and epigrams in the MS. Book, and in the aphorisms in his sibylline leaflet, the *Laocoon*. *Barry: a Poem* must unfortunately be numbered among lost works.

In the field of literature Blake's early study, as Malkin tells us, was of the Elizabethans. His attitude to eighteenth-century verse may be noted in his lines ' To the Muses,' or in the contemptuous reference to ' tinkling rhymes and elegances terse ' in the youthful *Poetical Sketches*. We meet here also with the imitations of Macpherson, continued in *Tiriel* and *Thel* ; but a more lasting and potent influence was that of Milton, to which may be attributed the metrical experiments of the Prophetic Books, the shorter rhythms being evidently suggested by the choruses in *Samson*, and the preface to *Jerusalem* showing that in this attempt at a new cadence Blake was deliberately following the example set by the author of *Paradise Lost*. Even Blake's phrases and subject-matter, which, except in the purely imitative *Poetical Sketches*, are almost entirely his own, may occasionally be traced to the same source, as in the opening lines of *Europe*, reminiscent of the ' Ode on the Morning of Christ's Nativity ' :—

> ' The deep of winter came ;
>   What time the secret child
> Descended thro' the orient gates of the eternal day.
> War ceas'd, & all the troops, like shadows, fled
>   to their abodes.'

Minor influences may be detected in the epigrams in the manner of Wolcot ; in the lyrics from the Prophetic Books which often recall the hymns of Charles Wesley, and in the grotesque Hudibrastic lilt of ' The Everlasting Gospel.'

Blake's Prophetic Books tell us what is known of his mystical religion and philosophy. It is in the message, rather than in the manner of its delivery, that their chief worth lies. As little as S. Paul's Epistle to the Romans can they be regarded as the practice of literature for its own sake. The value of Blake's letters to Butts, obviously written to a friend to whom he could speak without fear of misconception, is enhanced by the fact that they belong to the period when he conceived and in part produced his great works *Milton* and *Jerusalem*.

Most of the epigrams in the MS. Book illustrate Blake's relations with his friends and patrons ; while certain of them (as perhaps cxiv) throw light upon his private life, of which almost nothing is known.

2. A short but valuable account of Blake's early life and literary and artistic predilections is given by Malkin in his *Father's Memoirs of His Child*, in an introductory letter to Thomas Johnes, of Hafod, dated January 4, 1806. This was written when Blake was forty-nine years of age, and Doctor Malkin, for whose book Blake designed the frontispiece, twelve years his junior. The facts there given were evidently derived from the poet himself.

3. Hunt's *Examiner* for Sunday, September 17, 1809, contains a critique of 'Mr. Blake's Exhibition,' impugning the artist's sanity in offensive terms. This attack is indignantly referred to by Blake in several of the epigrams written in the Rossetti MS.

4. John Linnell, portrait and landscape painter, was introduced to Blake by Mr. George Cumberland, of Bristol, in 1818 (not 1813 as stated by Gilchrist), and thenceforward remained Blake's steadfast friend and supporter. To his assistance we owe the great work of Blake's old age, his 'Inventions to the Book of Job,' designs which had been executed for Butts, but were only engraved at the instance of his friend. Mr. Linnell left certain memoranda referring to the poet, while among other entries in his private journal are notes of several transactions made on Blake's behalf. These documents are now in the possession of Mr. John Linnell, junior.

5. Frederick Tatham, sculptor and miniature painter, was the son of Charles Heathcote Tatham, architect, who made Blake's acquaintance through Linnell. About 1825, when a youth of twenty or twenty-one, the younger Tatham met Blake and, unfortunately for the world, became one of the small group of neophytes. On the death of the poet's wife in October, 1831, Tatham acquired, or appropriated, the whole of Blake's literary remains, which he afterwards destroyed, as we are told, on 'religious grounds.' This person wrote a memoir of Blake which he appears to have parted with for purely secular reasons. Lost sight of for some time, and fruitlessly sought by Gilchrist, it reappeared in the Blamire sale in 1863, bound in with an illuminated copy of *Jerusalem* (see *Rossetti Papers*, 1862–1870 *passim*). This MS. life, which no one seems to have thought worth printing in full, has been used and quoted by Swinburne, Ellis and Yeats, and others, though they do not appear to have gleaned from this source any new facts of real importance. Those given, however, presumably possess the interest of having been derived from Catherine Blake, who, for a short time before her death, had been an inmate of the miniature painter's household. Tatham's misstatement of the date of Blake's birth (which misled Swinburne) does not suggest habits of accuracy ; and Richard Garnett, who met him later in life, refers to him as a man on whose word no reliance could be placed.

My knowledge of Tatham's Memoir, which I have not been able to see, is limited to the extracts quoted therefrom by Swinburne and others. The copy of *Jerusalem* with which it is bound up was re-sold at Sotheby's in June, 1887, to a London dealer, and is now the property of an owner who prefers that no description of its contents be given.

6. Henry Crabb Robinson, then in his fiftieth year, first met Blake at the home of Mr. Aders on December 10, 1825. His diary and letters contain accounts of Blake in his last years, interesting and valuable both as to his mystical opinions (not very clearly or sympathetically apprehended

by the diarist) and as to his views on the poetry of Words-
worth. These passages are reprinted together in Ellis and
Yeats' Memoir (*Works*, i. 142–150).

7. Blake died August 12, 1827. Short notices of his
life and works appeared in the *Literary Gazette*, the *Gentleman's Magazine*, and the *Annual Register* for the same
year.

8. In 1828 John Thomas Smith, Keeper of the Prints
and Drawings in the British Museum, published his *Nollekins and his Times*, which has been not inaptly described
as the most candid biography written in the English language. The second volume, as the title-page states, com-
prehends 'Memoirs of several contemporary Artists from
the time of Roubiliac, Hogarth, and Reynolds, to that of
Fuseli, Flaxman, and Blake.' Scant justice has hitherto
been done to this admirable little life, which gives for the
first time the greater part of the material upon which
Cunningham and Gilchrist based their biographies. Smith's
acquaintance with Blake dates from his early days at the
Mathews' to the close of the poet's life. This contemporary
picture drawn with intelligent sympathy by one who knew
him well is of the utmost value; and Smith's tribute to
Blake's genius, sanity, and lofty character, coming from the
pen of one who was the reverse of a hero-worshipper, is
sufficient refutation of the contrary view.

9. In 1830 Allan Cunningham published his *Lives of the
Most Eminent British Painters, Sculptors, and Architects*,
among which is a biography of Blake. This gaily and
rather irreverently written little life is mainly derived from
Smith's *Nollekins*, and while it shows no particular research
or regard for accuracy has preserved a few anecdotes of
Blake which probably would have otherwise disappeared.

10. About 1860, when Linnell, Tatham, Samuel Palmer,
Richmond, and a few other friends and contemporaries of
the poet were still living, Alexander Gilchrist began his *Life
of Blake*, "*Pictor Ignotus*." Gilchrist, in Rossetti's words,
'lived next door to Carlyle and was as near him in other

respects as he could manage,' and his style betrays the influence of his model. There is also a tendency to dwell unduly upon unimportant incidents such as the 'Visionary Heads,' which gives the portrait a lack of proportion. Practically the whole of the first volume had been written, and the first eight chapters printed, when Gilchrist died on the 30th of November, 1861. The book, which was published two years later, was completed by his widow, aided by D. G. and W. M. Rossetti, the former supplying a supplementary chapter to the biography, and editing the 'Selections' from Blake's prose and verse, and the latter contributing a serviceable list of his pictures and engravings. The letters to Butts, 1800–1803, appear here for the first time. A second edition, with some new letters, was published in 1880. This *Life*, handsomely produced, and embellished with facsimiles of Blake's own glorious designs, achieved its main purpose in popularizing the poet, and in preparing the way for Swinburne's great critical appreciation. Gilchrist incorporates most of the material drawn from the preceding sources, though his manner of writing sometimes leaves it doubtful whether he is supplementing our knowledge or merely embroidering facts more simply narrated by earlier biographers.

11. Ellis and Yeats' Memoir, prefixed to their large edition of the *Works*, 1893, is especially intended, as the editors state, to supply new facts, or to discuss in greater detail aspects of Blake's life which they consider unsatisfactorily dealt with by Gilchrist. Of much importance, if substantiable on good evidence, is the discovery that Blake was of Irish ancestry, his grandfather, a certain John O'Neill, of Rathmines, Dublin, having assumed the name of Blake borne by his second wife. James O'Neill, his son by a previous union, also took the name of Blake, and settled in London, where he became the father of the poet. This account, however, is at variance with another, first given in Mr. Alfred T. Storey's *William Blake*, published in the same year, where, on the authority of two ladies, daughters

of William John Blake, of Southampton, claiming to be second cousins of the poet, Blake's descent is traced to the Somersetshire family with which the Commonwealth Admiral was connected. Without attempting the difficult task of reconciling these rival claims, it may be pointed out that Blake's father was certainly a Protestant, and that the poet, who in one instance describes himself as ' English Blake,' nowhere claims Irish descent. Messrs. Ellis and Yeats interpret the mysterious reference to Hayley's having ' hirèd a villain to bereave my life,' in the sense of his having conspired with Flaxman to deprive Blake of his means of livelihood, and identify the hired villain with Hunt, the author of the article in the *Examiner*. I refer elsewhere to these editors' interpretation of Blake's mystical writings.

12. Biographies of Blake derived from the above sources, but of interest as embodying personal appreciations of Blake's work, will be found in Alfred T. Storey's *William Blake, his Life, Character, and Genius*, 1893, in Richard Garnett's monograph in the *Portfolio*, 1895, and in the introductions of W. M. Rossetti, Laurence Housman and W. B. Yeats to their editions of the poems. In pure aesthetic criticism D. G. Rossetti's prefatory notes to the ' Selections ' printed in Gilchrist, James Thompson's Essay, and Swinburne's masterpiece hold the first place. Henry G. Hewlett's curious essay in depreciation, entitled ' Imperfect Genius ' (*Contemporary Review*, vol. 28), should also be noticed. An elaborate attempt to expound Blake's symbolic system in detail is contained in Ellis and Yeats' edition of the *Works*, and, more concisely stated, in Maclagan and Russell's Introduction to their reprint of *Jerusalem*, 1905.

VI. EDITIONS

The following is a list of the editions quoted in the footnotes. I refer to those only where use has been made of the original printed and manuscript sources, and where the readings given might for this reason be understood to possess some authority.

1. *Malk.*   A Father's Memoirs of his Child.   By Benj. Heath Malkin, Esq., M.A., F.A.S.   Longman, Hurst, Rees, and Orme, London.   1806.   8º.

Contains five songs from *Poetical Sketches* and *Songs of Innocence and of Experience*, printed presumably from copies supplied by Blake to the author.   Malkin's version of 'The Tyger' contains an interesting variant reading of l. 12.

2. *Cunn.*   The Lives of the most eminent British Painters, Sculptors, and Architects, by Allan Cunningham.   John Murray, London.   1829–1833.   6 vols.   16º.

Volume ii contains poems from *Poetical Sketches* and *Songs of Innocence and of Experience.*   To Cunningham's corrupt version of ' The Tyger ' may be traced the second or later version ' on MS. authority,' which has deceived so many of Blake's editors.

3. *Wilk.*   Songs of Innocence and of Experience, Shewing the two Contrary States of the Human Soul. (Dedication of the Poem of the Grave.)   W. Pickering and W. Newbery, London.   1839.   8º.

The first letterpress edition of the *Songs.*   Edited with a short but excellent preface by J. J. Garth Wilkinson, the translator of Swedenborg. In the *Dictionary of National Biography* and elsewhere, the text of this edition is described as ' much altered,' but as a matter of fact Wilkinson's emendations are somewhat fewer than those of later editors.

4. *R¹.*   Dante Gabriel Rossetti's original transcript of a portion of Blake's MS. Book.   See Bibliographical Preface to ' Poems from the Rossetti MS.'   This transcript was probably made about 1847, when Rossetti was still a youth.

These readings, furnished me by Mr. White, are here quoted for the first time.

5. *Gil.*   Life of William Blake, ' Pictor Ignotus,' with Selections from his poems and other writings by the late Alexander Gilchrist. . . . Illustrated from Blake's own works in facsimile by W. J. Linton and in Photolithography ; with a few of Blake's original plates.   In two volumes.   Vol. i. Macmillan, London.   1863.   8º.

Poems quoted by Gilchrist in the first volume of the *Life.*

6. *DGR*. The same. Volume ii.

Poems printed in the 'Selections' from Blake's works, given by D. G. Rossetti, in the second volume of Gilchrist's *Life*. Rossetti rejects some of the changes made in his earlier transcript, but retains others, and not infrequently adopts the readings of Wilkinson. With reference to these and other attempts at emendation introduced by him into Blake's text we may note Rossetti's later statement 'that he would not now, if the work were before him to be done, make so many alterations.' (See WMR's *Dante Gabriel Rossetti*, p. 165.)

7. *Swinb*. William Blake: A Critical Essay. By Algernon Charles Swinburne. With illustrations from Blake's designs in facsimile, coloured and plain. J. C. Hotten, London. 1868. 8°.

Contains poems quoted by Swinburne from Blake's published works and from the Rossetti MS. Book. From the latter source Swinburne prints several poems omitted by Rossetti, including the greater portion of 'The Everlasting Gospel.'

8. *Shep*. The Poems of William Blake. Comprising *Songs of Innocence and of Experience*, together with *Poetical Sketches*, and some copyright poems not in any other edition. Basil Montague Pickering, London. 1874. 8°.

This edition collects in a single volume Richard Herne Shepherd's earlier text of the *Songs of Innocence and* [*of*] *Experience, with other poems*, 1866 (reprinted in 1868) ; and that of the *Poetical Sketches*, 1868, all of which were published by B. M. Pickering. Shepherd was not able to print in his edition any of the poems from the Rossetti MS. His text of the poems included is, however, by far the most accurate of any hitherto published.

9. *WMR*. The Poetical Works of William Blake, Lyrical and Miscellaneous. Edited with a Prefatory Memoir by William Michael Rossetti. [Aldine Edition.] George Bell and Sons, London. 1874. 8°.

This popular edition has been frequently reprinted. The readings quoted in my footnotes are taken from a copy of the fourth edition, 1883.

10. *W. Muir's facsim.* Mr. William Muir's coloured facsimiles of the *Songs of Innocence* and the *Songs of Experience*. In the footnotes to *The Gates of Paradise* I refer also to Mr. Muir's text of the prologue and of the

'Keys of the Gates' prefixed in ordinary typography to his facsimile of *The Gates of Paradise*.

Admirable as facsimiles of Blake's coloured illustrations, these reproductions cannot be followed with any certainty for the text of the poems.

11. *E Y*. The Works of William Blake, Poetic, Symbolic, and Critical. Edited with Lithographs of the Illustrated 'Prophetic Books,' and a Memoir and Interpretation by Edwin John Ellis and William Butler Yeats. In three volumes. Bernard Quaritch, London. 1893. Large 8°.

In this edition the somewhat confusing arrangement of the Poems may perhaps be due to the editors' scheme of interpretation. For some of their text apparently Messrs. Ellis and Yeats have trusted to the Aldine edition, while part has been derived from Mr. Ellis' transcripts of the MS. Book and *The Four Zoas*. These editors, in expounding Blake's system, lay claim to special knowledge 'produced by the evocations of symbolic magic' (i. 288 and *passim*) ; and some of their remarks (e. g. ii. 299) would seem to suggest their belief that the possession of these occult powers enables them to produce a text through which Blake's mind is reflected more accurately than in the MSS. left by himself.

12. *WBY*. The Poems of William Blake. Edited by W. B. Yeats. [The Muses' Library.] Lawrence and Bullen, London. 1893. 8°.

In some respects a more correct text than the preceding. Reprinted by Routledge (1905).

13. *LH*. Selections from the writings of William Blake with an introductory essay by Lawrence Housman. Kegan Paul, Trench, Trübner, and Co. 1893. 8°.

I quote this edition only for the variant reading in the song taken from *An Island in the Moon*, since this MS. was in Mr. Housman's hands.

14. *Russell and Maclagan*. The Prophetic Books of William Blake. Jerusalem. Edited by E. R. D. Maclagan and A. G. B. Russell [*on cover* A. G. B. Russell and E. R. D. Maclagan]. Bullen, London. 1904. 4°.

Apparently intended as the first of a series of typographical reprints of Blake's Prophetic Books. Purports to be a verbatim and literatim reprint, but contains such misreadings as 'course' for 'race,' and 'By his own hand shall surely die' for 'By his own law shall surely die.'

VII

In a work involving much reference to material not lying ready to hand in any public library an editor is necessarily dependent upon the goodwill and co-operation of the owners of precious books and manuscripts. It is with gratitude that I acknowledge the invaluable aid rendered me in various ways by collectors and students of the works of Blake.

My debt to Mr. W. A. White, of Brooklyn, New York, the owner of the Rossetti MS., the Pickering MS., and other Blake originals, can best be made clear by an explanation of his share in the work. Entering into my desire to produce an accurate and final text of Blake's poems, Mr. White has for the past three years collaborated with me in this endeavour by furnishing me with exact transcripts of the poems in the MS. Book, and answering a very great number of questions of detail. I owe also to Mr. White the correct text of the smaller Pickering MS., which after a disappearance of over thirty years was opportunely rediscovered while this edition was in the press. I should not omit to explain that it was Mr. White's conjecture that *The Gates of Paradise* belonged to a later date than had been previously supposed, which led me, after a study of the symbolic references in the couplets explanatory of the plates, to form the conclusion that the two issues ' For the Sexes,' in which the poems first appear, must have been produced, not in 1793, but somewhere nearer 1810. Lastly, I am indebted to Mr. White for the two facsimiles of the MS. Book given in this edition.

To Mr. John Linnell, junior, I owe the correct text of the songs, and passages quoted in the footnotes from *The Four Zoas*, as well as the description of this MS., and details of copies of *The Gates of Paradise*, *The Ghost of Abel*, and other Blake originals in the possession of the Linnell family. Mr. Linnell has also furnished me with photographs of obscurely written lines in *The Four Zoas*, and has replied with great minuteness to several questions of mine relating to different works of Blake. My thanks are also due to Miss Isabelle Linnell and Mr. William Linnell.

I owe to the kindness of Mr. C. Fairfax Murray the loan of the autograph MS. known as *An Island in the Moon*, since presented by him to the Fitzwilliam Museum, as well as extracts from original letters of Flaxman throwing light upon the cause of Blake's estranged attitude towards his former friend. A hitherto unprinted poem (see p. 218) courteously sent me by Mr. A. G. B. Russell illustrates the earlier and happier relationship between the two artists.

I have to thank Captain Butts for the loan of Blake's letters to his grandfather, Mr. Thomas Butts, the artist's lifelong friend and patron. I am obliged to Mr. Bernard Quaritch for lending me the MS. of *Tiriel*. To Signora Helen Rossetti Angeli I tender my thanks for her kindness in sending me from Italy the early and curious Blake MS. containing 'The Passions' and another piece.

I have to acknowledge the courtesy of the various owners of copies of the *Songs of Innocence* and the *Songs of Experience*, enumerated in my Bibliographical Preface (pp. 72–77), for collations and details of the several impressions.

Mr. W. M. Rossetti kindly furnished me with his recollection of the lost book, the *French Revolution*, and also of the Pickering MS. which has since come to light. Mr. John Pearson in several communications has given me the benefit of his expert knowledge of original issues and reprints of works of Blake, and Mr. John Lawler has been good enough to supply me with information as to Blake originals sold by auction. Mr. Frederick Macmillan has taken great pains to clear up the question of the process by which the plates of the *Songs* were reproduced in Gilchrist's *Life*.

I am indebted to Mrs. Beach for research work in the British Museum in the early stages of this book. I am grateful to Mr. Cowley of the Bodleian Library for a courteous response to questions submitted by me, in the first place, to Mr. Madan; to Mr. Fortescue of the British

General Preface

Museum for personal replies to like inquiries ; and to Mr. Peter Cowell of the Liverpool Public Library for obtaining for me the loan of certain rare books. To Mr. Wilberforce Eames I owe information regarding the unique example of Blake's *Milton* in the Astor-Lenox Library.

I have pleasure in acknowledging the help of Mr. T. Harkness Graham, assistant in the University Library, in the reading and correction of the proofs, and the aid in various ways given me by Miss May Allen, Librarian to the Biological Library. The help rendered by the members of my class in bibliography, especially by Miss M. E. Lyster and Miss D. E. Yates, has contributed greatly to the accuracy of this edition.

Professor John Macdonald Mackay has been good enough to read certain of my proofs and prefaces.

In concluding this long list of obligations I desire to add that it was at the suggestion of the late Professor York Powell that I undertook, in a somewhat light-hearted mood, the preparation of a small edition of Blake's Lyrical Poems for the Clarendon Press. A cursory comparison of existing texts showed me the impossibility of giving a reliable version of Blake, even in the form of selections, without preliminary collation of the original engraved and manuscript sources. This view was accepted by the Delegates of the Press, and the present critical edition undertaken besides the smaller work at first proposed. I wish to thank the authorities of the Press, and especially Mr. H. S. Milford, for the care and patience with which they have carried out the 'minute particulars' of this book. The untimely death of Professor York Powell deprived me of advantages of advice and encouragement, given by him so generously at the outset of my task, and robs me now of much of the pleasure with which I bring to completion this edition of one of his favourite poets, which, imperfect though it be, I am fain to dedicate to his memory.

JOHN SAMPSON.

LIVERPOOL,
Nov. 20, 1905.

CONTENTS

Contents

Contents

Contents

ILLUSTRATIONS

POEMS

from the

POETICAL SKETCHES

(Privately Printed, 1783)

BIBLIOGRAPHICAL PREFACE

TO THE

POETICAL SKETCHES

THE *Poetical Sketches*, Blake's earliest work, is a slender demy octavo volume of 38 leaves, privately issued, without publisher's or printer's name. The title-page reads: POETICAL | SKETCHES. | By W. B. | LONDON: | Printed in the Year MDCCLXXXIII. The first quire of two leaves contains the title and 'advertisement'; then nine quires in fours, signed B—K (K⁴ blank) and paginated 1–70. There are no half-titles to the section 'Miscellaneous Poems' or to 'King Edward the Third.' The book is without index or table of literary contents, which are as follows:—

The little book, which is exceedingly rare, is the only one of Blake's poetical writings, except the first book of the *French Revolution*, which made its appearance in ordinary type. As we learn from Cunningham, it was printed at the expense of Flaxman and Mathew, who handed the unbound sheets to the author to dispose of for his own advantage. The size of the edition is not stated; but it was probably a small one, and of it Blake seems to have issued a few copies only. The Preface, which was the composition of Mathew, runs :—

'ADVERTISEMENT

' The following Sketches were the production of untutored youth, commenced in his twelfth, and occasionally resumed by the author till his twentieth year ; since which time, his talents having been wholly directed to the attainment of excellence in his profession, he has been deprived of the leisure requisite to such a revisal of these sheets, as might have rendered them less unfit to meet the public eye.

' Conscious of the irregularities and defects to be found in almost every page, his friends have still believed that they possessed a poetical originality, which merited some respite from oblivion. These their opinions remain, however, to be now reproved or confirmed by a less partial public.'

While the book contains a few obvious misprints, such as 'cares' for 'ears' in 'An Imitation of Spencer,' and 'her' for 'his' in the fourth stanza of the 'Song' on p. 12 ; yet its general inaccuracy is far less than has been represented, and by no means warrants such violent changes as D. G. Rossetti's 'rustling birds of dawn' for 'rustling beds of dawn' in the 'Mad Song.' The printer, while generally respecting Blake's use of 'd or ed where the latter is to be pronounced as a separate syllable, has evidently corrected Blake's spelling, omitted capitals, and supplied his own punctuation, frequently a faulty one. See 'Gwin, King of Norway,' where the lines,

> 'Arouse thyself! the nations, black
> Like clouds, come rolling o'er!'

are printed:

> 'Arouse thyself! the nations black,
> Like clouds, come rolling o'er!'

In the present edition punctuation is amended and the indented lines of the printer abandoned in favour of Blake's own invariable and more artistic alinement. In every other respect the text of the original edition is exactly reproduced.

The lyrics in *Poetical Sketches* include the whole of the poems on pp. 1–28, to which Blake, or perhaps Mathew, gives the title 'Miscellaneous Poems.' The other pieces fall somewhat outside the scope of this edition, but are supplied in an appendix in order that the reader may be enabled to judge of Blake's first volume in its entirety. The 'Poems from the *Poetical Sketches*' together with the pieces in the first Appendix give therefore, in their proper order, the whole contents of the book.

In a second Appendix I have placed two short poems, 'Song by a Shepherd' and 'Song by an Old Shepherd.' These songs are not printed among the poems in the *Poetical Sketches*, but were found in Blake's handwriting on the fly-leaves of a copy which was lent to Mr. Basil Montague Pickering, the publisher, about 1868. They clearly belong to the same period as the *Poetical Sketches*, though all Blake's editors arrange them among poems written in a different manner and at a much later date. First printed by R. H. Shepherd in Pickering's editions of 1868 and 1874, where they are placed at the end of the poems from the Pickering MS., they were apparently unknown to D. G. Rossetti, and (as Pickering's copyright) could not be included in W. M. Rossetti's Aldine edition.

Selections from the *Poetical Sketches* were first given by Malkin and Cunningham, the former printing ' How sweet I roam'd from field to field,' and the latter the 'Address to the Muses,' with a few passages from ' King Edward the Third.' D. G. Rossetti, in the selection given in Gilchrist's *Life*, prints six of the eight songs (excluding the two last), 'To the Muses,' 'To the Evening Star,' 'To Spring,' 'To Summer,' 'Blind-man's Buff,' and selections from scenes i, iii, v, and vi of 'King Edward the Third.' R. H. Shepherd prints the whole book with his customary accuracy, separately in 1868 as a supplementary volume to the *Songs of Innocence and of Experience*, and together with that work in the edition of 1874. W. M. Rossetti and later editors have availed themselves of this excellent text. Shepherd makes a few trifling corrections ; he omits Blake's general heading 'Miscellaneous Poems' and inserts a half-title to 'King Edward the Third' which is not in the original. W. M. Rossetti places the pieces in an order of his own and omits the prose, with the exception of the 'Prologue to King John' and 'Samson' which he prints as blank verse. Ellis and Yeats follow the Aldine edition, omitting 'Samson.' W. B. Yeats omits 'Fair Elinor,' 'Gwin of Norway,' the two prologues, 'The Couch of Death,' 'Contemplation,' and 'Samson.' There is an excellent facsimile reproduction of the *Poetical Sketches* (fifty copies printed by W. Griggs in May, 1890).

POEMS FROM POETICAL SKETCHES

To Spring

O thou with dewy locks, who lookest down   1
Thro' the clear windows of the morning, turn
Thine angel eyes upon our western isle,
Which in full choir hails thy approach, O Spring!

The hills tell each other, and the list'ning   5
Vallies hear; all our longing eyes are turned
Up to thy bright pavillions: issue forth,
And let thy holy feet visit our clime.

Come o'er the eastern hills, and let our winds   9
Kiss thy perfumèd garments; let us taste
Thy morn and evening breath; scatter thy pearls
Upon our love-sick land that mourns for thee.

O deck her forth with thy fair fingers; pour   13
Thy soft kisses on her bosom; and put
Thy golden crown upon her languish'd head,
Whose modest tresses were bound up for thee!

Poetical Sketches, pp. 1, 2.
5 tell each] do tell each DGR : tell to each EY.   7 pavillions]
pavilion DGR.   14 soft] softest DGR.

To Summer

O thou who passest thro' our vallies in   1
Thy strength, curb thy fierce steeds, allay the heat
That flames from their large nostrils! thou, O Summer,
Oft pitched'st here thy golden tent, and oft
Beneath our oaks hast slept, while we beheld   5
With joy thy ruddy limbs and flourishing hair.

Poetical Sketches, p. 2.
6 ruddy . . . hair] Cp. MS. Book, xxv.

'Abstinence sows sand all over
The ruddy limbs & flaming hair.'

Beneath our thickest shades we oft have heard
Thy voice, when noon upon his fervid car
Rode o'er the deep of heaven; beside our springs
Sit down, and in our mossy vallies, on   10
Some bank beside a river clear, throw thy
Silk draperies off, and rush into the stream:
Our vallies love the Summer in his pride.

Our bards are fam'd who strike the silver wire:
Our youth are bolder than the southern swains: 15
Our maidens fairer in the sprightly dance:
We lack not songs, nor instruments of joy,
Nor echoes sweet, nor waters clear as heaven,
Nor laurel wreaths against the sultry heat.

11 thy] all DGR.   12 Silk] Thy DGR.   15 youth] youths DGR.

To Autumn

O Autumn, laden with fruit, and stained   1
With the blood of the grape, pass not, but sit
Beneath my shady roof; there thou may'st rest,
And tune thy jolly voice to my fresh pipe,
And all the daughters of the year shall dance!   5
Sing now the lusty song of fruits and flowers.

'The narrow bud opens her beauties to
The sun, and love runs in her thrilling veins;
Blossoms hang round the brows of morning, and
Flourish down the bright cheek of modest eve,   10
Till clust'ring Summer breaks forth into singing,
And feather'd clouds strew flowers round her head.

'The spirits of the air live on the smells
Of fruit; and joy, with pinions light, roves round
The gardens, or sits singing in the trees.'   15
Thus sang the jolly Autumn as he sat;
Then rose, girded himself, and o'er the bleak
Hills fled from our sight; but left his golden load.

Poetical Sketches, p. 3.

To Winter

'O Winter! bar thine adamantine doors: 1
The north is thine; there hast thou built thy dark
Deep-founded habitation. Shake not thy roofs,
Nor bend thy pillars with thine iron car.'

He hears me not, but o'er the yawning deep   5
Rides heavy; his storms are unchain'd, sheathèd
In ribbèd steel; I dare not lift mine eyes,
For he hath rear'd his sceptre o'er the world.

Lo! now the direful monster, whose skin clings   9
To his strong bones, strides o'er the groaning rocks:
He withers all in silence, and in his hand
Unclothes the earth, and freezes up frail life.

He takes his seat upon the cliffs,—the mariner   13
Cries in vain. Poor little wretch, that deal'st
With storms!—till heaven smiles, and the monster
Is driv'n yelling to his caves beneath mount Hecla.

Poetical Sketches, p. 4.
  1–4 no quotation marks in original.   15, 16 and the monster . . .
mount Hecla]
                  and drives the monster
        Yelling beneath Mount Hecla to his caves. EY.

To the Evening Star

Thou fair-hair'd angel of the evening,   1
Now, whilst the sun rests on the mountains, light
Thy bright torch of love; thy radiant crown
Put on, and smile upon our evening bed!
Smile on our loves, and while thou drawest the   5

Poetical Sketches, p. 5.
  3 bright] brilliant DGR, EY.   5, 6 while . . . dew]
                  whilst thou drawest round
      The curtains of the sky, scatter thy dew. DGR.
               while thou drawest round
     The sky's blue curtains, scatter silver dew. Swinb.

Blue curtains of the sky, scatter thy silver dew
On every flower that shuts its sweet eyes
In timely sleep. Let thy west wind sleep on
The lake; speak silence with thy glimmering eyes,
And wash the dusk with silver. Soon, full soon,   10
Dost thou withdraw; then the wolf rages wide,
And the lion glares thro' the dun forest:
The fleeces of our flocks are cover'd with
Thy sacred dew: protect them with thine influence.

6 silver] EY *omit.*   7 shuts] closes DGR, Swinb., EY.   12 And the]
And then the DGR, EY, WBY.   14 protect . . . influence] protect
with influence EY.

To Morning

O holy virgin! clad in purest white,   1
Unlock heav'n's golden gates, and issue forth;
Awake the dawn that sleeps in heaven; let light
Rise from the chambers of the east, and bring
The honied dew that cometh on waking day.   5
O radiant morning, salute the sun
Rouz'd like a huntsman to the chace, and with
Thy buskin'd feet appear upon our hills.

Poetical Sketches, p. 6.

Fair Elenor

The bell struck one, and shook the silent tower;   1
The graves give up their dead: fair Elenor
Walk'd by the castle gate, and lookèd in.
A hollow groan ran thro' the dreary vaults.

Poetical Sketches, pp. 7–10. The theme of this very juvenile poem was
evidently suggested by Walpole's 'Gothic story,' *The Castle of Otranto*,
first published in 1765. Compare the incident in the first chapter, where
Isabella descends into the vaults of the Castle, and shrieks on meeting what
she believes to be the ghost of Conrad.

She shriek'd aloud, and sunk upon the steps,   5
On the cold stone her pale cheeks. Sickly smells
Of death issue as from a sepulchre,
And all is silent but the sighing vaults.

Chill death withdraws his hand, and she revives;   9
Amaz'd, she finds herself upon her feet,
And, like a ghost, thro' narrow passages
Walking, feeling the cold walls with her hands.

Fancy returns, and now she thinks of bones   13
And grinning skulls, and corruptible death
Wrap'd in his shroud; and now fancies she hears
Deep sighs, and sees pale sickly ghosts gliding.

At length, no fancy but reality   17
Distracts her. A rushing sound, and the feet
Of one that fled, approaches.—Ellen stood
Like a dumb statue, froze to stone with fear.

The wretch approaches, crying: 'The deed is done;   21
Take this, and send it by whom thou wilt send;
It is my life—send it to Elenor:—
He's dead, and howling after me for blood!

'Take this,' he cry'd; and thrust into her arms   25
A wet napkin, wrap'd about; then rush'd
Past, howling: she receiv'd into her arms
Pale death, and follow'd on the wings of fear.

They pass'd swift thro' the outer gate; the wretch   29
Howling, leap'd o'er the wall into the moat,
Stifling in mud. Fair Ellen pass'd the bridge,
And heard a gloomy voice cry 'Is it done?'

As the deer wounded, Ellen flew over   33
The pathless plain; as the arrows that fly
By night, destruction flies, and strikes in darkness.
She fled from fear, till at her house arriv'd.

6 cheeks] cheek *all edd.*

Her maids await her; on her bed she falls,   37
That bed of joy, where erst her lord hath press'd:
'Ah, woman's fear!' she cry'd; 'Ah, cursèd duke!
Ah, my dear lord! ah, wretched Elenor!

'My lord was like a flower upon the brows   41
Of lusty May! Ah, life as frail as flower!
O ghastly death! withdraw thy cruel hand,
Seek'st thou that flow'r to deck thy horrid temples?

'My lord was like a star in highest heav'n   45
Drawn down to earth by spells and wickedness;
My lord was like the opening eyes of day
When western winds creep softly o'er the flowers;

'But he is darken'd; like the summer's noon   49
Clouded; fall'n like the stately tree, cut down;
The breath of heaven dwelt among his leaves.
O Elenor, weak woman, fill'd with woe!'

Thus having spoke, she raisèd up her head,   53
And saw the bloody napkin by her side,
Which in her arms she brought; and now, tenfold
More terrified, saw it unfold itself.

Her eyes were fix'd; the bloody cloth unfolds,   57
Disclosing to her sight the murder'd head
Of her dear lord, all ghastly pale, clotted
With gory blood; it groan'd, and thus it spake:

'O Elenor, I am thy husband's head,   61
Who, sleeping on the stones of yonder tower,
Was 'reft of life by the accursèd duke!
A hirèd villain turn'd my sleep to death!

'O Elenor, beware the cursèd duke;   65
O give not him thy hand, now I am dead;
He seeks thy love; who, coward, in the night,
Hirèd a villain to bereave my life.'

47 eyes] eye Swinb.   49 summer's] summer Swinb.   61 I am]
behold *all edd*.   68 Hirèd . . . life.] This line is repeated by Blake

She sat with dead cold limbs, stiffen'd to stone;   69
She took the gory head up in her arms;
She kiss'd the pale lips; she had no tears to shed;
She hugg'd it to her breast, and groan'd her last.

in one of his epigrams on Hayley (MS. Book, lxxviii). Blake's use of
'bereave' as a transitive verb is perhaps imitative of the line quoted by
him, from Chaucer, in his *Descriptive Catalogue*:

'Hath me bireft my beauty and my pith.'

Song

How sweet I roam'd from field to field   1
And tasted all the summer's pride,
'Till I the prince of love beheld
Who in the sunny beams did glide!

He shew'd me lilies for my hair,   5
And blushing roses for my brow;
He led me through his gardens fair
Where all his golden pleasures grow.

With sweet May dews my wings were wet,   9
And Phoebus fir'd my vocal rage;
He caught me in his silken net,
And shut me in his golden cage.

He loves to sit and hear me sing,   13
Then, laughing, sports and plays with me;
Then stretches out my golden wing,
And mocks my loss of liberty.

Poetical Sketches, p. 10. According to Malkin (pp. xxxiv, xxxvi), who
quotes this poem, it was written by Blake before the age of fourteen.
12 golden cage] Cp. *Island in the Moon* (c. 1785) iii:

'Come & be cured of all your pains
In Matrimony's Golden cage.'

Song

My silks and fine array,   1
My smiles and languish'd air,
By love are driv'n away;
And mournful lean Despair
Brings me yew to deck my grave: 5
Such end true lovers have.

His face is fair as heav'n
When springing buds unfold;
O why to him was't giv'n
Whose heart is wintry cold?   10
His breast is love's all worship'd tomb,
Where all love's pilgrims come.

Bring me an axe and spade,
Bring me a winding sheet;
When I my grave have made   15
Let winds and tempests beat:
Then down I'll lie as cold as clay.
True love doth pass away!

Poetical Sketches, p. 11.

Song

Love and harmony combine,   1
And around our souls intwine
While thy branches mix with mine,
And our roots together join.

Joys upon our branches sit,   5
Chirping loud and singing sweet;
Like gentle streams beneath our feet
Innocence and virtue meet.

Poetical Sketches, p. 12.
                    2 intwine] entwine *all except* Shep.

Thou the golden fruit dost bear,   9
I am clad in flowers fair;
Thy sweet boughs perfume the air,
And the turtle buildeth there.

There she sits and feeds her young,   13
Sweet I hear her mournful song;
And thy lovely leaves among,
There is love, I hear her tongue.

There his charming nest doth lay,   17
There he sleeps the night away;
There he sports along the day,
And doth among our branches play.

16 her] An obvious misprint for 'his.' All Blake's editors make the
necessary correction.   17 charming . . . lay,] charm'd nest he doth lay,
DGR.

Song

I love the jocund dance,   1
The softly-breathing song,
Where innocent eyes do glance,
And where lisps the maiden's tongue.

I love the laughing vale,   5
I love the echoing hill,
Where mirth does never fail,
And the jolly swain laughs his fill.

I love the pleasant cot,   9
I love the innocent bow'r,
Where white and brown is our lot,
Or fruit in the mid-day hour.

I love the oaken seat,   13
Beneath the oaken tree,
Where all the old villagers meet,
And laugh our sports to see.

Poetical Sketches, p. 13.
    4 And where] Where DGR.   5 vale] gale Malk.

I love our neighbours all,   17
But, Kitty, I better love thee;
And love them I ever shall;
But thou art all to me.

Song

Memory, hither come,   1
And tune your merry notes:
And, while upon the wind
Your music floats,
I'll pore upon the stream   5
Where sighing lovers dream,
And fish for fancies as they pass
Within the watery glass.

I'll drink of the clear stream,
And hear the linnet's song;   10
And there I'll lie and dream
The day along:
And when night comes, I'll go
To places fit for woe,
Walking along the darken'd valley   15
With silent Melancholy.

Poetical Sketches, p. 14.

Mad Song

The wild winds weep,   1
And the night is a-cold;
Come hither, Sleep,
And my griefs unfold:
But lo! the morning peeps   5
Over the eastern steeps,
And the rustling beds of dawn
The earth do scorn.

Poetical Sketches, p. 15.
4 unfold] infold Shep. ; enfold WMR, EY, WBY.   7 beds] birds
DGR, WBY.

Lo! to the vault
Of pavèd heaven,   10
With sorrow fraught
My notes are driven:
They strike the ear of night,
Make weep the eyes of day;
They make mad the roaring winds,   15
And with tempests play.

Like a fiend in a cloud,
With howling woe
After night I do croud,
And with night will go;   20
I turn my back to the east
From whence comforts have increas'd;
For light doth seize my brain
With frantic pain.

17 Like ... cloud] Cp. 'Infant Sorrow' in the *Songs of Experience*:
> 'Helpless, naked, piping loud,
> Like a fiend hid in a cloud.'

The picture was probably suggested in Blake's mind by passages in Macpherson's 'Ossian.'   22 From whence] Whence DGR.

Song

Fresh from the dewy hill, the merry year   1
Smiles on my head and mounts his flaming car;
Round my young brows the laurel wreathes a shade,
And rising glories beam around my head.

My feet are wing'd, while o'er the dewy lawn,   5
I meet my maiden risen like the morn:
Oh bless those holy feet, like angels' feet;
Oh bless those limbs, beaming with heav'nly light.

Like as an angel glitt'ring in the sky   9
In times of innocence and holy joy;
The joyful shepherd stops his grateful song
To hear the music of an angel's tongue.

Poetical Sketches, p. 16.
  5 like] with Gil.   6 angels'] angel's Gil.   9 Like as] As when
Gil.   12 an] that Gil.

So when she speaks, the voice of Heaven I hear;   13
So when we walk, nothing impure comes near;
Each field seems Eden, and each calm retreat;
Each village seems the haunt of holy feet.

But that sweet village where my black-ey'd maid   17
Closes her eyes in sleep beneath night's shade,
Whene'er I enter, more than mortal fire
Burns in my soul, and does my song inspire.

Song

When early morn walks forth in sober grey,   1
Then to my black ey'd maid I haste away;
When evening sits beneath her dusky bow'r,
And gently sighs away the silent hour,
The village bell alarms, away I go,   5
And the vale darkens at my pensive woe.

To that sweet village, where my black ey'd maid
Doth drop a tear beneath the silent shade,
I turn my eyes; and pensive as I go
Curse my black stars and bless my pleasing woe.   10

Oft when the summer sleeps among the trees,
Whisp'ring faint murmurs to the scanty breeze,
I walk the village round; if at her side
A youth doth walk in stolen joy and pride,
I curse my stars in bitter grief and woe,   15
That made my love so high and me so low.

O should she e'er prove false, his limbs I'd tear
And throw all pity on the burning air;
I'd curse bright fortune for my mixèd lot,
And then I'd die in peace and be forgot.   20

To the Muses

Whether on Ida's shady brow,   1
Or in the chambers of the East,
The chambers of the sun, that now
From antient melody have ceas'd;

Whether in Heav'n ye wander fair,   5
Or the green corners of the earth,
Or the blue regions of the air
Where the melodious winds have birth;

Whether on chrystal rocks ye rove,   9
Beneath the bosom of the sea
Wand'ring in many a coral grove,
Fair Nine, forsaking Poetry!

How have you left the antient love   13
That bards of old enjoy'd in you!
The languid strings do scarcely move!
The sound is forc'd, the notes are few!

Poetical Sketches, p. 18.
12 Poetry] poesie Cunn.   13 you] ye Cunn.   15 do] now Cunn.

Gwin, King of Norway

Come, Kings, and listen to my song: 1
When Gwin, the son of Nore,
Over the nations of the North
His cruel sceptre bore;

The Nobles of the land did feed   5
Upon the hungry Poor;
They tear the poor man's lamb, and drive
The needy from their door.

Poetical Sketches, pp. 19–23.

'The land is desolate; our wives   9
And children cry. for bread;
Arise, and pull the tyrant down!
Let Gwin be humblèd!'

Gordred the giant rous'd himself   13
From sleeping in his cave;
He shook the hills, and in the clouds
The troubl'd banners wave.

Beneath them roll'd, like tempests black,   17
The num'rous sons of blood;
Like lions' whelps, roaring abroad,
Seeking their nightly food.

Down Bleron's hills they dreadful rush,   21
Their cry ascends the clouds;
The trampling horse and clanging arms
Like rushing mighty floods!

Their wives and children, weeping loud,   25
Follow in wild array,
Howling like ghosts, furious as wolves
In the bleak wintry day.

'Pull down the tyrant to the dust,   29
Let Gwin be humblèd,'
They cry, 'and let ten thousand lives
Pay for the tyrant's head.'

From tow'r to tow'r the watchmen cry,   33
'O Gwin, the son of Nore,
Arouse thyself! the nations, black
Like clouds, come rolling o'er!'

Gwin rear'd his shield, his palace shakes,   37
His chiefs come rushing round;
Each, like an awful thunder cloud,
With voice of solemn sound:

9–12 The . . . humbled] *No quotation marks in original.*   21 hills]
hill EY.

Like reared stones around a grave   41
They stand around the King;
Then suddenly each seiz'd his spear,
And clashing steel does ring.

The husbandman does leave his plow   45
To wade thro' fields of gore;
The merchant binds his brows in steel,
And leaves the trading shore;

The shepherd leaves his mellow pipe,   49
And sounds the trumpet shrill;
The workman throws his hammer down
To heave the bloody bill.

Like the tall ghost of Barraton   53
Who sports in stormy sky,
Gwin leads his host, as black as night
When pestilence does fly,

With horses and with chariots—   57
And all his spearmen bold
March to the sound of mournful song,
Like clouds around him roll'd.

Gwin lifts his hand—the nations halt;   61
'Prepare for war!' he cries—
Gordred appears!—his frowning brow
Troubles our northern skies.

The armies stand, like balances   65
Held in th' Almighty's hand;—
'Gwin, thou hast fill'd thy measure up:
Thou'rt swept from out the land.'

53 Barraton] Probably a reminiscence of 'Berrathon' in Macpherson's
Ossian, a piece from which Blake would also seem to have borrowed the
name 'Leutha' in the *Visions of the Daughters of Albion* (1793).

And now the raging armies rush'd   69
Like warring mighty seas;
The Heav'ns are shook with roaring war,
The dust ascends the skies!

Earth smokes with blood, and groans and shakes   73
To drink her children's gore,
A sea of blood; nor can the eye
See to the trembling shore!

And on the verge of this wild sea   77
Famine and death doth cry;
The cries of women and of babes
Over the field doth fly.

The King is seen raging afar,   81
With all his men of might;
Like blazing comets scattering death
Thro' the red fev'rous night.

Beneath his arm like sheep they die,   85
And groan upon the plain;
The battle faints, and bloody men
Fight upon hills of slain.

Now death is sick, and riven men   89
Labour and toil for life;
Steed rolls on steed, and shield on shield,
Sunk in this sea of strife!

The god of war is drunk with blood;   93
The earth doth faint and fail;
The stench of blood makes sick the heav'ns;
Ghosts glut the throat of hell!

O what have Kings to answer for   97
Before that awful throne;
When thousand deaths for vengeance cry,
And ghosts accusing groan!

78, 80 doth] do WMR, EY.

Like blazing comets in the sky   101
That shake the stars of light,
Which drop like fruit unto the earth
Thro' the fierce burning night;

Like these did Gwin and Gordred meet,   105
And the first blow decides;
Down from the brow unto the breast
Gordred his head divides!

Gwin fell: the Sons of Norway fled,   109
All that remain'd alive;
The rest did fill the vale of death,
For them the eagles strive.

The river Dorman roll'd their blood   113
Into the northern sea;
Who mourn'd his sons, and overwhelm'd
The pleasant south country.

An Imitation of Spencer

Golden Apollo, that thro' heaven wide   1
Scatter'st the rays of light, and truth's beams,
In lucent words my darkling verses dight,
And wash my earthy mind in thy clear streams,
That wisdom may descend in fairy dreams,   5
All while the jocund hours in thy train
Scatter their fancies at thy poet's feet;
And when thou yields to night thy wide domain,
Let rays of truth enlight his sleeping brain.

Poetical Sketches, pp. 24-26. This piece has not the air of being one of Blake's earliest efforts, in spite of its metrical faults. Representing the Spenserian stanza by the formula *ababbcbcC*, Blake's successive attempts are: *ababbcbcc, ababbcbcB, ababbcbB, ababbabb, ababbcbcb, ababbcbcbB*—all different and all wrong.

Title] *All edd. correct* Spencer *to* Spenser.   2 truth's] truth his *all edd.*
8 yields] yield'st *all edd.*

For brutish Pan in vain might thee assay   10
With tinkling sounds to dash thy nervous verse,
Sound without sense; yet in his rude affray,
(For ignorance is Folly's leesing nurse
And love of Folly needs none other's curse)
Midas the praise hath gain'd of lengthen'd cares,   15
For which himself might deem him ne'er the worse
To sit in council with his modern peers,
And judge of tinkling rhimes and elegances terse.

And thou, Mercurius, that with wingèd brow
Dost mount aloft into the yielding sky,   20
And thro' Heav'n's halls thy airy flight dost throw,
Entering with holy feet to where on high
Jove weighs the counsel of futurity;
Then, laden with eternal fate, dost go
Down, like a falling star, from autumn sky,   25
And o'er the surface of the silent deep dost fly:

If thou arrivest at the sandy shore
Where nought but envious hissing adders dwell,
Thy golden rod, thrown on the dusty floor,
Can charm to harmony with potent spell.   30
Such is sweet Eloquence, that does dispel
Envy and Hate that thirst for human gore;
And cause in sweet society to dwell
Vile savage minds that lurk in lonely cell.

O Mercury, assist my lab'ring sense   35
That round the circle of the world wou'd fly,
As the wing'd eagle scorns the tow'ry fence
Of Alpine hills round his high aëry,
And searches thro' the corners of the sky,
Sports in the clouds to hear the thunder's sound,   40
And see the wingèd lightnings as they fly;
Then, bosom'd in an amber cloud, around
Plumes his wide wings, and seeks Sol's palace high.

13 leesing nurse] Read, with all Blake's editors, leasing nurse, i.e. one
who holds her charge in a lease or leash.   15 cares] *All edd. correct
this misprint for* ears.   19 brow] bow *all edd.*

And thou, O warrior maid invincible,
Arm'd with the terrors of Almighty Jove,   45
Pallas, Minerva, maiden terrible,
Lov'st thou to walk the peaceful solemn grove,
In solemn gloom of branches interwove?
Or bear'st thy Egis o'er the burning field,
Where, like the sea, the waves of battle move?   50
Or have thy soft piteous eyes beheld
The weary wanderer thro' the desert rove?
Or does th' afflicted man thy heav'nly bosom move?

Blind-man's Buff

When silver Snow decks Susan's cloaths,   1
And jewel hangs at th' shepherd's nose,
The blushing bank is all my care,
With hearth so red, and walls so fair;
'Heap the sea-coal, come, heap it higher,   5
The oaken log lay on the fire;'
The well-wash'd stools, a circling row,
With lad and lass, how fair the show!
The merry can of nut-brown ale,
The laughing jest, the love-sick tale,   10
'Till, tir'd of chat, the game begins.
The lasses prick the lads with pins;
Roger from Dolly twitch'd the stool,
She, falling, kiss'd the ground, poor fool!
She blush'd so red, with side-long glance   15
At hob-nail Dick, who griev'd the chance.
But now for Blind-man's Buff they call;
Of each incumbrance clear the hall—
Jenny her silken 'kerchief folds,
And blear-ey'd Will the black lot holds.   20

Poetical Sketches, pp. 26–28.
1, 2 When . . . nose] Compare the opening lines of 'Song by an Old Shepherd' (Appendix II) :—

> 'When silver snow decks Sylvia's clothes,
> And jewel hangs at shepherd's nose.'

3 blushing bank] chimney nook DGR.

Now laughing stops, with 'Silence! hush!'
And Peggy Pout gives Sam a push.
The Blind-man's arms, extended wide,
Sam slips between:—'O woe betide
Thee, clumsy Will!'—but titt'ring Kate   25
Is pen'd up in the corner strait!
And now Will's eyes beheld the play;
He thought his face was t'other way.
'Now, Kitty, now! what chance hast thou,
Roger so near thee!—Trips, I vow!'   30
She catches him—then Roger ties
His own head up—but not his eyes;
For thro' the slender cloth he sees,
And runs at Sam, who slips with ease
His clumsy hold; and, dodging round,   35
Sukey is tumbled on the ground!—
'See what it is to play unfair!
Where cheating is, there's mischief there.'
But Roger still pursues the chace,—
'He sees! he sees!' cries softly Grace;   40
'O Roger, thou, unskill'd in art,
Must, surer bound, go thro' thy part!'
Now Kitty, pert, repeats the rhymes,
And Roger turns him round three times,

29–31 Now . . . him] This seems to be the sense intended by the faulty
punctuation of the original:

> 'Now, Kitty, now; what chance hast thou,
> Roger so near thee, Trips; I vow!
> She catches him—'

DGR reads:

> 'Now, Kitty, now! what chance hast thou!
> Roger so near thee trips!—I vow
> She catches him!—'

Shep.:

> '"Now, Kitty, now; what chance hast thou,
> Roger so near thee trips, I vow!"
> She catches him—'

WMR, EY, and WBY:

> '"Now, Kitty, now! what chance hast thou?
> Roger so near thee trips, I vow!"
> She catches him—'

Then pauses ere he starts—but Dick　　　　　45
Was mischief bent upon a trick;
Down on his hands and knees he lay
Directly in the Blind-man's way,
Then cries out 'Hem!' Hodge heard, and ran
With hood-wink'd chance—sure of his man;　50
But down he came.—Alas, how frail
Our best of hopes, how soon they fail!
With crimson drops he stains the ground;
Confusion startles all around.
Poor piteous Dick supports his head,　　　55
And fain would cure the hurt he made;
But Kitty hasted with a key,
And down his back they strait convey
The cold relief; the blood is stay'd,
And Hodge again holds up his head.　　　60
Such are the fortunes of the game,
And those who play should stop the same
By wholesome laws; such as all those
Who on the blinded man impose
Stand in his stead; as, long a-gone,　　　65
When men were first a nation grown,
Lawless they liv'd, till wantonness
And liberty began t' increase,
And one man lay in another's way;
Then laws were made to keep fair play.　　70

57 hasted] hastens DGR.　　　65 as] So DGR.

APPENDIX I

TO THE POETICAL SKETCHES

[The latter portion of *Poetical Sketches* (pp. 29–70) containing the blank verse and prose pieces following the 'Miscellaneous Poems.' Reprinted from the original edition, but without variorum readings in footnotes.]

KING EDWARD THE THIRD.

PERSONS.

King Edward.	*Lord Audley.*
The Black Prince.	*Lord Percy.*
Queen Philippa.	*Bishop.*
Duke of Clarence.	*William*, Dagworth's
Sir John Chandos.	Man.
Sir Thomas Dagworth.	*Peter Blunt*, a common
Sir Walter Manny.	Soldier.

SCENE,

The Coast of France, King Edward and Nobles before it.   The Army.

King. O thou, to whose fury the nations are   1
But as dust, maintain thy servant's right !
Without thine aid, the twisted mail, and spear,
And forgèd helm, and shield of seven times beaten brass,
Are idle trophies of the vanquisher.   5
When confusion rages, when the field is in a flame,
When the cries of blood tear horror from heav'n,
And yelling death runs up and down the ranks,
Let Liberty, the charter'd right of Englishmen,   9
Won by our fathers in many a glorious field,
Enerve my soldiers ; let Liberty
Blaze in each countenance, and fire the battle.
The enemy fight in chains, invisible chains, but heavy ;   13
Their minds are fetter'd, then how can they be free ?
While, like the mounting flame,
We spring to battle o'er the floods of death !
And these fair youths, the flow'r of England,   17
Vent'ring their lives in my most righteous cause,
O sheathe their hearts with triple steel, that they
May emulate their fathers' virtues.
And thou, my son, be strong ; thou fightest for a crown   21
That death can never ravish from thy brow,
A crown of glory—but from thy very dust
Shall beam a radiance, to fire the breasts
Of youth unborn. Our names are written equal   25
In fame's wide trophied hall ; 'tis ours to gild
The letters, and to make them shine with gold

That never tarnishes: whether Third Edward,
Or the Prince of Wales, or Montacute, or Mortimer,   29
Or ev'n the least by birth, shall gain the brightest fame,
Is in his hand to whom all men are equal.
The world of men are like the num'rous stars
That beam and twinkle in the depth of night,   33
Each clad in glory according to his sphere;
But we, that wander from our native seats
And beam forth lustre on a darkling world,
Grow larger as we advance: and some, perhaps   37
The most obscure at home, that scarce were seen
To twinkle in their sphere, may so advance
That the astonish'd world, with upturn'd eyes,
Regardless of the moon, and those that once were bright,   41
Stand only for to gaze upon their splendor.

            [*He here knights the Prince, and other young Nobles.*]

Now let us take a just revenge for those
Brave Lords, who fell beneath the bloody axe
At Paris. Thanks, noble Harcourt, for 'twas   45
By your advice we landed here in Brittany,
A country not yet sown with destruction,
And where the fiery whirlwind of swift war
Has not yet swept its desolating wing.   49
Into three parties we divide by day,
And separate march, but join again at night;
Each knows his rank, and Heav'n marshal all.   [*Exeunt.*

       SCENE, *English Court. Lionel, Duke of Clarence;*
          Queen Philippa; Lords; Bishop; &c.

   Clarence. My Lords, I have by the advice of her   1
Whom I am doubly bound to obey, my Parent
And my Sovereign, call'd you together.
My task is great, my burden heavier than
My unfledg'd years;   5
Yet, with your kind assistance, Lords, I hope
England shall dwell in peace; that, while my father
Toils in his wars, and turns his eyes on this
His native shore, and sees commerce fly round   9
With his white wings, and sees his golden London
And her silver Thames, throng'd with shining spires
And corded ships, her merchants buzzing round
Like summer bees, and all the golden cities   13
In his land overflowing with honey,
Glory may not be dimm'd with clouds of care.
Say, Lords, should not our thoughts be first to commerce?
My Lord Bishop, you would recommend us agriculture?   17
   Bishop. Sweet Prince, the arts of peace are great,
And no less glorious than those of war,

Perhaps more glorious in the philosophic mind.
When I sit at my home, a private man, 21
My thoughts are on my gardens and my fields,
How to employ the hand that lacketh bread.
If Industry is in my diocese,
Religion will flourish ; each man's heart 25
Is cultivated and will bring forth fruit.
This is my private duty and my pleasure;
But, as I sit in council with my prince,
My thoughts take in the gen'ral good of the whole, 29
And England is the land favour'd by Commerce ;
For Commerce, tho' the child of Agriculture,
Fosters his parent, who else must sweat and toil,
And gain but scanty fare. Then, my dear Lord, 33
Be England's trade our care ; and we, as tradesmen,
Looking to the gain of this our native land.
   Clar. O my good Lord, true wisdom drops like honey
From your tongue, as from a worship'd oak. 37
Forgive, my Lords, my talkative youth, that speaks
Not merely what my narrow observation has
Pick'd up, but what I have concluded from your lessons.
Now, by the Queen's advice, I ask your leave 41
To dine to-morrow with the Mayor of London :
If I obtain your leave, I have another boon
To ask, which is the favour of your company.
I fear Lord Percy will not give me leave. 45
   Percy. Dear Sir, a prince should always keep his state,
And grant his favours with a sparing hand,
Or they are never rightly valuèd.
These are my thoughts : yet it were best to go : 49
But keep a proper dignity, for now
You represent the sacred person of
Your father ; 'tis with princes as 'tis with the sun ;
If not sometimes o'er-clouded, we grow weary 53
Of his officious glory.
   Clar. Then you will give me leave to shine sometimes,
My Lord ?
   Lord. Thou hast a gallant spirit, which I fear 57
Will be imposed on by the closer sort.   [*Aside.*
   Clar. Well, I'll endeavour to take
Lord Percy's advice ; I have been used so much
To dignity that I'm sick on't. 61
   Queen Phil. Fie, Fie, Lord Clarence ! you proceed not to business,
But speak of your own pleasures.
I hope their Lordships will excuse your giddiness.
   Clar. My Lords, the French have fitted out many 65
Small ships of war, that, like to ravening wolves,
Infest our English seas, devouring all
Our burden'd vessels, spoiling our naval flocks.
The merchants do complain, and beg our aid. 69

Percy. The merchants are rich enough ;
Can they not help themselves ?
  Bish. They can, and may ; but how to gain their will
Requires our countenance and help.   73
  Percy. When that they find they must, my Lord, they will:
Let them but suffer awhile, and you shall see
They will bestir themselves.
  Bish. Lord Percy cannot mean that we should suffer   77
This disgrace : if so, we are not sovereigns
Of the sea—our right, that Heaven gave
To England, when at the birth of nature
She was seated in the deep ; the Ocean ceas'd   81
His mighty roar, and fawning play'd around
Her snowy feet, and own'd his awful Queen.
Lord Percy, if the heart is sick, the head
Must be aggriev'd ; if but one member suffer,   85
The heart doth fail. You say, my Lord, the merchants
Can, if they will, defend themselves against
These rovers : this is a noble scheme,
Worthy the brave Lord Percy, and as worthy   89
His generous aid to put it into practice.
  Percy. Lord Bishop, what was rash in me is wise
In you ; I dare not own the plan. 'Tis not
Mine. Yet will I, if you please,   93
Quickly to the Lord Mayor, and work him onward
To this most glorious voyage ; on which cast
I'll set my whole estate,
But we will bring these Gallic rovers under.   97
  Queen Phil. Thanks, brave Lord Percy ; you have the thanks
Of England's Queen, and will, ere long, of England.   [*Exeunt.*

SCENE, *At Cressey. Sir Thomas Dagworth and*
Lord Audley, meeting.

  Aud. Good morrow, brave Sir Thomas ; the bright morn   1
Smiles on our army, and the gallant sun
Springs from the hills like a young hero
Into the battle, shaking his golden locks
Exultingly : this is a promising day.   5
  Dagw. Why, my Lord Audley, I don't know.
Give me your hand, and now I'll tell you what
I think you do not know. Edward's afraid of Philip.
  Aud. Ha, Ha, Sir Thomas ! you but joke ;   9
Did you ere see him fear ? At Blanchetaque,
When almost singly he drove six thousand
French from the ford, did he fear then ?
  Dagw. Yes, fear—that made him fight so.   13
  Aud. By the same reason I might say 'tis fear
That makes you fight.

Dagw. Mayhap you may : look upon Edward's face,
No one can say he fears. But when he turns   17
His back, then I will say it to his face,
He is afraid : he makes us all afraid.
I cannot bear the enemy at my back.
Now here we are at Cressy; where to-morrow,   21
To-morrow we shall know. I say, Lord Audley,
That Edward runs away from Philip.
　　Aud. Perhaps you think the Prince too is afraid?
　　Dagw. No ; God forbid ! I'm sure he is not.   25
He is a young lion. O I have seen him fight
And give command, and lightning has flashed
From his eyes across the field : I have seen him
Shake hands with death, and strike a bargain for   29
The enemy ; he has danc'd in the field
Of battle, like the youth at morrice play.
I'm sure he 's not afraid, nor Warwick, nor none,
None of us but me, and I am very much afraid.   33
　　Aud. Are you afraid too, Sir Thomas?
I believe that as much as I believe
The King 's afraid : but what are you afraid of?
　　Dagw. Of having my back laid open; we turn   37
Our backs to the fire, till we shall burn our skirts.
　　Aud. And this, Sir Thomas, you call fear! Your fear
Is of a different kind then from the King's;
He fears to turn his face, and you to turn your back.   41
I do not think, Sir Thomas, you know what fear is.

Enter Sir John Chandos.

　　Chand. Good morrow, Generals; I give you joy:
Welcome to the fields of Cressy. Here we stop,
And wait for Philip.   45
　　Dagw. I hope so.
　　Aud. There, Sir Thomas, do you call that fear?
　　Dagw. I don't know; perhaps he takes it by fits.
Why, noble Chandos, look you here,   49
One rotten sheep spoils the whole flock ;
And if the bell-weather is tainted, I wish
The Prince may not catch the distemper too.
　　Chand. Distemper, Sir Thomas ! what distemper?   53
I have not heard.
　　Dagw. Why, Chandos, you are a wise man,
I know you understand me ; a distemper
The King caught here in France of running away.   57
　　Aud. Sir Thomas, you say you have caught it too.
　　Dagw. And so will the whole army; 'tis very catching,
For, when the coward runs, the brave man totters.
Perhaps the air of the country is the cause.   61
I feel it coming upon me, so I strive against it ;

You yet are whole; but, after a few more
Retreats, we all shall know how to retreat
Better than fight.—To be plain, I think retreating   65
Too often takes away a soldier's courage.

   Chand. Here comes the King himself: tell him your thoughts
Plainly, Sir Thomas.

   Dagw. I've told him before, but his disorder   69
Makes him deaf.

Enter King Edward and Black Prince.

   King. Good morrow, Generals; when English courage fails,
Down goes our right to France.
But we are conquerors every where; nothing   73
Can stand our soldiers; each man is worthy
Of a triumph. Such an army of heroes
Ne'er shouted to the Heav'ns, nor shook the field.
Edward, my son, thou art   77
Most happy, having such command: the man
Were base who were not fir'd to deeds
Above heroic, having such examples.

   Prince. Sire, with respect and deference I look   81
Upon such noble souls, and wish myself
Worthy the high command that Heaven and you
Have given me. When I have seen the field glow,
And in each countenance the soul of war   85
Curb'd by the manliest reason, I have been wing'd
With certain victory; and 'tis my boast,
And shall be still my glory, I was inspir'd
By these brave troops.   89

   Dagw. Your Grace had better make
Them all Generals.

   King. Sir Thomas Dagworth, you must have your joke,
And shall, while you can fight as you did at   93
The Ford.

   Dagw. I have a small petition to your Majesty.

   King. What can Sir Thomas Dagworth ask that Edward
Can refuse?   97

   Dagw. I hope your Majesty cannot refuse so great
A trifle; I've gilt your cause with my best blood,
And would again, were I not forbid
By him whom I am bound to obey: my hands   101
Are tied up, my courage shrunk and wither'd,
My sinews slacken'd, and my voice scarce heard;
Therefore I beg I may return to England.

   King. I know not what you could have ask'd, Sir Thomas,   105
That I would not have sooner parted with
Than such a soldier as you have been, and such a friend:
Nay, I will know the most remote particulars
Of this your strange petition; that if I can   109
I still may keep you here.

Dagw. Here on the fields of Cressy we are settled
'Till Philip springs the tim'rous covey again.
The Wolf is hunted down by causeless fear;   113
The Lion flees, and fear usurps his heart,
Startled, astonish'd at the clam'rous Cock;
The Eagle, that doth gaze upon the sun,
Fears the small fire that plays about the fen.   117
If, at this moment of their idle fear,
The Dog doth seize the Wolf, the Forester the Lion,
The Negro in the crevice of the rock
Doth seize the soaring Eagle; undone by flight,   121
They tame submit: such the effect flight has
On noble souls. Now hear its opposite.
The tim'rous Stag starts from the thicket wild,
The fearful Crane springs from the splashy fen,   125
The shining Snake glides o'er the bending grass,
The Stag turns head and bays the crying Hounds,
The Crane o'ertaken fighteth with the Hawk,
The Snake doth turn, and bite the padding foot.   129
And if your Majesty's afraid of Philip,
You are more like a Lion than a Crane:
Therefore I beg I may return to England.
King. Sir Thomas, now I understand your mirth,   133
Which often plays with Wisdom for its pastime,
And brings good counsel from the breast of laughter.
I hope you'll stay, and see us fight this battle,
And reap rich harvest in the fields of Cressy;   137
Then go to England, tell them how we fight,
And set all hearts on fire to be with us.
Philip is plum'd, and thinks we flee from him,
Else he would never dare to attack us. Now,   141
Now the quarry's set! and Death doth sport
In the bright sunshine of this fatal day.
Dagw. Now my heart dances, and I am as light
As the young bridegroom going to be married.   145
Now must I to my soldiers, get them ready,
Furbish our armours bright, new plume our helms,
And we will sing like the young housewives busied
In the dairy: my feet are wing'd, but not   149
For flight, an please your grace.
King. If all my soldiers are as pleas'd as you,
'Twill be a gallant thing to fight or die;
Then I can never be afraid of Philip.   153
Dagw. A raw-bon'd fellow t'other day pass'd by me;
I told him to put off his hungry looks—
He answer'd me, 'I hunger for another battle.'
I saw a little Welchman with a fiery face;   157
I told him he look'd like a candle half
Burn'd out; he answer'd, he was 'pig enough
To light another pattle.' Last night, beneath

The moon I walk'd abroad, when all had pitch'd   161
Their tents, and all were still ;
I heard a blooming youth singing a song
He had compos'd, and at each pause he wip'd
His dropping eyes. The ditty was, 'if he   165
Return'd victorious, he should wed a maiden
Fairer than snow, and rich as midsummer.'
Another wept, and wish'd health to his father.
I chid them both, but gave them noble hopes.   169
These are the minds that glory in the battle,
And leap and dance to hear the trumpet sound.
   King. Sir Thomas Dagworth, be thou near our person ;
Thy heart is richer than the vales of France :   173
I will not part with such a man as thee.
If Philip came arm'd in the ribs of death,
And shook his mortal dart against my head,
Thou'dst laugh his fury into nerveless shame !   177
Go now, for thou art suited to the work,
Throughout the camp ; enflame the timorous,
Blow up the sluggish into ardour, and
Confirm the strong with strength, the weak inspire,   181
And wing their brows with hope and expectation :
Then to our tent return, and meet to council.   [*Exit Dagworth.*
   Chand. That man's a hero in his closet, and more
A hero to the servants of his house   185
Than to the gaping world ; he carries windows
In that enlargèd breast of his, that all
May see what's done within.
   Prince. He is a genuine Englishman, my Chandos,   189
And hath the spirit of Liberty within him.
Forgive my prejudice, Sir John ; I think
My Englishmen the bravest people on
The face of the earth.   193
   Chand. Courage, my Lord, proceeds from self-dependence.
Teach man to think he's a free agent,
Give but a slave his liberty, he'll shake
Off sloth, and build himself a hut, and hedge   197
A spot of ground ; this he'll defend ; 'tis his
By right of nature : thus set in action,
He will still move onward to plan conveniences,
'Till glory fires his breast to enlarge his castle ;   201
While the poor slave drudges all day, in hope
To rest at night.
   King. O Liberty, how glorious art thou !
I see thee hov'ring o'er my army, with   205
Thy wide-stretch'd plumes ; I see thee
Lead them on to battle ;
I see thee blow thy golden trumpet, while
Thy sons shout the strong shout of victory !   209
O noble Chandos, think thyself a gardener,

My son a vine, which I commit unto
Thy care : prune all extravagant shoots, and guide
Th' ambitious tendrils in the paths of wisdom ;   213
Water him with thy advice ; and Heav'n
Rain fresh'ning dew upon his branches. And,
O Edward, my dear son ! learn to think lowly of •
Thyself, as we may all each prefer other—   217
'Tis the best policy, and 'tis our duty.   [*Exeunt King Edward.*
    Prince. And may our duty, Chandos, be our pleasure.
Now we are alone, Sir John, I will unburden,
And breathe my hopes into the burning air,   221
Where thousand deaths are posting up and down,
Commission'd to this fatal field of Cressy.
Methinks I see them arm my gallant soldiers,
And gird the sword upon each thigh, and fit   225
Each shining helm, and string each stubborn bow,
And dance to the neighing of our steeds.
Methinks the shout begins, the battle burns.
Methinks I see them perch on English crests,   229
And roar the wild flame of fierce war upon
The throngèd enemy. In truth I am too full ;
It is my sin to love the noise of war.
Chandos, thou seest my weakness ; strong nature   233
Will bend or break us : my blood, like a springtide,
Does rise so high to overflow all bounds
Of moderation ; while Reason, in her
Frail bark, can see no shore or bound for vast   237
Ambition. Come, take the helm, my Chandos,
That my full-blown sails overset me not
In the wild tempest : condemn my 'ventrous youth,
That plays with danger as the innocent child   241
Unthinking plays upon the viper's den :
I am a coward in my reason, Chandos.
    Chand. You are a man, my prince, and a brave man,
If I can judge of actions ; but your heat   245
Is the effect of youth, and want of use :
Use makes the armèd field and noisy war
Pass over as a summer cloud, unregarded,
Or but expected as a thing of course.   249
Age is contemplative ; each rolling year
Brings forth fruit to the mind's treasure-house :
While vacant youth doth crave and seek about
Within itself, and findeth discontent,   253
Then, tir'd of thought, impatient takes the wing,
Seizes the fruits of time, attacks experience,
Roams round vast Nature's forest, where no bounds
Are set, the swiftest may have room, the strongest   257
Find prey ; till tir'd at length, sated and tired
With the changing sameness, old variety,
We sit us down, and view our former joys

With distaste and dislike.   261
 Prince. Then, if we must tug for experience,
Let us not fear to beat round Nature's wilds,
And rouze the strongest prey: then if we fall,
We fall with glory. I know the wolf   265
Is dangerous to fight, not good for food,
Nor is the hide a comely vestment; so
We have our battle for our pains. I know
That youth has need of age to point fit prey,   269
And oft the stander-by shall steal the fruit
Of th' other's labour. This is philosophy;
These are the tricks of the world; but the pure soul
Shall mount on native wings, disdaining   273
Little sport, and cut a path into the heaven of glory,
Leaving a track of light for men to wonder at.
I'm glad my father does not hear me talk;
You can find friendly excuses for me, Chandos.   277
But do you not think, Sir John, that if it please
Th' Almighty to stretch out my span of life,
I shall with pleasure view a glorious action
Which my youth master'd?   281
 Chand. Considerate age, my Lord, views motives,
And not acts; when neither warbling voice
Nor trilling pipe is heard, nor pleasure sits
With trembling age, the voice of Conscience then,   285
Sweeter than music in a summer's eve,
Shall warble round the snowy head, and keep
Sweet symphony to feather'd angels, sitting
As guardians round your chair; then shall the pulse   289
Beat slow, and taste and touch and sight and sound and smell,
That sing and dance round Reason's fine-wrought throne,
Shall flee away, and leave them all forlorn;
Yet not forlorn if Conscience is his friend.   293
          [*Exeunt.*

  SCENE, *in Sir Thomas Dagworth's Tent. Dagworth and*
       William his Man.

 Dagw. Bring hither my armour, William.
Ambition is the growth of ev'ry clime.
 Will. Does it grow in England, Sir?
 Dagw. Aye, it grows most in lands most cultivated.
 Will. Then it grows most in France; the vines here
Are finer than any we have in England.
 Dagw. Aye, but the oaks are not.
 Will. What is the tree you mentioned? I don't think
I ever saw it.
 Dagw. Ambition.
 Will. Is it a little creeping root that grows in ditches?
 Dagw. Thou dost not understand me, William
It is a root that grows in every breast;

Ambition is the desire or passion that one man
Has to get before another, in any pursuit after glory ;
But I don't think you have any of it.

Will. Yes, I have ; I have a great ambition to know every thing, Sir.

Dagw. But when our first ideas are wrong, what follows must all be wrong of course ; 'tis best to know a little, and to know that little aright.

Will. Then, Sir, I should be glad to know if it was not ambition that brought over our King to France to fight for his right?

Dagw. Tho' the knowledge of that will not profit thee much, yet I will tell you that it was ambition.

Will. Then, if ambition is a sin, we are all guilty in coming with him, and in fighting for him.

Dagw. Now, William, thou dost thrust the question home ; but I must tell you that, guilt being an act of the mind, none are guilty but those whose minds are prompted by that same ambition.

Will. Now, I always thought that a man might be guilty of doing wrong without knowing it was wrong.

Dagw. Thou art a natural philosopher, and knowest truth by instinct ; while reason runs aground, as we have run our argument. Only remember, William, all have it in their power to know the motives of their own actions, and 'tis a sin to act without some reason.

Will. And whoever acts without reason may do a great deal of harm without knowing it.

Dagw. Thou art an endless moralist.

Will. Now there's a story come into my head, that I will tell your honour if you'll give me leave.

Dagw. No, William, save it till another time ; this is no time for story-telling : but here comes one who is as entertaining as a good story.

Enter Peter Blunt.

Peter. Yonder's a musician going to play before the King ; it's a new song about the French and English, and the Prince has made the minstrel a 'squire, and given him I don't know what, and I can't tell whether he don't mention us all one by one ; and he is to write another about all us that are to die, that we may be remembered in Old England, for all our blood and bones are in France ; and a great deal more that we shall all hear by and by ; and I came to tell your honour, because you love to hear war-songs.

Dagw. And who is this minstrel, Peter, dost know?

Peter. O aye, I forgot to tell that ; he has got the same name as Sir John Chandos, that the prince is always with—the wise man that knows us all as well as your honour, only e'nt so good natur'd.

Dagw. I thank you, Peter, for your information, but not for your compliment, which is not true ; there's as much difference between him and me as between glittering sand and fruitful mold ; or shining glass and a wrought diamond, set in rich gold, and fitted to the finger of an emperor ; such is that worthy Chandos.

Peter. I know your honour does not think any thing of yourself, but every body else does.

Dagw. Go, Peter, get you gone; flattery is delicious, even from the lips of a babbler. [*Exit Peter.*

Will. I never flatter your honour.

Dagw. I don't know that.

Will. Why you know, Sir, when we were in England, at the tournament at Windsor, and the Earl of Warwick was tumbled over, you ask'd me if he did not look well when he fell; and I said No, he look'd very foolish; and you was very angry with me for not flattering you.

Dagw. You mean that I was angry with you for not flattering the Earl of Warwick. [*Exeunt.*

SCENE, *Sir Thomas Dagworth's Tent. Sir Thomas Dagworth—to him*

Enter Sir Walter Manny.

Sir Walter. Sir Thomas Dagworth, I have been weeping   1
Over the men that are to die to-day.

Dagw. Why, brave Sir Walter, you or I may fall.

Sir Walter. I know this breathing flesh must lie and rot,
Cover'd with silence and forgetfulness.   5
Death wons in cities' smoke, and in still night,
When men sleep in their beds, walketh about.
How many in walled cities lie and groan,
Turning themselves upon their beds,   9
Talking with death, answering his hard demands.
How many walk in darkness, terrors are round
The curtains of their beds, destruction is
Ready at the door. How many sleep   13
In earth, cover'd with stones and deathy dust,
Resting in quietness, whose spirits walk
Upon the clouds of heaven to die no more.
Yet death is terrible, tho' borne on angels' wings.   17
How terrible then is the field of death,
Where he doth rend the vault of heaven,
And shake the gates of hell.
O Dagworth, France is sick, the very sky,   21
Tho' sunshine light it, seems to me as pale
As the pale fainting man on his death-bed,
Whose face is shewn by light of sickly taper.
It makes me sad and sick at very heart,   25
Thousands must fall to-day.

Dagw. Thousands of souls must leave this prison-house,
To be exalted to those heavenly fields,
Where songs of triumph, palms of victory,   29
Where peace and joy and love and calm content,
Sit singing in the azure clouds, and strew
Flowers of heaven's growth over the banquet-table.

Bind ardent Hope upon your feet like shoes,   33
Put on the robe of preparation,
The table is prepar'd in shining heaven,
The flowers of immortality are blown;
Let those that fight fight in good stedfastness,   37
And those that fall shall rise in victory.
   Sir Walter. I've often seen the burning field of war,
And often heard the dismal clang of arms;
But never, till this fatal day of Cressy,   41
Has my soul fainted with these views of death.
I seem to be in one great charnel-house,
And seem to scent the rotten carcases;
I seem to hear the dismal yells of death,   45
While the black gore drops from his horrid jaws;
Yet I not fear the monster in his pride—
But O! the souls that are to die to-day!
   Dagw. Stop, brave Sir Walter; let me drop a tear,   49
Then let the clarion of war begin;
I'll fight and weep, 'tis in my country's cause;
I'll weep and shout for glorious liberty.
Grim war shall laugh and shout, deckèd in tears,   53
And blood shall flow like streams across the meadows,
That murmur down their pebbly channels, and
Spend their sweet lives to do their country service:
Then shall England's verdure shoot, her fields shall smile,   57
Her ships shall sing across the foaming sea,
Her mariners shall use the flute and viol,
And rattling guns, and black and dreary war,
Shall be no more.   61
   Sir Walter. Well, let the trumpet sound, and the drum beat;
Let war stain the blue heavens with bloody banners;
I'll draw my sword, nor ever sheath it up
'Till England blow the trump of victory,   65
Or I lay stretch'd upon the field of death.   [*Exeunt.*

SCENE, *in the Camp. Several of the Warriors meet at the King's Tent
with a Minstrel, who sings the following Song:*

O sons of Trojan Brutus, cloath'd in war,   1
Whose voices are the thunder of the field,
Rolling dark clouds o'er France, muffling the sun
In sickly darkness like a dim eclipse,
Threatening as the red brow of storms, as fire   5
Burning up nations in your wrath and fury!

Your ancestors came from the fires of Troy,
(Like lions rouz'd by light'ning from their dens,
Whose eyes do glare against the stormy fires),   9
Heated with war, fill'd with the blood of Greeks,
With helmets hewn, and shields covered with gore,
In navies black, broken with wind and tide:

They landed in firm array upon the rocks   13
Of Albion; they kiss'd the rocky shore;
'Be thou our mother and our nurse,' they said;
'Our children's mother, and thou shalt be our grave,
The sepulchre of ancient Troy, from whence   17
Shall rise cities, and thrones, and arms, and awful pow'rs.'

Our fathers swarm from the ships. Giant voices
Are heard from the hills, the enormous sons
Of Ocean run from rocks and caves ; wild men,   21
Naked and roaring like lions, hurling rocks,
And wielding knotty clubs, like oaks entangled
Thick as a forest, ready for the axe.

Our fathers move in firm array to battle ;   25
The savage monsters rush like roaring fire ;
Like as a forest roars with crackling flames,
When the red lightning, borne by furious storms,
Lights on some woody shore; the parchèd heavens   29
Rain fire into the molten raging sea.

The smoking trees are strewn upon the shore,
Spoil'd of their verdure. O how oft have they
Defy'd the storm that howlèd o'er their heads !   33
Our fathers, sweating, lean on their spears, and view
The mighty dead : giant bodies streaming blood,
Dread visages frowning in silent death.

Then Brutus spoke, inspir'd; our fathers sit   37
Attentive on the melancholy shore :
Hear ye the voice of Brutus—'The flowing waves
Of time come rolling o'er my breast,' he said ;
'And my heart labours with futurity :   41
Our sons shall rule the empire of the sea.

'Their mighty wings shall stretch from east to west.
Their nest is in the sea, but they shall roam
Like eagles for the prey; nor shall the young   45
Crave or be heard; for plenty shall bring forth,
Cities shall sing, and vales in rich array
Shall laugh, whose fruitful laps bend down with fulness.

19, 35 Giant voices . . . giant bodies] Cp. 'Giants ancient inhabitants of
England,' the first entry in Blake's list of subjects for a history of England
(MS. Book, p. 116). In the prospectus of 'Works now published and on
sale at Mr. Blake's, No. 13, Hercules Buildings, Lambeth,' October 10, 1793,
is included 'The History of England, a small book of Engravings. Price 3*s.*'
This work, no copy of which is known to exist, would seem to show that
Blake engraved these subjects as a companion volume to *The Gates of
Paradise*, which is described in the same leaflet in identical terms.

'Our sons shall rise from thrones in joy,   49
Each one buckling on his armour ; Morning
Shall be prevented by their swords gleaming,
And Evening hear their song of victory :
Their towers shall be built upon the rocks,   53
Their daughters shall sing, surrounded with shining spears.

'Liberty shall stand upon the cliffs of Albion,
Casting her blue eyes over the green ocean ;
Or, tow'ring, stand upon the roaring waves,   57
Stretching her mighty spear o'er distant lands ;
While, with her eagle wings, she covereth
Fair Albion's shore, and all her families.'

Prologue, intended for a Dramatic Piece of King Edward the Fourth

O for a voice like thunder, and a tongue   1
To drown the throat of war! When the senses
Are shaken, and the soul is driven to madness,
Who can stand? When the souls of the oppressed
Fight in the troubled air that rages, who can stand?   5
When the whirlwind of fury comes from the
Throne of God, when the frowns of his countenance
Drive the nations together, who can stand?
When Sin claps his broad wings over the battle,   9
And sails rejoicing in the flood of Death;
When souls are torn to everlasting fire,
And fiends of Hell rejoice upon the slain,
O who can stand? O who hath causèd this?   13
O who can answer at the throne of God?
The Kings and Nobles of the Land have done it!
Hear it not, Heaven, thy Ministers have done it!

Prologue to King John

Justice hath heaved a sword to plunge in Albion's breast ; for Albion's
sins are crimson dy'd, and the red scourge follows her desolate sons. Then
Patriot rose ; full oft did Patriot rise, when Tyranny hath stain'd fair
Albion's breast with her own children's gore. Round his majestic feet
deep thunders roll ; each heart does tremble, and each knee grows slack.
The stars of heaven tremble ; the roaring voice of war, the trumpet, calls
to battle. Brother in brother's blood must bathe, rivers of death. O land
most hapless ! O beauteous island, how forsaken ! Weep from thy silver

fountains, weep from thy gentle rivers! The angel of the island weeps!
Thy widowed virgins weep beneath thy shades! Thy aged fathers gird
themselves for war! The sucking infant lives to die in battle; the weeping
mother feeds him for the slaughter! The husbandman doth leave his
bending harvest! Blood cries afar! The land doth sow itself! The
glittering youth of courts must gleam in arms! The aged senators their
ancient swords assume! The trembling sinews of old age must work the
work of death against their progeny, for Tyranny hath stretch'd his purple
arm, and 'blood' he cries; 'the chariots and the horses, the noise of shout,
and dreadful thunder of the battle heard afar!' Beware, O Proud, thou
shalt be humbled; thy cruel brow, thine iron heart, is smitten, though
lingering Fate is slow. O yet may Albion smile again, and stretch her
peaceful arms, and raise her golden head exultingly! Her citizens shall
throng about her gates, her mariners shall sing upon the sea, and myriads
shall to her temples crowd! Her sons shall joy as in the morning! Her
daughters sing as to the rising year!

A War Song to Englishmen

Prepare, prepare the iron helm of war,   1
Bring forth the lots, cast in the spacious orb;
Th' Angel of Fate turns them with mighty hands,
And casts them out upon the darken'd earth!
               Prepare, prepare.   5

Prepare your hearts for Death's cold hand! prepare
Your souls for flight, your bodies for the earth;
Prepare your arms for glorious victory!
Prepare your eyes to meet a holy God!
               Prepare, prepare.   10

Whose fatal scroll is that? Methinks 'tis mine!
Why sinks my heart, why faultereth my tongue?
Had I three lives, I'd die in such a cause,
And rise, with ghosts, over the well-fought field.
               Prepare, prepare.   15

The arrows of Almighty God are drawn!
Angels of Death stand in the low'ring heavens!
Thousands of souls must seek the realms of light,
And walk together on the clouds of heaven!
               Prepare, prepare.   20

Soldiers, prepare! Our cause is Heaven's cause;
Soldiers, prepare! Be worthy of our cause:
Prepare to meet our fathers in the sky:
Prepare, O troops, that are to fall to-day!
               Prepare, prepare.   25

Alfred shall smile, and make his harp rejoice;
The Norman William, and the learnèd Clerk,
And Lion Heart, and black-brow'd Edward, with
His loyal queen shall rise, and welcome us!
                                Prepare, prepare.   30

The Couch of Death

The veiled Evening walked solitary down the western hills, and Silence
reposed in the valley; the birds of day were heard in their nests, rustling
in brakes and thickets; and the owl and bat flew round the darkening
trees: all is silent when Nature takes her repose. In former times, on
such an evening, when the cold clay breathed with life, and our ancestors,
who now sleep in their graves, walked on the stedfast globe, the remains
of a family of the tribes of Earth, a mother and a sister, were gathered to
the sick bed of a youth. Sorrow linked them together; leaning on one
another's necks alternately, like lilies dropping tears in each other's bosom,
they stood by the bed like reeds bending over a lake, when the evening
drops trickle down. His voice was low as the whisperings of the woods
when the wind is asleep, and the visions of Heaven unfold their visitation.
'Parting is hard and death is terrible; I seem to walk through a deep
valley, far from the light of day, alone and comfortless! The damps of death
fall thick upon me! Horrors stare me in the face! I look behind, there is
no returning; Death follows after me; I walk in regions of Death, where no
tree is; without a lantern to direct my steps, without a staff to support me.'
Thus he laments through the still evening, till the curtains of darkness were
drawn. Like the sound of a broken pipe, the aged woman raised her voice.
'O my son, my son, I know but little of the path thou goest. But lo, there
is a God, who made the world; stretch out thy hand to Him.' The youth
replied, like a voice heard from a sepulchre, 'My hand is feeble, how should
I stretch it out? My ways are sinful, how should I raise mine eyes? My
voice hath used deceit, how should I call on Him who is Truth? My breath
is loathsome, how should he not be offended? If I lay my face in the dust,
the grave opens its mouth for me; if I lift up my head, sin covers me as a
cloak. O my dear friends, pray ye for me! Stretch forth your hands that
my helper may come! Through the void space I walk, between the sinful
world and eternity! Beneath me burns eternal fire! O for a hand to pluck
me forth!' As the voice of an omen heard in the silent valley, when the
few inhabitants cling trembling together; as the voice of the Angel of Death,
when the thin beams of the moon give a faint light; such was this young
man's voice to his friends. Like the bubbling waters of the brook in the
dead of night, the aged woman raised her cry, and said, 'O Voice, that
dwellest in my breast, can I not cry, and lift my eyes to Heaven? Thinking
of this, my spirit is turned within me into confusion. O my child, my child,
is thy breath infected? So is mine. As the deer wounded, by the brooks
of water, so the arrows of sin stick in my flesh; the poison hath entered

into my marrow.' Like rolling waves upon a desert shore, sighs succeeded sighs, they covered their faces and wept. The youth lay silent, his mother's arm was under his head ; he was like a cloud tossed by the winds, till the sun shine, and the drops of rain glisten, the yellow harvest breathes, and the thankful eyes of the villagers are turned up in smiles. The traveller that hath taken shelter under an oak, eyes the distant country with joy. Such smiles were seen upon the face of the youth, a visionary hand wiped away his tears, and a ray of light beamed around his head. All was still. The moon hung not out her lamp, and the stars faintly glimmered in the summer sky ; the breath of night slept among the leaves of the forest ; the bosom of the lofty hill drank in the silent dew, while on his majestic brow the voice of Angels is heard, and stringed sounds ride upon the wings of night. The sorrowful pair lift up their heads, hovering Angels are around them, voices of comfort are heard over the Couch of Death, and the youth breathes out his soul with joy into eternity.

Contemplation

Who is this, that with unerring step dares tempt the wilds, where only Nature's foot hath trod ? 'Tis Contemplation, daughter of the grey Morning ! Majestical she steppeth, and with her pure quill on every flower writeth Wisdom's name. Now lowly bending, whispers in mine ear, ' O man, how great, how little thou ! O man, slave of each moment, lord of eternity ! seest thou where Mirth sits on the painted cheek ? doth it not seem ashamed of such a place, and grow immoderate to brave it out ? O what an humble garb true Joy puts on ! Those who want Happiness must stoop to find it ; it is a flower that grows in every vale. Vain foolish man, that roams on lofty rocks, where, 'cause his garments are swoln with wind, he fancies he is grown into a giant ! Lo, then, Humility, take it, and wear it in thine heart ; lord of thyself, thou then art lord of all. Clamour brawls along the streets, and destruction hovers in the city's smoak ; but on these plains, and in these silent woods, true joys descend : here build thy nest ; here fix thy staff ; delights blossom around ; numberless beauties blow ; the green grass springs in joy, and the nimble air kisses the leaves ; the brook stretches its arms along the velvet meadow, its silver inhabitants sport and play ; the youthful sun joys like a hunter rouzed to the chace, he rushes up the sky, and lays hold on the immortal coursers of day, the sky glitters with the jingling trappings. Like a triumph, season follows season, while the airy music fills the world with joyful sounds.' I answered, ' Heavenly goddess ! I am wrapped in mortality, my flesh is a prison, my bones the bars of death, Misery builds over our cottage roofs, and Discontent runs like a brook. Even in childhood, Sorrow slept with me in my cradle ; he followed me up and down in the house when I grew up ; he was my schoolfellow : thus he was in my steps and in my play, till he became to me as my brother. I walked through dreary places with him, and in church-yards ; and I oft found myself sitting by Sorrow on a tomb-stone.'

Samson

Samson, the strongest of the children of men, I sing; how he was foiled by woman's arts, by a false wife brought to the gates of death. O Truth, that shinest with propitious beams, turning our earthly night to heavenly day, from presence of the Almighty Father thou visitest our darkling world with blessed feet, bringing good news of Sin and Death destroyed. O white-robed Angel, guide my timorous hand to write as on a lofty rock with iron pens the words of truth, that all who pass may read. Now Night, noon-tide of damned spirits, over the silent earth spreads her pavilion, while in dark council sat Philista's lords; and, where strength failed, black thoughts in ambush lay. Their helmèd youth and aged warriors in dust together ly, and Desolation spreads his wings over the land of Palestine: from side to side the land groans, her prowess lost, and seeks to hide her bruised head under the mists of night, breeding dark plots. For Dalila's fair arts have long been tried in vain; in vain she wept in many a treacherous tear. 'Go on, fair traitress; do thy guileful work; ere once again the changing moon her circuit hath performed, thou shalt overcome, and conquer him by force unconquerable, and wrest his secret from him. Call thine alluring arts and honest-seeming brow, the holy kiss of love, and the transparent tear; put on fair linen that with the lily vies, purple and silver; neglect thy hair, to seem more lovely in thy loose attire; put on thy country's pride, deceit; and eyes of love decked in mild sorrow; and sell thy Lord for gold.' For now, upon her sumptuous couch reclined in gorgeous pride, she still intreats, and still she grasps his vigorous knees with her fair arms. 'Thou lov'st me not! thou'rt war, thou art not love! O foolish Dalila! O weak woman! it is death cloathed in flesh thou lovest, and thou hast been incircled in his arms! Alas, my Lord, what am I calling thee? Thou art my God! To thee I pour my tears for sacrifice morning and evening. My days are covered with sorrow. Shut up, darkened. By night I am deceived. Who says that thou wast born of mortal kind? Destruction was thy father, a lioness suckled thee, thy young hands tore human limbs, and gorgèd human flesh. Come hither, Death, art thou not Samson's servant? 'Tis Dalila that calls; thy master's wife; no, stay, and let thy master do the deed: one blow of that strong arm would ease my pain; then should I lay at quiet and have rest. Pity forsook thee at thy birth! O Dagon furious, and all ye gods of Palestine, withdraw your hand! I am but a weak woman. Alas, I am wedded to your enemy! I will go mad, and tear my crispèd hair; I'll run about, and pierce the ears o' th' gods! O Samson, hold me not; thou lovest me not! Look not upon me with those deathful eyes! Thou wouldst my death, and death approaches fast.' Thus, in false tears, she bath'd his feet, and thus she day by day oppressed his soul: he seemed a mountain, his brow among the clouds; she seemed a silver stream, his feet embracing. Dark thoughts rolled to and fro in his mind, like thunder clouds troubling the sky; his visage was troubled; his soul was distressed. 'Though I should tell her all my heart, what can I fear? Though I should tell this secret of my birth, the utmost may be warded off as well when told as now.' She saw him moved, and thus resumes her wiles. 'Samson, I'm thine; do with me what thou wilt; my friends are enemies; my life is death; I am a traitor to my nation, and despised; my joy is given into the hands of him who hates me, using deceit to the wife of his bosom. Thrice hast thou mocked me and grieved my soul. Didst thou not tell me with green withs to bind thy nervous arms, and, after that, when I had found thy falsehood, with new ropes to bind thee fast? I knew thou didst but mock me. Alas, when in thy sleep I bound thee with them to try thy truth, I cried, "The Philistines be upon thee, Samson!" Then did suspicion wake thee; how didst thou rend the feeble ties! Thou fearest nought, what shouldst thou fear? Thy power is more than mortal, none can hurt thee; thy bones are brass, thy sinews are iron. Ten thousand spears are like the summer grass; an army of mighty men are as flocks in the vallies; what canst thou fear? I drink my tears like water; I live upon sorrow! O worse than wolves and tygers, what canst thou give when such a trifle is denied me? But O! at last thou mockest me, to shame my over-fond inquiry. Thou toldest me to weave thee to the beam by thy strong hair; I did even that to try thy truth; but, when I cried "The Philistines be upon thee!" then didst thou leave me to bewail that Samson loved me not.' He sat, and inward griev'd, he saw and lov'd the beauteous suppliant, nor could conceal aught that might appease her: then, leaning on her bosom, thus he spoke. 'Hear, O Dalila! doubt no more of Samson's love; for that fair breast was made the ivory palace of my inmost heart, where it shall lie at rest: for sorrow is the lot of all of woman born: for care was I brought forth, and labour is my lot: nor matchless might, nor wisdom, nor every gift enjoyed, can from the heart of man hide sorrow. Twice was my birth foretold from heaven, and twice a sacred vow enjoined me that I should drink no wine, nor eat of any unclean thing, for holy unto Israel's God I am, a Nazarite even from my mother's womb. Twice was it told, that it might not be broken. "Grant me a son, kind Heaven," Manoa cried; but Heaven refused. Childless he mourned, but thought his God knew best. In solitude, though not obscure, in Israel he lived, till venerable age came on: his flocks increased, and plenty crowned his board: beloved, revered of man. But God hath other joys in store. Is burdened Israel his grief? The son of his old age shall set it free. The venerable sweet'ner of his life receives the promise first from Heaven. She saw the maidens play, and blessed their innocent mirth; she blessed each new-joined pair; but from her the long-wished deliverer shall spring. Pensive, alone she sat within the house, when busy day was fading, and calm evening, time for contemplation, rose from the forsaken east, and drew the curtains of heaven: pensive she sat, and thought on Israel's grief, and silent prayed to Israel's God; when lo, an angel from the fields of light entered the house. His form was manhood in the prime, and from his spacious brow shot terrors through the evening shade. But mild he hailed her, "Hail, highly favoured!" said he; "for lo, thou shalt conceive, and bear a son, and Israel's strength shall be upon his shoulders, and he shall be called Israel's Deliverer. Now, therefore, drink no wine, and eat not any unclean thing, for he shall be a Nazarite to God." Then, as a neighbour, when his evening tale is told, departs, his blessing leaving, so seemed he to depart: she wondered with exceeding joy, nor knew he was an angel. Manoa left his fields to sit in the house, and take his evening's rest from labour—the sweetest time that God has allotted mortal man. He sat, and heard with joy, and praised God, who Israel still doth keep. The time rolled on, and Israel groaned oppressed. The sword was bright, while the plow-share rusted, till hope grew feeble, and was ready to give place to doubting: then prayed Manoa: "O Lord, thy flock is scattered on the hills. The wolf teareth them, Oppression stretches his rod over our land, our country is plowed with swords, and reaped in blood. The echoes of slaughter reach from hill to hill. Instead of peaceful pipe the shepherd bears a sword, the ox goad is turned into a spear. O when shall our Deliverer come? The Philistine riots on our flocks, our vintage is gathered by bands of enemies. Stretch forth thy hand, and save." Thus prayed Manoa. The aged woman walked into the field, and lo, again the angel came. Clad as a traveller fresh risen on his journey, she ran and called her husband, who came and talked with him. "O man of God," said he, "thou comest from far. Let us detain thee while I make ready a kid, that thou mayest sit and eat, and tell us of thy name and warfare; that, when thy sayings come to pass, we may honour thee." The Angel answered, "My name is wonderful; enquire not after it, seeing it is a secret: but, if thou wilt, offer an offering unto the Lord."'

APPENDIX II

[The two songs referred to in editor's introduction, found in Blake's autograph on the fly-leaves of a copy of the original edition of *Poetical Sketches*, and here reprinted from Shepherd's text (ed. 1874, p. 154). See also his Introduction to that edition, p. vi.]

Song by a Shepherd

Welcome, stranger, to this place,   1
Where joy doth sit on every bough,
Paleness flies from every face;
We reap not what we do not sow.

Innocence doth like a rose   5
Bloom on every maiden's cheek;
Honour twines around her brows,
The jewel health adorns her neck.

Shepherd, p. 154.
                     1 stranger] little stranger EY.

Song by an Old Shepherd

When silver snow decks Sylvia's clothes,   1
And jewel hangs at shepherd's nose,
We can abide life's pelting storm,
That makes our limbs quake, if our hearts be warm.

Whilst Virtue is our walking-staff,   5
And Truth a lantern to our path,
We can abide life's pelting storm,
That makes our limbs quake, if our hearts be warm.

Blow, boisterous wind, stern Winter frown,   9
Innocence is a Winter's gown.
So clad, we'll abide life's pelting storm,
That makes our limbs quake, if our hearts be warm.

Shepherd, p. 154.
1, 2 When . . . nose]. Cp. Blind-man's Buff (*Poetical Sketches*), ll. 1-2.
8 That] Which EY.

SONGS

from

AN ISLAND IN THE MOON

(an untitled Autograph MS., circa 1784)

BIBLIOGRAPHICAL PREFACE

TO

AN ISLAND IN THE MOON

The Blake MS. known as *An Island in the Moon*, is a thin foolscap folio volume of sixteen leaves, lacking two (or perhaps four) leaves through the loss of one (or two) sheets from the centre of the single quire of which it is composed.

The autograph is in Blake's early hand, and begins at the head of the first page (recto of first leaf):—

'In the Moon is a certain Island, near by a mighty continent, which small island seems to have some affinity to England, & what is more extraordinary the people are so much alike, & their language so much the same, that you would think you was among your friends. in this Island dwells three Philosophers, Suction the Epicurean, Quid the Cynic, and Sipsop the Pythagorean. I call them by the names of those sects; tho' the sects are not ever mention'd there, as being quite out of date. however the things still remain, and the vanities are the same. the three Philosophers sat together thinking of nothing. in comes Etruscan Column, the Antiquarian, & after an abundance of Enquiries to no purpose sat himself down & described something that nobody listen'd to. so they were employ'd when Mrs. Gimblet came in.'

It ends abruptly—or rather is left unfinished by the author—on line nineteen of the recto of the leaf following the lacuna in the text, now the seventeenth page, but which, when the book was complete, must have been page 21 or 25. The remaining pages are blank, with the exception of the verso of the last leaf, which is scribbled over with rough sketches and pen-trials, among them Blake's signature written backwards as if engraved on copper-plate. The soiled appearance of this last verso proves it to have been the original outer leaf of the MS., and since it is also, as

the watermarks show, the other half of the sheet on which
the work begins, there are no grounds for Messrs. Ellis
and Yeats' conjecture that the MS. at one time possessed
a first leaf containing a title-page.

The brochure itself, which may be described as a somewhat incoherent and pointless precursor of the *Headlong
Hall* type of novel, was perhaps intended by the author as
a satire on the little coterie of distinguished personages
which met at Mrs. Mathews' salon in Rathbone Place ;
but, if so, the originals of the portraits are not now to be
identified, though Quid the Cynic may possibly stand for
Blake himself. I am unable to agree with Mr. Yeats'
surmise that *An Island in the Moon* preceded and even
led to the publication of the *Poetical Sketches* in 1783, and
that Blake's gratitude for Mr. Mathews' share in defray-
ing the cost of printing the little volume caused the author
to leave the present work unfinished. This is to attach
unnecessary importance to a trifle evidently dashed off by
Blake for his own amusement without thought of publication ; nor, as we know from the epigrams in the MS. Book,
was it the poet's wont to allow social patronage or material
assistance to interfere with his Celtic privilege of free
satire. The MS., moreover, contains the first drafts of
' Holy Thursday ' and the ' Nurse's Song,' and had these
beautiful lyrics been written in 1783 it is difficult to believe
that Blake would not have included them in his first
published work. The doggerel lines on Dr. Johnson
are more likely to have been written before than after
Johnson's death. We may therefore, with tolerable certainty, date it between the publication of the *Poetical
Sketches* in 1783, and December 20, 1784, probably in the
latter year, when, as J. T. Smith tells us, Blake's relations
with the Mathews and their circle had become somewhat
strained. In chapters 5 and 7 there are references to the
Chatterton controversy, which reached its height in 1782,
and would seem, when Blake wrote, to have been still a
topic of conversation.

Messrs. Ellis and Yeats have given a synopsis of the
chapters, with copious though rather inaccurately printed
extracts, from this MS. in their edition of Blake's works,
vol. i. pp. 186–201 ; and Mr. Lawrence Housman, who
dates the MS. *circa* 1789, has reprinted three chapters
as specimens of his prose, while, strangely, placing one of
the songs among the ' Later Poems.' The work has never
been printed as a whole ; nor, were this done, would it

add to Blake's literary reputation. Its chief interest to general readers must lie in its giving us the first drafts of three of the *Songs of Innocence*, in its evidence, even at this early date, of Blake's rooted antipathy to science and experiment, and in its foreshadowing, some years beforehand, the 'illuminated printing' which he afterwards employed in the *Songs of Innocence* and in the Prophetic Books.

I do not repeat here the early versions of 'Holy Thursday,' 'Nurse's Song,' or 'The Little Boy Lost,' the variant readings to which are given in the footnotes to the *Songs of Innocence*. Besides the six songs which follow, a number of choruses and nonsense verses are placed in the mouths of several of the characters. Some of these, such as 'This frog he would a wooing ride' and the London street-cry, 'I cry my matches as far as Guildhall,' are plainly not Blake's at all; while others are, as the writer intended them, trivialities or doggerel sung by children or drunken boon-companions. Since these pieces have been referred to and partly quoted by Messrs. Ellis and Yeats, I have thought it necessary to print the whole of them in an Appendix, which all lovers of Blake may pass over.

My text of these poems is taken from my transcript of the original MS., kindly lent to me by Mr. Charles Fairfax Murray, who has since presented it to the Fitzwilliam Museum, Cambridge.

FROM THE ISLAND IN THE MOON

i

1

When old corruption first begun,   1
Adorn'd in yellow vest,
He committed on flesh a whoredom—
O, what a wicked beast!

2

From then a callow babe did spring,   5
And old corruption smil'd
To think his race should never end,
For now he had a child.

3

He call'd him Surgery & fed   9
The babe with his own milk;
For flesh & he could ne'er agree:
She would not let him suck.

4

And this he always kept in mind;   13
And form'd a crooked knife,
And ran about with bloody hands
To seek his mother's life.

Isl. in Moon, chap. vi—'"Ah!" said Sipsop, "I only wish Jack Tearguts had had the cutting of Plutarch; he understands anatomy better than any of the Ancients; he'll plunge his knife up to the hilt in a single drive, and thrust his fist in, and all in the space of a Quarter of an hour: he does not mind their crying—tho' they cry ever so, he'll Swear at them, & keep them down with his fist, & tell them that he'll scrape their bones if they don't lay still & be quiet—What the devil should the people in the hospital, that have it done for nothing, make such a piece of work for?" "Hang that!" said Suction, "let us have a song." Then the Cynic sang :—'
Only printed by EY i. p. 193.
      5 then] there EY.   13 in] on EY.

5

And as he ran to seek his mother   17
He met with a dead woman.
He fell in love & married her—
A deed which is not common!

6

She soon grew pregnant, & brought forth   21
Scurvy & spott'd fever.
The father grinn'd & skipt about,
And said 'I'm made for ever!

7

'For now I have procured these imps   25
I'll try experiments.'
With that he tied poor scurvy down,
& stopt up all its vents.

8

And when the child began to swell   29
He shouted out aloud—
'I've found the dropsy out, & soon
Shall do the world more good.'

9

He took up fever by the neck,   33
And cut out all its spots;
And, thro' the holes which he had made,
He first discover'd guts.

20 which] that EY.

ii

[The Song of Phebe and Jellicoe]

Phebe drest like beautie's Queen,   1
Jellicoe in faint peagreen,
Sitting all beneath a grot,
Where the little lambkins trot.

Maidens dancing, loves a sporting,   5
All the country folks a courting,
Susan, Johnny, Bob, & Joe,
Lightly tripping on a row.

Happy people, who can be   9
In happiness compar'd with ye?
The Pilgrim with his crook & hat
Sees your happiness compleat.

Isl. in Moon, chap. viii—'Then said Miss Gittipin, "Mr. Scopprell, do you know the song of 'Phebe and Jellicoe'?"—"No, Miss," said Scopprell. Then she repeated these verses, while steelyard walk'd about the room.' EY i. p. 196, WBY p. 95 with title 'The Pilgrim.'   LH p. 144.
  5 loves a sporting] lovers sporting EY, WBY.   7 Bob] Bab LH.
10 with] to EY, WBY.

iii

Hail Matrimony, made of Love!   1
To thy wide gates how great a drove
On purpose to be yok'd do come;
Widows & maids & Youths also,
That lightly trip on beauty's toe,
Or sit on beauty's bum.

Isl. in Moon, chap. ix—'"Hang Italian songs! let's have English," said Quid, "English Genius for ever—here I go—."'   The subject and metre of this song were perhaps suggested by 'He that intends to take a wife,' *Pills to purge Melancholy*, iii. p. 106. EY (i. p. 198) print ll. 7, 8, 13, 18, and 25-7.

Hail fingerfooted lovely Creatures!   7
The females of our human Natures,
Formed to suckle all Mankind.
Tis you that come in time of need,
Without you we shoud never Breed,
Or any Comfort find.

For if a Damsel's blind or lame,   13
Or Nature's hand has crooked her frame,
Or if she's deaf, or is wall-eyed;
Yet, if her heart is well inclined,
Some tender lover she shall find
That panteth for a Bride.

The universal Poultice this,   19
To cure whatever is amiss
In damsel or in Widow gay!
It makes them smile, it makes them skip;
Like Birds, just curèd of the pip,
They chirp & hop away.

Then come, ye maidens! come, ye swains!   25
Come & be cured of all your pains
In Matrimony's Golden cage—

7 Hail] EY *omit.*   17 Some tender lover] Some (?friend) or EY.
25 maidens] maids, and EY.   27] Here the song abruptly breaks off.
' "Go and be hanged!" said Scopprell, " how can you have the face to make
game of matrimony?"' The phrase in the last line, as EY point out, explains
the 'golden cage' in the third stanza of 'How sweet I roam'd from field to
field'; see *Poetical Sketches*, 1783, p. 10.

iv

To be or not to be   1
Of great capacity,
Like Sir Isaac Newton,
Or Locke, or Doctor South,
Or Sherlock upon death—
I'd rather be Sutton!

Isl. in Moon, chap. ix—'Then Quid called upon Obtuse Angle for a Song,
& he, wiping his face, & looking on the corner of the cieling, sang:—'
Printed here for the first time.
6 Sutton] Thomas Sutton, founder of the Charterhouse (1532-1611).

For he did build a house   7
For aged men & youth,
With walls of brick & stone;
He furnish'd it within
With whatever he could win,
And all his own.

He drew out of the Stocks   13
His money in a box,
And sent his servant
To Green the Bricklayer,
And to the Carpenter;
He was so fervent.

The chimneys were three score,   19
The windows many more;
And, for convenience,
He sinks & gutters made,
And all the way he pav'd
To hinder pestilence.

Was not this a good man—   25
Whose life was but a span,
Whose name was Sutton—
As Locke, or Doctor South,
Or Sherlock upon Death,
Or Sir Isaac Newton?

V

This city & this country has brought forth many
        mayors   1
To sit in state, & give forth laws out of their old oak
        chairs,
With face as brown as any nut with drinking of strong
        ale—
Good English hospitality, O then it did not fail!

Isl. in Moon, chap. ix—'The Lawgiver was very attentive [to the
preceding song] & beg'd to have it sung over again & again; till the

With scarlet gowns & broad gold lace, would make
    a yeoman sweat ;   5
With stockings roll'd above their knees & shoes as black
    as jet ;
With eating beef & drinking beer, O they were stout
    & hale—
Good English hospitality, O then it did not fail!

Thus sitting at the table wide the Mayor & Alder-
    men   9
Were fit to give law to the city; each eat as much as
    ten :
The hungry poor enter'd the hall to eat good beef
    & ale—
Good English hospitality, O then it did not fail!

company were tired, & insisted on the Lawgiver singing a song himself,
which he readily complied with :—'

    Cp. 'Old English hospitality is long since deceased,' in Chatterton's
'Antiquity of Christmas Games,' an essay reprinted in the *Miscellanies* of
1778, with which work Blake appears to me to have been familiar.

    EY i. pp. 198–9. WBY (p. 135) entitles this song 'Old English Hospitality,'
following the inaccurate version given of the refrain in the first and second
stanza by EY.

    1 has] have WBY.   4 and 8 Good] Old EY, WBY.   10 law]
laws EY, WBY.

vi

    Leave, O leave [me] to my sorrows ;   1
    Here I'll sit & fade away,
    Till I'm nothing but a spirit,
    And I lose this form of clay.

    Then if chance along this forest   5
    Any walk in pathless ways,
    Thro' the gloom he'll see my shadow,
    Hear my voice upon the Breeze.

    Isl. in Moon, chap. xi—'Here a laugh began, and Miss Gittipin sung—.'
EY i. p. 200. WBY (p. 102) prints as a single stanza, with title 'A Song of
Sorrow.'

    1 me] *omitted in orig.* ; me EY, WBY.   sorrows] sorrow EY, WBY.
4 lose] love EY, WBY.

APPENDIX

TO

AN ISLAND IN THE MOON

a

Little Phebus came strutting in,   1
With his fat belly & his round chin.
What is it you would please to have?
Ho! Ho!
I won't let it go at only so & so!   5

Isl. in Moon, chap. iii.   Sung by Quid the Cynic.   EY i. p. 189.
5 so & so] so so EY.

b

Honour & Genius is all I ask,
And I ask the Gods no more!
            No more! No more! ⎱ *the three Philosophers*
            No more! No more! ⎰   *bear chorus.*

Isl. in Moon, chap. iii.   Sung by Quid the Cynic.   EY i. p. 190.

c

Hear then the pride & knowledge of a Sailor!   1
His sprit sail, fore sail, main sail, & his mizen.
A poor frail man—god wot! I know none frailer,
I know no greater sinner than John Taylor.

Isl. in Moon, chap. viii.   Sung by Steelyard, the Lawgiver.   Not in EY.

d

Lo! the Bat with Leathern wing,   1
Winking & blinking,
Winking & blinking,
Winking & blinking,
Like Dr. Johnson.

Quid. 'O ho!' said Dr. Johnson   6
To Scipio Africanus,
'If you don't own me a Philosopher
*** **** **** ***** ****.'

Isl. in Moon, chap. ix—'"I say, this evening we'll all get drunk.   I say,

Suction. 'A ha!' to Dr. Johnson   10
          Said Scipio Africanus,
          **** ** ** ***** **********
          *** **** ** ***** ****'
     And the Cellar goes down with a step (*Grand*
                                    Chorus).

dash, an Anthem! an Anthem!" said Suction—.'   EY (i. p. 196) print this
stanza.

e

     1*st Vo*. Want Matches?   1
     2*nd Vo*. Yes! Yes! Yes!
     1*st Vo*. Want Matches?
     2*nd Vo*. No!

     1*st Vo*. Want Matches?   5
     2*nd Vo*. Yes! Yes! Yes!
     1*st Vo*. Want Matches?
     2*nd Vo*. No!

Isl. in Moon, chap. **ix**.   Song of boy match-sellers.   Not in EY.

f

     I cry my matches as far as Guildhall:
     God bless the duke & his aldermen all!

Isl. in Moon, chap. ix.   Probably an old London street-cry.   Here sung
by Mrs. Nannicantipol.   Not in EY.

g

     As I walk'd forth one may morning   1
     To see the fields so pleasant & so gay,
     O! there did I spy a young maiden sweet,
     Among the Violets that smell so sweet,
                         smell so sweet,
                         smell so sweet,
     Among the Violets that smell so sweet.   7

Isl. in Moon, chap. ix—' Then said Suction, " come, Mr. Lawgiver, your
song!" and the Lawgiver sang ... " Hang your Violets! here's your Rum
and water."'   Not in EY.

h

This frog he would a wooing ride,
Kitty alone! Kitty alone!
This frog he would a wooing ride,
Kitty alone & I!
Ting cock, I cary, Kitty alone!
Kitty Alone! Kitty alone!
Cock I cary Kitty alone,
Kitty alone & I!

Isl. in Moon, chap. ix—' " Miss Gittipin," said he, " you sing like a harpsi-chord ; let your bounty descend to our fair ears, and favour us with a fine song." Then she sung—.' Cp. variant of this song, with same refrain, in Halliwell's *Nursery Rhymes of England* (Percy Society), 1842. Not in EY.

i

O, I say, you Joe,	1
Throw us the ball!	
I've a good mind to go	
And leave you all.	
I never saw such a bowler	5
To bowl the ball in a tansey,	
And to clean it with my hankercher	
Without saying a word.	
That Bill's a foolish fellow;	9
He has given me a black eye.	
He does not know how to handle a bat	
Any more than a dog or a cat :	
He has knock'd down the wicket,	13
And broke the stumps,	
And runs without shoes to save his pumps.	

Isl. in Moon, chap. xi—' Here nobody could sing any longer, till Tilly Lally pluck'd up a spirit, & he sung—.' Not in EY.

k

There's Doctor Clash,	1
And Sinior Falalasole,	
O they sweep in the cash	
Into their purse hole!	
Fa me la sol La me fa Sol!	

Isl. in Moon, chap. xi—' The Lawgiver all the while sat delighted to see

Great A, little A,   6
Bouncing B !
Play away, Play away,
You'r out of the key!
Fa me la sol La me fa sol!

Musicians should have   11
A pair of very good ears,
And Long fingers & thumbs,
And not like clumsy bears.
Fa me la sol La me fa sol!

Gentlemen ! Gentlemen !   16
Rap ! Rap ! Rap !
Fiddle ! Fiddle ! Fiddle !
Clap ! Clap ! Clap !
Fa me la sol La me fa sol!

them in such a serious humour. " Mr. Scropprell," said he, " you must be
acquainted with a great many songs?" " O, dear sir, Ho ! Ho ! Ho ! I am
no singer ; I must beg of one of these tender hearted ladies to sing for me."
They all declined, & he was forced to sing himself.'   Not in EY.

1

A crowned king,
On a white horse sitting,
With his trumpets sounding,
And Banners flying ;
Thro' the clouds of smoke he makes his way,
And the shout of his thousands fills his heart with
    rejoicing & victory.
And the shout of his thousands fills his heart with
    rejoicing & victory.
Victory ! Victory ! 'twas William the prince of Orange.

Isl. in Moon, chap. ix—' Then said the Lawgiver, " funny enough, let's
have handel's waterpiece."   Then Sipsop sung—.'   Not in EY, who refer
to it as a song in praise of William the Conqueror.

SONGS

OF INNOCENCE

and

OF EXPERIENCE

BIBLIOGRAPHICAL PREFACE

TO THE

SONGS OF INNOCENCE AND OF EXPERIENCE

THE *Songs of Innocence* (1789) was the first of Blake's works produced by the novel method which, in his prospectus of 1793, he styles 'illuminated printing.' The text and surrounding design were written in reverse, in a medium impervious to acid, upon small copper plates about 5″ by 3″, which were then etched in a bath of aqua fortis until the work stood in relief as on a stereotype. From these plates, which to economize copper were in many cases engraved upon both sides, impressions were printed, in the ordinary manner, in tints meant to harmonize with the colour scheme afterwards applied in water-colours by the artist. In the dexterous interweaving of text and design Blake anticipates the modern school of book illustration. Gilchrist's statement (*Life*, i. 68) that 'by the end of 1788 ... the illustrated designs in colour ... had been executed' conveys the impression that before engraving Blake had completed an entire series of coloured illustrations to the *Songs of Innocence*. This would seem to be pure assumption, and it is evident that no such sketches were known to Mr. W. M. Rossetti, or he would undoubtedly have included them in his exhaustive 'Annotated Catalogue of Blake's Pictures and Drawings' (Gilchrist, ii. 201–64). The only original designs known to the present writer are the following :—
(1) In Quaritch's *General Catalogue* (1887, p. 935) there is an entry of three coloured sketches for the *Songs of Innocence* 'from the collection of a friend of Blake's.' These designs, which are described as being 'in Blake's usual rich style of colouring' and as 'differing considerably from the published engravings,' are the Piper frontispiece, ·the Introduction ('Piping down the valleys wild'), and a third drawing called 'An Ideal Hell,' which is probably attributed by a cataloguer's error to the *Songs of Innocence*.

(2) There are besides in the Rossetti MS. Book the original designs for two of the *Songs of Experience*, ' The Angel ' and ' The Sick Rose '—the latter different in many respects from the version subsequently engraved. We have no reason to believe that Blake first executed for all the songs coloured sketches which have since disappeared. Probably many of the originals were merely pencil drawings ' with nothing to seek '—to quote Blake's own phrase in his recipe for engraving on pewter—which would naturally be destroyed in the process of rubbing off on to the copper.

The engraved version of the *Songs*, issued by the author without change during a period of nearly forty years, must of course be regarded as the only authoritative text ; even where, as in a few cases, the earlier manuscript readings seem preferable. Original autograph versions of three of the *Songs of Innocence* are found in the unpublished Blake manuscript known as *An Island in the Moon*. Manuscript versions of eighteen of the twenty-six *Songs of Experience* form some of the first entries in the Rossetti MS. Book. Several of the latter have the appearance of being fair copies, transcribed, at one time, from an earlier notebook or from loose scraps of paper, while others, such as ' The Tyger,' are evidently the first rough draft. All these variant readings are here given in the footnotes to the *Songs*.

The *Songs of Innocence* was at first issued as a separate work, complete copies of the little book in its original form containing thirty-one plates. These include five—' The Little Girl Lost,' ' The Little Girl Found,' ' The Voice of the Ancient Bard,' and ' The School Boy '—which were afterwards generally transferred by Blake to the *Songs of Experience*, though the two last were still sometimes placed by him among the *Songs of Innocence*. With the exception of the frontispiece, title-page, and introduction, the plates in this earliest issue were printed upon both sides of octavo paper, the thirty-one plates occupying seventeen leaves. These loose leaves were then stitched by Mrs. Blake into paper covers, in most cases by the rough process known as ' stabbing,' a cord being laced through holes punctured an inch or two apart.

In 1793 Blake completed the engraving of the *Songs of Experience*. His prospectus, dated Oct. 10 of the same year, addressed ' To the Public,' and giving a list of ten

works 'now published and on Sale at Mr. Blake's, no. 13
Hercules Buildings, Lambeth,' advertises the *Songs of
Innocence* and the *Songs of Experience* as two separate
books, each being priced at 5s. and described as containing
twenty-five designs. Blake here, according to his practice
in other cases, does not include either frontispiece or title-
page, which would make the entire number of plates in the
two series fifty-four. As this is the full number in a perfect
copy of the *Songs of Innocence and of Experience*, including
the general title-page which had not then been engraved,
Blake in this prospectus must have reckoned 'A Divine
Image' ('Cruelty has a Human Heart') among the number.
Though this poem is inserted without question in all
editions of Blake since Shepherd's, it would seem to have
been deliberately rejected by the poet himself. The plate
containing it is not found in any authentic copy of the
Songs issued in the lifetime of the artist or his wife, and
is known to us by only two examples. One of these is in
the uncoloured copy of the *Songs* in the Reading Room of
the British Museum, which, as the watermark shows, was
printed not earlier than 1832, and the other is a proof
impression in the possession of Mr. William Muir, which he
has reproduced at the end of his facsimile of *The Marriage
of Heaven and Hell*.

In 1794 Blake added a general title-page to both series,
which thenceforward were issued by him as one work, the
plates printed on one side of the leaf only and numbered
by hand consecutively one to fifty-four. This is the form
in which most copies of the *Songs* occur. It should be
noted that there was never any true *edition*, in the ordinary
sense of the term, of this or of any other of Blake's engraved
works. Sets of impressions were struck off as required,
the issue of the *Songs* extending from the completion of
the *Songs of Innocence* in 1789 to the close of Blake's life.
In 1863 ten of the original plates, yielding sixteen impressions (six being engraved on both sides of the copper),
were still in existence, and were used by Mr. Gilchrist in
the second volume of his *Life* of Blake. The outline
designs there, as I learn from Mr. Frederick Macmillan,
were printed from electrotypes which have every appearance of having been made from the actual plates engraved
by Blake. The present whereabouts of these plates I have
been unable to trace.

According to Gilchrist (*Life*, i. 125) a few copies were

' issued plain in black and white, or blue and white.' This
agrees with the modest price (5s. each) at which Blake
advertises the *Songs of Innocence* and the *Songs of Experience* in his Prospectus of 1793. The thirty shillings
or two guineas which Gilchrist (i. 124) tells us the artist
received for the first issue of the collected *Songs* probably
refers to coloured impressions. The only uncoloured copy
of the *Songs of Innocence and of Experience* known to the
present writer is the very unworthy example, already referred to, in the Reading Room of the British Museum.
This is a made-up copy, in which part of the plates at least
were printed after the death of Blake and his wife, perhaps
by Mr. F. Tatham, into whose possession they passed after
Catherine Blake's death in October, 1831.

The earlier examples of the *Songs of Innocence* are distinguished by the simplicity and delicacy of their colouring,
contrasting in this respect with some of the later more
elaborately illuminated copies of the *Songs of Innocence and*
of Experience. These last issues are printed upon larger
paper and upon one side of the leaf only. The Monckton
Milnes copy, produced after 1818, measures $13'' \times 10\frac{5}{8}''$, and
each plate has the additional embellishment of a wide wash
border instead of the simple red line with which Blake
ordinarily surrounded the designs. In a copy exhibited at
the Grolier Club at New York in 1905, the plates are surrounded by delicate borders of trees, vines, and even drapery.
These frames, which are not more than a quarter of an
inch in width, were added with a fine brush.

Besides the sixteen plates reprinted by Gilchrist, which,
as Mr. D. G. Rossetti points out, are ' as absolutely the
originals as those appearing in the copies printed by
Blake'—except of course in having been printed from
electros instead of direct from the plates, and in lacking the
superadded water-colour tinting—there are three modern
facsimiles of the *Songs*. The first of these is given in *The
Works of William Blake, reproduced in facsimile from the
original editions* (100 *copies printed for private circulation*),
1876. This has evidently been prepared from the very
poor uncoloured copy of the *Songs* acquired by the British
Museum in January, 1864, and, while it affords a fairly good
general idea of Blake's designs, is coarsely executed and exceedingly inaccurate as to the text. The second is the very
beautiful reproduction made by Mr. William Muir in 1884
and 1885, the edition being limited to fifty copies. The out-

line drawings are here facsimilized by lithography, and the colouring added by hand from the finest examples accessible to the artist. The tinting of the *Songs of Innocence* is copied from the volume which Blake gave to Flaxman—though the plates, it may be noted, are arranged in a different order—that of the *Songs of Experience* from the famous Beckford Library copy, originally belonging to a Mr. Edwards, purchased by Mr. Quaritch at the Hamilton Palace sale, July 4, 1882, and now the property of Mr. W. A. White of Brooklyn. These exquisite facsimiles leave little to be desired in their general fidelity to the originals. Blake's cameo plates have, however, a sharpness and definiteness of outline impossible to achieve by printing from stone, and partly no doubt for this reason Mr. Muir fails in the difficult technical feat of reproducing the grace, beauty, and delicacy of Blake's lettering.

There is also a useful facsimile of the outlines of the *Songs*, edited by Mr. Edwin J. Ellis (Quaritch, 1903). The plates are here reproduced by a photographic process, which, as the editor points out, fails to represent the clearness of the originals where the copies have been made from tinted impressions. Neither of these facsimiles, however, though much more accurate than the reproduction of 1876, is a trustworthy guide for Blake's text.

In Blake's *Songs of Innocence* (including, as in the first issue, 'The Little Girl Lost,' 'The Little Girl Found,' and 'The School Boy') the body of the text is in minuscule roman, with the exception of 'The Voice of the Ancient Bard,' which is in italic. In the *Songs of Experience*, on the contrary, Blake substituted for roman the more easily formed italic characters which he first adopted in the *Book of Thel* (1789) and used in all his subsequent works; only four songs, 'The Tyger,' 'Ah! Sunflower,' 'London,' and 'A Poison Tree,' with the introductory stanza to 'A Little Girl Lost,' being written in the former style of lettering.

There is no engraved Table of Contents, and a collation of various copies of the *Songs* shows that the order in which the plates are arranged varies in almost every instance. The plates are without engraved foliation or pagination, and catchwords are only used where one of the longer songs is continued on to a second plate. The early issues of the *Songs of Innocence* are without manuscript pagination or border lines. Later issues of the two series, printed upon one side of the leaf only, are foliated at the top right-hand corner, in the same brown or red ink with which Blake added the border lines surrounding the plates.

Blake's earliest arrangement is found in the extremely rare first issue of the *Songs* printed upon both sides of the leaf. In Table I I give the collations of five copies of the *Songs of Innocence* and in Table II of one copy of the *Songs of Innocence and of Experience*, plates printed upon the same leaf being bracketed together and those on the recto being placed first.

The first three plates of the *Songs of Innocence*, the frontispiece, title-page, and Introduction, are printed upon one side of the leaf only ; the frontispiece was generally bound, as if printed on the verso, to face the title-page.

It will be seen from these tables that although the order of plates is not identical in any of these six copies, yet in four of these the same designs are invariably found either as recto or verso of the same leaf. A further instance of the same juxtaposition is the example in the Print Room of the British Museum. This is evidently a made-up copy, the deficiency of the original being supplied by two leaves of the earlier issue, in which, as in A, B, and C, ' The Ecchoing Green' (two plates) and the ' Nurse's Song' and 'Holy Thursday' are printed upon either side of the same leaf. In a sale at Sotheby's of the library of J. B. Ditchfield, M.D., April 24, 1893, among the books sold is recorded an incomplete copy of the *Songs of Innocence* in which these four plates are wanting. This volume was bound by C. Lewis in 1782, so that the two missing leaves, which we may reasonably conjecture have gone to supply the lacunae in the Print Room copy, must have disappeared at an early date. These coincidences of arrangement, however, are as likely to have arisen from the fact of a number of impressions having been printed at one time, as from any deliberate intention on the part of the author.

Some copies bearing Blake's own foliation seem to be arranged regardless of system, and it was probably with the intention of rectifying this defect that Blake compiled, either for his own guidance or that of his wife, the table showing the order in which the songs should be paged and arranged, which Mr. Muir has given in facsimile at the end of his reproduction of *The Marriage of Heaven and Hell*. This index, which is written on two opposite leaves of quarto paper, may be dated approximatelv by the watermark (1818) of the Monckton Milnes copy, with which it coincides in arrangement.

'The Order in which the *Songs of Innocence & of Experience* ought to be paged & placed.

'Page 1. General Title. 2. Frontispiece of Piper. 3. Title page to *Songs of Innocence.* 4. Introduction—Piping down the Valleys, &c. 5. Ecchoing Green. 6. Ditto. 7. The Lamb. 8. The Shepherd. 9. Infant Joy. 10. Little Black Boy. 11. Ditto. 12. Laughing Song. 13. Spring. 14. Ditto. 15. Cradle Song. 16. Ditto. 17. Nurse's Song. 18. Holy Thursday. 19. The Blossom. 20. The Chimney Sweeper. 21. The Divine Image. 22. Night. 23. Ditto. [2nd leaf of index begins] page 24. A dream. 25. On Another's Sorrow. 26. The Little Boy Lost. 27. The Little Boy Found.

'End of *Songs of Innocence:* then Begins *Songs of Experience.* [page] 28. Frontispiece of Child on the Shepherd's head. 29. Title Page of *Songs of Experience.* 30. Introduction—Hear the voice of the Bard, &c. 31. Earth's Answer. 32. Nurse's Song. 33. The Fly. 34. The Tyger. 35. Little Girl Lost. 36. Ditto. 37. Ditto. 38. The Clod & Pebble. 39. The Little Vagabond. 40. Holy Thursday. 41. A Poison Tree. 42. The Angel. 43. The Sick Rose. 44. To Tirzah. 45. The Voice of the Ancient Bard. 46. My pretty Rose Tree. 47. The Garden of Love. 48. A Little Boy Lost. 49. Infant Sorrow. 50. The School Boy. 51. London. 52. A Little Girl Lost. 53. The Chimney Sweeper. A little Black thing, &c. 54. The Human Abstract.'

This arrangement, as the only one in which Blake is known to have laid down explicit instructions regarding the order of the songs, is followed in the present edition. Later issues, however, show an entirely different order, five copies (N, O, P, Q, R) placing the plates in identical sequence, and others approximating closely to the same standard. This later arrangement of the *Songs* is as follows:—

1. General Title. 2. Frontispiece. 3. Title-page to *Songs of Innocence.* 4. Introduction. 5. The Shepherd. 6, 7. The Ecchoing Green. 8. The Lamb. 9, 10. The Little Black Boy. 11. The Blossom. 12. The Chimney Sweeper. 13. The Little Boy Lost. 14. The Little Boy Found. 15. Laughing Song. 16, 17. Cradle Song. 18. The Divine Image. 19. Holy Thursday. 20, 21. Night. 22, 23. Spring. 24. Nurse's Song. 25. Infant Joy. 26. A Dream. 27. On

Another's Sorrow. [End of *Songs of Innocence*.] 28. Frontispiece. 29. Title-page to *Songs of Experience*. 30. Introduction. 31. Earth's Answer. 32. The Clod and Pebble. 33. Holy Thursday. 34–6. The Little Girl Lost. The Little Girl Found. 37. The Chimney Sweeper. 38. Nurse's Song. 39. The Sick Rose. 40. The Fly. 41. The Angel. 42. The Tyger. 43. My pretty Rose Tree. 44. The Garden of Love. 45. The Little Vagabond. 46. London. 47. The Human Abstract. 48. Infant Sorrow. 49. A Poison Tree. 50. A Little Boy Lost. 51. A Little Girl Lost. 52. To Tirzah. 53. The School Boy. 54. The Voice of the Ancient Bard. [End of *Songs of Experience*.]

A fairly satisfactory test of the date of a copy of the later issue of the *Songs of Innocence and of Experience*, printed upon one side of the leaf only, may be obtained by noting the positions of 'The School Boy' and 'The Voice of the Ancient Bard.' In earlier copies these two songs are included in the *Songs of Innocence*, as in Blake's first impression printed upon recto and verso; in later issues both are placed among the *Songs of Experience*; while, in two of the very last copies produced, 'The School Boy' is retained among the *Songs of Experience* and 'The Voice of the Ancient Bard' is retransferred to the end of the *Songs of Innocence*.

In Table III I give the collation of the sixteen examples known to me. The copies described in this and in the two preceding tables are:

A. *Songs of Innocence*. 31 plates, printed upon 17 leaves. Without pagination. No dated watermark. Printed in golden brown. Simple colouring. In the original blue-grey paper binding. Size $7\frac{1}{2} \times 5\frac{1}{4}$ inches.

    Sold at Sotheby's. Now in the possession of Mrs. George Barclay Moffat, New York.

B. *The same*. 31 plates, printed upon 17 leaves. Without pagination. No dated watermark. Coloured with predominating tone of yellow brown. Originally in worn-out red leather binding, now re-bound in red levant morocco. Size $7\frac{3}{8} \times 5\frac{3}{16}$ inches.

    The property of Robert Hoe, Esq., New York.

C. *The same*. 31 plates, printed upon 17 leaves. Without pagination. No dated watermark. Printed in yellow. Coloured very beautifully with extreme finish. Bound in citron morocco by Bedford. Size $6\frac{7}{16} \times 5$ inches.

    Flaxman's copy, with autograph of his sister. Now

the property of J. Pearson, Esq., Cecil House, Syden-
ham. This was the copy used by Mr. William Muir
in his coloured facsimile of the *Songs of Innocence.*

D. *The same.* 31 plates, printed upon 17 leaves. Paginated in pencil. No dated watermark. Coloured in
green tone throughout. Bound in original mottled
calf. Size $7\frac{1}{8} \times 5$ inches.

Copy presented by Blake to his physician. Sold
at Sotheby's, Feb. 22, 1897. Now the property of
Robert Hoe, Esq., New York.

E. *The same.* An incomplete copy forming part of a
miscellaneous collection sold at Sotheby's, Nov. 20,
1900.

F. *Songs of Innocence and of Experience.* 55 plates on
32 leaves. There are duplicate impressions of 'The
Laughing Song,' one being placed among the *Songs
of Experience.* Paginated consecutively throughout.
Coloured. Size 7 inches in height. Bound in green
morocco by Bedford.

Formerly in the possession of Mr. Butts, Blake's
friend. The volume was cut down by a later
owner to meet the dimensions of an old weekly
washing book, from the covers of which it was rescued
by Mr. Locker-Lampson. Now in the Rowfant
Library.

G. *Songs of Innocence.* 28 plates, printed on one side of
the leaf only. Foliated consecutively by Blake.
Watermarks dated 1802 and 1804. Printed in golden
brown. Coloured. Without border lines. Size
$6\frac{15}{16} \times 4\frac{13}{16}$ inches. In olive green calf binding.

Copy in the possession of Mr. Perry of Providence,
America. Purchased in 1900 from Quaritch, who
describes it, probably in mistake, as John Linnell's
copy. The error may have originated through the
fact that a pen and ink portrait of Blake, by Linnell,
and an autograph letter of Blake's to the same friend
were inserted in, though not bound up with, this copy.
Pasted upon a fly-leaf at the end of the book is a pen
and ink sketch by Blake, representing a woman and
nude boy.

H. *Songs of Innocence and of Experience.* 54 plates, each
on separate leaf. Foliated consecutively by Blake.
No dated watermark. Printed in sepia. Coloured.
Bound in cloth, about 1830.

Copy bearing the autographs, in ink, of H. W. Phillips the painter, and later, in pencil, of Gerald Massey the poet. Now the property of Mr. Bernard Quaritch.

I. *The same.* Presumably a copy followed by Shepherd in Pickering's three editions of 1866, 1868, and 1874, but no bibliographical details are available. The inclusion of 'The School Boy' among the *Songs of Innocence* points to the original having been rather an earlier than a later issue. Shepherd includes among the *Songs of Experience* the rare poem 'A Divine Image,' which he may, however, have taken from the posthumously printed copy in the British Museum Reading Room.

K. *The same.* 54 plates, printed on one side of the leaf only. Each book is separately foliated, the general title-page being without foliation. The watermark of the *Songs of Innocence* is 'Whatman 1808.' Very beautifully coloured. In old calf binding *circa* 1830. Following the general title-page the *Songs of Experience*, by an error of the binder, are placed before the *Songs of Innocence*. A sheet of brown paper is inserted between the two series, possibly part of the original binding. Size 5 × 7½ inches.

Copy in the possession of Mrs. John R. Wade, Brooklyn, New York.

L. *The same.* 54 plates, printed upon one side of the leaf. General title-page without foliation and the remaining leaves numbered by Blake 1–53, in the same sepia as the border lines. Watermark without date. Printed in greenish grey. Coloured. Bound in the original white vellum binding. Size 12 × 8½ inches.

This copy, which was bought from Blake by Mr. John Linnell, August 27, 1819, is now in the possession of William Linnell, Esq.

M. *The same.* 54 plates, each printed on a separate leaf. Foliated by Blake 1–54. Dated watermark 1818. Plates are printed in brown. Delicately coloured, with wide wash borders. Modern binding. Size 13 × 10⅝ inches.

Formerly the property of Mr. R. Monckton Milnes, afterwards Lord Houghton, and sold at the Crewe sale, March 30, 1903.

N. *The same.* 54 plates, on separate leaves. Foliated consecutively by Blake. Watermark 1815. Printed in red. Richly and elaborately coloured. Bound in green morocco by C. Lewis. Size $8\frac{3}{4} \times 5\frac{7}{16}$ inches.

A pencil note in this copy reads 'Edwards May 1828' [? R. Edwards the publisher of Young's *Night Thoughts*, 1797, illustrated by Blake]. Afterwards the Beckford copy, sold at the Hamilton Palace sale, 1882, and now the property of W. A. White, Esq., of Brooklyn, New York. This copy was used by Mr. W. Muir in his reproduction of the *Songs of Experience*, who considered it the best he had seen.

O. *The same.* 54 plates, printed upon one side of the leaf only. Foliated by Blake 1–54 consecutively. Printed in dull orange-red, with added border lines of same colour. Coloured with extreme finish and beauty. The size of the drawing paper upon which the plates are printed is $10\frac{3}{4} \times 8\frac{3}{8}$ inches. These sheets were originally bound in boards covered with light green calico. They are now mounted in a book of white drawing paper, 12×10 inches. Half-bound in morocco.

This was the copy which T. G. Wainewright ('Janus Weathercock') bought from Blake, probably during his connexion with the *London Magazine* 1820–3, or shortly afterwards. Subsequently in the library of James Weales, Esq., now in the possession of John Linnell, Esq., whose father purchased it Dec. 13, 1842, from a Mr. White.

P. *The same.* 54 plates, printed on one side of the leaf only. Foliated consecutively by Blake 1–54. Printed in reddish orange, with added border lines of same colour. Richly and splendidly coloured. The plates in this copy are printed upon pieces of drawing paper varying in height from 6 to $7\frac{1}{4}$ inches, and in width from $4\frac{1}{2}$ to 5 inches. These sheets are mounted on white paper $11\frac{1}{4} \times 9$ inches, and bound in boards covered with unglazed calico or holland of a warm red colour.

This is the copy bought, through Mr. Linnell, from Blake by Mr. Aders in July, 1826, for the sum of five guineas, which was then considered to be a somewhat enhanced price for a coloured copy of the *Songs*. Acquired by Mr. J. Linnell from Mr. or Mrs. Aders, and now in the possession of James T. Linnell, Esq.

Q. *The same.* 54 plates, printed on recto only. Paginated consecutively by Blake in red. Watermark dated 182– (last figure wanting). Printed in orange. Richly coloured and gilt. Bound in morocco *circa* 1830. Size $8\frac{1}{2} \times 5\frac{1}{8}$ inches.

Crabb Robinson's copy, with MS. note: 'This copy I received from Blake himself and coloured by his own hand, which I present with great pleasure to Edwin W. Field. H. C. Robinson. March 11, 1863.' Crabb Robinson, as Mr. Linnell informs me, bought this copy in April, 1826, for the sum of five guineas, paid through the elder Mr. Linnell to Blake at the same date. Now in the possession of C. Fairfax Murray, Esq., to whom it was bequeathed by Sir F. W. Burton, who had received it from Mrs. Field as a gift in memory of her husband.

R. *The same.* 54 plates, printed upon one side of the leaf only. Foliated consecutively in ink 1–54. Watermark dated 1825. Printed in golden brown. Brilliantly coloured and gilt, with added borders of floral tracery. Size $6\frac{1}{16} \times 5\frac{1}{2}$ inches. Modern mount binding.

Formerly the property of the artist Edward Calvert, Blake's friend. Now in the possession of Mr. Perry of Providence, N. Y.

S. *The same.* 54 plates, printed upon 52 leaves. This set of impressions is apparently made up from three different copies. Supplied from the early issue of the *Songs of Innocence*, printed upon both sides of the leaf, are the second plate of 'The Ecchoing Green' printed as recto to 'The Lamb' (verso) and 'The Chimney Sweeper' recto with 'The Blossom' verso. The majority of the plates, 38 in number, belong to a copy which, as the watermark shows, was issued not earlier than 1825. These, all printed in a reddish brown, are foliated by Blake between the outer and inner borders with which he surrounded the designs. Supplied from a third copy are twelve plates of the *Songs of Experience*, viz.: 28, 32, 33, 38, 40, 41, 42, 43, 47, 49, 50, 51. These plates, which lack the border lines, and are foliated in pencil, are printed in a variety of tints. The colouring of some of the plates is rather muddy, and the copy, as Rossetti points out, is a very poor one. In modern binding. Size $7\frac{3}{4} \times 4\frac{1}{2}$ inches.

Purchased by the British Museum (Print Room) in 1836.

T. *The same.* 54 plates, printed on recto only. Foliated by Blake. Watermark dated 1825. The colour, according to Gilchrist, is not as delicately executed or as harmonious as some of the earlier examples. It was sent by Mrs. Blake, marked 'Blake's own,' to Dr. Jebb, Bishop of Limerick, as a return for a sum of twenty guineas which he had handed to her through Mr. Haviland Burke. In 1863 this copy was in the possession of the Rev. Charles Forster. This is the copy followed by Gilchrist and most later editors in the arrangement of the *Songs.*

V. *Songs of Experience* only, but, as the foliation shows, having at one time formed part of a copy which contained the *Songs of Innocence* also. 25 plates, printed on one side of the leaf only. Foliated 30–54. No dated watermark. Richly coloured and gilt. Bound in modern English maroon morocco. Size $7\frac{3}{4} \times 5\frac{1}{4}$ inches.

Now in the possession of Robert Hoe, Esq., New York.

X. *Songs of Innocence and of Experience.* 54 plates, printed on recto only. Foliated in pencil. Obviously printed from the original plates after Blake's death. Ff. 1–40 and 42 printed with leaden grey ink upon thick paper, some sheets of which bear the watermark 1831. Ff. 41, 43, 44, printed in somewhat darker ink upon larger and thinner paper, f. 43 bearing the watermark 1832. Ff. 45–54 are printed in reddish sepia upon large thin paper. Uncoloured. In a modern binding, each leaf separately mounted on a guard. Size, larger paper $10\frac{3}{4} \times 7\frac{1}{2}$, smaller paper $9\frac{1}{2} \times 7\frac{1}{2}$ inches.

Copy in the Reading Room of the British Museum, purchased January 7, 1864.

Y. *The same.* Under this heading I give the order of the *Songs* as they occur in the first letterpress edition edited by Wilkinson in 1839. This is not traceable to any engraved original, and may be the editor's own arrangement.

It is not probable that the whole impression of the *Songs* issued by Blake much exceeded in number the twenty-two copies described above. The 'Public,' to whom the author appeals in his Prospectus and elsewhere, had thus only the remotest opportunity of becoming acquainted with his poems save by the two or three examples quoted by Malkin and Cunningham[1]. It was not until 1839, twelve years after Blake's death, that the *Songs of Innocence and of Experience* were printed for the first time in ordinary types. This little volume, published by Pickering and edited by James John Garth Wilkinson (Swedenborgian, 1812–99), is now itself somewhat of a bibliographical rarity, and only a very small edition can have been printed. The Gilchrists (*Life*, i. 124, and *Dict. Nat. Biog.*, v. 184) speak of Wilkinson's text as 'much altered.' In reality his reprint compares not unfavourably in this respect with those of later editors, who make greater pretensions to literal fidelity. Wilkinson omits 'The Little Vagabond,' and prints the poems in an order which apparently is not derivable from any engraved authority. In 1863 the *Songs* were reprinted in the second volume of Gilchrist's *Life* of Blake; the biographer states the poems are 'now given in strict fidelity to the original, the correction of some few glaring grammatical blemishes alone excepted, which seemed a pious duty.' These 'corrections' are the work of Mr. D. G. Rossetti, who has in several instances retained Wilkinson's alterations, and in others introduced new readings of his own which cannot always be commended. His text of 'The Tyger' is based upon the corrupt version of Cunningham, and such changes as 'ta'en' for 'took' in the lines—

> 'Farewell green fields and happy groves
> Where flocks have took delight'

take away something of the charm of the original. He introduces into the *Songs of Experience* the 'Cradle Song' taken from the MS. Book, and from the same source prefixes two stanzas, in themselves a complete poem, to 'The Garden of Love.' A far more accurate edition of the *Songs*, together with other of Blake's poems, was published by Pickering in 1866, passed into a second edition two years later, and was reprinted, with the *Poetical Sketches*, in 1874. The order of the songs in this edition differs from that of Wilkinson or Rossetti, but, while the particular copy from which this arrangement is borrowed has not been traced by me, it is most improbable that so faithful

---

[1] In Malkin's *Father's Memoirs of His Child* (1806), and Cunningham's *Lives of British Painters* (1830).

an editor as Mr. R. Herne Shepherd would have rearranged the poems in a way of his own. The *Song of Experience* with the title 'A Divine Image' ('Cruelty has a Human Heart') appears in Shepherd's edition for the first time, taken perhaps from the copy in the British Museum. The Aldine edition of Blake's Poems, edited by Mr. W. M. Rossetti, was published in 1874, and has been frequently reprinted. The editor's remarks on the last pages of his Prefatory Memoir may have given rise to some misconception. Referring to the changes introduced by Mr. D. G. Rossetti into the poems printed in Gilchrist's *Life*, he says :—'These emendations were indeed great improvements, and they rectify various annoying and inexcusable laxities in point of metre or syntax, or here and there of expression. It is therefore with considerable reluctance that I abandon them, and do Blake the disservice of again presenting him without their aid,' and later :—'At any rate, as the compositions in question have been already reproduced at a date inter-mediate between that of my brother's editing and of the present volume, and were then printed in their original shape (which term includes their occasional original shape-lessness), I have not felt justified in recurring to another form of the same poems, which, if better, as it assuredly is, is also less absolutely exact.' This explanation hardly renders it sufficiently clear that Blake's text has been restored only in the case of the *Poetical Sketches*, and that the *Songs of Innocence and of Experience* are still printed with Mr. D. G. Rossetti's emendatory readings. Since 1874 the Aldine edition appears to have been generally accepted as the standard text of Blake's Poems. It is followed in most of the subsequent editions and selections, among others, with a few fresh changes, in the large *Collected Works of William Blake* edited by Messrs. Ellis and Yeats. A different and more accurate text is given by Mr. W. B. Yeats in his smaller 'Muses' Library' edition of Blake.

TABLE I

FIRST ISSUES OF *SONGS OF INNOCENCE.*

(Printed upon both sides of leaf.)

A.

LEAF.	
1.	Frontispiece (verso)
2.	Title-page (recto)
3.	Introduction (recto)
4.	A Dream
5.	{ The Little Girl Lost ; The Little Girl Lost }
6.	{ The Little Girl Found ; The Lamb }
7.	{ The Blossom ; The Ecchoing Green (2 plates) }
8.	{ The Divine Image ; The Chimney Sweeper }
9.	{ Infant Joy ; The Shepherd }
10.	Night (2 plates)
11.	A Cradle Song (2 plates)
12.	{ The Little Boy Lost ; The Little Boy Found }
13.	{ Nurse's Song ; Holy Thursday }
14.	{ On Another's Sorrow ; Spring }
15.	The School Boy
16.	{ Laughing Song ; The Little Black Boy }
17.	{ The Little Black Boy ; The Voice of the An- }

B.

LEAF.	
1.	Front.
2.	Title-page
3.	Intr.
4.	{ Shepherd ; Inf. Joy }
5.	{ Crad. Song (2 pl.) ; Laugh. Song }
6.	{ Lit. Blk. Boy ; Lit. Blk. Boy }
7.	{ Voice Anc. Bard ; Ecch. Grn. (2 pl.) }
8.	{ Nurse's Song ; Holy Thurs. }
9.	On Anoth. Sor.
10.	{ Spring ; Spring }
11.	Sch. Boy
12.	{ Dream ; Lit. Gl. Lost }
13.	{ Lit. Gl. Lost ; Lit. Gl. Fd. }
14.	{ Blossom ; Lamb }
15.	{ Lit. Boy Lost ; Lit. Boy Fd. }
16.	{ Night (2 pl.) ; Chim. Sweeper }
17.	Divine Im.

C.

LEAF.	
1.	Front.
2.	Title-page
3.	Intr.
4.	{ Ecch. Grn. (2 pl.) ; Laugh. Song }
5.	{ Lit. Blk. Boy ; Lit. Blk. Boy }
6.	{ Voice Anc. Bard ; Blossom }
7.	Lamb
8.	{ Dream ; Lit. Gl. Lost }
9.	{ Lit. Gl. Fd. (2 pl.) ; Nurse's Song }
10.	{ Holy Thurs. ; Inf. Joy }
11.	Shepherd
12.	{ Night (2 pl.) ; Lit. Boy Lost }
13.	{ Lit. Boy Fd. ; Divine Im. }
14.	Chim. Sweeper
15.	{ Crad. Song (2 pl.) ; On Anoth. Sor. }
16.	{ Spring ; Spring }
17.	Sch. Boy

D.

LEAF.	
1.	Title-page
2.	Front.
3.	Intr.
4.	{ Shepherd ; Lit. Blk. Boy }
5.	{ Lit. Blk. Boy ; Voice Anc. Bard }
6.	{ Crad. Song (2 pl.) ; Blossom }
7.	{ Lit. Gl. Lost ; Lit. Gl. Lost }
8.	{ Lit. Gl. Fd. ; Lamb }
9.	Nurse's Song
10.	{ Inf. Joy ; On Anoth. Sor. }
11.	{ Lit. Boy Lost ; Lit. Boy Fd. }
12.	Chim. Sweeper
13.	{ Spring ; Spring }
14.	Sch. Boy
15.	{ Laugh. Song ; Dream }
16.	{ Holy Thurs. ; Divine Im. }
17.	{ Ecch. Grn. (2 pl.) ; Night (2 pl.) }

E.

LEAF.	
1.	Front.
2.	Title-page
3.	Intr.
4.	{ Shepherd ; Lit. Blk. Boy }
5.	{ Lit. Blk. Boy ; Voice Anc. Bard }
6.	{ Divine Image ; Dream }
7.	{ Ecch. Grn. (2 pl.) ; On Anoth. Sor. }
8.	{ Inf. Joy ; Lamb }
9.	{ Spring ; Spring }
10.	{ Blossom ; Nurse's Song }
11.	Chim. Sweeper
12.	Crad. Song (2 pl.)

TABLE II

FIRST ISSUE OF *SONGS OF INNOCENCE AND OF EXPERIENCE*

(Printed upon both sides of leaf)

F

LEAF		LEAF	
1.	General Title-page	1.	Frontispiece to *Songs of Experience*
2.	Frontispiece		
3.	Title-page to *Songs of Innocence*	2.	Title-page
4.	Introduction	3.	{ Introduction / Earth's Answer
5.	{ The Shepherd / Infant Joy	4.	{ Laughing Song / The Little Girl Lost
6.	{ The Blossom / The Lamb	5.	{ The Little Girl Lost / The Little Girl Found
7.	{ Laughing Song / Little Black Boy	6.	{ A Little Boy Lost / The Chimney Sweeper
8.	{ Little Black Boy / The Voice of the Ancient Bard	7.	{ The Tyger / London
9.	{ The Divine Image / The Chimney Sweeper	8.	{ The Garden of Love / The Sick Rose
10.	Cradle Song (2 plates)	9.	{ Nurse's Song / The Angel
11.	The Ecchoing Green (2 plates)	10.	{ The Little Vagabond / The Human Abstract
12.	{ On Another's Sorrow / Spring	11.	{ The Fly / A Poison Tree
13.	{ Spring / The School Boy	12.	{ Infant Sorrow / A Little Girl Lost
14.	{ Nurse's Song / Holy Thursday	13.	{ Holy Thursday / My Pretty Rose Tree. Ah! Sunflower. The Lilly.
15.	{ The Little Boy Lost / The Little Boy Found	14.	{ To Tirzah / The Clod and the Pebble
16.	Night (2 plates)		
17.	A Dream		

TABLE III

LATER ISSUES OF *SONGS OF INNOCENCE AND OF EXPERIENCE*

(Printed upon one side of leaf only)

Plates (Songs of Innocence)	I. including 'School Boy' and 'Voice of Ancient Bard'					II. lacking 'Sch. Boy' and 'Voice of Anc. Bard'			III. lacking 'Sch. Boy'		IV. Unauthenticated	
	G	H	I	K	L	M	N O P Q R	S	T	V	X	Y
General Title-page	wtg.	2	1	[o]	[o]	1	1	1	1		1	[1]
Frontispiece (Piper and Child on Cloud)	1	1	[2]	1	1	2	2	2	2		2	[2]
Title-page to *Songs of Innocence*	2	3	3	2	2	3	3	3	3		3	[3]
Introduction (Piping down the Valleys wild)	3	4	4	3	3	4	4	4	4		4	4
Ecchoing Green (2 plates)	4, 5	12, 13	6, 7	5, 6	5, 6	5, 6	6, 7	6, 7	6, 7		6, 7	16, 17
The Lamb	19	15	8	7	7	7	8	8	8		8	12
The Shepherd	11	5	5	4	4	8	5	5	5		5	5
Infant Joy	9	14	24	25	25	9	25	25	25		24	15
The Little Black Boy (2 plates)	12, 13	7, 8	9, 10	8, 9	8, 9	10, 11	9, 10	9, 10	9, 10		9, 10	13, 14
Laughing Song	23	17	26	14	14	12	15	15	15			9
Spring (2 plates)	7, 8	9, 10	21, 22	22, 23	22, 23	13, 14	22, 23	23, 24	22, 23		21, 22	6, 7
A Cradle Song (2 plates)	15, 16	24, 25	15, 16	15, 16	15, 16	15, 16	16, 17	16, 17	16, 17	wtg.	15, 16	18, 19
Nurse's Song	24	16	23	24	24	17	24	20	24		23	10
Holy Thursday	18	11	18	18	18	18	19	19	19		18	8
The Blossom	6	6	11	10	10	19	11	11	11		11	27
The Chimney Sweeper	20	18	12	11	11	20	12	12	12		12	28
The Divine Image	17	19	17	17	17	21	18	18	18		17	11
Night (2 plates)	27, 28	26, 27	19, 20	19, 20	19, 20	22, 23	20, 21	21, 22	20, 21		19, 20	21, 22
A Dream	21	20	25	27	27	24	26	26	26		25	24
On Another's Sorrow	14	21	28	28	28	25	27	27	27		26	23
The Little Boy Lost	25	28	13	12	12	26	13	13	13		13	25
The Little Boy Found	26	29	14	13	13	27	14	14	14		14	26
[The Voice of the Ancient Bard]	10	23	29	26	26				28		29	29
[The School Boy]	22	22	27	21	21						20	20

Songs of Experience Plates	G	I lacking 'School Boy' and 'Voice of Ancient Bard'				II including 'Sch. Boy' and 'Voice of Anc. Bard'			III lacking 'Voice of Anc. Bard'		IV Unauthenticated	
		H	I	K	L	M	N O P Q R	S	T	V	X	Y
Frontispiece (Shepherd carrying winged child on head)		30	[30]	1	29	28	28	28	29	1	27	[30]
Title-page to *Songs of Experience*		31	31	2	30	29	29	29	30	30	28	[31]
Introduction. Hear the voice of the bard		32	32	3	31	30	30	30	31	31	45	32
Earth's Answer		33	33	4	32	31	31	31	32	32	46	33
Nurse's Song		49	37	6	39	32	38	38	40	53	33	43
The Fly		39	40	23	41	33	40	40	41	38	35	37
The Tyger		50	41	7	43	34	42	42	43	37	37	38
The Little Girl Lost } (3 plates)		51, 52	45, 46	17, 18	35, 36	35, 36	34, 35	34, 35	35, 36	41, 42	30, 31	44, 45
The Little Girl Found }		52, 53	46, 47	18, 19	36, 37	36, 37	35, 36	35, 36	36, 37	43, 44	31, 32	45, 46
The Clod and the Pebble		34	38	5	33	38	32	32	33	33	49	35
The Little Vagabond		44	55	10	46	39	45	45	46	51	54	wtg.
Holy Thursday		35	43	11	34	40	33	33	34	52	29	40
A Poison Tree		45	52	9	50	41	49	51	50	35	40	50
The Angel		37	44	15	42	42	41	41	42	46	36	42
The Sick Rose		38	36	22	40	43	39	39	39	39	34	53
To Tirzah		54	49	25	51	44	52	52	40	49	41	49
The Voice of the Ancient Bard	wtg.	wtg.	wtg.	wtg.	wtg.	45	54	54	wtg.	wtg.	44	wtg.
My Pretty Rose Tree. Ah! Sunflower. The Lilly		42	35	12	44	46	43	43	44	47	38	41
The Garden of Love		46	39	21	45	47	44	44	45	45	53	36
A Little Boy Lost		40	42	14	53	48	50	49	51	48	52	39
Infant Sorrow		36	34	16	49	49	48	48	49	36	43	34
The School Boy		wtg.	wtg.	wtg.	wtg.	50	53	53	53	54	42	wtg.
London		47	48	20	47	51	46	46	47	50	39	52
A Little Girl Lost.		41	53	24	52	52	51	50	52	wtg.	51	51
The Chimney Sweeper		43	51	8	38	53	37	37	38	34	48	48
The Human Abstract		48	50	13	48	54	47	47	48	40	47	47
[A Divine Image]		wtg.	54	wtg.	wtg.	wtg.	wtg.	wtg.	wtg.	wtg.	50	wtg.

SONGS

Of

INNOCENCE

and Of

EXPERIENCE

*Shewing the Two Contrary States
of the Human Soul*

The general title-page to both series of the *Songs*, issued together as one work. This plate was probably engraved after Oct. 10, 1793, when Blake issued his prospectus 'To the Public.'

Omitted in the editions of DGR, WMR, EY, and WBY; Shep. writes 'showing' for 'shewing.' In notes DGR and WBY incorrectly read *Songs of Innocence and Experience.*

In the MS. Book (p. 101) are two stanzas entitled 'Motto to the Songs of Innocence & of Experience,' which, under the title 'A Motto,' W. M. Rossetti prefixes to the *Songs* in the Aldine edition. These lines, however, were never engraved or published by Blake, nor are they known to occur as an inscription in any copy of the *Songs.*

S O N G S

of

I n n o c e n c e

1789

The Author & Printer, W. Blake.

The engraved title to the *Songs of Innocence*, when published either as
a separate work, or in conjunction with the *Songs of Experience*. In the
earlier, as well as in the later issue, this plate is printed on the recto of the
leaf, with verso blank, facing the engraved frontispiece of the piper, which
is printed on the verso of the preceding leaf (recto blank).

Reprinted in Gilchrist (*Life*, ii. *end*) from an electrotype of the original plate.

SONGS OF INNOCENCE

Introduction

Piping down the valleys wild,   1
Piping songs of pleasant glee,
On a cloud I saw a child,
And he laughing said to me:

'Pipe a song about a Lamb!'   5
So I piped with merry chear.
'Piper, pipe that song again;'
So I piped: he wept to hear.

'Drop thy pipe, thy happy pipe;   9
Sing thy songs of happy chear:'
So I sang the same again,
While he wept with joy to hear.

'Piper, sit thee down and write   13
In a book, that all may read.'
So he vanish'd from my sight,
And I pluck'd a hollow reed,

In the first and subsequent issues of the *Songs of Innocence* printed on the recto of leaf, verso blank. This poem was first printed in ordinary type in Cunningham's *Lives of British Painters*, ii. 150 (1830).

11 sang] sung Cunn., Wilk., Shep., WBY.

Thus translated, with the omission of the second and third stanzas, by Dr. N. H. Julius, in the *Vaterländisches Museum*, Jahrg. 1811, Bd. II, Heft i :—

'Pfeifend ging ich durch das Thal,
Pfeifend Lieder ohne Zahl;
Sah ein Kind von Luft getragen,
Hört' es lächelnd zu mir sagen:

"Pfeifer, setz dich hin und schreib,
Dass dein Lied im Sinn verbleib'."
So erklang's vor meinem Ohr,
Und ich schnitt ein hohles Rohr,

Schnitzte eine Feder dran,
Macht' aus Wasser Tinte dann,
Schrieb die Lieder hin zur Stund,
Dass sie sing' der Kinder Mund.'

And I made a rural pen,   17
And I stain'd the water clear,
And I wrote my happy songs
Every child may joy to hear.

The Ecchoing Green

The Sun does arise,   1
And make happy the skies;
The merry bells ring
To welcome the Spring;
The sky lark and thrush,
The birds of the bush,
Sing louder around
To the bells' chearful sound,
While our sports shall be seen
On the Ecchoing Green.

Old John, with white hair,   11
Does laugh away care,
Sitting under the oak,
Among the old folk.
They laugh at our play,
And soon they all say:
'Such, such were the joys
When we all, girls & boys,
In our youth time were seen
On the Ecchoing Green.'

Till the little ones, weary,   21
No more can be merry;
The sun does descend,
And our sports have an end.

This song was engraved on two plates. The first of these (to fourth line of second stanza) is among the remnant reprinted by Gilchrist (*Life*, ii. *end*). In the first issue of the *Songs of Innocence* the two plates are always printed as recto and verso of the same leaf.

8 bells'] *No apostrophe in orig.*   18 When we all, girls & boys] *No punctuation in orig.* ; When we, all girls and boys Wilk., Shep.

Round the laps of their mothers
Many sisters and brothers,
Like birds in their nest,
Are ready for rest,
And sport no more seen
On the darkening Green.

The Lamb

Little Lamb who made thee?   1
Dost thou know who made thee?
Gave thee life, & bid thee feed,
By the stream & o'er the mead ;
Gave thee clothing of delight,
Softest clothing, wooly, bright ;
Gave thee such a tender voice,
Making all the vales rejoice?
Little Lamb who made thee?
Dost thou know who made thee?

Little Lamb, I'll tell thee,   11
Little Lamb, I'll tell thee:
He is callèd by thy name,
For he calls himself a Lamb.
He is meek, & he is mild ;
He became a little child.
I a child, & thou a lamb,
We are callèd by his name.
Little Lamb, God bless thee !
Little Lamb, God bless thee !

This is among the original plates reprinted by Gilchrist (*Life*, ii. *end*). In
the first issue of the *Songs of Innocence* this plate is found as recto or verso
to ' The Blossom,' or as recto to ' Nurse's Song ' or ' Spring.'
3 bid] bade DGR, WMR, EY.

The Shepherd

How sweet is the Shepherd's sweet lot!   1
From the morn to the evening he strays;
He shall follow his sheep all the day,
And his tongue shall be fillèd with praise.

For he hears the lamb's innocent call,   5
And he hears the ewe's tender reply;
He is watchful while they are in peace,
For they know when their Shepherd is nigh.

In the first issue of the *Songs of Innocence* this plate is printed as verso to
'Infant Joy,' or as recto to 'The Little Black Boy.'   In almost all later issues it
follows the 'Introduction.'
5, 6 lamb's . . . ewe's] *No apostrophe in orig.* ; lambs' . . . ewes' *all edd.*
8 when] that Wilk., DGR.

Infant Joy

'I have no name: 1
I am but two days old.'
What shall I call thee?
'I happy am,
Joy is my name.'
Sweet joy befall thee!

Pretty joy!   7
Sweet joy, but two days old.
Sweet joy I call thee:
Thou dost smile,
I sing the while,
Sweet joy befall thee!

In the first issue of the *Songs of Innocence* this plate is printed either as
recto or verso to 'The Shepherd,' or as verso to 'On Another's Sorrow.'

The Little Black Boy

My mother bore me in the southern wild,   1
And I am black, but O my soul is white;
White as an angel is the English child,
But I am black, as if bereav'd of light.

My mother taught me underneath a tree,   5
And, sitting down before the heat of day,
She took me on her lap and kissèd me,
And, pointing to the east, began to say:

'Look on the rising sun,—there God does live,   9
And gives his light, and gives his heat away;
And flowers and trees and beasts and men recieve
Comfort in morning, joy in the noon day.

'And we are put on earth a little space,   13
That we may learn to bear the beams of love;
And these black bodies and this sun-burnt face
Is but a cloud, and like a shady grove.

'For when our souls have learn'd the heat to bear,   17
The cloud will vanish, we shall hear his voice,
Saying: "come out from the grove, my love & care,
And round my golden tent like lambs rejoice."'

Thus did my mother say, and kissèd me;   21
And thus I say to little English boy.
When I from black, and he from white cloud free,
And round the tent of God like lambs we joy,

I'll shade him from the heat, till he can bear   25
To lean in joy upon our father's knee;
And then I'll stand and stroke his silver hair,
And be like him, and he will then love me.

Engraved on two plates of four and three stanzas respectively. In the earliest issue of the *Songs of Innocence* the former is printed as verso to the 'Laughing Song' or 'The Shepherd,' the latter as recto to 'The Voice of the Ancient Bard.'

9 does] doth Muir's *facsim.*   11 beasts] beast Shep.   ·16 Is ... cloud] Are ... cloud *all edd.* ; Are like a cloud Swinb. p. 115.   17 learn'd] learnt Shep.   18 cloud] clouds Wilk., Shep.   19 Wilk. *omits* out.   23-28 When I from ... will then love me] *Quoted* Shep.

Laughing Song

When the green woods laugh with the voice of joy,   1
And the dimpling stream runs laughing by;
When the air does laugh with our merry wit,
And the green hill laughs with the noise of it;

When the meadows laugh with lively green,   5
And the grasshopper laughs in the merry scene,
When Mary and Susan and Emily
With their sweet round mouths sing ' Ha, Ha, He!'

When the painted birds laugh in the shade,   9
Where our table with cherries and nuts is spread,
Come live, & be merry, and join with me,
To sing the sweet chorus of ' Ha, Ha, He!'

In the first issue of the *Songs of Innocence* this plate is generally printed as recto to the first plate of ' The Little Black Boy.' In the Brit. Mus. Rdg. Rm. copy this plate is lacking. This song was first printed in ordinary type in Malkin's *Father's Memoirs of His Child* (1806).

6 the merry] this merry Malk. 10 Where] When Wilk., Shep.
11 merry] happy Wilk., Shep.

Spring

Sound the Flute!   1
Now it 's mute.
Birds delight
Day and Night;
Nightingale
In the dale,
Lark in Sky,
Merrily,
Merrily, Merrily, to welcome in the Year.

Upon two plates in the engraved original. In the first issue of the *Songs of Innocence* the former is usually found as verso to ' On Another's Sorrow,' and the latter as recto to ' The School Boy.'

2 it 's] 'tis DGR, WMR, EY, Muir's *facsim.*

Little Boy,   10
Full of joy;
Little Girl,
Sweet and small;
Cock does crow,
So do you;
Merry voice,
Infant noise,
Merrily, Merrily, to welcome in the Year.

Little Lamb,   19
Here I am;
Come and lick
My white neck;
Let me pull
Your soft Wool;
Let me kiss
Your soft face:
Merrily, Merrily, we welcome in the Year.

A Cradle Song

Sweet dreams, form a shade   1
O'er my lovely infant's head;
Sweet dreams of pleasant streams
By happy, silent, moony beams.

Sweet sleep, with soft down   5
Weave thy brows an infant crown.
Sweet sleep, Angel mild,
Hover o'er my happy child.

Engraved on two plates of six and two stanzas respectively, which in the first issue of the *Songs of Innocence* are always printed as recto and verso of the same leaf. The first of the two plate is among the number reprinted by Gilchrist (*Life*, ii. *end*). Compare with this the 'Cradle Song' on p. 114 reversed, of the MS. Book, which DGR and most editors insert among the *Songs of Experience*. The poem, however, was never engraved or published by Blake.

Sweet smiles, in the night   9
Hover over my delight;
Sweet smiles, Mother's smiles,
All the livelong night beguiles.

Sweet moans, dovelike sighs,   13
Chase not slumber from thy eyes.
Sweet moans, sweeter smiles,
All the dovelike moans beguiles.

Sleep, sleep, happy child,   17
All creation slept and smil'd;
Sleep, sleep, happy sleep,
While o'er thee thy mother weep.

Sweet babe, in thy face   21
Holy image I can trace.
Sweet babe, once like thee,
Thy maker lay and wept for me.

Wept for me, for thee, for all,   25
When he was an infant small.
Thou his image ever see,
Heavenly face that smiles on thee,

Smiles on thee, on me, on all;   29
Who became an infant small.
Infant smiles are his own smiles;
Heaven & earth to peace beguiles.

11, 12 smiles ... beguiles] smile ... beguile Wilk., DGR, WMR, EY.
14 thy] thine Wilk., DGR, WMR, EY.   15 moans] moan DGR, WMR,
EY.   15, 16 smiles ... beguiles] smile ... beguile Wilk., DGR, WMR,
EY.   20 thy] doth DGR, WMR, EY.   31, 32 Infant ... beguiles]

> 'Infant smiles, like His own smile
> Heaven and earth to peace beguile.'

Wilk., DGR.

Nurse's Song

When the voices of children are heard on the green, 1
And laughing is heard on the hill,
My heart is at rest within my breast,
And everything else is still.

'Then come home, my children, the sun is gone down, 5
And the dews of night arise;
Come, come, leave off play, and let us away
Till the morning appears in the skies.'

'No, no, let us play, for it is yet day, 9
And we cannot go to sleep;
Besides, in the sky the little birds fly,
And the hills are all cover'd with sheep.'

'Well, well, go & play till the light fades away, 13
And then go home to bed.'
The little ones leapèd & shoutèd & laugh'd
And all the hills ecchoèd.

Nurses Song *orig.* Reprinted in Gilchrist (*Life*, ii. *end*) from the original plate.   In the first issue of the *Songs of Innocence* this plate occurs as recto to 'Holy Thursday' (generally) or as verso to 'The Lamb,' or as recto to 'The Chimney Sweeper.'   The original version of this song is found in the MS. known as *The Island in the Moon* (chap. xi):—'After this ['Holy Thursday' sung by Mr. Obtuse Angle] they all sat silent for a quarter of an hour, and Mrs. Nannicantipol said "it puts me in mind of my [*grand*-]mother's song : When the tongues of children are heard on the green," *etc.*'

1 voices] tongues *Isl. in Moon.*   2 And ... hill] And laughing upon the hill *ibid. 2nd rdg.* (afterwards re-corrected to its earlier and present form). 5 Then ... down] Then come home children, the sun is down *ibid. 1st rdg.*   8 DGR, WMR, EY, and WBY divide this poem into two eight-line stanzas.   10 And ... sleep] And we cannot sleep till it's dark *Isl. in Moon 1st rdg.*   11 Besides ... fly] The flocks are at play & we can't go away *ibid. 1st rdg.*   12 And ... sheep] And the meadows are cover'd with sheep *ibid.*   14 go] come Wilk.   15 leapèd ... laugh'd] leap'd, and shouted, and laughed Wilk., Shep.; leaped and shouted and laughed WMR, EY, WBY.   16 ecchoèd] I have found in a library copy of Blake's poems the joyous emendation of some youthful reader :

'And all the hills echoèd, èd, èd!'

Holy Thursday

'Twas on a Holy Thursday, their innocent faces clean, 1
The children walking two & two, in red & blue & green,
Grey headed beadles walk'd before, with wands as white
    as snow,
Till into the high dome of Paul's they like Thames'
    waters flow.

O what a multitude they seem'd, these flowers of London
    town! 5
Seated in companies, they sit with radiance all their own.
The hum of multitudes was there, but multitudes of
    lambs,
Thousands of little boys & girls raising their innocent
    hands.

Now like a mighty wind they raise to heaven the voice
    of song, 9
Or like harmonious thunderings the seats of heaven
    among.
Beneath them sit the agèd men, wise guardians of the
    poor;
Then cherish pity, lest you drive an angel from your
    door.

In the first issue of the *Songs of Innocence* this plate is generally printed as
verso to ' Nurses Song,' or (once) as recto to ' The Divine Image.' The original
MS. version of this song is found in *The Island in the Moon* (chap. xi), where
it is sung by Mr. Obtuse Angle. The erased passages, which E and Y have
pronounced illegible, are here given in the footnotes. This poem was first
printed in ordinary type in Malkin's *Father's Memoirs of His Child* (1806).

1 'Twas on a] Upon a *Isl. in Moon.* 2 The] Came DGR, WMR,
EY. red] grey *Isl. in Moon.* 6 Seated . . . sit] Seated in companies
they were Wilk., DGR. 7 was] were *Isl. in Moon.* 8 Thousands
. . . hands] And all in order sit waiting the chief chanter's commands *Isl. in
Moon 1st rdg. deleted*; Thousands of little girls & boys, *etc. ibid. 2nd rdg.*
9 Now] Then *Isl. in Moon.* 11 agèd] rev'rend *Isl. in Moon.* wise]
the *Isl. in Moon* 9–12 In Blake's first draft (in the *Island in the Moon*)
this stanza stood : —
    ' Then like a mighty wind they raise to heav'n the voice of song,
    Or like harmonious thunderings the seats of heav'n among,
    When the whole multitude of innocents their voices raise
    Like angels on the throne of heav'n, raising the voice of praise.'

Blake then deleted the entire stanza, and began :—

'Let cherubim and seraphim now raise their voices high.'

This also was cancelled, and the stanza rewritten with the slight changes noted above. This song is thus translated by Dr. Julius (*Vaterländisches Museum*, II. 1, 1811):—

'Es war am grünen Donnerstag, man sähe die Kinder ziehn,
  Sauber gewaschen, paarweis', gekleidet in roth und in blau und in grün;
  Grauköpfige Zuchtmeister mit schneeweissen Ruthen voran.
  In St. Pauls hohen Dom wie der Themse Fluthen strömen sie dann.

'O! wie zahllos erscheinen sie da, diese Blumen von Londons Macht;
  Abgetheilt sitzend in Rotten, ganz in der eignen Unschuld Pracht!
  Es ersummt wie eine Menge, doch der Lämmer Menge nur allein,
  Tausend kleine Knaben und Mädchen erheben ihre Händchen so rein.

'Jetzt wie ein Wirbelwind steigt zum Himmel Gesanges Chor
  Wie ein harmonisch Gewitter zu den Sitzen der Engel empor.
  Zwischen den Kleinen die Alten, der Armuth weiser Hort—
  Drum erbarme dich vor deiner Thür, oder du treibst einen Engel fort.'

The Blossom

Merry, Merry Sparrow!   1
Under leaves so green,
A happy Blossom
Sees you, swift as arrow,
Seek your cradle narrow
Near my Bosom.

Pretty, Pretty Robin!   7
Under leaves so green,
A happy Blossom
Hears you sobbing, sobbing,
Pretty, Pretty Robin,
Near my Bosom.

In the first issue of the *Songs of Innocence* this plate is found as recto or verso to 'The Lamb,' as recto to 'The Little Girl Lost,' and as verso to the second plate of 'Spring.'

EY and WBY print as one stanza.

The Chimney Sweeper

When my mother died I was very young,   1
And my father sold me while yet my tongue
Could scarcely cry ''weep! 'weep! 'weep! 'weep!'
So your chimneys I sweep, & in soot I sleep.

There's little Tom Dacre, who cried when his head,   5
That curl'd like a lamb's back, was shav'd: so I said
'Hush, Tom! never mind it, for when your head's bare
You know that the soot cannot spoil your white hair.'

And so he was quiet, & that very night,   9
As Tom was a sleeping, he had such a sight!—
That thousands of sweepers, Dick, Joe, Ned & Jack,
Were all of them lock'd up in coffins of black.

And by came an Angel who had a bright key,   13
And he open'd the coffins & set them all free;
Then down a green plain leaping, laughing, they run,
And wash in a river, and shine in the Sun.

Then naked & white, all their bags left behind,   17
They rise upon clouds and sport in the wind;
And the Angel told Tom, if he'd be a good boy,
He'd have God for his father, & never want joy.

And so Tom awoke; and we rose in the dark,   21
And got with our bags & our brushes to work.
Tho' the morning was cold, Tom was happy & warm:
So if all do their duty they need not fear harm.

In the first issue of the *Songs of Innocence* this plate is found printed as recto or verso to ' The Divine Image,' as recto to the first plate of ' Spring,' or as verso to ' Nurse's Song.' This poem was first printed in ordinary type in James Montgomery's *Chimney-sweeper's Friend and Climbing-boy's Album* (1824) from a copy supplied to the editor by Charles Lamb.

3 'weep !] *No apostrophe in orig.*   5 Dacre] Toddy *in* J. Montgomery (Ch. Lamb).

The Divine Image

To Mercy, Pity, Peace, and Love   1
All pray in their distress;
And to these virtues of delight
Return their thankfulness.

For Mercy, Pity, Peace, and Love   5
Is God, our father dear,
And Mercy, Pity, Peace, and Love
Is Man, his child and care.

For Mercy has a human heart,   9
Pity a human face,
And Love, the human form divine,
And Peace, the human dress.

Then every man, of every clime,   13
That prays in his distress,
Prays to the human form divine,
Love, Mercy, Pity, Peace.

And all must love the human form,   17
In heathen, turk, or jew;
Where Mercy, Love, & Pity dwell,
There God is dwelling too.

In the first issue of *Songs of Innocence* this plate occurs either as recto or verso to 'The Chimney Sweeper,' or as verso to 'Holy Thursday,' or recto to 'A Dream.' The original plate is among the number reprinted in Gilchrist's *Life* (ii. *end*). This poem was first printed in ordinary type in Malkin's *Father's Memoirs of His Child* (1806).

'The Divine Image,' with the omission of stanza 2, has for many years been used as one of the hymns of the Positivist congregation in a northern city.

Night

The sun descending in the west,   1
The evening star does shine ;
The birds are silent in their nest,
And I must seek for mine.
The moon, like a flower,
In heaven's high bower,
With silent delight
Sits and smiles on the night.

Farewell, green fields and happy groves,   9
Where flocks have took delight.
Where lambs have nibbled, silent moves
The feet of angels bright ;
Unseen they pour blessing,
And joy without ceasing,
On each bud and blossom,
And each sleeping bosom.

They look in every thoughtless nest,   17
Where birds are cover'd warm ;
They visit caves of every beast,
To keep them all from harm.
If they see any weeping
That should have been sleeping,
They pour sleep on their head,
And sit down by their bed.

Engraved upon two plates, which, in the first issue, of the *Songs of Innocence*, are always found as recto and verso of the same leaf.   The poem, or part of a poem, on p. 105 of the MS. Book, entitled 'Day' and beginning 'The Sun arises in the East,' may have been designed by Blake as the antithesis of this Song of Innocence.

3 nest] nests W. Muir.   9 groves] grove DGR, WMR, EY.   10 took] ta'en *all except* Shep. *and* WBY.   11 moves] move DGR, WMR, EY.   13 blessing] blessings W. Muir.   23 head] heads W. Muir. 24 by] on Wilk.

H 2

When wolves and tygers howl for prey,   25
They pitying stand and weep;
Seeking to drive their thirst away,
And keep them from the sheep.
But if they rush dreadful,
The angels, most heedful,
Recieve each mild spirit,
New worlds to inherit.

And there the lion's ruddy eyes   33
Shall flow with tears of gold,
And pitying the tender cries,
And walking round the fold,
Saying 'wrath, by his meekness,
And, by his health, sickness
Is driven away
From our immortal day.

'And now beside thee, bleating lamb,   41
I can lie down and sleep;
Or think on him who bore thy name,
Graze after thee and weep.
For, wash'd in life's river,
My bright mane for ever
Shall shine like the gold
As I guard o'er the fold.'

33 eyes] eye W. Muir.   36 fold] folds W. Muir.   39 Is] Are
DGR, WMR, EY.   46 mane] name Wilk.

A Dream

Once a dream did weave a shade   1
O'er my Angel-guarded bed,
That an Emmet lost its way
Where on grass methought I lay.

In the first issue of the *Songs of Innocence* this plate is printed as reoto to
'The Little Girl Lost,' or as verso to 'Laughing Song' or to 'The Divine
Image.'

Troubled, 'wilder'd, and forlorn,   5
Dark, benighted, travel-worn,
Over many a tangled spray,
All heart-broke I heard her say:

'O, my children! do they cry?   9
Do they hear their father sigh?
Now they look abroad to see:
Now return and weep for me.'

Pitying, I drop'd a tear;   13
But I saw a glow-worm near,
Who replied: 'What wailing wight
Calls the watchman of the night?

'I am set to light the ground,   17
While the beetle goes his round:
Follow now the beetle's hum;
Little wanderer, hie thee home.'

On Another's Sorrow

Can I see another's woe,   1
And not be in sorrow too?
Can I see another's grief,
And not seek for kind relief?

Can I see a falling tear,   5
And not feel my sorrow's share?
Can a father see his child
Weep, nor be with sorrow fill'd?

Can a mother sit and hear   9
An infant groan, an infant fear?
No, no! never can it be!
Never, never can it be!

In the first issue of the *Songs of Innocence* this plate is found as recto to the first plate of 'Spring,' and as recto or verso to 'Infant Joy.' The original plate is reprinted in Gilchrist's *Life* (ii. *end*).

And can he who smiles on all   13
Hear the wren with sorrows small,
Hear the small bird's grief & care,
Hear the woes that infants bear,

And not sit beside the nest,   17
Pouring pity in their breast;
And not sit the cradle near,
Weeping tear on infant's tear;

And not sit both night & day,   21
Wiping all our tears away?
O, no! never can it be!
Never, never can it be!

He doth give his joy to all;   25
He becomes an infant small;
He becomes a man of woe;
He doth feel the sorrow too.

Think not thou canst sigh a sigh,   29
And thy maker is not by;
Think not thou canst weep a tear,
And thy maker is not near.

O! he gives to us his joy   33
That our grief he may destroy;
Till our grief is fled & gone
He doth sit by us and moan.

30 by] nigh Wilk.   34 grief] griefs Wilk., DGR.

The Little Boy Lost

'Father! father! where are you going?   1
O, do not walk so fast.
Speak, father, speak to your little boy,
Or else I shall be lost.'

In the first issue of the *Songs of Innocence* this plate is always found as recto to 'The Little Boy Found.' The original draft of this poem is found in the *Island in the Moon* (chap. xi), introduced by the words 'Then sung Quid—.'
  1 Father! father!] O father, father *Isl. in Moon.*   3 Speak] O speak *Isl. in Moon.*

The night was dark, no father was there;   5
The child was wet with dew;
The mire was deep, & the child did weep,
And away the vapour flew.

5 The . . . there] The night it was dark & no father was there
Isl. in Moon.   6 The child] And the child *Isl. in Moon.*

The Little Boy Found

The little boy lost in the lonely fen,   1
Led by the wand'ring light,
Began to cry; but God, ever nigh,
Appear'd like his father, in white.

He kissèd the child, & by the hand led,   5
And to his mother brought,
Who in sorrow pale, thro' the lonely dale,
Her little boy weeping sought.

In the first issue of the *Songs of Innocence* this plate always occurs as verso to the preceding.
8 Her] The DGR, WMR, EY.

SONGS

of

EXPERIENCE

1794

The Author & Printer, W. Blake

The engraved title to the *Songs of Experience*, when published either in conjunction with the *Songs of Innocence* or separately. The plate is printed on the recto of the leaf, facing the frontispiece of the Shepherd on the verso of the preceding leaf.

Reprinted in Gilchrist's *Life* (ii. *end*) from an electrotype of the original plate. This title-page would appear to have been twice engraved by Blake. In Gilchrist's reprint the date 1794 is omitted and the cross stroke to the letter *f* has a downward instead of an upward curve. In some copies the date has evidently been inserted by hand.

SONGS OF EXPERIENCE

Introduction

Hear the voice of the Bard !   1
Who Present, Past, & Future, sees ;
Whose ears have heard
The Holy Word
That walk'd among the ancient trees,

Calling the lapsèd Soul,   6
And weeping in the evening dew ;
That might controll
The starry pole,
And fallen fallen light renew !

'O Earth, O Earth, return !   11
Arise from out the dewy grass ;
Night is worn,
And the morn
Rises from the slumberous mass.

'Turn away no more ;   16
Why wilt thou turn away ?
The starry floor,
The wat'ry shore,
Is giv'n thee till the break of day.'

One engraved plate. Not found in any MS. version. Closely connected
with this poem are 'The Voice of the Ancient Bard,' by which it is immediately
preceded in some copies of the *Songs*, and 'Earth's Answer,' by which it is
followed in all copies.

1-10] Swinb. prints as a single stanza.   4 Holy] ancient Swinb.
5 ancient] silent Swinb.   11-20] Swinb. prints as a single stanza.
18 floor] shore Swinb.   19 shore] floor Swinb.   20 Is] Are Swinb.,
WMR, EY.

Earth's Answer

Earth rais'd up her head   1
From the darkness dread & drear.
Her light fled,
Stony dread!
And her locks cover'd with grey despair.

'Prison'd on wat'ry shore,   6
Starry Jealousy does keep my den:
Cold and hoar,
Weeping o'er
I hear the father of the ancient men.

'Selfish father of men!   11
Cruel, jealous, selfish fear!

'*The* Earth's Answer' (MS. Book) first word deleted. Engraved on a single plate from what is obviously the original draft in the MS. Book (p. 111 reversed). Cp. the lines immediately preceding this poem in the MS' Book, beginning:—

> 'Why art thou silent & invisible,
> Father of Jealousy?'

Cp. also the final stanza of *Ahania* (*engraved* 1795):—

> 'But now alone, over rocks, mountains,
> Cast out from thy lovely bosom
> Cruel jealousy, selfish fear,
> Self-destroying; how can delight
> Renew in these chains of darkness
> Where bones of beasts are strown,
> On the bleak and snowy mountains
> Where bones from the birth are buried
> Before they see the light?'

3 Her ... fled] Blake's successive changes of this line are :—

> Her *eyes fled*
>   *orbs dead*
>   light fled (pencil).

4 Stony dread!] *Punctuation as in* MS. Book *and engraved* Songs; (Stony dread!) DGR; Stony, dread, WMR, EY, WBY.   6 Prison'd ... shore] Prisoned on this watery shore Swinb.   7 my den:] *Punctuation as in* Wilk., Shep.; *so also in* Swinb. *Essay,* p. 118; *other edd. read* ... my den Cold and hoar;   10 father of the] *del. in* MS. Bk. *and replaced by some illegible word erased.*   11–15 MS. Book *cancelled.* The original rime-arrangement *a b aa b* breaks down in this and the next stanza.   11 Selfish] Cruel MS. Book *1st rdg. del.*   12 selfish] weeping MS. Book *1st rdg. del.*

Can delight,
Chain'd in night,
The virgins of youth and morning bear?

' Does spring hide its joy   16
When buds and blossoms grow?
Does the sower
Sow by night,
Or the plowman in darkness plow?

' Break this heavy chain   21
That does freeze my bones around.
Selfish! vain!
Eternal bane!
That free Love with bondage bound.'

14 Chain'd] Clog'd MS. Book *1st rdg. del.*   16-20 This stanza was
an addition written in place of the third, which Blake cancelled, but restored when engraving.   16 joy] delight MS. Book *1st rdg. del.*
18, 19 Does . . . night] Does the sower sow His seed by night MS. Book
1st rdg. del. : Can the sower sow by night Swinb.   22 freeze] close
MS. Book *1st rdg. del.*   24, 25 Eternal . . . bound] Thou, my bane Hast
my love with bondage bound MS. Book *1st rdg. del.*

Nurse's Song

When the voices of children are heard on the green   1
And whisp'rings are in the dale,
The days of my youth rise fresh in my mind,
My face turns green and pale.

Then come home, my children, the sun is gone down, 5
And the dews of night arise;
Your spring & your day are wasted in play,
And your winter and night in disguise.

Engraved without material change from a fair copy (without title) in the
MS. Book (p. 109 reversed).
  Nurse's Song] *No apostrophe in original*; Nurses' Song Wilk.   3 my]
R¹ *omits.*   rise] are MS. Book.   4 My] And my R¹.   green]
grave R¹.

The Fly

Little Fly,　　　　　　　　　　　1
Thy summer's play
My thoughtless hand
Has brush'd away.

Am not I　　　　　　　　　　　5
A fly like thee?
Or art not thou
A man like me?

For I dance,　　　　　　　　　　9
And drink, & sing,
Till some blind hand
Shall brush my wing.

Engraved on a single plate, in double columns, from what is evidently the first draft, without title, on p. 101 of the MS. Book. An uncompleted and deleted stanza shows that before hitting upon this felicitous tiny metre Blake began to write the song in a less sprightly strain—

> 'Woe! alas! my guilty hand
> Brush'd across thy summer joy;
> All thy gilded painted pride
> Shatter'd, fled . . .'

He then turned to the shorter metre, preserving the 'guilty hand' in the first draft of stanza 1. Then follows a deleted stanza, omitted by him in the engraved version, probably because, since writing the poem, he had used its first two lines as one of his 'Proverbs of Hell' (*Marriage of Heaven and Hell*) :

> 'The cut worm
> Forgives the plow,
> And dies in peace,
> And so do thou.'

Then come the second, third, and fifth stanzas in their present form, followed by two versions of stanza four, which is an afterthought. Blake then prefixed numbers to the stanzas indicating their present order. A few trifling deviations from the engraved text are given in the footnotes.

2 summer's] summer MS. Book.　　3 thoughtless] guilty MS. Book *1st rdg. del.*　　8 A pictorial representation of the same idea occurs in *The Gates of Paradise* (engraved 1793, from the original pencil sketches in the MS. Book), in which a youth, hat in hand, chases a butterfly of human shape, while another, which he has just struck down, lies crushed at his feet. Below is the inscription 'Alas !'　Cp. also *Milton*, f. 18, ll. 27-30.

If thought is life   13
And strength & breath,
And the want
Of thought is death;

Then am I   17
A happy fly,
If I live
Or if I die.

13-16 If . . . death]
            'Thought is life
            And strength & breath;
            But the want
            Of thought is death.'
MS. Book *1st rdg. del.*

The Tyger

Tyger! Tyger! burning bright   1
In the forests of the night,
What immortal hand or eye
Could frame thy fearful symmetry?

In what distant deeps or skies   5
Burnt the fire of thine eyes?
On what wings dare he aspire?
What the hand dare sieze the fire?

Engraved on a single plate from the first draft of the poem on pp. 109, 108 (reversed) of the MS. Book. The MS. readings, too numerous to be readily intelligible in footnotes, are given in full in the appended note on the different versions of 'The Tyger.' This poem was first printed in ordinary type in Malkin's *Father's Memoirs* (1806), p. xxxix, from a copy probably supplied by Blake himself, which exhibits an important variant reading of the last line of the third stanza. An early corrupt version also appeared in Cunningham's *Lives of the British Painters* (1830), ii. 144.

2 forests] forest Malk., Cunn., R¹; Thro' the desarts Chas. Lamb (quoting from memory, in a letter to Bernard Barton, May 15, 1824). 4 Could frame] Framed Cunn., DGR, WMR (2nd version). 6 Burnt] Burned Cunn., DGR., WMR (2nd version); burn'd Wilk. the] that DGR, WMR (2nd version). fire] fervour Cunn., R¹. of] within DGR, WMR (2nd version). 7, 8 dare] dared DGR, WMR (2nd version).

And what shoulder, & what art, 9
Could twist the sinews of thy heart?
And when thy heart began to beat,
What dread hand? & what dread feet?

What the hammer? what the chain? 13
In what furnace was thy brain?
What the anvil? what dread grasp
Dare its deadly terrors clasp?

When the stars threw down their spears, 17
And water'd heaven with their tears,
Did he smile his work to see?
Did he who made the Lamb make thee?

Tyger! Tyger! burning bright 21
In the forests of the night,
What immortal hand or eye,
Dare frame thy fearful symmetry?

10 thy] thine Wilk. 11 And . . . heart] When thy heart, Malk., Cunn., DGR, WMR (2nd version). 12 What . . . feet?] What dread hand forged thy dread feet? Malk. ; What dread hand formed thy dread feet? Cunn., DGR, WMR (2nd version) ; What dread hand and what dread feet WMR, EY, WBY ; What dread hand framed thy dread feet? Swinb. *See also editor's note to this poem.* 13, 14 What . . . brain] What the hammer! what the chain! Formed thy strength and forged thy brain? Cunn., R¹ ; What the hammer, what the chain, Knit thy strength and forged thy brain? DGR, WMR (2nd version). 16 Dare] Dared Malk., Cunn., DGR, WMR (2nd version). its] thy Cunn., DGR, WMR (2nd version). 17 spears] spheres Cunn., R¹. 18 water'd] watered Malk., Wilk., WMR, EY, WBY ; sprinkled Cunn. their] shining Cunn. 21-24 This stanza is omitted by Cunn., DGR and WMR (2nd version).

NOTE ON 'THE TYGER.'

The original draft of 'The Tyger,' written upon two opposite pages (pp. 109, 108 reversed) of the MS. Book, enables us to follow every step in the composition of the poem. On the left page is found the first rough draft of stanzas 1, 2, 3, 4, and 6. In stanza 3 the manuscript version throws light upon a verse which has proved a crux to many of Blake's readers and commentators. It will be seen that Blake at first intended the line—

'What dread hand and what dread feet'

merely as the beginning of a sentence running on into the next stanza. Unable to complete this stanza to his satisfaction he cancelled it altogether, leaving the preceding line as it stood. This, of course, did not escape his notice when engraving the poem for the *Songs of Experience*, and by a change of punctuation he converted the unfinished passage into its present shape—

'What dread hand? & what dread feet?'

a line exactly parallel in form to—

'What the hammer? what the chain?'

of the following stanza. The terrible, compressed force of these two short sentences, which burst forth with a momentary pause between them like shells from a mortar, is altogether lost in the languid punctuation of the Aldine edition—

'And, when thy heart began to beat,
What dread hand and what dread feet?'

and it is only the failure of critics to observe the significance of the revised pointing of the engraved version which caused Swinburne to speak of this passage as a ' rock of offence,' or Mr. Yeats to remark that when engraving the poem Blake 'forgot to alter the last line of the third stanza.' At a later date, in the version which there is no reason to doubt was supplied by the author to Dr. Malkin, Blake again remodelled this line into the slow and solemn form—

'What dread hand forged thy dread feet?'

where the gain in definiteness and technical accuracy is at the sacrifice of much of the fiery energy and vague suggestion of terror conveyed by the earlier text. It is probably with an imperfect remembrance of this final emendation of Blake's, misled by the spurious version of Gilchrist, that Swinburne (*Critical Essay*, p. 120) refers to 'the recovery of that nobler reading—

'What dread hand *framed* thy dread feet?'

a variant for which there is no printed or manuscript authority. The word ' frame' moreover had already been used in the first stanza.

On the opposite page of the MS. Book is the first draft of the fifth stanza, the composition of which Mr. W. A. White, the present owner of the MS. Book, thus explains to me in a letter :—

' I think that [Blake] wrote first " What the shoulder? What the knee?" and then, seeing that he had used the word "shoulder" before, he struck it out and inserted the word over it, which seems to be " ankle," but is not very clearly written.

'Then I think the glorious line occurred to him, " Did He who made the lamb make thee?" Probably after that he erased the line above, and wrote above it " And did He laugh His work to see?" and then added the two lines about the stars. Then Blake re-arranged the order of the lines in the stanza, and numbered them in order to make this order clear ; and also at the same time numbered the stanzas, making this the fifth. I think that he struck out the number "3" in front of the first line of this stanza by accident, meaning to erase the first word " And." '

Above the fifth stanza, though probably written after it, is a revised version of stanza 2, which differs from that finally adopted. The difficult line—

'Could heart descend, or wings aspire?'

has been interpreted by Swinburne: 'Could God bring down his heart to the making of a thing so deadly and strong? Or could any lesser daemonic force of nature take to itself wings and fly high enough to assume power equal to such a creation? Could spiritual force so far descend, or material force so far aspire?'

Upon the same page, to the right of these two stanzas, follows a fair copy of stanzas 1, 3, 5, and 6, which, except for unimportant differences of capitalization, and the readings 'dare frame' for 'could frame' in the first, and 'hand and eye' for 'hand or eye' in the first and last stanzas, is identical with the text of the engraved *Songs*.

The following is a faithful transcript of the original draft of 'The Tyger' in the MS. Book, Blake's variant readings being indicated typographically by placing them in consecutive order, one below another, deleted words or lines being printed in italics. The manuscript itself is unpunctuated throughout. It will be seen that this version differs in important details from that given by Messrs. Ellis and Yeats (iii. pp. 91, 92), which not only fails to make clear the sequence of Blake's alterations, but contains such inexplicable misreadings as 'filch' for 'fetch,' 'horn'd' for 'horrid,' 'inspire' for 'aspire,' and 'did' for 'dare'—errors repeated in Mr. Yeats' 'Muses' Library' edition of Blake (notes, pp. 238, 239).

THE TYGER.

  1. Tyger, Tyger, burning bright
    In the forests of the night,
    What immortal hand &' eye
             or
    Could frame thy fearful symmetry?
    Dare

  2. *In what* distant deeps or skies
    Burnt in
    Burnt the fire of thine eyes?
    The cruel
    On what wings dare he aspire?
    What the hand dare sieze the fire?

  3. And what shoulder, & what art
    Could twist the sinews of thy heart?
    And when thy heart began to beat
    What dread hand & what dread feet

    Could fetch it from the furnace deep,
    And in thy horrid ribs dare steep?
    In the well of sanguine woe—
    In what clay & in what mould
    Were thy eyes of fury roll'd?

  4. *What* the hammer? *what* the chain?
    Where   *where*
    In what furnace was thy brain?

What the anvil ? what *the arm*
                                arm
                                grasp
                                clasp
                   dread grasp
Could its deadly terrors *clasp* ?
Dare   *grasp* ?
                           clasp ?

6. Tyger, Tyger, burning bright
   In the forests of the night,
   What immortal hand & eye
   Dare *form* thy fearful symmetry ?
      frame

   [*On the opposite page*]

   Burnt in distant deeps or skies
   The cruel fire of thine eyes ?
   Could heart descend, or wings aspire ?
   What the hand dare sieze the fire ?

5. *3.* And *did he laugh* his work to see ?
         dare he *smile*
              laugh
    What the shoulder ? what the knee ?
         ankle ?

    4. *Did* he who made the lamb make thee ?
       Dare

    1. When the stars threw down their spears,

    2. And water'd heaven with their tears.

A few words must be added with regard to the so-called ' second version '
of ' The Tyger ' in the Aldine edition, and thence reprinted by later editors
under such headings as ' a later MS. version ' and the like. This, Mr. W. M.
Rossetti explains in a footnote, is ' the version which figures in Mr. Gilchrist's
book,' adding that it ' shows certain variations on MS. authority.' What
MS., as Mr. Yeats complains, is not stated, and as there is obviously no
warrant for these readings in the MS. Book, he assumes that they owe
their origin to changes introduced into the text by D. G. Rossetti. The
version given by the latter, however, as he himself states in a note prefixed
to his first transcript (R^1), is based upon that printed by Cunningham in his
Lives of British Painters (1830, ii, 144), where the last three stanzas run :—

> ' And what shoulder and what art
>   Could twist the sinews of thy heart ?
>   When thy heart began to beat
>   What dread hand formed thy dread feet ?

> ' What the hammer ! what the chain !
>   Formed thy strength and forged thy brain ?
>   What the anvil ! What dread grasp
>   Dared its deadly terrors clasp ?

'When the stars threw down their spheres,
And sprinkled heaven with shining tears,
Did he smile, his work to see?
Did he who made the lamb make thee?'

A comparison of the versions of the other poems and passages quoted by Cunningham with their originals in the *Poetical Sketches* shows that unauthorized readings are introduced into almost every line, and it is plain that Cunningham treated Blake's text with the same freedom which he would have thought himself entitled to use in an old Scots ballad. No manuscript authority of Blake's can therefore be claimed for this version. The interest attaching to everything relating to this poem, called by Swinburne 'the most famous of Blake's lyrics,' may be thought sufficient excuse for adding to the length of this note by reprinting Dr. Julius's German translation of 'The Tyger' from the *Vaterländisches Museum*, Bd. II, Heft i. (Hamburg, 1806). This spirited and admirably literal rendering appeared, it will be noticed, at a time when Blake's *Songs* were almost unknown to his own countrymen.

'DER TIGER.

'Tiger, Tiger, Flammenpracht
In den Wäldern düstrer Nacht!
Sprich, welch Gottes Aug' und Hand
Dich so furchtbar schön verband?

'Stammt vom Himmel, aus der Höll',
Dir der Augen Feuerquell'?
Welche Flügel trägst du kühn?
Wer wagt wohl, zu nah'n dem Glüh'n?

'Welche Stärke, welche Kunst,
Wob so sinnreich Herzensbrunst?
Als dein Herz den Puls empfand,
Welch ein Fuss und welche Hand?

'Was ist Hammer, Kettenklirr'n?
Welche Esse schmolz dein Hirn?
Was ist Amboss? Welcher Held
Muth in deinem Arm behält?

'Aus den Sternen flog der Speer,
Thränend ward der Himmel Meer:
Schaut' er lächelnd da auf dich?
Der das Lamm schuf, schuf er dich?

'Tiger, Tiger, Flammenpracht
In den Wäldern düstrer Nacht!
Sprich, wess Gottes Aug' und Hand
Dich so furchtbar schön verband?'

The Little Girl Lost

In futurity   1
I prophetic see
That the earth from sleep
(Grave the sentence deep)

Shall arise and seek   5
For her maker meek ;
And the desart wild
Become a garden mild.

In the southern clime,   9
Where the summer's prime
Never fades away,
Lovely Lyca lay.

Seven summers old   13
Lovely Lyca told ;
She had wander'd long
Hearing wild birds' song.

'Sweet sleep, come to me   17
Underneath this tree.
Do father, mother, weep ?
Where can Lyca sleep ?

'Lost in desart wild   21
Is your little child.
How can Lyca sleep
If her mother weep ?

'If her heart does ake   25
Then let Lyca wake ;
If my mother sleep,
Lyca shall not weep.

This song, and its sequel 'The Little Girl Found,' are engraved upon three plates, the first of which contains the first ten stanzas of the present poem, and the second the conclusion of the same with the first three stanzas and half of the fourth of the next song. The first and last plates are among the number reprinted from the originals by Gilchrist. No manuscript versions of these songs are known to exist.

2 I . . . see] I prophesy WBY.   17-32 Wilk. *and* Shep. *omit quotation marks.*

'Frowning, frowning night,   29
O'er this desart bright,
Let thy moon arise
While I close my eyes.'

Sleeping Lyca lay   33
While the beasts of prey,
Come from caverns deep,
View'd the maid asleep.

The kingly lion stood,   37
And the virgin view'd,
Then he gambol'd round
O'er the hallow'd ground.

Leopards, tygers, play   41
Round her as she lay,
While the lion old
Bow'd his mane of gold.

And her bosom lick,   45
And upon her neck
From his eyes of flame
Ruby tears there came;

While the lioness   49
Loos'd her slender dress,
And naked they convey'd
To caves the sleeping maid.

45 And ... lick] And her breast did lick DGR, WMR, EY, Muir's *facsim.*
(*Songs of In.*)

The Little Girl Found

All the night in woe   1
Lyca's parents go
Over vallies deep,
While the desarts weep.

See note to 'The Little Girl Lost.'

Tired and woe-begone,   5
Hoarse with making moan,
Arm in arm seven days
They trac'd the desert ways.

Seven nights they sleep   9
Among shadows deep,
And dream they see their child
Starv'd in desert wild.

Pale, thro' pathless ways   13
The fancied image strays
Famish'd, weeping, weak,
With hollow piteous shriek.

Rising from unrest,   17
The trembling woman prest
With feet of weary woe:
She could no further go.

In his arms he bore   21
Her, arm'd with sorrow sore;
Till before their way
A couching lion lay.

Turning back was vain: 25
Soon his heavy mane
Bore them to the ground.
Then he stalk'd around,

Smelling to his prey;   29
But their fears allay
When he licks their hands,
And silent by them stands.

They look upon his eyes   33
Fill'd with deep surprise;
And wondering behold
A spirit arm'd in gold.

22 sorrow] sorrows DGR.   26 his] the Wilk.

On his head a crown ;   37
On his shoulders down
Flow'd his golden hair.
Gone was all their care.

'Follow me,' he said,   41
'Weep not for the maid ;
In my palace deep
Lyca lies asleep.'

Then they followèd,   45
Where the vision led,
And saw their sleeping child
Among tygers wild.

To this day they dwell   49
In a lonely dell ;
Nor fear the wolvish howl
Nor the lions' growl.

38 shoulders] shoulder Wilk.   52 lions'] lions *orig.*; lion's *all edd.*

The Clod and the Pebble

'Love seeketh not Itself to please,   1
Nor for itself hath any care,
But for another gives its ease,
And builds a Heaven in Hell's despair.'

So sung a little Clod of Clay,   5
Trodden with the cattle's feet,
But a Pebble of the brook
Warbled out these metres meet :

Engraved on a single plate from the fair copy on p. 115 (reversed) of the MS. Book. Without title in the MS.

3 another] another's R¹.   4 in] to R¹.   5 sung] sang MS. Book, DGR, WMR, EY.   7 brook] wood R¹.

'Love seeketh only Self to please,   9
To bind another to Its delight,
Joys in another's loss of ease,
And builds a Hell in Heaven's despite.'

9–12 Cp. *Visions of the Daughters of Albion* (engraved 1793) f. 10 : 'Can
that be Love, that drinks another as a sponge drinks Water?'   9 Self]
Self DGR, WMR, EY.   10 bind] bend R¹.

The Little Vagabond

Dear Mother, dear Mother, the Church is cold,   1
But the Ale-house is healthy & pleasant & warm ;
Besides I can tell where I am used well,
Such usage in heaven will never do well.

But if at the Church they would give us some Ale,   5
And a pleasant fire our souls to regale,
We'd sing and we'd pray all the live-long day,
Nor ever once wish from the Church to stray.

Then the Parson might preach, & drink, & sing,   9
And we'd be as happy as birds in the spring ;
And modest dame Lurch, who is always at Church,
Would not have bandy children, nor fasting, nor birch.

And God, like a father, rejoicing to see   13
His children as pleasant and happy as he,
Would have no more quarrel with the Devil or the Barrel,
But kiss him, & give him both drink and apparel.

Engraved on a single plate from the version in pencil, MS. Book (p. 105
reversed) entitled 'The little *pretty* Vagabond' ['pretty' *del.*].   This poem is
omitted in Wilkinson's edition of the *Songs*.
   4 Such... well] Such usage in heaven makes all go to hell MS. Book 1*st
rdg. del.*; The poor parsons with wind like a blown bladder swell MS.
Book 2*nd rdg.*, DGR, WMR, EY.   13 rejoicing to see] that joys for
to see MS. Book 1*st rdg. del.*   16 But ... apparel] But shake hands
& kiss him & there'd be no more hell MS. Book 1*st rdg. del. and* R¹; But
kiss him & give him both *food* [*del.* changed to 'drink'] & apparel MS. Book
2*nd rdg.*

Holy Thursday

Is this a holy thing to see   1
In a rich and fruitful land,
Babes reduc'd to misery,
Fed with cold and usurous hand?

Is that trembling cry a song?   5
Can it be a song of joy?
And so many children poor?
It is a land of poverty!

And their sun does never shine,   9
And their fields are bleak & bare,
And their ways are fill'd with thorns:
It is eternal winter there.

For where-e'er the sun does shine,   13
And where-e'er the rain does fall,
Babe can never hunger there,
Nor poverty the mind appall.

Engraved on a single plate from the fair copy on p. 103 (reversed) of the MS. Book. This plate is reprinted from an electrotype of the original in Gilchrist's *Life* (ii. *end*).

4 Fed . . . hand] Fed with a cold usurious hand DGR.   7 And . . . poor] And so great a number poor MS. Book.   8, 12 It is] 'Tis MS. Book.   13 For] But MS. Book.   15 Babe] Babes Wilk., DGR, WMR, EY. can] should DGR, WMR, EY.

A Poison Tree

I was angry with my friend: 1
I told my wrath, my wrath did end.
I was angry with my foe:
I told it not, my wrath did grow.

Engraved on a single plate from the copy in the MS. Book (p. 114 reversed). The title, 'Christian Forbearance,' of the MS. (written later in pencil) has been adopted by DGR, WMR, and EY, in preference to that in the engraved version.

4 A line drawn below this stanza in the MS. Book shows that Blake originally intended the poem to end at this point.

And I water'd it in fears,   5
Night & morning with my tears ;
And I sunnèd it with smiles,
And with soft deceitful wiles.

And it grew both day and night,   9
Till it bore an apple bright ;
And my foe beheld it shine,
And he knew that it was mine,

And into my garden stole   13
When the night had veil'd the pole :
In the morning glad I see
My foe outstretch'd beneath the tree.

9 both] by MS. Book.   11 And ... shine] And I gave it to my
foe MS. Book *1st rdg. del.*

The Angel

I Dreamt a Dream ! what can it mean ?   1
And that I was a maiden Queen,
Guarded by an Angel mild :
Witless woe was ne'er beguil'd !

And I wept both night and day,   5
And he wip'd my tears away,
And I wept both day and night,
And hid from him my heart's delight.

So he took his wings and fled ;   9
Then the morn blush'd rosy red ;
I dried my tears, & arm'd my fears
With ten thousand shields and spears.

Engraved on a single plate, from the fair copy, written in pencil, on p. 103
(reversed) of the MS. Book.   The title written later.   The original coloured
design of this plate is found on p. 65 of the MS. Book.

Soon my Angel came again: 13
I was arm'd, he came in vain;
For the time of youth was fled,
And grey hairs were on my head.

15, 16 For . . . head] The same lines, with the change of 'were' to 'are,'
are used by Blake as the final couplets to 'Infant Sorrow' (MS. Book x`,
and the first version of 'In a Mirtle Shade' (MS. Book xiii).   15 For]
But MS. Book *1st rdg. del.*

The Sick Rose

O Rose, thou art sick!   1
The invisible worm,
That flies in the night,
In the howling storm,

Has found out thy bed   5
Of crimson joy;
And his dark secret love
Does thy life destroy.

Engraved from the copy in the MS. Book (p. 107 reversed). The original
coloured design is found on p. 21 of the MS. Book. It differs considerably
from the engraved illustration. Instead of the worm preying upon the heart
of the rose there is a youth prostrate on the ground, as if in regret at seeing
the spirit of the rose, symbolized by a female figure, take flight.
    5 Has] Hath MS. Book.   7, 8 And . . . destroy] A dark-secret love
Doth life destroy MS. Book *1st rdg. del.*   7 his] her MS. Book, *above
an erased and illegible word.*

To Tirzah

Whate'er is Born of Mortal Birth   1
Must be consumèd with the Earth,
To rise from Generation free:
Then what have I to do with thee?

Not in MS. Book. Engraved on a single plate. On the robe of one of
the figures in the design at the foot of the page is written 'It is Raised a
Spiritual Body.' Shepherd prints this; the rest omit.
    By the name Tirzah, taken from Canticles vi. 4, Blake personifies Natural
Religion. In *Jerusalem* and *Milton, passim,* Tirzah, generally associated
with Rahab, or Moral Law, is represented as a bright and beautiful being,

The Sexes sprung from Shame & Pride   5
Blow'd in the morn ; in evening died ;
But Mercy chang'd Death into Sleep ;
The Sexes rose to work & weep.

Thou Mother of my Mortal part   9
With cruelty didst mould my Heart,
And with false self-decieving tears
Didst bind my Nostrils, Eyes, & Ears ;

Didst close my Tongue in senseless clay,   13
And me to Mortal Life betray :
The Death of Jesus set me free :
Then what have I to do with thee ?

preying upon and pitying her victims, and perverting the mild influences of
the lovely Enitharmon, or Space : cp. *Milton*, f. 20, ll. 41-45 :—

> 'Rahab created Voltaire : Tirzah created Rousseau,
> Asserting the Self-righteousness against the Universal Saviour,
> Mocking the Confessors & Martyrs, claiming Self-righteousness
> With cruel Virtue, making War upon the Lambs Redeemed
> To perpetuate War & Glory, to perpetuate the Laws of Sin.'

Cf. also Swinburne, *Essay*, p. 122 : ' "Tirzah," in his mythology, represents the mere separate and human nature, mother of the perishing body
and daughter of the " religion," which occupies itself with laying down laws
for the flesh ; which, while pretending (and that in all good faith) to despise
the body and bring it into subjection as with control of bit and bridle, does
implicitly overrate its power upon the soul for evil or good, and thus falls
foul of fact on all sides by assuming that spirit and flesh are twain, and that
things pleasant and good for the one can properly be loathsome or poisonous
to the other.'

5 sprung] sprang DGR, WMR, EY.   6 Blow'd] Blown DGR, WMR,
EY.   11 tears] fears Swinb.   12 bind] blind WBY.

The Voice of the Ancient Bard

Youth of delight, come hither,   1
And see the opening morn,
Image of truth new-born.
Doubt is fled, & clouds of reason,
Dark disputes & artful teazing.   5

Not in the MS. Book.   This poem is generally found as one of the
Songs of Innocence, though sometimes placed by Blake among the *Songs of
Experience.*   In all the early issues of the former it occurs as verso to ' The

Folly is an endless maze,
Tangled roots perplex her ways.
How many have fallen there!
They stumble all night over bones of the dead,
And feel they know not what but care,   10
And wish to lead others, when they should be led.

Little Black Boy,' while in the latest issues it is commonly placed last,
forming a connecting link with the Introduction to the *Songs of Experience*.
See editor's Bibliographical Preface to the *Songs*.
  9 stumble] tumble Muir's *facsimile* (*Songs of Experience*).   10 And . . .
care] And feel—they know not what but care Wilk., WMR, EY, WBY :
And feel—they know not what save care DGR.   11 when] where Muir's
facsimiles.

My Pretty Rose Tree

A flower was offer'd to me,   1
Such a flower as May never bore ;
But I said ' I've a Pretty Rose-tree,'
And I passèd the sweet flower o'er.

Then I went to my Pretty Rose-tree,   5
To tend her by day and by night,
But my Rose turn'd away with jealousy,
And her thorns were my only delight.

The first poem in the MS. Book (on p. 115 reversed).   Without title in the
original draft.   This and the two following songs are engraved upon a single
plate, reprinted in Gilchrist's *Life* (ii, *end*).
  4 passèd] DGR, Shepherd and other editors ruin the melody of this line
by reading ' passed ' or ' pass'd ' for ' passèd.'   It was Blake's almost
invariable practice, not only in manuscript but in engraved poems, to omit
the *e* of the final *ed* in the preterite or participial termination, where he did
not intend it to be pronounced as a separate syllable.   The only exception
to this rule is in the case of words where the omission of the *e* might
possibly lead to confusion with another word, e. g. ' pined ' not ' pin'd.'
  6 To . . . by night] In the silence of the night MS. Book *1st rdg. del.*   her]
it MS. Book *2nd rdg.* R¹.   by night] R¹ *omits* by.   7 turn'd] turned
all except Shep. : turn'd . . . jealousy] was turnèd from me MS. Book *1st
rdg. del. and replaced by* was fillèd with Jealousy.   8 Blake's first version
of this stanza seems to me preferable to that of the engraved *Songs :—*

          ' Then I went to my pretty rose tree
            In the silence of the night ;
            But my rose was turnèd from me,
            And her thorns were my only delight.'

Ah ! Sun Flower

Ah, Sun-flower! weary of time,   1
Who countest the steps of the Sun;
Seeking after that sweet golden clime,
Where the traveller's journey is done;

Where the Youth pined away with desire,   5
And the pale Virgin shrouded in snow,
Arise from their graves, and aspire
Where my Sun-flower wishes to go.

Not in the MS. Book.   Engraved on the same plate as the preceding
and following song.

3 clime] prime DGR.

The Lilly

The modest Rose puts forth a thorn,   1
The humble Sheep a threat'ning horn;
While the Lilly white shall in Love delight,
Nor a thorn, nor a threat, stain her beauty bright.

Engraved on the same plate as the two preceding songs, from the first
rough draft without title on p. 109 (reversed) of the MS. Book. In its
present form this beautiful little poem might more fitly rank as a Song of
Innocence than a Song of Experience; but the first draft, with its successive
alterations as seen in the MS. Book, shows that Blake originally conceived
it in its 'contrary state.'   Beginning by writing—

'The rose puts envious . . .'

he felt that 'envious' did not express his full meaning, and deleted the last
three words, writing above them 'lustful rose,' and finishing the line with
the words 'puts forth a thorn.'   He then went on—

'The coward sheep a threat'ning horn;
While the lilly white shall in love delight,
And the lion increase freedom & peace.'

at which point he drew a line under the poem to show that it was finished.
On a subsequent reading he deleted the last line, substituting for it—

'The priest loves war, & the soldier peace,'

but here, perceiving that his rime had disappeared, he cancelled this line
also, and gave the poem an entirely different turn by changing the word
'lustful' to 'modest,' and 'coward' to 'humble,' and completing the quatrain
(as in the engraved version) by a fourth line simply explanatory of the first
three.

The Garden of Love

I went to the Garden of Love,   1
And saw what I never had seen :
A Chapel was built in the midst,
Where I used to play on the green.

And the gates of this Chapel were shut,   5
And 'Thou shalt not' writ over the door ;
So I turn'd to the Garden of Love
That so many sweet flowers bore ;

And I saw it was fillèd with graves,   9
And tomb-stones where flowers should be :
And Priests in black gowns were walking their rounds,
And binding with briars my joys & desires.

Engraved on a single plate from the fair transcript on the first page (p. 115 reversed) of the MS. Book. Without title in the MS.

DGR followed by WMR and EY prefix as the first two stanzas of this poem the lines beginning—

'I laid me down upon a bank
Where Love lay sleeping . . .'

There is no authority for this in the engraved version, and Rossetti was evidently misled by the immediate juxtaposition of these two songs in the MS. Book, where however they are clearly divided by Blake's usual line of separation. Swinburne (*Essay*, p. 141) falls into the same error.

2 And saw] And I saw MS. Book.   5 this] the R¹.   were] was Wilk.   7 So] And MS. Book *1st rdg. del.*   9 fillèd] filled MS. Book *and orig.; all edd. read* 'filled' (= fill'd *in all except* Wilk. *and* Shep.). 11 in] with R¹.   12 binding] choking R¹.

This is another of the poems translated by Dr. Julius in the *Vaterländisches Museum*, II. i. (1806) :—

'Ich ging einst zum Garten der Liebe,
Und sah, was ich nimmer gesehn.
Am Rasen stand eine Capelle,
Wo sonst ich pflog spielend zu gehn.

'Und zu war die Thür der Capelle,
Und "du sollst nicht" stand auf dem Thor,
So kehrt' ich zum Garten der Liebe,
Der Blumen sonst brachte hervor.

'Und ich sah ihn mit Gräbern gefüllet,
Und Grabstein', wo Liebe sollt' sein ;
Und Priester in Trau'r umgingen die Mau'r,
Und senkten in Schmerz mein liebendes Herz.

A Little Boy Lost

'Nought loves another as itself,   1
Nor venerates another so,
Nor is it possible to Thought
A greater than itself to know:

'And, Father, how can I love you   5
Or any of my brothers more?
I love you like the little bird
That picks up crumbs around the door.'

The Priest sat by and heard the child,   9
In trembling zeal he siez'd his hair:
He led him by his little coat,
And all admir'd the Priestly care.

And standing on the altar high,   13
'Lo! what a fiend is here,' said he,
'One who sets reason up for judge
Of our most holy Mystery.'

Engraved on a single plate from the rough draft on p. 106 (reversed) of the MS. Book.

5 And] Then MS. Bk. *1st rdg. del.*   how . . . you] I cannot love you MS. Book *1st rdg. del.*   6 Or] Nor MS. Book *1st rdg. del.*   7 I . . . bird] I love myself: so does the bird MS. Book *1st rdg. del.*   11, 12 The first reading of these two lines in the MS. Book was—

> 'The mother follow'd, weeping loud,
> "O, that I such a fiend should bear!"'

These are deleted and replaced by—

> 'Then led him by his little coat,
> To shew his zealous priestly care.'

The last line is again cancelled and rewritten—

> 'And all admir'd his priestly care,'

the word 'Then' in the preceding line being deleted and replaced by '&.'   12 the] his Muir's *facsimile*.   13-16 This stanza appears to have followed the fifth in order of composition.

> The weeping child could not be heard,   17
> The weeping parents wept in vain ;
> They strip'd him to his little shirt,
> And bound him in an iron chain ;
>
> And burn'd him in a holy place,   21
> Where many had been burn'd before :
> The weeping parents wept in vain.
> Are such things done on Albion's shore ?

19 They] And MS. Book *1st rdg. del.*   19, 20 They . . . chain] They bound the little ivory limbs In a cruel iron chain MS. Book *1st rdg. del.* 21 And . . . place] They burn'd him in a holy fire MS. Book *1st rdg.* with first and last words *del.* and changed to above.   24 Are . . . shore ?] Such things are done on Albion's shore MS. Book *1st rdg.* altered as above.

Swinb. comments (*Essay*, p. 126), 'To the surprising final query, "Are such things done on Albion's shore ?" one is provoked to respond, " On the whole, not, as far as we can see " ; but the " Albion " of Blake's verse is never this weaving and spinning country of our working days ; it is rather some inscrutable remote land of Titanic visions, moated with silent white mist instead of solid and sonorous surf, and peopled with vague pre-Adamite giants, symbolic of more than we can safely define or conceive.'

Infant Sorrow

> My mother groan'd, my father wept,   1
> Into the dangerous world I leapt ;
> Helpless, naked, piping loud,
> Like a fiend hid in a cloud.
>
> Struggling in my father's hands,   5
> Striving against my swadling bands,
> Bound and weary, I thought best
> To sulk upon my mother's breast.

Engraved upon a single plate, the original of which is among the number reprinted by Gilchrist (*Life*, ii. *end*).

Compare the much fuller form of this song found on p. 113 (reversed) of the MS. Book, only the first two stanzas of which were engraved by Blake for the *Songs of Experience*. The complete poem will be found among 'Poems from the Rossetti MS. Book' (x).

The School Boy

I love to rise in a summer morn   1
When the birds sing on every tree;
The distant huntsman winds his horn,
And the sky-lark sings with me.
O! what sweet company.

But to go to school in a summer morn,   6
O! it drives all joy away;
Under a cruel eye outworn,
The little ones spend the day
In sighing and dismay.

Ah! then at times I drooping sit,   11
And spend many an anxious hour,
Nor in my book can I take delight,
Nor sit in learning's bower,
Worn thro' with the dreary shower.

How can the bird that is born for joy   16
Sit in a cage and sing;
How can a child, when fears annoy,
But droop his tender wing,
And forget his youthful spring?

O! father & mother, if buds are nip'd   21
And blossoms blown away,
And if the tender plants are strip'd
Of their joy in the springing day,
By sorrow and care's dismay,

Engraved upon a single plate, reprinted from an electrotype of the original copper in Gilchrist's *Life* (ii. *end*). Not in the MS. Book. This song, like 'The Little Girl Lost,' 'The Little Girl Found,' and 'The Voice of the Ancient Bard,' originally formed one of the *Songs of Innocence*, where, in the early issues, it is always printed as verso to the last plate of 'Spring.' On the completion of the *Songs of Experience* Blake, in most cases, transferred these poems to the latter series. In the editions of Wilkinson and Shepherd 'The School Boy' appears among the *Songs of Innocence*. See Bibliographical Preface to the *Songs*.

   1 in] on *all except* Shep., WBY.   2 When . . . sing] When birds are singing DGR, WMR, EY.

How shall the summer arise in joy,   26
Or the summer fruits appear?
Or how shall we gather what griefs destroy,
Or bless the mellowing year,
When the blasts of winter appear?

London

I wander thro' each charter'd street,   1
Near where the charter'd Thames does flow,
And mark in every face I meet
Marks of weakness, marks of woe.

In every cry of every Man,   5
In every Infant's cry of fear,
In every voice, in every ban,
The mind-forg'd manacles I hear.

How the Chimney sweeper's cry   9
Every black'ning Church appalls;
And the hapless Soldier's sigh
Runs in blood down Palace walls.

But most thro' midnight streets I hear   13
How the youthful Harlot's curse
Blasts the new born Infant's tear,
And blights with plagues the Marriage hearse.

Engraved on a single plate, with some important changes from the first
draft of this poem found on p. 109 (reversed) of the MS. Book. This plate is
among the number reprinted by Gilchrist (*Life*, ii. *end*).

1, 2 charter'd] dirty MS. Book.   3 And mark] And see MS. Book
1*st rdg. del.* ; A mark WMR (corrected, however, in some later editions), EY,
WBY.   6 In . . . fear] In every voice of every child MS. Book 1*st rdg.
del.*   8 The . . . hear] The german forged links I hear MS. Book 1*st
rdg. del.*   9 How] But most *etc.* MS. Book 1*st rdg. del.* It would appear
to have been Blake's first intention to close the poem with this stanza.
10 Blackens o'er the churches walls MS. Book 1*st rdg. del.*   14 Harlot's]
No apostrophe in orig. ; harlots' Wilk. ; harlot's *rest.*   13–16 In the MS.
Book this stanza was at first written—

'But most the midnight harlot's curse
From every dismal street I hear,
Weaves around the marriage hearse,
And blasts the new born infant's tear.'

K 2

This was cancelled and followed by—

> 'But most *from every* [*alt. to* through wintry] streets I hear,
> How the midnight harlot's curse
> Blasts the new born infant's tear,
> And *hangs* [*alt. to* smites] with plagues the marriage hearse.'

Compare Blake's use of the same epithets in a quatrain twice repeated in the MS. Book (pp. 107 and 99 reversed):—

'*An Ancient Proverb.*

> 'Remove away that black'ning church,
> Remove away that marriage hearse,
> Remove away that *place* [*alt. to* man] of blood,
> '*Twill* [*alt. to* You'll] quite remove the ancient curse.'

A Little Girl Lost

Children of the future Age,   1
Reading this indignant page,
Know that in a former time,
Love, sweet Love, was thought a crime!

In the Age of Gold,   5
Free from winter's cold,
Youth and maiden bright
To the holy light,
Naked in the sunny beams delight.

Once a youthful pair,   10
Fill'd with softest care,
Met in garden bright
Where the holy light
Had just remov'd the curtains of the night.

There, in rising day,   15
On the grass they play;
Parents were afar,
Strangers came not near,
And the maiden soon forgot her fear.

Engraved on a single plate.   Not in the MS. Book.

1–4 In the engraved original this introductory stanza is written indented in roman characters, the body of the poem being in italic.   15 There] Then *all except* Shep., WBY.

Tired with kisses sweet,   20
They agree to meet
When the silent sleep
Waves o'er heaven's deep,
And the weary tired wanderers weep.

To her father white   25
Came the maiden bright;
But his loving look,
Like the holy book,
All her tender limbs with terror shook.

'Ona! pale and weak!   30
To thy father speak:
O! the trembling fear,
O! the dismal care,
That shakes the blossoms of my hoary hair!'

The Chimney Sweeper

A little black thing among the snow,   1
Crying ''weep! 'weep!' in notes of woe!
'Where are thy father & mother, say?'—
'They are both gone up to the church to pray.

'Because I was happy upon the heath,   5
And smil'd among the winter's snow,
They clothèd me in the clothes of death,
And taught me to sing the notes of woe.

Engraved on a single plate. The original draft of this song in the MS.
Book shows that Blake at first intended the second and third stanzas (on
p. 103 reversed) to form a poem complete in itself. The first stanza and title
are an afterthought, written in pencil upon a different page (106 reversed).
    3 Where . . . say] Where are they, father and mother, say? MS. Book.
4 to the church] to church MS. Book.   6 winter's snow] wintery *wind*
[*alt. to* snow] MS. Book.   7 clothèd] clothed MS. Book, *orig.*, Shep.
[= clothèd]; cloth'd Wilk.; *the rest* clothed [= cloth'd].

'And because I am happy & dance & sing,   9
They think they have done me no injury,
And are gone to praise God & his Priest & King,
Who make up a heaven of our misery.'

12 Who ... misery] Who wrap themselves up in our misery MS. Book
1st rdg. del.

The Human Abstract

Pity would be no more   1
If we did not make somebody Poor;
And Mercy no more could be
If all were as happy as we.

And mutual fear brings peace,   5
Till the selfish loves increase;
Then Cruelty knits a snare,
And spreads his baits with care.

He sits down with holy fears,   9
And waters the ground with tears;
Then Humility takes its root
Underneath his foot.

Soon spreads the dismal shade   13
Of Mystery over his head;
And the Catterpiller and Fly
Feed on the Mystery.

And it bears the fruit of Deceit,   17
Ruddy and sweet to eat;
And the Raven his nest has made
In its thickest shade.

Engraved on a single plate, reprinted in Gilchrist (ii. *end*) from the draft
in the MS. Book (p. 107 reversed). The first title of the poem was 'The
Earth.' This is erased, and 'The human Image' substituted: the present
title is not in the MS. Book.

Compare with this song the fine variant version, beginning 'I heard an
Angel singing,' MS. Book (p. 114 reversed).

1 would] could MS. Book.   2 If there was nobody poor MS. Book
1st rdg. del.   9 with ... fears] with his holy fears EY.   20 its]
the Swinb.   thickest] blackest MS. Book.

> The Gods of the earth and sea   21
> Sought thro' Nature to find this Tree;
> But their search was all in vain :
> There grows one in the Human Brain.

23, 24 'But their search was all in vain
        Till they sought in the human brain.'
                                MS. Book 1*st rdg., last line del.*
The 'Tree of Mystery' signifies 'Moral Law.'   See *Jerusalem*, f. 28,
ll. 14-19 :—

'He [Albion] sat by Tyburn's brook, and underneath his heel shot up
A deadly Tree : he nam'd it Moral Virtue, and the Law
Of God, who dwells in Chaos, hidden from the human sight.
The Tree spread over him its cold shadows (Albion groan'd),
They bent down, they felt the earth, and again enrooting
Shot into many a Tree, an endless labyrinth of woe.'

A very similar description of the growth of the Tree is found in *Ahania*
(*engr.* 1795), chap. iii, thus condensed by Swinburne (*Essay*, p. 121):
'Compare the passage ... where the growth of it is defined ; rooted in the
rock of separation, watered with the tears of a jealous God, shot up from
sparks and fallen germs of material seed ; being after all a growth of mere
error, and vegetable (not spiritual) life ; the topmost stem of it made into
a cross whereon to nail the dead redeemer and friend of men.'

[TO THE *SONGS OF EXPERIENCE*]

A Divine Image

> Cruelty has a Human Heart,   1
> And Jealousy a Human Face;
> Terror the Human Form Divine,
> And Secrecy the Human Dress.
>
> The Human Dress is forgèd Iron,   5
> The Human Form a fiery Forge,
> The Human Face a Furnace seal'd,
> The Human Heart its hungry Gorge.

I place this poem as appendix to the *Songs of Experience* in the absence of
evidence that it was included in any authentic copy of the *Songs* issued
during Blake's lifetime.   Out of fifteen examples of the *Songs of Experience*

known to me, one only, the uncoloured copy in the Reading Room of the British Museum, contains this plate, and there the watermark of the paper, which is dated 1832, proves that it must have been printed *at least* five years after Blake's death.   The only other existing specimen of the engraved song is a proof impression (also uncoloured) in the possession of Mr. William Muir, which he has reproduced in facsimile at the end of his beautiful edition of *The Marriage of Heaven and Hell.*   It is quite clear that Blake engraved this poem with a view to its forming one of the *Songs of Experience*; and the total number of plates specified as belonging to this work in his prospectus 'To the Public' (see Bibliographical Preface to the *Songs*) would seem to show that this was his intention in October, 1793, when this advertisement was issued.   It is fairly plain too that Blake rejected the plate without destroying it—perhaps because it was one of those which were engraved on both sides of the copper—leaving it possible for it to be inadvertently introduced into one or two copies which may have been printed when the plates passed into other hands, after the death of Mrs. Blake in October, 1831.   This poem seems to have been unknown to Blake's first editor, Wilkinson, as well as to Gilchrist, who rightly represents 54 as the number of plates belonging to a complete set of both series of the *Songs*.   It is first introduced into the *Songs of Experience* by R. H. Shepherd (1866), who probably took it from the posthumously printed copy which the British Museum had acquired two years before.   Since then it has been included among the *Songs* without comment by W. M. Rossetti and all Blake's later editors, who follow Shepherd in placing it immediately after 'A Little Girl Lost.'

POEMS

from

THE ROSSETTI MANUSCRIPT

(circa 1793–1811)

commonly known as

'THE MANUSCRIPT BOOK'

BIBLIOGRAPHICAL PREFACE

TO THE

ROSSETTI MANUSCRIPT

THE Rossetti MS. is the name used in this edition as a descriptive title for Blake's book of notes and sketches, commonly called 'The MS. Book,' and sometimes, less correctly, 'Ideas of Good and Evil.' The latter title, partially covered by a pencil sketch, is found written, in bold script characters, on the verso of the second leaf. In all probability Blake intended it to refer to the series of designs, beginning on p. 15, afterwards engraved and published as *The Gates of Paradise*. The poems which some editors include under this title had not then been written.

The Rossetti MS. is a foolscap quarto volume $(7\frac{3}{4} \times 6\frac{3}{8}$ inches) of 58 leaves, paginated consecutively 1–116 by its present owner. The drawing paper is without watermark; but the stitching in the centre of the quires after ff. 5, 18, 30, 42, and 54, shows that the book is made up of one gathering of 10 leaves and four gatherings of 16 and 8 leaves alternately. Bound in at the end is a folded sheet of different and smaller paper forming two leaves, upon which are written part of 'The Everlasting Gospel' and part of the first draft of Blake's description of his 'Canterbury Pilgrims.'

A pencil note on the verso of the flyleaf, signed 'D.G.C.R.,' Rossetti's earlier signature, tells how he became possessed of the volume : 'I purchased this original MS. of Palmer, an attendant in the Antique Gallery at the British Museum, on the 30th April, '47. Palmer knew Blake personally, and it was from the artist's wife that he had the present MS. which he sold me for 10s. Among the sketches there are one or two profiles of Blake himself.'

Rossetti transcribed certain of the contents, heading them 'Verse and Prose by William Blake (Natus 1757 : obiit 1827). All that is of any value in the foregoing pages has here been copied out. D. G. C. R.' Rossetti's transcript (in my footnotes referred to as R¹) contains a number of emendatory readings, some of which he subsequently rejected in his version of the poems printed in Gilchrist's *Life*. This transcript, bound in at the end of the MS. Book proper, consists of 33 leaves, of which 5 (evidently containing Epigrams 1–19) have been cut out. Part of the paper bears the watermark 1844. The volume is bound in half-calf and labelled ' Blake MS.'

The MS. Book covers a period of at least twenty years of Blake's life. He first used it for sketches only, and when it had served this purpose, converted it into a note-book for poetry, and, still later, for prose. The sketches include two drawings of the figure of Nebuchadnezzar which Blake afterwards engraved in the undated *Marriage of Heaven and Hell*, all the designs for *The Gates of Paradise* (engraved 1793), most of those for the *Visions of the Daughters of Albion* (engraved 1793), and some for the *Songs of Experience*, *Urizen*, and *America* (all engraved 1794). As there are no designs for Blake's earlier works, the *Songs of Innocence* and *The Book of Thel* (both engraved 1789), we may infer that his use of the sketch-book began not earlier, but probably not much later, than the year 1789. Some of the sketches are full page, a few are in colour or sepia, but the greater number are small finished or rough pencil drawings occupying the centre of the page.

About 1793, when most of the leaves were thus filled, Blake began to use the sketch-book for the transcription of some of his poems, reversing the volume and beginning on the three blank pages at the end of the book. Here he copied, in most cases apparently from earlier rough drafts, certain of the *Songs of Experience*, besides other lyrical poems which he himself never published. These pieces, as our facsimile shows, were neatly written in two columns in a small, but fairly clear hand, separation lines being drawn between the different poems. In most cases the titles were afterthoughts. Vertical pencil lines are drawn through those poems which Blake engraved as part of the *Songs of Experience*. Avoiding at first the pages on which sketches of any importance appeared, Blake continued to write from the reversed end as far as p. 98. All the poems in this section of the book—Songs of Experience or lyrics of the same character—must have been written before the end of the year 1793.

After writing these poems, which form the first section of the MS. Book (i–xxxvi), Blake discontinued the use of it as a notebook for several years. Taking it up again about the beginning of his Felpham period, he added some new poems, writing them, not as before from the reversed end, but from the original beginning of the sketch-book. On pp. 3 and 2 is the fine poem 'My spectre around me night and day,' which, as Swinburne points out, embodies precisely the same theme as *Jerusalem* (1804). On p. 12 are the lines 'Each man is in his spectre's power,' and the long poem 'I saw a monk of Charlemaine,' both of which were afterwards engraved as part of *Jerusalem*. On p. 21 begins the series of epigrams which may be dated from the end of Blake's stay at Felpham to the year 1809; they relate to his differences with Hayley, Cromek, Stothard, and Hunt, and were obviously written down, *animum solvere*, without view to publication. To the same period evidently belong the epigrams on art and artists, which are probably, as Ellis and Yeats conjecture, an overflow from his marginal notes to his copy of Reynolds's *Discourses*, now preserved in the British Museum. Among the last entries in the MS. are Blake's 'Advertisement' and 'Additions to the Catalogue for the year 1810,' which are scattered here and there throughout the book with frequent encroachments upon the sketches. In the same category should be placed his great unfinished poem 'The Everlasting Gospel,' the last written piece in the MS. Book. Fragments of this are drafted or copied on blank spaces left on the now crowded pages, part of the poem being written, obviously after the exhaustion of other space, upon a scrap of paper bound in at the end of the book.

The earliest dated entry in the MS. Book is the note on p. 10, 'I say I shan't live five years. And if I live one it will be a Wonder. June 1793'; the latest, on p. 59, is an extract 'From *Bell's Weekly Messenger*, Aug. 4th, 1811.'

A few of the poems in the Rossetti MS., such as 'Fayette,' were left in an unfinished state, while others have elsewhere received Blake's revision. The lines beginning 'Three virgins at the break of day' appear in a more perfect form in the Pickering MS., where I print them with the readings from the MS. Book in footnotes. The MS. Book version of 'I saw a monk of Charlemaine' was afterwards split up by Blake into two separate poems—'The Grey Monk' of the Pickering MS. and the 'Address to the Deists' in *Jerusalem*.

In the following Index to the Rossetti MS., the sketches, poems, and prose contents are given in the order in which they occur in the volume ; inverted pieces, written from the reversed end, are marked by an asterisk. To follow roughly Blake's own order of writing the poems enumerated, the Index should be read backwards page by page, from p. 115 to p. 98, and continued straightforwardly from p. 3 to the same point. Italics indicate sketches or prose. For prose passages, of which only the few first or last words are quoted in this Index, reference may be made to Gilchrist (vol. ii) or to Ellis and Yeats (vol. ii. pp. 383–403). The following contractions are used :—S.E., *Songs of Experience* ; MS. Book, Rossetti Manuscript (followed by number of poem in the present edition) ; Advt., *Advertisement to Blake's Canterbury Pilgrims from Chaucer, containing anecdotes of Artists* (apparently intended as Blake's own title for piece which Rossetti and others call 'Public Address') ; Cat. 1810, *For the year* 1810. *Additions to Blake's Catalogue of Pictures,* &c. ; WMR., W. M. Rossetti's 'Annotated Lists of Blake's Paintings, Drawings, and Engravings,' List 2, no. 25 (Gilchrist's *Life*, ii. pp. 242–243).

INDEX TO 'THE ROSSETTI MS.'

p. 1. *Prose.*—If men of weak capacities . . . without which the art is lost. [Advt.]

p. 2. *Sketch* (pencil).—Daphne.
My spectre *continued* (stanzas 9, 10, 11, 12, 13, *1, *2, and *3). [MS. Book xxxvii.]

p. 3. My spectre around me night & day. [MS. Book xxxvii.]

p. 4. *Title-page.*—Ideas of Good & Evil.
Sketch (pencil).—A young woman dressing.
When a man has married a wife. [MS. Book xxxviii.]

p. 5. When Klopstock England defied. [MS. Book xxxix.]

p. 6. *Sketch* (pen and ink) [see WMR (a)].
On the Virginity of the Virgin Mary & Johanna Southcott. [MS. Book xl.]

p. 7. Mock on, Mock on, Voltaire, Rousseau. [MS. Book xli.]

p. 8. *Sketch.*

p. 9. *Sketch* (sepia).

p. 10. *Note.*—Tuesday Jan^r 20, 1807, between Two & seven in the Evening Despair.
Note.—I say I shan't live five years. And if I live one it will be a Wonder. June 1793.
Memoranda.—To engrave on pewter. To woodcut on pewter. To engrave on copper. [*See* Gil. ii. 158.]

p. 11. *Sketch.*

p. 12. I saw a Monk of Charlemaine. [MS. Book xlii.]
Morning : To find the Western path. [MS. Book xliii.]
Terror in the house does roar. [MS. Book xliv.]
Each man is in his spectre's power. [*Jerusalem.*]

p. 13. *Sketch* (sepia).

p. 14. Three Virgins at the Break of day. [Pickering MS. The Golden Net.]
The Birds. [MS. Book xlv.]

p. 15. *Sketch.—For Gates of Paradise.*
Sketch.—? Lucifer discovering Judas. (*Inferno*, Canto xxxiv.) [See
WMR (b)].

p. 16. *Sketch.*—(The same.)

p. 17. *Sketch.*—(The same.)
Sketch.—[See WMR (f¹.)]
Note.—I wonder who can say 'speak no ill of the dead' *etc.*
Note.—Columbus discovered America *etc.*

p. 18. *Prose.*—There is not because there cannot be any difference . . .
should consider the following. [Advt.]
Note.—Princes appear to me to be fools *etc.*

p. 19. *Sketch.—For Gates of Paradise.*
Prose.—Rubens' Luxembourg gallery is confessed . . . as guilty of
mental high treason. [Advt.]
Prose.—Who that has eyes . . . Oh rare wisdom. [Advt.]

p. 20. *Prose.*—The wretched state of the arts in this country . . . I demand
therefore of the Amateurs of [Advt.]

p. 21. *Sketch.—For Songs of Experience—*'The Sick Rose.' [See WMR (g)].
No real style of colouring ever appears. [MS. Book xlvi.]
You don't believe, I won't attempt to make ye. [MS. Book xlvii.]
Prose.—Art the encouragement which is my due . . . nothing can
hinder my course. [Advt.]
And in melodious accents I. [MS. Book xlviii.]
You don't believe *continued.* [MS. Book xlvii.]

p. 22. And his legs cover'd it like a long fork. [MS. Book xlix.]

p. 23. *Sketch.*—[See WMR (h).]
Prose.—The painters of England are unimployed . . . storehouse of
intellectual riches. [Advt.]
Was I angry with Hayley who used me so ill. [MS. Book l.]
Anger & Wrath my bosom rend. [MS. Book li.]

p. 24. The Sussex Men are Noted Fools. [MS. Book lii.]
Prose.—(continued from p. 25) . . . as a public duty. William
Blake. [Advt.]

p. 25. *Sketch.—For Gates of Paradise.*
Madman I have been called. Fool they call thee. [MS. Book liii.]
To H —— : You think Fuseli is not a Great Painter. I'm glad.
[MS. Book liv.]
Prose.—In a commercial nation . . . in the journeyman's labour.
[Advt.]
Prose.—P.S. I do not believe . . . (continued on p. 24) [Advt.]

p. 26. To F —— : I mock thee not, though I by thee am Mockèd. [MS.
Book lv.]

p. 26. Can there be anything more mean. [MS. Book lvi.]

p. 27. S—— in Childhood on the nursery floor. [MS. Book lvii.]

To Nancy F——: How can I help thy husband's copying me. [MS. Book lviii.]

Of H——'s birth this was the happy lot. [MS. Book lix.]

p. 28. *Sketch* (pencil).—For *Visions of the Daughters of Albion.*

Sir Joshua praises Michael Angelo. [MS. Book lx.]

He's a Blockhead who wants a proof of what he can't Perceive. [MS. Book lxi.]

p. 29. Cr—— loves artists as he loves his Meat. [MS. Book lxii.]

A Petty Sneaking Knave I knew. [MS. Book lxiii.]

Sir Joshua praised Rubens with a smile. [MS. Book lxiv.]

He is a Cock would. [MS. Book lxv.]

p. 30. *Sketch.*—[See WMR. (i)].

He has observ'd the Golden Rule. [MS. Book lxvi.]

To S——d: You all your Youth observ'd the Golden Rule. [MS. Book lxvii.]

p. 31. Mr. Stothard to Mr. Cromek: For Fortune's favours you your riches bring. [MS. Book lxiii.]

Mr. Cromek to Mr. Stothard: Fortune favours the Brave, old proverbs say. [MS. Book lix.]

I am no Homer's Hero you all know. [MS. Book lxx.]

p. 32. The Angel that presided o'er my birth. [MS. Book lxxi.]

Florentine Ingratitude: Sir Joshua sent his own portrait to. [MS. Book lxxii.]

p. 33. A Pitiful Case: The villain at the gallows tree. [MS. Book lxxiii.]

To the Royal Academy: A Strange Erratum in all the Editions. [MS. Book lxxiv.]

If it is true, what the Prophets write. [MS. Book lxxv.]

[The Everlasting Gospel. *a.*]

p. 34. *Sketch.*—For *Gates of Paradise.*

On F—— and S——: I found them blind, I taught them how to see. [MS. Book lxxvi.]

P—— loved me not as he lov'd his friends. [MS. Book lxxvii.]

To forgive enemies H—— does pretend. [MS. Book lxxviii.]

p. 35. To F——: You call me Mad; 'tis folly to do so. [MS. Book lxxix.]

On H——y's Friendship: When H——y finds out what you cannot do. [MS. Book lxxx.]

To forgive enemies H—— does pretend *continued* (ll. 3, 4). [MS. Book lxxviii.]

p. 36. *Sketch.*—[See WMR. (j).]

Some men created for destruction come. [MS. Book lxxxi.]

On S——: You say reserve and modesty he has. [MS. Book lxxxii.]

p. 37. Imitation of Pope, & a compliment to the Ladies. [MS. Book lxxxiii.]

To H——: Thy friendship oft has made my heart to ake. [MS. Book lxxxiv.]

Cosway Frazer & Baldwin of Egypt's Lake. [MS. Book lxxxv.]

p. 37. An Epitaph: Come knock your heads against this stone. [MS. Book lxxxvi.]

Another: I was buried near this dyke. [MS. Book lxxxvii.]

Another: Here lies John Trot, the Friend of all mankind. [MS. Book lxxxviii.]

p. 38. My title as a Genius thus is prov'd. [MS. Book lxxxix.]

I, Rubens, am a Statesman and a Saint. [MS. Book xc.]

To English Connoisseurs: You must agree that Rubens was a fool. [MS. Book xci.]

Note.—There is just the same science in Lebrun or Rubens or even Vanloo that there is in Raphael or Michael Angelo, but not the same genius. Science is soon got; the other never can be acquired but must be born.

Swelled limbs with no outline that you can descry. [MS. Book xcii.]

A Pretty Epigram for the encouragement of those Who have paid great sums in the Venetian and Flemish ooze. [MS. Book xciii.]

These are the Idiots' chiefest arts. [MS. Book xciv.]

p. 39. Raphael Sublime Majestic Graceful Wise. [MS. Book xcv.]

Learn the laborious stumble of a Fool. [MS. Book xcvi.]

If I e'er Grow to Man's Estate. [MS. Book xcvii.]

The cripple every step drudges & labours. [MS. Book xcviii.]

p. 40. *Sketch.*—For *Gates of Paradise.*

On the great encouragement given by English Nobility. [MS. Book xcix.]

Give Pensions to the Learned Pig. [MS. Book c.]

All pictures that's painted with sense and with thought. [MS. Book ci.]

p. 41. On H—— the Pickthank: I write the rascal thanks, till he and I [MS. Book cii.]

Cromek speaks: I always take my judgement from a Fool. [MS. Book ciii.]

When you look at a picture you always can see. [MS. Book civ.]

English Encouragement of Art. Cromek's opinions put into rhyme. [MS. Book cv.]

p. 42. You say their Pictures well painted be. [MS. Book cvi.]

Sketch.

The Washerwoman's Song: I wash'd them out and wash'd them in. [MS. Book cvii.]

p. 43. When I see a Rubens Rembrandt Correggio. [MS. Book cviii.]

Great things are done when Men & Mountains meet. [MS. Book cix.]

p. 44. *Sketch* (pencil).—For *Marriage of Heaven and Hell*—'Nebuchadnezzar.'

Note.—Let a Man who has made a drawing go on & on & he will produce a Picture or Painting, but if he chooses to leave it before he has spoil'd it he will do a Better Thing.

p. 45. *Sketch.*—For *Gates of Paradise*—I have said to corruption *etc.*

p. 46. *Sketch.*—Murder. [See WMR. (k).]

Prose.—They say there is no straight line in nature ... Machination. [Advt.]

Prose.—Delicate Hands & Heads will never appear While Titian &c. as in the Book of Moonlight, p. 5.

p. 46. *Prose.*—Woollett I know . . . (continued on p. 47). [Advt.]
  *I give you the end of a golden string. [*Jerusalem.*]
p. 47. *Prose.*—(Continued from p. 46) . . . master's touch. [Advt.]
  Prose.—Every line is the line of beauty. It is only fumble and bungle
    which cannot draw a line. This only is ugliness, But that is not
    a line which doubts and hesitates in the midst of its course. [Advt.]
  If you play a Game of chance. [MS. Book cx.]
p. 48. *Sketch.*—Nebuchadnezzar.
  Note.—This was spoke by My Spectre to Voltaire Bacon &c.
  [The Everlasting Gospel. ʒ. ll. 1–26.]
  [The Everlasting Gospel. δ.]
p. 49. [The Everlasting Gospel. ʒ. ll. 27–52.]
p. 50. [The Everlasting Gospel. ʒ. ll. 53–71.]
  The only Man that e'er I knew. [MS. Book cxi.]
  For this is being a Friend just in the nick. [MS. Book cxii.]
p. 51. [The Everlasting Gospel. ʒ. ll. 72–92.]
  Prose.—In this plate Mr. B. has resumed . . . in condemnation.
    [Advt.]
p. 52. *Sketch* (pencil).
  Prose.—Of my Work & approbation . . . reputation as a draughtsman.
    [Advt.]
  [The Everlasting Gospel. ʒ. ll. 93–96.]
  [The Everlasting Gospel. η.]
  The Everlasting Gospel. (γ². ll. 1–25.)
  Prose.—The manner in which my character has been blasted . . . paid
    for what they put in on these ungracious subjects. [Advt.]
  I will tell you what Joseph of Arimathea. [MS. Book cxiii.]
p. 53. *Prose.*—Flaxman cannot deny . . . as Machlin told me at the time
    [Advt.]
  [The Everlasting Gospel. γ². ll. 26–83.]
  Prose.—Many people are so foolish . . . asserted that Woollett's.
    [Advt.]
p. 54. [The Everlasting Gospel. γ². ll. 84–106.]
  Grown old in Love from Seven till Seven times Seven. [MS.
    Book cxiv.]
  [The Everlasting Gospel. θ.]
p. 55. *Prose.*—Prints were superior to Basire's because . . . beginnings of
    art. [Advt.]
p. 56. *Sketch.*—[See WMR. (1).]
  Why was Cupid a Boy. [MS. Book cxv.]
  Note.—This day is Publish'd Advertizements to Blake's Canterbury
    Pilgrims from Chaucer, containing anecdotes of Artists.
  Prose.—I hope this print . . . It is very true what you have said.
    [Advt.]
p. 57. *Sketch.*
  Prose.—For these thirty-two Years . . . [Advt.]
  Prose.—Woollett's best works . . . I forget. [Advt.]
  Prose.—The Cottager's . . . is never correct. [Advt.]
  Prose.—I do not pretend to Paint better than Rafael (or Mich. Ang.)
    . . . which they understand not. [Advt.]

p. 58. *Prose.*—In this manner the English public . . . but dey do not draw de draw. [Advt.]

    Prose.—Resentment for Personal Injuries has had some share in this public address but love to my art and zeal for my country a much greater. [Advt.]

p. 59. *Sketch.*—For *Gates of Paradise.*

    Prose.—Men think they can Copy Nature . . . manifest to all. [Advt.]

    Extract.—From Bell's Weekly Messenger, Aug. 4th 1811 *etc.*

p. 60. I asked my Dear Friend Orator Prig. [MS. Book cxvi.]

    That God is Colouring Newton does show. [MS. Book cxviii.]

    Prose.—Cooke wished to give to Hogarth . . . but he could not. [Adv.]

p. 61. *Sketch.*—For *Gates of Paradise*—What we hope we see.

    O dear Mother Outline of wisdom most sage. [MS. Book cxvii.]

    To Venetian Artists : Perhaps this little Fable may make us merry. [MS. Book cxviii.]

    Prose.—Englishmen rouse yourselves . . . Hogarth's works prove. [Advt.]

p. 62. *Prose.*—A detestable Falsehood . . . God or man. [Advt.]

    Prose.—I do not mean smooth'd up & Nigled & Poco Pen'd and all the beauties [picked out] blurr'd & blotted but Drawn with a firm & decided hand at once, like Fuseli & Michael Angelo, Shakespeare & Milton. [Advt.]

    Some laugh at what others can see no crime in. [MS. Book cxx.]

p. 63. *Sketch.*—For *Gates of Paradise*—I found him beneath a tree.

    I've given great Provision to my Foes. [MS. Book cxx.]

    Prose.—Whoever looks at any . . . to look at his print. [Advt.]

    Later Note.—He who could represent Christ . . . fine art. [Advt.]

    *Great Men and Fools do often me inspire. [MS. Book cxix.]

p. 64. *Extract.*—From Cratelos. Me time has crook'd, no good workman Is he, Infirm is all that he does.

    Prose.—I do not know whether Homer . . . trading competition. [Advt.]

    Note.—I always thought that Jesus Christ was a snubby or I should not have worshipped him if I thought he had been one of those long spindled nosed rascals.

p. 65. Having given great offence by writing in Prose. [MS. Book cxx.]

    Prose.—Chaucer's Canterbury Pilgrims. Being a complete Index of Human Characters as they exist age after age. [Title for Advt.]

    If men will act like a maid smiling over a churn. [MS. Book cxxi.]

    Sketch.—For *Songs of Experience*—The Angel.

p. 66. *Prose.*—The English artist . . . Vasari tells us. [Advt.]

    Call that the Public Voice which is their Error. [MS. Book cxxii.]

    Prose.—What kind of intellect . . . & not the forms of Things. [Advt.]

    Prose.—Let us teach Buonaparte & whomsoever else it may concern that it is not Arts that follow & attend upon Empire but Empire that attends upon & follows The Arts. [Advt.]

    Prose.—It is nonsense for Noblemen . . . but not to make a Man. [Advt.]

p. 67. *Sketch.*—Profile of Blake. [See WMR. (c).]

p. 67. *Prose.*—The originality of this production . . . whitloes on their fingers. [Advt.]

Prose.—No man of sense . . . as to believe this. [Advt.]

Note.—23 May 1810 found the Word Golden.

Prose.—A man sets himself . . . yourselves to be disgraced. [Advt.]

p. 68. *Sketch.*—For *Gates of Paradise*—(frontispiece).

Prose.—The Last Judgment is not Fable . . . [Cat. 1810.]

Prose.—Note here that Fable or allegory . . . [Cat. 1810.]

p. 69. *Sketch.*—For *Gates of Paradise*—At last for hatching ripe.

Prose.—[Cat. 1810.]

p. 70. *Prose.*—For the year 1810 Addition to Blake's Catalogue of Pictures &c. [Title for Cat. 1810.]

Some people admire the work of a Fool. [MS. Book cxxiii.]

Prose.—[Cat. 1810.]

p. 71. (*A quarter of this leaf has been cut out.*)

Sketch.—For *Gates of Paradise*—Death's Door.

Prose.—The—when they assert that Jupiter . . . [Cat. 1810.]

Note.—A jockey that is anything of a jockey will never buy a horse by the colour & a man who has got any brains will never buy a picture by the colour.

Note.—When I tell any truth it is not for the sake of convincing those who do not know it, but for the sake of defending those who do.

p. 72. *Prose.*—And heal Visions . . . the golden Age. [Cat. 1810.]

p. 73. *Sketches.*—[See WMR. (m).]

To God. [MS. Book cxxviii.]

Since all the Riches of this World. [MS. Book cxxiv.]

p. 74. *Sketches.*

p. 75. *Sketches.*—[See WMR. (d).]

p. 76. *Prose.*—No Man of Sense . . . a Male & Female chain'd [Cat. 1810.]

p. 77. *Prose.*—together by the feet . . . a Cruel Church. [Cat. 1810.]

p. 78. *Prose.*—The greatest part of what are call'd . . . cord in his hand. [Cat. 1810.]

To Chloe's breast young Cupid slily stole. [MS. Book cxxvi.]

p. 79. Now Art has lost its mental Charms. [MS. Book cxxvii.]

Prose.—In Eternity one Thing . . . vegetable Nature also. [Cat. 1810.]

Nail his neck to the Cross, nail it with a nail. [MS. Book cxxviii.]

p. 80. *Prose.*—Between the Figures . . . on the brink of [Cat. 1810.]

p. 81. *Prose.*—perdition . . . of the Hebrew. [Cat. 1810.]

p. 82. *Prose.*—Just above . . . & Intentions. [Cat. 1810.]

p. 83. *Prose.*—The Characters . . . removing the [Cat. 1810.]

p. 84. *Prose.*—old heavens . . . Art in proportion to his means. [Cat. 1810.]

Prose—(continued from p. 83.) [Cat. 1810.]

Sketch—[See WMR (n).]

p. 85. *Prose.*—Over the head . . . for a Protection. [Cat. 1810.]

p. 86. *Prose.*—The painter hopes that his Friends Amytus Melitus & Lycon will perceive . . . begs public protection and all will be well. [Cat. 1810.]

Prose.—The Combats of Good & Evil . . . Knowledge of good & evil.

p. 87. The Caverns of the Grave I've seen. [MS. Book cxxix.]

    Prose.—(Description of Last Judgment.) [Cat. 1810.]

p. 88. *Note and Quotations* from Aphra Behn & Dryden, dated Sunday,
    August 1807. [See Swinb. *Essay,* pp. 130–1.]

p. 89. *Note.*—(The same.)

    I rose up at the dawn of day. [MS. Book cxxx.]

p. 90. *Prose.*—Shall know them . . . be Painting. [Cat. 1810.]

p. 91. *Sketch.*—For *Gates of Paradise*—Fire, he rears from the pool his mighty
    stature.

    Prose.—Such as Rafael . . . Mercy I have. [Cat. 1810.]

p. 92. *Prose.*—Represented those who are . . . Envy the Success. [Cat. 1810.]

p. 93. *Sketch.*—For *Gates of Paradise*—Earth.

    Prose.—Of Satan or of Og . . . Angels happier than. [Cat. 1810.]

p. 94. *Sketch* (sepia)—For *Gates of Paradise*—Air.

    Prose.—Men because . . . Last Judgment &c. [Cat. 1810.]

p. 95. *Sketch.*—For *Gates of Paradise*—Water.

    Prose.—that Bad art . . . not with it. [Cat. 1810.]

p. 96. *Extract.*—Lines written . . . surrender of Copenhagen.

p. 97. *Sketch.*—For *Europe*—an assassin.

    Extract.—Continued (from p. 96) signed 'Birmingham I.'

p. 98. [The Everlasting Gospel. γ^1. ll. 1–38.]

    Do what you will this life's a fiction. [MS. Book cxxxi.]

    *Fayette (Stanzas 1, 4, 6). [MS. Book xxxv.]

p. 99. *Several Questions Answered. [MS. Book xxxvi.]

    Fayette (Stanzas 3, 9, 10). [MS. Book xxxv.]

p. 100. [The Everlasting Gospel. β. ll. 1–37.]

    *Her whole Life is an Epigram. [MS. Book xxxiii.]

    *An Old maid early e'er I knew. [MS. Book xxxiv.]

p. 101. [The Everlasting Gospel. β. ll. 38–57.]

    *Little fly. [SE.]

    *Motto to the Songs of Innocence & of Experience. [MS.
    Book xxxii.]

p. 102. *Sketch.*—Adam and Eve.

p. 103. *The Angel: I dreamt a Dream! what can it mean. [SE.]

    *Because I was happy upon the heath. [SE.: The Chimney
    Sweeper, stanzas 2, 3.]

    *The Question Answer'd: What is it men in women do require
    [MS. Book xxxvi, 4.]

    *Lacedemonian Instruction: Come hither, my boy, tell me what
    thou seest there. [MS. Book xxix.]

    *Riches: The countless gold of a merry heart. [MS. Book xxx,
    stanza 2.]

    *An answer to the parson: Why of the sheep do you not learn
    peace? [MS. Book xxxi.]

    *The look of love alarms. [MS. Book xxxvi, 2.]

    *Holy Thursday: Is this a holy thing to see. [SE.]

p. 104. *Sketch.*

p. 105. *Day: The sun arises in the East. [MS. Book xxii.]

    *The Fairy: Come hither, my sparrows. [MS. Book xxiii.]

    *The sword sung on the barren heath. [MS. Book xxiv.]

p. 105. *Abstinence sows sand all over. [MS. Book xxv.]
 *In a wife I would desire. [MS. Book xxvi.]
 *If you trap the moment before it 's ripe. [MS. Book xxvii.]
 *Eternity: He who bends to himself a joy. [MS. Book xxxvi, 1.]
 *The Kid: Thou, little Kid, did'st play. [MS. Book xxviii.]
 *The little Vagabond: Dear Mother, Dear Mother, the Church is cold. [SE.]

p. 106. *To my Mirtle: To a lovely mirtle bound. [MS. Book xiii.]
 *Nought loves another as itself. [A Little Boy Lost. SE.]
 *Love to faults is always blind *continued* (stanza 2). [MS. Book xvii.]
 *The Chimney Sweeper (stanza 1). [SE.]
 *Merlin's prophecy: The harvest shall flourish in wintry weather. [MS. Book xxi.]

p. 107. *The human Image: Pity would be no more. [The Human Abstract. SE.]
 *They said this mystery never shall cease. [MS. Book xvi.]
 *Love to faults is always blind. [MS. Book xvii.]
 *There souls of men are bought & sold. [MS. Book xviii.]
 *The wild flower's song: As I wander'd the forest (stanza 1). [MS. Book xix.]
 *The sick Rose: O Rose, thou art sick. [SE.]
 *Soft Snow: I walkèd abroad on a snowy day. [MS. Book xx.]
 *An ancient Proverb: Remove away that black'ning church. [MS. Book xxxvi, 5.]

p. 108. *Sketches* (pencil).
 *The Tyger: Tyger, Tyger, burning bright (first draft of stanzas 1, 2, 3, 4 and 6). [SE.]

p. 109. *London: I wander thro' each charter'd street. [SE.]
 *The wild flower's song: *continued* (stanzas 2, 3). [MS. Book xix.]
 *To Nobodaddy: Why art thou silent & invisible. [MS. Book xiv.]
 *The modest rose puts forth a thorn. [The Lilly. SE.]
 *When the voices of children are heard on the green. [Nurse's Song. SE.]
 *Are not the joys of morning sweeter. [MS. Book xv.]
 *The Tyger: Tyger, Tyger, burning bright (stanzas 1, 3, 5, 6). [SE.]

p. 110. *Sketch.*—Suggests Urizen.

p. 111. *Sketch.*—Continuation of above.
 *Thou hast a lap full of seed. [MS. Book xii.]
 *Earth's Answer: Earth rais'd up her head. [SE.]
 *In a mirtle shade: Why should I be bound to thee. [MS. Book xiii.]

p. 112. *Sketch.*

p. 113. *Silent Silent Night. [MS. Book vii.]
 *O lapwing thou fliest around the heath. [MS. Book viii.]
 *I fear'd the fury of my wind. [MS. Book ix.]
 *Infant Sorrow: My mother groan'd, my father wept. [MS. Book x, also SE.]
 *Why should I care for the men of thames. [MS. Book xi.]

p. 114. *I asked a thief to steal me a peach. [MS. Book iv.]
　　　　 *I heard an Angel singing. [MS. Book v.]
　　　　 *A cradle Song : Sleep Sleep beauty bright. [MS. Book vi.]
　　　　 *Christian Forbearance : I was angry with my friend. [A Poison Tree. SE.]
p. 115. *A flower was offer'd to me. [My Pretty Rose Tree. SE.]
　　　　 *I told my love I told my love. [MS. Book i.]
　　　　 *Love seeketh not itself to please. [The Clod and the Pebble. SE.]
　　　　 *I laid me down upon a bank. [MS. Book ii.]
　　　　 *I went to the garden of love. [The Garden of Love. SE.]
　　　　 *I saw a chapel all of gold. [MS. Book iii.]
p. 116. *List* (in ink).—*Of twenty-two subjects for history of England.*
　　　　　　 1. Giants ancient inhabitants of England.
　　　　 List (in pencil).—*Of plagues of Egypt.*
　　　　　　 Lice, Boils, Hail, Locusts, *etc.*

[Here follow the contents of the two leaves bound in at the end of the MS.]

p. [117]. *Prose.*—(Description of Canterbury Pilgrims.) [*Descriptive Cat.*]
p. [118]. *Prose.*—(The same.)
p. [119]. *Prose.*—[Cat. 1810.]
p. [120]. [The Everlasting Gospel. ε.]

[End of the Rossetti MS.]

INDEX TO THE ROSSETTI TRANSCRIPT (R¹)

The Everlasting Gospel (*part*).
My Spectre around me night and day.
To find the western path.
Three virgins at the break of day.
I see, I see, the mother said.
Where thou dwellest, in what grove.
Why was Cupid a boy.
If e'er I grow to man's estate.
Sleep, sleep, beauty bright.
When the voices of children are heard on the green.
The look of love alarms.
I heard an angel singing.
I give you the end of a golden string.
I laid me down upon a bank.
A flower was offer'd to me.
The angel who presided o'er my birth.
I saw a chapel all of gold.
Never seek to tell thy love.
Great things are done when men and mountains meet.
I wander'd the forest.

The errors of a wise man make your rule.

O rose thou art sick.

Nought loves another as itself.

Tyger, Tyger, burning bright.

I walk'd abroad on a snowy day.

Love seeketh not itself to please.

I was angry with my friend.

Mock on, mock on, Voltaire, Rousseau.

What do I care for the men of Thames.

I rose up at the dawn of day.

Dear mother, dear mother, the church is cold.

I asked a thief to steal me a peach.

To Chloe's heart young Cupid slily stole.

The caverns of the grave I've seen.

The countless gold of a merry heart.

He's a blockhead who wants a proof of what he can't perceive.

[*Hiatus of five leaves.*]

Five epigrams numbered 20–4.

Prose descriptions of Blake's pictures, Canterbury Pilgrims and
Vision of the Last Judgment.

In making his transcript, Rossetti appears to have contemplated publication of part of the contents of the MS.
Book, edited by his brother, or by his friend, William
Allingham, the poet. In a letter to the latter dated
November 1, 1860, he writes : ' A man (one Gilchrist, who
lives next door to Carlyle, and is as near him in other
respects as he can manage) wrote to me the other day,
saying he was writing a life of Blake, and wanted to
see my manuscript by that genius. Was there not some
talk of *your* doing something in the way of publishing
its contents ? I know William thought of doing so, but
fancy it might wait long for his efforts, and I have no time,
but really think its contents ought to be edited, especially
if a new Life gives a " shove to the concern " (as Spurgeon
expressed himself in thanking a liberal subscriber to his
Tabernacle). I have not yet engaged myself any way
to said Gilchrist on the subject, though I have told him he
can see it here if he will give me a day's notice.' Rossetti,
as we know, did lend the MS. to Gilchrist in the following
year, and on the death of the latter helped to complete his
unfinished work by editing the selection from Blake's
poetical and prose works given in the second volume of
the *Life*. Under the heading ' Poems hitherto unpublished,'
Rossetti, without distinguishing between the two separate
sources, prints for the first time a number of poems from the
Blake autograph in his own possession, together with others

from the borrowed Pickering MS. He takes considerable liberty with the text and gives to several of the pieces titles of his own. From the MS. Book also he excerpts the prose manifesto which he calls 'Public Address,' Blake's Memoranda on his modes of engraving, and his 'Vision of the Last Judgment' (i.e. Additions to Catalogue 1810).

Swinburne was the next to make use of the MS. Book in his *Critical Essay* (1868). He adds to the number of new poems printed, and, by his copious extracts and illuminative comment, gives for the first time some adequate conception of Blake's great and extraordinary poem 'The Everlasting Gospel.'

About the same time the Pickering MS., which has since disappeared, became the property of Basil Montague Pickering, the publisher, who printed the whole of it for the first time in his editions of 1866, 1868, and 1874, edited by R. H. Shepherd. Pickering's last edition, and the Aldine edition which appeared in the same year, mutually supplement each other. W. M. Rossetti was able to use that part only of the Pickering MS. which had already been printed by his brother, while Shepherd was prohibited from using any part of the larger MS. Book. W. M. Rossetti, who generally follows his brother's text, prints more, though not as stated all, of 'The Everlasting Gospel,' as well as a few new poems, chiefly epigrams.

The Rossetti MS. Book was purchased January 26, 1887, by its present owner, Mr. W. A. White, who soon after lent it for a time to the publisher of Ellis and Yeats' large edition of Blake's *Works*, 1893. A copy of the manuscript, made for Mr. Ellis, was used for their three-volume edition, as well as by Mr. Yeats' in his small 'Muses' Library' Blake, published in the same year. Mr. Ellis' transcript, if one may judge by the text of these editors, bears obvious marks of having been made in haste by a copyist unfamiliar with Blake's hand. In their description of the MS. Book (vol. i. pp. 202–32) Ellis and Yeats include for the first time a few minor poems which had been rejected or ignored by former editors. Their versions of some of the longer poems and prose pieces in the MS. Book must be sought elsewhere, e.g. 'Fayette' (vol. ii. pp. 24–7), 'My spectre around me night and day' (vol. ii. pp. 37, 38), 'The Everlasting Gospel' (vol. ii. pp. 42–60), and 'To the Deists' in *Jerusalem* (vol. ii. pp. 221–4), and the prose 'Advertisement' and 'Additions to Blake's Catalogue' (vol. ii. pp. 333–403).

My own text of the poems has been prepared from transcripts of the MS. Book made by Mr. White for the present edition. These transcripts, which faithfully reproduce the relative positions of poems or stanzas on the original page, with all Blake's deletions, insertions, and corrections, together with his marks of transposition and successive numerations of stanzas and lines (without careful observance of which many of the poems would be unintelligible), possess the advantage of having been made by a Blake student thoroughly familiar with his author's handwriting and mode of composition. The aid of the magnifying glass or of photography has also been resorted to, and any obscure passage submitted to minute scrutiny.

From these transcripts copies of the poems have been made by the present editor, and collated with the chief existing texts, any differences of reading being again referred to Mr. White for further examination. Some idea of the care bestowed upon this part of the work may be gathered from the fact that in more than one instance the original transcription of a single page has cost Mr. White four or five hours' close labour. Similar care has been given by the editor to unravelling Blake's method of building up a poem, enabling the reader to follow the same process by reference to the notes. The proofs have lastly been read by Mr. White, and the text and notes again checked from the original manuscript. This edition therefore, while it serves every purpose of a facsimile, presents he matter in a much clearer and more intelligible form.

Not the least important result of the plan here pursued— besides the light which it throws upon Blake's self-criticism apparent in his successive changes—is the new form in which a number of the most familiar poems now appear. One may hesitate to change the generally received line 'Sweet morning leads me on' (xliii) to 'Sweet mercy leads me on,' yet the latter is not only as Blake wrote it, but also imparts a deeper meaning to the poem. The lyric 'To a lovely mirtle bound' (MS. Book xiii, D. G. Rossetti's 'In a Myrtle Shade') gains by the recovery of Blake's final version. Blake's final readings, whether for the worse or for the better, are here uniformly adopted. Instances will be noted where, as in 'Cupid' (MS. Book cxv), these changes are the reverse of improvements, or where the MS. version of some of the *Songs of Experience* may be preferred to the text of the engraved book.

The poetical pieces forming part of the MS. Book, but not printed in this section of my edition, are part of the *Songs of Experience*, the variant readings of which are supplied in the footnotes to that work—' Three virgins at the break of day,' which I print in the poems from the Pickering MS. with the readings of the MS. Book version, and the two quatrains ' Each man is in his spectre's power' and ' I give you the end of a golden string,' afterwards engraved as part of *Jerusalem* and here printed among poems from the Prophetic Books.

POEMS

FROM

THE ROSSETTI MS.

I

MS. Book i–xxxvi, pp. 115–98

Written in the reversed book
circa 1793

I

ROSSETTI MANUSCRIPT

i

I told my love, I told my love,   1
I told her all my heart;
Trembling, cold, in ghastly fears,
Ah! she doth depart.

Soon as she was gone from me,   5
A traveller came by,
Silently, invisibly—
O! was no deny.

MS. Book, p. 115.   Printed by DGR and later edd. under the title ' Love's
Secret.'   Not in Swinb.   All edd. print the first stanza deleted by Blake :—

> ' Never pain [seek *del.*] to tell thy love,
> Love that never told can be ;
> For the gentle wind does move
> Silently, invisibly.'

All edd. read seek *for* pain; WBY *reads* shall *for* can; *all edd. except*
WBY *read* doth *for* does.

2, 3 heart ... fears] *All edd. punctuate by comma after* heart *and period
after* fears.   4 doth] did *all edd.*   5 Soon as] Soon after *all edd.*
8 O! . . . deny] He took her with a sigh MS. Book *1st rdg. del. and
all edd.*

ii

I laid me down upon a bank,   1
Where love lay sleeping;
I heard among the rushes dank
Weeping, Weeping.

Then I went to the heath & the wild,   5
To the thistles & thorns of the waste ;
And they told me how they were beguil'd,
Driven out, & compel'd to be chaste.

MS. Book, p. 115.   DGR, Swinb., WMR and EY print these as the first
two stanzas of 'The Garden of Love,' ignoring the separation line drawn
between the two poems.   EY however note this, iii. p. 93.   WBY prints
separately with title ' The Thistles and Thorns.'

iii

I saw a chapel all of gold   1
That none did dare to enter in,
And many weeping stood without,
Weeping, mourning, worshipping.

I saw a serpent rise between   5
The white pillars of the door,
And he forc'd & forc'd & forc'd;
Down the golden hinges tore,

And along the pavement sweet,   9
Set with pearls & rubies bright,
All his shining length he drew,
Till upon the altar white

Vomiting his poison out   13
On the bread & on the wine.
So I turn'd into a sty,
And laid me down among the swine.

MS. Book, p. 115. DGR and all later editors entitle this 'The Defiled Sanctuary.' Not in Swinb.

8 Down . . . tore] Till he broke the pearly door MS. Book *1st rdg. del.*; Till he the golden hinges tore *all except* WBY, *who reads*, Till down the golden hinges tore.   13 Vomiting] He vomited DGR, WMR, EY; Vomited WBY.

iv

I askèd a thief to steal me a peach: 1
He turnèd up his eyes.
I ask'd a lithe lady to lie her down:
Holy & meek, she cries.

MS. Book, p. 114. Not in DGR. Swinb. (p. 141) and later edd. entitle this 'The Will and the Way.'

1 askèd] asked = ask'd *all edd.*   steal] steel EY (Index to MS. Book, i. 205).   2 He] And he MS. Book *1st rdg. del.*   turnèd] turned = turn'd *all edd.*

As soon as I went an angel came:　　5
He wink'd at the thief,
And smil'd at the dame;

And without one word said　　8
Had a peach from the tree,
And still as a maid
Enjoy'd the Lady.

5 As . . . came] *all edd. print as two lines.*　　6 He] And he MS. Book
1*st rdg. del.*　　8 said] spoke MS. Book 1*st rdg. del. and all edd.*
10 And . . . maid] And 'twixt earnest & joke MS. Book 1*st rdg. del. and
all edd.*　　11 Enjoy'd] He enjoy'd MS. Book 1*st rdg. del.*

V

I heard an Angel singing　　1
When the day was springing:
'Mercy, Pity, Peace
Is the world's release.'

Thus he sang all day　　5
Over the new mown hay,
Till the sun went down,
And haycocks lookèd brown.

I heard a Devil curse　　9
Over the heath & the furze:
'Mercy could be no more
If there was nobody poor,

'And pity no more could be,　　13
If all were as happy as we.'
At his curse the sun went down
And the heavens gave a frown.

MS. Book, p. 114.　An earlier version of 'The human Image' (engraved
under the title 'The Human Abstract' in the *Songs of Experience*).　DGR
and later edd. name this 'The Two Songs.'　Swinb. p. 147.
3 Pity, Peace] Pity and Peace *all edd.*　　4 Is] Are *all edd.*　　5
Thus] So *all except* WBY.　　12 was] were *all edd.*　　13 could]
would Swinb.　14 as happy] *All edd. omit.* 'as.'　we] ye *all except* Swinb.,
EY correcting later in note iii. p. 97.　15 At his curse] Thus he sang &
MS. Book 1*st rdg. del.*　　16 frown] Here, as Blake's line drawn beneath

this stanza shows, the poem originally ended. Later he added a fifth
stanza :—

> '*Down* [at first *And down*] *pour'd the heavy rain*   [17]
> *Over the new reap'd grain,*
> *And Mercy & Pity & Peace descended ;*
> *The Farmers were ruined & harvest was ended*'

and again indicated the completion of the poem by a fresh terminal line. This
stanza Blake afterwards deleted. Lastly follow several attempts at a new
stanza, the final form of the only completed couplet of which reads :

> 'And Miseries' increase   [21]
> Is Mercy, Pity, Peace ' ;

the rejected readings, which are not very legibly written, being :—

> '*And Mercy Pity* [*&* del.] *Peace*
> (? *Joy'd*) *at their increase*
> (? *With*) *Poverty's Increase*
> *Are*
> *And by distress increase*
> *Mercy, Pity, Peace*
> *By Misery to increase*
> *Mercy, Pity, Peace.*'

Swinb. (p. 147) re-arranges and prints ll. [17], [18], [21], and [22] as his last
stanza:—

> 'Down poured the heavy rain
> Over the new-reaped grain ;
> And Misery's increase
> Is Mercy, Pity, Peace.'

DGR prints as his third stanza ll. 9–14, l. 5 of 'The Human Abstract' version
(*Songs of Experience*) and ll. [21], [22] (slightly altered) :—

> 'I heard a Devil curse
> Over the heath and the furze :
> "Mercy could be no more
> If there were nobody poor,
> And Pity no more could be
> If all were happy as ye :
> And mutual fear brings Peace.
> Misery's increase
> Are Mercy, Pity, Peace "' ;

concluding, as a separate couplet, with ll. 15, 16 :—

> 'At his curse the sun went down,
> And the heavens gave a frown.'

WMR, EY, and WBY follow DGR. EY however, in their 'Notes to the
Poetical Sketches, Songs, &c.' iii. p. 97, print the poem as it is found in the
MS. Book, their readings of the partially illegible words being rather different
from mine.

vi

A Cradle Song

Sleep! Sleep! beauty bright,   1
Dreaming o'er the joys of night;
Sleep! Sleep! in thy sleep
Little sorrows sit & weep.

Sweet Babe, in thy face   5
Soft desires I can trace,
Secret joys & secret smiles,
Little pretty infant wiles.

As thy softest limbs I feel,   9
Smiles as of the morning steal
O'er thy cheek, & o'er thy breast
Where thy little heart does rest.

O! the cunning wiles that creep   13
In thy little heart asleep.
When thy little heart does wake
Then the dreadful lightnings break,

MS. Book, p. 114. Obviously written as the contrary of the 'Cradle Song'
in the *Songs of Innocence ;* but never engraved by Blake.   DGR and all later
editors include this poem among the *Songs of Experience,* in most cases with
explanatory note.   This song, as the line drawn below it shows, at first consisted of stanzas 1, 3, 4.   Stanza 2 was then added and a second boundary
line drawn, while still later Blake added the final stanza and numbered the
whole in their present order.
    1-4 Sleep . . . weep] The two couplets were written in reverse order,
Blake indicating the change by prefixed numerals.   2 Dreaming . . .
night] Thou shalt taste the joys of night MS. Book *1st rdg. del.*   o'er] in
all edd.   4 Little . . . weep] Thou wilt every secret keep MS. Book *1st
rdg. del.* ; Canst thou any secret keep *ibid. 2nd rdg. del.*   8 Little . . .
wiles] Such as burning youth beguiles MS. Book *1st rdg. del.*   9 As *etc.*]
Yet a little while the moon Silent . . . MS. Book *abandoned opening
of this stanza.*   feel] touch MS. Book *1st rdg. del.* ; stroke *ibid. 2nd rdg.
del.*   10 steal] broke *ibid. 1st rdg. del.*   12, 15 does] doth *all edd.*
16 lightnings] light shall *all edd.*

From thy cheek & from thy eye, 17
O'er the youthful harvests nigh.
Infant wiles & infant smiles
Heaven & Earth of peace beguiles.

17-20 From . . . beguiles] all edd. omit this stanza. It has been printed,
however, by Swinb., p. 124, who reads 'thine eye' for ' thy eye' in
l. 17. 19 Infant . . . infant] Female . . . female MS. Book *1st rdg. del.*

vii

Silent, Silent Night, 1
Quench the holy light
Of thy torches bright;

For possess'd of Day,
Thousand spirits stray 5
That sweet joys betray.

Why should joys be sweet
Usèd with deceit,
Nor with sorrows meet?

But an honest joy 10
Does itself destroy
For a harlot coy.

MS. Book, p. 113. Without any corrections, and obviously transcribed
from an earlier draft. No title in original. DGR and later edd. name
'Night and Day.' Swinb. p. 133. EY omit in their Table of Contents to
the MS. Book (i. 205).
  7 joys] love Swinb. 11 does] doth DGR, WMR, EY, WBY.

viii

O lapwing! thou fliest around the heath,
Nor seest the net that is spread beneath.
Why dost thou not fly among the corn fields?
They cannot spread nets where a harvest yields.

MS. Book, p. 113. Without correction. Only printed by EY, i. 206.
    1 thou] that EY.

ix

I fear'd the fury of my wind   1
Would blight all blossoms fair & true;
And my sun it shin'd & shin'd,
And my wind it never blew.

But a blossom fair or true   5
Was not found on any tree;
For all blossoms grew & grew
Fruitless, false, tho' fair to see.

MS. Book, p. 113. Printed by DGR and later edd. with the title 'Barren Blossom.' Not in Swinb.

 1 fury] roughness MS. Book 1st *rdg. del.*   wind] word EY (in their very inaccurate index to the MS. Book, i. 205).   4 And] But MS. Book 1st *rdg. del.*

x

Infant Sorrow

My mother groan'd, my father wept;   1
Into the dangerous world I leapt,
Helpless, naked, piping loud,
Like a fiend hid in a cloud.

Struggling in my father's hands,   5
Striving against my swaddling bands,
Bound & weary, I thought best
To sulk upon my Mother's breast.

MS. Book, p. 113, with title added later, as the different ink shows. The two first stanzas were afterwards engraved by Blake as one of the *Songs of Experience.* First printed by Swinb., pp. 137–139, who numbers the stanzas with roman numerals. Not in DGR or WMR. EY (Notes to the Poetical Sketches, Songs, &c.) iii. 93, 94; WBY (Notes), p. 240.

 To understand Blake's successive changes in the last part of this poem it should be noted that, beginning with l. 21, he changed 'a Priest' (afterwards, as in xiii, altered to 'my father') to 'many a Priest,' making corresponding changes in the other stanzas where required. Cp. with this poem 'In a Mirtle Shade' (MS. Book xiii).

 4 Like . . . cloud] See note to 'Infant Sorrow' (*Songs of Exp.*) l. 4.

When I saw that rage was vain,   9
And to sulk would nothing gain,
Turning many a trick & wile
I began to soothe & smile.

And I sooth'd day after day,   13
Till upon the ground I stray;
And I smil'd night after night,
Seeking only for delight.

And I saw before me shine   17
Clusters of the wand'ring vine;
And, beyond, a mirtle tree
Stretch'd its blossoms out to me.

But a Priest with holy look,   21
In his hands a holy book,
Pronouncèd curses on his head
Who the fruits or blossoms shed.

I beheld the Priest by night;   25
He embrac'd my mirtle bright:
I beheld the Priest by day,
Where beneath my vines he lay.

Like a serpent in the day   29
Underneath my vines he lay:
Like a serpent in the night
He embrac'd my mirtle bright.

9-12 When . . . smile] This stanza is an afterthought.   11 Turning . . . wile] I began to MS. Book *1st rdg. del.*; Seeking many an artful wile MS. Book *2nd rdg. del.*; Twining many a trick and wile Swinb. 13 sooth'd] grew MS. Book *1st rdg. del.*; Swinb. *retains this*; smil'd MS. Book *2nd rdg. del.*; EY *omit.*   14 stray] lay Swinb., EY, WBY. 15 smil'd] grew MS. Book *1st rdg. del.*, Swinb.   17, 18 And . . . vine]
    'But upon the earthly ground
    No delight was to be found.'
MS. Book first beginning of this stanza *del.* EY put asterisks for 'was to.'
17 And I . . .] From this point onwards I give the earlier (and preferable) form of the remaining stanzas; and print in a final note the revised form of stanzas 6-9. These changes are all dependent upon the substitution of 'many a Priest' for 'a Priest' in l. 21.   21 But a Priest] My father then MS. Book *2rd rdg.* look] book EY   book (? look) WBY (Notes), p. 240.   24 fruits] fruit Swinb., EY.   28 vines] vine EY.   29-32 I beheld . . . bright] The two couplets of this stanza were originally written in

So I smote him, & his gore   33
Stain'd the roots my mirtle bore;
But the time of youth is fled,
And grey hairs are on my head.

the reverse order, the final position of the lines being afterwards indicated
in Blake's usual manner by Arabic numerals added in the left-hand margin.
17–36 And I saw . . . head] I append here the final version of the last five
stanzas (see note to l. 17). The verses were not re-copied, the changes being
deletions and additions.

And I saw before me shine   *17
Clusters of the wand'ring vine;
And many a lovely flower & tree
Stretch'd their blossoms out to me.

But many a Priest with holy look,   *21
In their hands a holy book,
Pronounc'd curses on my head
And bound me in a mirtle shade.

I beheld the Priests by night;   *25
They embrac'd the blossoms bright:
I beheld the Priests by day;
Underneath the vines they lay.

Like to holy men by day   *29
Underneath the vines they lay:
Like to serpents in the night
They embrac'd my mirtle bright.

So I smote them, & their gore   *33
Stain'd the roots my mirtle bore;
But the time of youth is fled,
And grey hairs are on my head.

*21 look] book EY.   *25–*32 I beheld . . . bright] WBY (Notes) *omits.*
*28 vines] vine EY.

xi

Why should I care for the men of thames,   1
Or the cheating waves of charter'd streams;
Or shrink at the little blasts of fear
That the hireling blows into my ear?

MS. Book, p. 113.   Printed by DGR and later edd. with title 'Thames and
Ohio.'   Not in Swinb.
1 thames] the Thames EY (Index to MS. Book, i. 205).   2 Or] And
all edd.   waves] waters DGR, WMR, EY, WBY.   4 my] mine *all edd.*

Tho' born on the cheating banks of Thames,   5
Tho' his waters bathèd my infant limbs,
The Ohio shall wash his stains from me:
I was born a slave, but I go to be free.

6 bathèd] bathed *all edd.*   7 The ... me] I spurn'd his waters away
from me MS. Book *1st rdg. del.*   8 go] long MS. Book *1st rdg. del.*

xii

Thou hast a lap full of seed,   1
And this is a fine country.
Why dost thou not cast thy seed,
And live in it merrily?

Shall I cast it on the sand   5
And turn it into fruitful land?
For on no other ground
Can I sow my seed,
Without tearing up
Some stinking weed.   10

MS. Book, p. 111, where it precedes 'Earth's Answer' (*Songs of Exp.*).
Printed by DGR and later edd. with title 'Seed Sowing.' Not in Swinb. or
WBY. Cp. *Ahania*, chap. v, stanza 12 :—

> 'Then thou, with thy lap full of seed,
> With thy hand full of generous fire,
> Walked forth from the clouds of morning,
> On the virgins of springing joy,
> On the human soul to cast
> The seed of eternal science.'

1 lap full] lapful DGR, WMR, EY.   2 fine] fair DGR, WMR, EY.
5, 6 Shall I ... turn] Oft I've ... turn'd MS. Book *1st rdg. del.*   7–10
For . . . weed] DGR, WMR and EY print these four lines as two. This
may have been Blake's first intention, as he wrote 'can' at the end of l. 7.
but he erased it and arranged the lines as here printed.   7 For] But MS.
Book *1st rdg. del.*   9 tearing] pulling MS. Book *1st rdg. del.*

xiii

[First Version]

In a Mirtle Shade

Why should I be bound to thee,   1
O my lovely mirtle tree?
Love, free love, cannot be bound
To any tree that grows on ground.

O! how sick and weary I   5
Underneath my mirtle lie;
Like to dung upon the ground,
Underneath my mirtle bound.

Oft my mirtle sigh'd in vain   9
To behold my heavy chain:
Oft my father saw us sigh,
And laugh'd at our simplicity.

So I smote him, & his gore   13
Stain'd the roots my mirtle bore.
But the time of youth is fled,
And grey hairs are on my head.

MS. Book, p. 111.   DGR and WMR omit this version; Swinb., pp. 137, 138, quotes stanzas 1 and 3.   EY (Notes to the Poetical Sketches, Songs, &c.) iii. 94 ; WBY (Notes), p. 245.   Cp. with this poem the fuller form of ' Infant Sorrow ' (MS. Book x).

5–8 O . . . bound] This stanza was added after the rest were written, in the left-hand column, prefixed numerals to ll. 5 and 9 indicating the relative position of the second and third stanzas.   WBY, by omitting these and printing the stanzas as written, misrepresents the true order.   Blake began stanza 2 with the couplet, afterwards deleted :

        ' To a lovely mirtle bound,
          Blossoms show'ring all around.'

Both EY and WBY print this couplet without marking the deletion, as elsewhere, by italics.   5 sick] weak EY, WBY.   11 Oft . . . saw] Oft the priest beheld MS. Book 1*st rdg. del.* : cp. MS. Book x.   13–16 So . . . head] cp. ' Infant Sorrow,' ll. 33–6 (MS. Book x).

[*Final Version*]

To My Mirtle

To a lovely mirtle bound,   1
Blossoms show'ring all around,
O how sick & weary I
Underneath my mirtle lie!
Why should I be bound to thee,   5
O my lovely mirtle tree?

MS. Book, p. 106, where it immediately precedes ' Nought loves another
as itself' ('A Little Boy Lost'). The simple and faultless form into which
Blake here compresses the sixteen lines of the preceding version has been
obscured by editorial changes. As this poem has never been correctly
printed, it may be well to reproduce it in the exact form in which it is found
in the MS. Book, indicating deleted lines by italics :—

TO MY MIRTLE.

5	Why should I be bound to thee	*1
6	O my lovely mirtle tree	
	Love free love cannot be bound	
	To any tree that grows on ground.	
1	To a lovely mirtle bound	*5
2	Blossoms showring all around	
	Like to dung upon the ground	
	Underneath my mirtle bound	
3	O how sick & weary I	*9
4	Underneath my mirtle lie.	

It will thus be seen that Blake began by transcribing, as it stood, the first
stanza of the earlier version, beginning his second stanza with the couplet
which he had rejected in the previous draft and adding—but in transposed
order—two accepted couplets of the same stanza. He then struck out ll. *3,
*4 and *7, *8, prefixing marginal numbers in his usual manner to indicate the
position of the lines retained. Blake's intention is perfectly plain ; yet we
find all Blake's editors following DGR in restoring the deleted lines *3, *4,
and printing the poem as two four-line stanzas. The original arrangement
of the verses must have misled Mr. Rossetti into supposing that two more
lines were required, otherwise he would have been the first to perceive how
greatly the poem gains in freshness and sweetness by the omission of the
rhetorical tag:—

Love, free love, cannot be bound
To any tree that grows on ground!

All edd. follow DGR's text. EY (Notes to the Poetical Sketches, Songs,
&c.) iii. 95, and WBY (Notes), print the lines in the order in which they
were written in the MS. Book, but leave them meaningless by the omission
of Blake's marginal numbers, and by ignoring deletions. DGR and all edd.
give this poem the title used in the earlier version, ' In a Myrtle Shade.'

3 sick] weak *all edd.*   4 lie] *All edd. end first stanza here.*   6 tree]
All edd. add ll. *3, *4.

xiv

To Nobodaddy

Why art thou silent & invisible,   1
Father of Jealousy?
Why dost thou hide thyself in clouds
From every searching Eye?

Why darkness & obscurity   5
In all thy words & laws,
That none dare eat the fruit but from
The wily serpent's jaws?
Or is it because Secresy gains females' loud applause?

MS. Book, p. 109. The title added later in different ink. Not in DGR.
Swinb., p. 264; EY, iii. 91, i. 209. Printed by WMR under the title 'Father
of Jealousy,' and by WBY in text as 'To Old Nobodaddy,' and in notes as
'To Nobodady' (*sic*). 'Nobodaddy' (obviously 'Nobody's Daddy,' anti-
thetical to 'Father of All') was Blake's jocular nickname for Urizen, the
Father of Jealousy. The same name occurs also in 'Fayette' and in the lines
on Klopstock (MS. Book xxxvi, xxxix).

2 Father] Man MS. Book *1st rdg. del.*   4 searching] passing EY.
5 EY and WBY print both stanzas as one.   7 dare] can EY.   9 Or
... applause] a later addition in pencil. All edd. print as two lines. Secresy]
Jealousy (with note querying 'secrecy' as the true reading) Swinb.: gains]
gives Swinb.: females' loud] feminine MS. Book *1st rdg. del.*, Swinb., EY, WBY.

XV

Are not the joys of morning sweeter   1
Than the joys of night?
And are the vig'rous joys of youth
Ashamèd of the light?

MS. Book, p. 109. Printed by DGR and later edd. with title 'Young
Love.' Swinb. (first two lines only), p. 140.
Cp. *Visions of the Daughters of Albion* (1793):—

               'Innocence! honest, open, seeking
The vigorous joys of morning light; open to virgin bliss,
Who taught thee modesty, subtil modesty, child of night & sleep?'

               4 Ashamèd] Ashamed DGR.

Let age & sickness silent rob   5
The vineyards in the night;
But those who burn with vig'rous youth
Pluck fruits before the light.

6 vineyards] vineyard *all edd.*

xvi

They said this mystery never shall cease:
The priest promotes war, & the soldier peace.

MS. Book, p. 107.   Cp. note to ' The Lilly ' (*Songs of Experience*).
2 promotes] loves MS. Book *1st rdg. del.*

xvii

Love to faults is always blind;   1
Always is to joy inclin'd,
Lawless, wing'd & unconfin'd,
And breaks all chains from every mind.

Deceit to secresy confin'd,   5
Lawful, cautious & refin'd;
To anything but interest blind,
And forges fetters for the mind.

MS. Book, written in pencil at top right-hand corners of pp. 107, 106.
I print the two stanzas as one poem, their connexion being obvious, though
not indicated by Blake himself. Not in DGR, WMR, or Swinb. EY and
WBY (the latter with the title ' Freedom and Captivity') print the first
stanza and an altered version of the fragment by which it is immediately
followed in the MS. (' There souls of men are bought & sold') as a single
poem. See also WBY (Notes), p. 246.
    3 Lawless . . . unconfin'd] Always . . . unconfin'd MS. Book *1st rdg.*
' Always ' is underlined, which was probably a hasty attempt at erasure ;
Lawless, wingèd, unconfined EY, WBY.   5–8 Deceit . . . mind] MS.
Book *1st rdg.* :—

> ' Deceit to secresy inclin'd,
> Modest, prudish & confin'd,
> Never is to interest blind,
> And chains in fetters every mind.'

xviii

There souls of men are bought & sold,　　　1
And milk fed infancy for gold ;
And youth to slaughter houses led,
And beauty, for a bit of bread.

MS. Book, p. 107.　Not in DGR and WMR.　Swinb., p. 127.　EY and
WBY print as second stanza to preceding poem.　See note to xvii.
　　1 There] The EY, WBY.　　　2 And] In EY, WBY: milk fed . . . gold]
cradled infancy is sold MS. Book 1st *rdg. del.*　　　3 youth] youths Swinb.,
EY, WBY.　　　4 beauty] maidens MS. Book 1st *rdg. del.*, Swinb.

xix

The Wild Flower's Song

As I wander'd the forest,　　　1
The green leaves among,
I heard a wild flower
Singing a song.

' I slept in the Earth　　　5
In the silent night,
I murmur'd my fears
And I felt delight.

' In the morning I went,　　　9
As rosy as morn,
To seek for new Joy ;
But I met with scorn.'

MS. Book, pp. 107, 109.　The second and third stanzas on p. 109 at first
formed the entire poem : later Blake added on p. 107 the introductory stanza
and catchwords (' I slept in the dark, &c.'), and finally the title.
　　1 wander'd the] wandered in the *all edd.*　　　3 flower] thistle MS. Book
1st *rdg. del.*　　　5 I . . . Earth] I was found in the dark *ibid.*　　　7
fears] thoughts R[1] (though correctly in DGR), WMR, EY, WBY.

XX

Soft Snow

I walkèd abroad on a snowy day: 1
I ask'd the soft snow with me to play:
She play'd & she melted in all her prime;
And the winter call'd it a dreadful crime.

MS. Book, p. 107.   The last line is in pencil.   Title added later.   DGR,
WMR, EY and WBY ('Couplets and Fragments,' i), Swinb. pp. 135, 136
(*note*).
  1 walkèd] walked MS. Book *and all edd.* : snowy] sunny Swinb.   2
ask'd] wooed Swinb., WBY.   4 And . . . crime] Oh, that sweet love
should be thought a crime! MS. Book *1st rdg. del.* ; Ah! that, &c. R¹,
Swinb. (*note*).

xxi

Merlin's Prophecy

The harvest shall flourish in wintry weather   1
When two virginities meet together:
The King & the Priest must be tied in a tether
Before two virgins can meet together.

MS. Book, p. 106.   Only printed by EY, i. 207.
  1 wintry] windy EY (Index to MS. Book), i. 205.   3 The King &
the Priest] The king and priest EY.

xxii

Day

The sun arises in the East,   1
Cloth'd in robes of blood & gold;
Swords & spears & wrath increast
All around his bosom roll'd,
Croun'd with warlike fires & raging desires.   5

MS. Book, p. 105.   Printed here for first time.   EY quote title and first
line in their index to the MS. Book, i. 205.
  1 sun] day MS. Book *1st rdg. del.*, EY (*Index*).   4 bosom] ancles
MS. Book *1st rdg. del.*

xxiii

The Fairy

'Come hither, my sparrows,   1
My little arrows.
If a tear or a smile
Will a man beguile,
If an amorous delay   5
Clouds a sunshiny day,
If the step of a foot
Smites the heart to its root,
'Tis the marriage ring—   9
Makes each fairy a king.'

So a fairy sung.
From the leaves I sprung;
He leap'd from the spray   13
To flee away;
But in my hat caught,
He soon shall be taught.
Let him laugh, let him cry,   17
He's my butterfly;
For I've pulled out the sting
Of the marriage ring.

MS. Book, p. 105. Title in pencil. Only in Swinb., pp. 142, 143, and EY, iii. 96. Blake's first title (afterwards erased) was 'The Marriage Ring.' Swinb. gives this instead of the later title : EY print both titles, without indicating the author's deletion of the first.

7 step] tread MS. Book *1st rdg. del.*   10, 11 Swinb. prints both stanzas as one.   11 sung] sang Swinb., EY.   12 sprung] sprang Swinb., EY.   13 the] his Swinb.   15 hat caught] Cp. a sketch in the MS. Book, afterwards engraved by Blake for *The Gates of Paradise*, no. 7, reproduced in Gilchr., i. 99.   19, 20 For . . . ring] l. 19 is an addition, the poem originally ending with l. 20 and a line now thoroughly erased :

'And the marriage ring'
.   .   .   .

20 Of] And MS. Book *1st rdg. del.* See preceding note.

xxiv

The sword sung on the barren heath,
The sickle in the fruitful field:
The sword he sung a song of death,
But could not make the sickle yield.

MS. Book, p. 105.　Not in DGR or Swinb.　WMR, EY, WBY ('Couplets and Fragments,' vii).

1, 3 sung] sang *all edd.*

XXV

Abstinence sows sand all over
The ruddy limbs & flaming hair,
But Desire Gratified
Plants fruits of life & beauty there.

MS. Book, p. 105.　DGR, WMR, EY (ii) and WBY (3) 'Couplets and Fragments,' Swinb., p. 137.

2 flaming] ? flowering ? flowery Swinb.

xxvi

In a wife I would desire
What in whores is always found—
The lineaments of Gratified desire.

MS. Book, p. 105.　Cp. 'Several Questions Answered' (xxxv).

xxvii

If you trap the moment before it's ripe,
The tears of repentance you'll certainly wipe;
But if once you let the ripe moment go
You can never wipe off the tears of woe.

MS. Book, p. 105.　In pencil.　Printed by DGR and all later edd. as the second stanza of the poem immediately following in the MS. Book (xxxv, 'Eternity') under the title 'Opportunity.'

1 trap] catch MS. Book *1st rdg. del.*　　4 You can] You'll MS. Book *1st rdg. del.*

xxviii

The Kid

Thou, little Kid, did'st play
&c.

So in MS. Book, p. 105. Blake here, according to his usual practice, uses
' &c.' to signify that the poem had already been noted elsewhere. He never
transcribed it into the MS. Book, and the remainder of this piece is therefore
lost to us.

xxix

Lacedemonian Instruction

Come hither, my boy, tell me what thou seest there.
A fool tangled in a religious snare.

MS. Book, p. 103. Title added later. Only in EY.
1 tell . . . there] what see you there ? EY.   2 tangled] caught EY.

xxx

Riches

The countless gold of a merry heart.
The rubies & pearls of a loving eye,
The indolent never can bring to the mart,
Nor the secret hoard up in his treasury.

MS. Book, p. 103 (reversed). All edd. follow DGR in printing this as
second stanza of cxxv, WBY with title ' The Two Kinds of Riches.'
2 of a loving eye] *In the MS., written in error,* ' of a loving of a loving eye.
3 indolent] idle man MS. Book 1*st rdg. del., and all edd.*   4 secret] cunning
MS. Book 1*st rdg. del., and all edd.*

xxxi

An Answer to the Parson

Why of the sheep do you not learn peace?
Because I don't want you to shear my fleece.

MS. Book, p. 103. DGR and WMR ('Couplets and Fragments,' xiii). Not in Swinb., EY, or WBY.

xxxii

Motto to the Songs of Innocence and of Experience

The Good are attracted by Men's perceptions,   1
And think not for themselves;
Till Experience teaches them to catch
And to cage the Fairies & Elves.

And then the Knave begins to snarl,   5
And the Hypocrite to howl;
And all his good Friends shew their private ends,
And the Eagle is known from the Owl.

MS. Book, p. 101. Not in DGR or EY. Swinb., p. 124. WMR prefixes to *Songs of Innocence and of Experience* with the title 'A Motto.' WBY (Notes) p. 238.
     3 to catch] how to catch Swinb.   7 ends] end WBY.

xxxiii

Her Whole Life is an Epigram smart, smooth & neatly
     pen'd,
Platted quite neat to catch applause, with a hang-noose
     at the end.

MS. Book, p. 100. Placed among 'Couplets and Fragments' by DGR (x), WMR, EY (xii), and WBY (14). Not in Swinb.
     1 Her] Not plainly written; possibly 'His': smart] smack *all edd.*
2 hang-noose] strong noose *all edd.*

xxxiv

An Old maid early e'er I knew   1
Ought but the love that on me grew ;
And now I'm cover'd o'er & o'er,
And wish that I had been a Whore.

O ! I cannot cannot find   5
The undaunted courage of a Virgin Mind ;
For Early I in love was crost,
Before my flower of love was lost.

MS. Book, p. 100. Printed only by EY, i. 206. The second stanza was originally the first, Blake afterwards renumbering them in their present order.
     1 e'er] *Read* ere.   3 I'm cover'd] I am covered EY.

xxxv

Several Questions Answered

[Eternity]   1.

He who bends to himself a joy
Doth the wingèd life destroy ;
But he who kisses the joy as it flies
Lives in Eternity's sunrise.

MS. Book, p. 99. Under the general title ' Several Questions Answered,' Blake here transcribes hastily in pencil, short pieces, the first drafts of which are written elsewhere in the MS. Book. The original order of pieces was 4, 2, 3, 1, 5, the revised sequence being indicated by Blake's usual marginal figures. None of Blake's editors print these fragments together. Title incorrectly given in EY's Index (i. 206) as ' Questions answered (again).'
     1–4 He . . . sunrise] First written on p. 105 with title ' Eternity.' Printed by DGR and later edd. with the title ' Opportunity,' as the first stanza of xxvii, the first draft of which immediately precedes it, on p. 105 of the MS. Book.   2 Doth] Does MS. Book, p. 105 *and all edd.* : wingèd] winged WMR, EY, WBY.   3 kisses] just kisses MS. Book, p. 105 1*st rdg. del.*
     Eternity's] an eternal MS. Book, p. 105 1*st rdg. del.*

2.

The look of love alarms,   5
Because it's fill'd with fire;
But the look of soft deceit
Shall win the lover's hire.

3.

Soft deceit & Idleness,   9
These are Beauty's sweetest dress.

4.

[The Question Answer'd]
What is it men in women do require?   11
The lineaments of Gratified Desire.
What is it women do in men require?
The lineaments of Gratified Desire.

5.

An ancient Proverb
Remove away that black'ning church,   15
Remove away that marriage hearse,
Remove away that [man] of blood—
You'll quite remove the ancient curse.

5-8 The ... hire] Transcribed from p. 103 of the MS. Book. Among
'Couplets and Fragments' (III), DGR, WMR, EY (4), WBY.   6 it's]
'tis MS. Book *1st version*, p. 103, *and all edd.*   fill'd] filled *all edd.*   9, 10
Soft ... dress] Transcribed from MS. Book, p. 103, where it follows the preceding quatrain but with Blake's usual line of separation. DGR and later
edd. print as the two last lines of 'The look of love alarms.' Blake at
first began this couplet with the deleted line 'Which are beauties sweetest
dress?'   10 Beauty's] beauties MS. Book *1st version*, p. 103.   11-14
What ... Desire] Transcribed from MS. Book, p. 103, where it bears the
title 'The Question Answer'd.' Not in DGR or WMR. Swinb., p. 182.
EY, i. 206. WBY (title omitted) 'Couplets and Fragments' (2).   11, 13
in] of MS. Book *1st version, 1st rdg. del.*   15-18 Transcribed from MS.
Book, p. 107, where the title is an addition. Only in WBY (Notes),
p. 240. Cp. note to 'London' (*Songs of Exp.*).   15 black'ning]
blackening WBY.   17 man] dash in MS.; place MS. Book *1st version, 1st rdg. del.* I supply 'man' from the last rdg. of the earlier
version.   18 You'll] 'Twill MS. Book *1st version, 1st rdg. del.*   the]
that WBY.

xxxvi

Prefatory Note

MS. Book, pp. 99, 98. Without title. Probably written about 1793. Blake has left no fair copy of this piece. Some of the stanzas are erased, some re-written, some separated from the rest by boundary lines, and some numbered with a bewildering series of marginal figures marking successive attempts at the arrangement of lines into stanzas, and stanzas into different orders. Reproduced as it stands in the MS., this rough draft would prove a chaos to the reader, and I have therefore endeavoured to represent the various stages in the development of the poem by printing it separately in its initial, mediate, and final forms. I call these three versions A, B, and C, and refer to the stanzas in each by lower-case roman numerals.

Blake began his first attempt at the head of the second column of p. 99 to the right of the space filled by 'Several Questions Answer'd.' This version (A) he next altered by erasing ll. 13, 14, 15; prefixing the marginal numerals 4, 2, 3 to A ii, A iii, A iv, to denote that the original second stanza was to be placed last.

His next change consisted in placing smaller figures 1–12 before the lines which he meant to retain in the order specified. The effect of this is to interpolate between A i and A ii a new second stanza [A *3], formed by uniting the first couplet of A iv and the second couplet of A iii:—

> Then he swore a great & solemn oath :
> 'To kill the people I am loth,'
> And said 'I love hanging & drawing & quartering
> Every bit as well as war & slaughtering.'

This re-arrangement, however—unless with WMR we transpose the relative positions of the second and third stanzas—leaves the pronoun 'he' without antecedent, and Blake accordingly erased the whole passage from 'Then old Nobodaddy aloft' to 'They shall have a Priest and a passing bell' (A ll. 9–19), leaving only the first two stanzas of A as originally written. To the latter of these ('The King awoke on his couch of gold') he now added, below the deleted passage, a companion stanza in the same metre ('The Queen of France just touched this Globe'), erasing and re-writing three lines in the process. These three stanzas form the beginning of B.

Turning to the vacant space in the first column below 'Several Questions Answer'd' Blake added three Fayette stanzas (B iv–vi) followed by a fourth ('Fayette, Fayette, thou'rt bought & sold') in the second column underneath B iii. This last he erased, and finished his work on p. 99 by drawing a line of separation between the Fayette stanzas in both columns and the matter immediately above. Resuming in the first column of p. 98 he began a new stanza ('Fayette beside his banner stood') which he cancelled before completion, adding the three verses 'Who will exchange his own fireside,' 'Will the mother exchange her new born babe,' and 'Fayette, Fayette, thou'rt bought & sold'—the last being an amended version of the deleted stanza at the foot of the second column of the preceding page. These three stanzas were then numbered 3, 2, 1 to show that their position was to be inverted, and later the figure 3 was struck out to mark the cancellation of ' Who will exchange ... dungeon floor,' a boundary line being drawn around the two retained stanzas. This gives us the poem in its fullest and best form B.

Blake's next alteration was to erase the two Fayette stanzas on p. 99 (B iv, v), leaving only that beginning ' Fayette beheld the King & Queen,' which he re-transcribed below, B vii. Cancelling the two stanzas above (B vii and B viii) Blake then added a slightly amended form of the lines beginning ' Who will exchange his own fireside,' and, at the head of the second column, the stanza ' O who would smile on the wintry seas,' the prefixed numbers 2, 1, 3, added later, indicating a new but not very happy revision of the arrangement of the three last stanzas. These changes are manifestly for the worse. Blake seems to have lost his grip of the poem, and to have abandoned any further attempt at completion. In version C I print the poem as he left it.

Under the title ' Lafayette,' WMR prints the stanzas in the following order : B i B ii A *iii B iv B v B iii (*1st rdg.*) C v B vii B viii. EY (ii. 24-27) give a not very accurate account of the evolution of the poem, omitting one stanza (A iv) altogether and ignoring or misinterpreting the successive re-arrangements of lines and stanzas indicated by Blake's marginal numbers.

On p. 98 we reach the point at which Blake reversed the MS. Book and began writing from the other end. Passages of ' The Everlasting Gospel ' and one epigram are found upside down upon the same page.

A

[i]

' Let the Brothels of Paris be openèd   1
With many an alluring dance,
To awake the Physicians thro' the city,'
Said the beautiful Queen of France.

[ii]

The King awoke on his couch of gold,   5
As soon as he heard these tidings told :
' Arise & come, both fife & drum,
And the [Famine] shall eat both crust & crumb.'

---

3 Physicians] Pestilence MS. Book *1st rdg. del.*, EY.   8 Famine] MS. Book *1st rdg. del.* ; no word substituted.

[iii]

Then old Nobodaddy aloft   9
****** & belched & cough'd,
And said, 'I love hanging & drawing & quartering
Every bit as well as war & slaughtering.
Damn praying & singing,   13
Unless they will bring in
The blood of ten thousand by fighting or swinging.'

[iv]

Then he swore a great & solemn oath: 16
'To kill the people I am loth;
But if they rebel, they must go to hell:
They shall have a Priest & a passing bell.'

15 swinging] surgery EY.   16–19 Then ... bell] EY *omit.*

B

[i]

'Let the Brothels of Paris be openèd   1
With many an alluring dance,
To awake the Physicians thro' the city'
Said the beautiful Queen of France.

[ii]

The King awoke on his couch of gold,   5
As soon as he heard these tidings told:
'Arise & come, both fife & drum,
And the Famine shall eat both crust and crumb.'

[iii]

The Queen of France just touch'd this Globe, 9
And the Pestilence darted from her robe;
But our good Queen quite grows to the ground,
And a great many suckers grow all around.

11, 12 But ... around]
'But the bloodthirsty people across the water
Will not submit to the gibbet & halter.'
MS. Book 1*st rdg. del.*, WMR.   12 And ... around] There is just such a tree at Java found MS. Book 2*nd rdg. del.*

[iv]

Fayette beside King Lewis stood ;　　　　13
He saw him sign his hand ;
And soon he saw the famine rage
About the fruitful land.

[v]

Fayette beheld the Queen to smile　　　　17
And wink her lovely eye ;
And soon he saw the pestilence
From street to street to fly.

[vi]

Fayette beheld the King & Queen　　　　21
In tears & iron bound ;
But mute Fayette wept tear for tear,
And guarded them around.

[vii]

Fayette, Fayette, thou'rt bought & sold　　　　25
And sold is thy happy morrow ;
Thou gavest the tears of Pity away
In exchange for the tears of sorrow.

17 beheld] liked EY.　　22 tears & iron] curses and iron WMR ; tears
of iron EY.　　24 Here follow in the MS. the deleted stanza :—

'Fayette, Fayette, thou'rt bought & sold
For well I see thy tears
Of Pity are exchanged for those
Of selfish slavish fears.'

and the deleted beginning of a stanza :—

'Fayette beside his banner stood,
His captains false around,
Thou'rt bought & sold—— '

EY reading 'I will see' for 'well I see,' and 'King Lewis' for 'his banner.'
This again is followed by the stanza marked for erasure :—

'Who will exchange his own fireside
For the steps of another's door?
Who will exchange his wheaten loaf
For the links of a dungeon floor ?'

and the two deleted lines :—

'Who will exchange his own heart's blood
For the drops of a Harlot's eye?'

25-32 Fayette … floor] These stanzas were at first written in reversed order.

[viii]

Will the mother exchange her new born babe   29
For the dog at the wintry door?
Yet thou dost exchange thy pitying tears
For the links of a dungeon floor!

C

[First three stanzas as B, concluding as below.]

[iv]

Who will exchange his own fireside   13
For the stone of another's door?
Who will exchange his wheaten loaf
For the links of a dungeon floor?

[v]

Fayette beheld the King & Queen   17
In curses & iron bound;
But mute Fayette wept tear for tear,
And guarded them around.

[vi]

O who would smile on the wintry seas   21
& Pity the stormy roar?
Or who will exchange his new born child
For the dog at the wintry door?

13-20 Who . . . around] These two stanzas were originally written in reversed order.   14 stone] steps MS. Book *1st rdg. del.*   18 curses] tears MS. Book *1st rdg. del.*

POEMS

FROM

THE ROSSETTI MS.

II

MS. Book, pp. 2–98. § xxxvii–cxxxi
Written circa 1800–1810

ROSSETTI MANUSCRIPT

Prefatory Note

MS. Book, pp. 3 and 2. In the first column of the former page are stanza 1, two deleted stanzas beginning 'Her weeping she shall ne'er give o'er,' and 'Thou hast parted from my side,' with stanzas 3, 5, 6, 8. In the second column of the same page are the cancelled first version of stanza 2, the cancelled stanza 'When my love did first begin' and stanza 4 (marked for insertion between stanzas 3 and 5, afterwards cancelled and then again marked 'to come in' in the position originally indicated). Last follow stanzas 2 and 7, the latter marked for insertion between 6 and 8. The whole of these are written in ink, with one or more arabic numbers at the head of each, showing clearly Blake's successive arrangements, and his final order of the eight retained stanzas. In either column, at the head of page 2, are stanzas 9 and 10, and near the foot of the page, in either column, stanzas 11 and 12 (all four written and numbered in ink) followed by stanza 13 (written in pencil and centred at foot of page). Intermediately between these and the two top stanzas, and written later in pencil around a sketch of Daphne, in the centre of the page, are to the left a stanza numbered 2 ('What transgressions I commit'), a stanza without number ('Poor, pale, pitiable form') and another which is almost illegible. To the right, numbered 1, is the stanza beginning 'O'er my sins thou sit and moan,' and numbered 14 (i.e. consecutive to 'Let us agree to give up love'), the final stanza 'Throughout all Eternity.' The stanzas, written in pencil, numbered 1 and 2, and the unnumbered stanza 'Poor pale pitiable form' are not cancelled, and Blake may have intended to arrange them as part of the poem in a final draft. If so, their natural place would seem to be after stanza 3.

The position of this poem in the MS. Book—the first piece written from the original beginning of the volume after it had been half filled by earlier poems written from the reversed end—proves that it was composed soon after Blake removed to Felpham, when he resumed his use of the old sketch-book as a notebook for poetry. The next piece of any importance is the poem (xli), three pages further on, which contains internal evidence of having been written about the same time as the lines to Butts in Blake's letter of October 2, 1800: xxxvii may therefore be dated October or November, 1800.

Swinburne (*Essay*, pp. 278, 279) describes 'My Spectre' as 'perfect *Jerusalem* both for style and matter,' and 'meant for insertion in some fresh instalment of prophetic rhapsody by way of complement or sequel' to that work. It is, however, rather an offshoot of *The Four Zoas*, written in 1797, the argument and symbolism of which are practically the same as those of *Milton* and *Jerusalem*.

Blake's use of the terms 'spectre' and 'emanation,' the former to signify the reasoning power in man, and the latter his imagination and emotion, supplies the clue to the meaning of this beautiful but obscure poem. The theme is identical with that of the later Prophetic Books, i.e. the separation of reason and emotion into two contrary and conflicting selves, and their reunion in a state of regained humanity and moral liberty, through self-annihilation achieved by the infinite tolerance and forgiveness of sin. Cp. the author's invocation to the Muses—in Blake's mythology the Daughters, not of Memory, but of Imagination—in the opening lines of *The Four Zoas* :—

'Daughters of Beulah, sing
His fall into Division and his resurrection into Unity,
His fall into the generation of decay and death, and his
Regeneration by resurrection from the dead.'

Of this poem, with the title 'Broken Love,' descriptive of the meaning which he reads into it, Mr. D. G. Rossetti gives a very corrupt text, printing stanzas 1, 2, 3, a fourth and fifth stanza, formed by amalgamating couplets taken from the unplaced or rejected stanzas :—

'Poor pale pitiable form
That I follow in a storm,
From sin I never shall be free
Till thou forgive and come to me.

'A deep winter dark and cold
Within my heart thou dost unfold ;
Iron tears and groans of lead
Thou bind'st around my aching head.'

then stanza 4, the unplaced stanza *1, the rejected stanza 'Thy weeping thou shall ne'er give o'er,' the unplaced stanza *2, and stanzas 5, 6, 7, 8, 14. The same version is adopted by Mr. W. M. Rossetti, and has been accepted without question by the majority of editors who follow the text of the Aldine edition. Mr. Swinburne (pp. 278, 279) prints with commentary the two rejected stanzas 'Thou hast parted from my side,' and 'When my love did first begin,' and stanzas 8–14, transposing the position of 11 and 12, which he thinks Blake must have so numbered 'by some evident slip of mind or pen.' In vol. ii, pp. 37–41, Messrs. Ellis and Yeats print fourteen stanzas with symbolic 'interpretation.' They conclude with the note : 'The text of the poem here is reprinted from the Aldine edition, the present editors not having seen the MS.' ; which must mystify readers who find, three pages before, 'the above is the true text of this poem with the numberings of the verses as finally arranged after three re-considerations by Blake. Not a word is altered from the original. The poem as printed in the Aldine Edition and elsewhere is erroneously arranged, partly from numberings of verses put experimentally and then erased by Blake.' The latter of these two contradictory statements, it may be explained, is the nearer to the truth ; though the editors have rendered their third stanza meaningless by printing the second in its earlier and cancelled, instead of in its revised form; and their text contains one or two of their customary deviations from verbal accuracy. Under the title 'Spectre and Emanation,' the poem is rather more correctly given by Mr. W. B. Yeats, who prints the fourteen approved and numbered stanzas in the text, and the three unplaced stanzas ('apparently rejected') in the notes (p. 249).

I

My Spectre around me night & day   1
Like a Wild beast guards my way;
My Emanation far within
Weeps incessantly for my Sin.

2

A Fathomless & boundless deep,   5
There we wander, there we weep;
On the hungry craving wind
My Spectre follows thee behind.

1 around] before EY, WBY.

1 Spectre] Cp. *Jerusalem*, f. 74, ll. 10–13:—

'The Spectre is the Reasoning Power in Man; & when separated
From Imagination, and closing itself as in steel in a Ratio
Of the Things of Memory, It thence frames Laws & Moralities
To destroy Imagination, the Divine Body, by Martyrdoms and Wars.'

See also *Jerusalem*, f. 8, l. 30; f. 10, ll. 15, 16; f. 36, l. 23; f. 54, l. 7; f. 56, l. 18; *Milton*, f. 42, l. 34; and *passim*.   3 Emanation] In Blake's mythology the Emanation is always personified as a female (cp. *Milton*, f. 14, ll. 13, 14, 'gave forth their Emanations Like Females of sweet beauty'), in contradistinction to the Spectre, who is male. The Emanation represents imagination and self-annihilation; the Spectre, reason, self-hood, pride and self-righteousness, cp. *Milton*, f. 12, ll. 28–31:—

'What do I here before the Judgement without my Emanation?
With the daughters of memory, & not with the daughters of inspiration;
I in my Selfhood am that Satan: I am that Evil One:
He is my Spectre.'

4 Here followed the two cancelled stanzas:—

'Thy [1st rdg. *Her*] weeping thou [*she*] shall ne'er give o'er.
I sin against thee [*her*] more & more;
And never will from sin be free
Till she forgives & comes to me.

'Thou hast parted from my side:
Once thou wast a virgin bride:
Never shalt thou a true love [*lover*] find:
My Spectre follows thee Behind.'

DGR and WMR print the former as their eighth stanza, making the necessary changes, overlooked by Blake, of 'shall' to 'shalt' in l. 1, 'she forgives' to 'thou forgive,' and 'comes' to 'come' in l. 4.   5–8 A...
behind] EY adopt the first rejected form of this stanza:—

'A deep winter, dark & cold,
Within my heart thou didst unfold;
A Fathomless & boundless deep;
There we wander, there we weep.'

3

He scents thy footsteps in the snow, 9
Wheresoever thou dost go,
Thro' the wintry hail & rain.
When wilt thou return again?

4

Dost thou not in Pride & Scorn 13
Fill with tempests all my morn,
And with jealousies & fears
Fill my pleasant nights with tears?

5

Seven of my sweet loves thy knife 17
Has bereavèd of their life.
Their marble tombs I built with tears,
And with cold & shuddering fears.

Blake's previous deleted readings are l. 1 'winter night dark' for 'winter dark,' and then ' On a dark cold winter night Within my Heart.' This is followed by another deleted stanza quoted only by Swinb. :—

> 'When my Love did first begin,
> Thou didst call that Love a sin :
> Secret trembling, night & day,
> Driving all my Loves away.'

8 Cp. *Jerusalem*, f. 30, ll. 2, 3 :—

> 'for wherever the Emanation goes, the Spectre
> Attends her as her Guard.'

9–12 He . . . again] Originally the fourth stanza. Cp. *Milton*, f. 32*, ll. 4, 5 :—

> ' My Spectre still wandering thro' them follows my Emanation,
> He hunts her footsteps thro' the snow & the wintry hail & rain.'

13–15 Dost . . . fears] Dost . . . fears? DGR, WMR. 13 Dost] Didst MS. Book *1st rdg. del.* 16 Fill] And fill DGR, WMR. 17, 18 Cp. *Milton*, f. 32, ll. 3–7 :—

> ' I thought that you would love my loves and joy in my delights,
> Seeking for pleasures in my pleasures, O Daughter of Babylon,
> Then thou wast lovely mild and gentle, now thou art terrible
> In jealousy, and unlovely in my sight, because thou hast cruelly
> Cut off my loves in fury till I have no love left for thee.'

17 my] thy EY. 18 Has] Hath DGR, WMR. 19 built . . . tears] build . . . fears EY, WBY. 20 shuddering fears] shadowy fears DGR, WMR ; shadowy tears EY, WBY.

6

Seven more loves weep night & day   21
Round the tombs where my loves lay,
And seven more loves attend each night
Around my couch with torches bright.

7

And seven more Loves in my bed   25
Crown with wine my mournful head,
Pitying & forgiving all
Thy transgressions great & small.

8

When wilt thou return & view   29
My loves, & them to life renew?
When wilt thou return & live?
When wilt thou pity as I forgive?

9

'Never, Never, I return: 33
Still for Victory I burn.
Living, thee alone I'll have;
And when dead I'll be thy Grave.

10

'Thro' the Heaven & Earth & Hell   37
Thou shalt never, never quell:
I will fly and thou pursue:
Night & Morn the flight renew.'

---

23 each] at DGR, WMR, EY, WBY.   24 Around] About R¹
26 wine] vine *all edd.*   28 Thy] My WBY.   30 to life] in life
DGR, WMR.   32 as I] and MS. Book 1*st rdg. del.*   33–40 EY
omit inverted commas (wtg. also in MS.)

11

Till I turn from Female Love   41
And root up the Infernal Grove,
I shall never worthy be
To step into Eternity.

12

And, to end thy cruel mocks,   45
Annihilate thee on the rocks,
And another form create
To be subservient to my Fate.

41 I] thou MS. Book *1st rdg. del.*   42 root] dig MS. Book *1st rdg. del.* :
Infernal Grove] See *Jerusalem*, f. 43, ll. 8–11, *and passim.*   43 I] Thou
MS. Book *1st rdg. del.*   45–49 And . . . Let] Swinb. transposes these
two stanzas.   45 And, to] And I to MS. Book *1st rdg. del.*, Swinb., EY,
WBY.   46 What is meant by 'annihilation' is rendered clear by the
following passage from *Milton*, f. 42, l. 37 ; f. 43, ll. 1–10 :—

'To cleanse the Face of my Spirit by Self-examination,
To bathe in the waters of Life, to wash off the Not Human,
I come in Self annihilation & the grandeur of Inspiration
To cast off Rational Demonstration by Faith in the Saviour,
To cast off the rotten rags of Memory by Inspiration,
To cast off Bacon Locke and Newton from Albion's covering,
To take off his filthy garments and clothe him with Imagination,
To cast aside from Poetry all that is not Inspiration,
That it no longer shall dare to mock with the aspersion of Madness
Cast on the Inspired by the tame high finisher of paltry Blots,
Indefinite or paltry Rhymes, or paltry Harmonies.'

47, 48 Cp. *The Four Zoas*, Night vii, ll. 298–306 :—

'I will destroy
That body I created; then shall we unite again in bliss ;
For, till these terrors planted round the Gates of Eternal life
Are driven away & annihilated, we never can repass the Gates.
Thou knowest that the Spectre is in Every Man insane, brutish,
Deformed; that I am thus a ravening devouring lust continually
Craving & devouring ; but my Eyes are always upon thee Oh lovely
Delusion, & I cannot crave for any thing but thee : not so
The Spectres of the Dead, for I am as the Spectre of the Living!'

also *The Four Zoas*, Night vii, ll. 339–345 :—

'Thou art united with thy Spectre, consummating by pains & labours
That coy mortal body, & by Self-annihilation back returning
To Life Eternal ; To be assur'd I am thy real self . . .
Thou didst subdue me in old times by thy Immortal Strength,
When I was a ravening, hungering, & thirsting, cruel lust of murder. . . .

13

Let us agree to give up Love,   49
And root up the infernal grove ;
Then shall we return & see
The worlds of happy Eternity.

14

& Throughout all Eternity   53
I forgive you, you forgive me.
As our dear Redeemer said :
' This the Wine, & this the Bread.'

But if thou dost refuse, Another body will be prepared
For me, & thou annihilate evaporate & be no more.'

See also *Jerusalem*, f. 92, ll. 8–12.   53 & Throughout] Through-out DGR, WMR. Cp. *Jerusalem*, f. 98, l. 23, 'In Forgiveness of Sins which is Self Annihilation.'   55 our dear Redeemer said] I, dear Redeemer, said EY.

[Appendix : Unplaced Stanzas]

*1

O'er my sins thou sit & moan :   *1
Hast thou no sins of thy own ?
O'er my sins thou sit & weep,
And lull thy own sins fast asleep.

See note above. DGR, followed by WMR and others, use the first couplet of *3 as ll. 1, 2 of their fourth stanza, the last couplet of *3, slightly altered as ll. 3, 4 of their fifth stanza ; and *1 and *2 as their seventh and ninth stanzas. Swinb. and EY omit, WBY quotes in Notes.

*1, *2 Cp. *Jerusalem*, f. 9, ll. 14, 15 :—

' Every Emanative joy forbidden as a Crime
And the Emanations buried alive in the earth with pomp of religion.'

*1 my] thy MS. Book 1*st rdg. del.* ; *my* WMR.   thou] I *ibid.*   thou sit] thou dost sit DGR, WMR, WBY.   *2 Hast thou] Have I MS. Book 1*st rdg. del.*   thy] my *ibid.* ; thine DGR, WMR, WBY.   *3 my] thy *ibid.* ; *my* WMR.   thou] I MS. Book 1*st rdg. del.*   thou sit] thou dost sit DGR, WMR, WBY.   *4 thy] my MS. Book 1*st rdg. del.* ; thine DGR, WMR.

*2

What Transgressions I commit   *5
Are for thy Transgressions fit.
They thy Harlots, thou their slave;
And my bed becomes their Grave.

*3

Poor, pale, pitiable form   *9
That I follow in a storm;
Iron tears & groans of lead
Bind around my aching head.

*5-*8 This stanza was written after the following one.   *6 Trans-
gressions] transgression WBY.   *8 my] thy WBY   *9 Cp. *Jerusalem,*
f. 67, ll. 43, 44 :—

'O thou poor Human Form! said she, O thou poor child of woe!
Why wilt thou wander away from Tirzah, why compel me to bind thee?'

*12 Followed in the MS. Book by the partly illegible but unerased
stanza :—

'And let [*us go*] to the . . . . . [? day]
With many wiles . . . .
Woman that does not love your [? wiles]
Will never [? win back] your smiles.'

XXXViii

When a Man has Married a Wife, he finds out whether
Her knees & elbows are only glued together.

MS. Book, p. 4.   Below a graceful little sketch of man in bed, and
a young woman sitting on the edge of it in a very elementary stage of
dressing. EY's reproduction of this drawing (vol. iii, without pagination)
conveys the idea that it is found on the same page as 'Daphne,' which is
not the case. EY (i. 208) print as a quatrain :—

'When a man marries a wife,
He finds out whether
Her elbows and knees are only
Glued together.'

The lines are certainly so divided in the MS., but the absence of initials in
the second and fourth, as well as the indentation, prove that Blake meant
them to form a couplet. In altering 'has Married' to 'marries,' and calling
the piece 'droll and *risqué*,' EY miss the point of the allusion to 'knees and
elbows,' which the colloquial 'elbow-grease' might have suggested.

xxxix

When Klopstock England defied,   1
Uprose William Blake in his pride;
For old Nobodaddy aloft
****** & Belch'd & cough'd;
Then swore a great oath that made heaven quake,   5
And called aloud to English Blake.
Blake was giving his body ease,
At Lambeth beneath the poplar trees.
From his seat then started he   9
And turned him round three times three.
The Moon at that sight [blushed scarlet red,]
The stars threw down their [cups and fled,
And all the devils that were in hell,   13
Answerèd with a ninefold yell.]
Klopstock felt the intripled turn,
And all his bowels began to churn,

MS. Book, p. 5.   Although written from the unreversed end this piece
probably belongs to the same date as those in the earlier section of the
MS. Book.   Swinb., pp. 31, 32, refers the origin of this Rabelaisian jeu
d'esprit to the passages from Klopstock rendered into English by Hayley
for Blake's benefit during the latter's stay at Felpham in 1803 (Hayley's
Diary, Mar. 26, 29); but the reference to Lambeth, and the repetition
of l. 4 in 'Fayette,' point rather to its having been written about 1793. Blake
may of course have been familiar with Collyer's translation of the *Messias*,
which had reached a second edition in 1769.   This piece is very faintly
written in pencil and a considerable portion of it is no longer legible.
I supply in square brackets from Swinb. and EY a few words which the
present owner of the MS. Book is unable to decipher.

   3 aloft] EY *omit*.   4 ****** . . . cough'd] EY *omit*. The same line
occurs in the first version of 'Fayette' (xxxvi. A).   5 made] would make
EY.   7, 8 Blake . . trees]

              ' Blake was away. His body was free
              At Lambeth beneath the poplar tree.'

EY.   9 From . . . he] From Lambeth then shouted he EY.   10
turned him round] EY *omit*.   11 sight] EY *omit*.   blushed . . . red]
Supplied from Swinb.   scarlet] quite EY.   12–14 cups . . . yell] *Supplied
from* Swinb.   12 cups] spears EY.   13, 14 And . . . yell] EY *omit*.
15 Klopstock] Astonished EY.   intripled] ninefold MS. Book 1*st rdg.
del*.   16 churn] burn MS. Book 1*st rdg. del*.

And his bowels turned round three times three,   17
And locked in his soul with a ninefold key ;
That from his body it ne'er could be . . . .
Till to the last [judgment] it was . . . .
Then again old Nobodaddy swore   21
He ne'er [had seen] such a thing before,
Since Noah was shut in the ark,
Since Eve first chose her hellfire spark,
Since 'twas the [fashion] to [go naked.   25
Since] the old Anything [was created,]
And so feeling, he beg'd me to turn again
And . . . poor Klopstock never . . . pain
Then   29
And . . . .
If Blake would do this when he **** ** **** *****
What might he not do if he sat down to write ?

17 And . . . round] They turned around MS. Book 1*st rdg. del.* ; EY *omit*
And.   19 ne'er] never EY.   20 to] EY *omit*   judgment]
Supplied from EY   it] EY *omit*.   22 ne'er] never Swinb., EY :
had seen] *supplied from* Swinb.   24 chose] EY *omit* : hellfire]
hell-found EY.   25 fashion : go naked] *Supplied from* Swinb., EY.
26 Since] *Supplied from* Swinb.   Anything] EY *omit*   was created]
Supplied from Swinb.   29, 30] Of these lines, which apparently were
legible when he had the MS. Book before him, Swinburne writes : 'Only
in choice Attic or in archaic French could the rest be endured by modern
eyes ; but Panurge could hardly have improved on the manner of retribution
devised for flaccid fluency and devout sentiment always running at the
mouth.'   31, 32 *A marginal addition.*

xl

On the Virginity of the Virgin Mary & Johanna Southcott

Whate'er is done to her she cannot know,
And if you'll ask her she will swear it so.
Whether tis good or evil none's to blame :
No one can take the pride, no one the shame.

MS. Book, p. 6, the title added later.   Only printed by EY i. 210.
2 you'll] you EY.   swear it] tell you MS. Book 1*st rdg. del.*   4 No one]
And none EY.

xli

Mock on, Mock on, Voltaire, Rousseau;   1
Mock on, Mock on; 'tis all in vain!
You throw the sand against the wind,
And the wind blows it back again.

And every sand becomes a Gem   5
Reflected in the beams divine;
Blown back they blind the mocking eye,
But still in Israel's paths they shine.

The Atoms of Democritus   9
And Newton's Particles of light
Are sands upon the Red sea shore,
Where Israel's tents do shine so bright.

MS. Book, p. 7. Without title. Printed by DGR and later editors with title 'Scoffers.' As one of the very few pieces which had hitherto, by some oversight, escaped at the hands of Blake's editors, this beautiful little poem might well have been spared Mr. W. B. Yeats' textual alterations.

     3 sand] dust WBY.   5 sand] stone WBY.

xlii

Prefatory Note

The first draft of this piece, written without title on p. 12 of the MS. Book, consists of fourteen stanzas which Blake later split up into two separate poems, 'To the Deists' in *Jerusalem*, and 'The Grey Monk' in the Pickering MS. This page therefore cannot be dated later than April, 1803. In the first column are found stanzas 1–9 and the first two lines of stanza 10, which is continued at the head of the second column. A line of separation drawn beneath this stanza, before ll. 41–56 were added, shows that Blake's first intention was to end with the lines:—

     ' The Hermit's prayer & the widow's tear
     Alone can free the world from fear.'

Below stanza 14 comes the beautiful lyric ' Morning ' (see xliii), which, it will be seen, is a different treatment of the same idea—

     ' The war of swords & spears
     Melted by dewy tears.'

being obviously suggested by ll. 51, 52 of this poem :—

     ' The tear shall melt the sword of steel
     And every wound it has made shall heal.'

The reading 'mercy,' which has hitherto been invariably misprinted 'morning' in the line 'Sweet Mercy leads me on,' gains additional force in this connexion, and we find Blake still dwelling on the same thought in the couplet which immediately follows :—

> 'Terror in the house does roar
> But Pity stands before the door.'

It was probably when about to engrave *Jerusalem* that Blake returned to this poem. His first change was to reduce its length to seven stanzas by drawing a separation line between stanzas 4 and 5, and marking stanzas 12, 13, and 14 to come in after stanza 4. Then below the couplet on Terror and Pity, he wrote the revised version of stanza 12 :—

> 'When Satan first the black bow bent
> And the Moral Law from the Gospel rent
> He forg'd the Law into a Sword
> And spill'd the blood of Mercy's Lord.'

At the same time he added in the margin the stanza :—

> 'Titus! Constantine! Charlemaine!
> O Voltaire! Rousseau! Gibbon! vain
> Your Grecian mocks [*mocks & iron* del.] & Roman sword
> Against this image of his Lord—'

linked to stanza 14 by the catchword 'A tear is &c.,' and between the columns and in the right-hand margin he made two attempts to rewrite stanza 2 which were not adopted in either of the final versions. Lastly he indicated clearly the order of the seven stanzas to be used in *Jerusalem* by marking the first four stanzas 1-4, and prefixing the numbers 5-7 to 'When Satan first the black bow bent,' 'Titus Constantine, Charlemaine,' and 'For a tear is an intellectual thing.' This, except for a few unimportant verbal changes, gives us the poem entitled 'To the Deists' engraved at the foot of f. 52 of *Jerusalem*. See 'Poems from the Prophetic Books.'

Of the stanzas thus rejected Blake made a separate poem which he transcribed into the Pickering MS., with the title 'The Grey Monk.' This poem begins with the original fifth stanza ; the line 'I see, I see, the Mother said' being changed to 'I die, I die, the Mother said.' The remaining stanzas (6-11) are arranged in the order of the MS. Book, with the interpolation of stanza 4 between 5 and 6, and stanza 14 between 10 and 11. These two stanzas are common to both versions.

In the footnotes to the present poem I give such variant readings only as are derived from the MS. Book, or from the text of Messrs. Ellis and Yeats, who, in their preface to Chapter III of *Jerusalem* (ii. 220-26), print the rejected readings and omitted stanzas. Blake's later text of 'To the Deists' and 'The Grey Monk' with editors' emendations will be found among poems from *Jerusalem* and 'The Pickering MS.'

I saw a Monk of Charlemaine   1
Arise, before my sight :
I talk'd to the Grey Monk where he stood
In beams of infernal light.

3 to] with EY   where] as EY.

Gibbon arose with a lash of steel,   5
And Voltaire with a wracking wheel :
The schools, in Clouds of learning roll'd,
Arose with War in iron & gold.

'Thou lazy Monk,' they said afar,   9
'In vain condemning Glorious War,
And in thy Cell thou shall ever dwell.
Rise, War, & bind him in his Cell!'

The blood red ran from the Grey Monk's side,   13
His hands & feet were wounded wide,
His body bent, his arms & knees
Like to the roots of ancient trees.

'I see, I see,' the Mother said,   17
'My Children will die for lack of bread.
What more has the merciless tyrant said ?'
The Monk sat down on her stony bed.

5–8 Gibbon . . . gold] Variants of this stanza are :—
(*a*) *Sideways, middle column, top of page :*

> 'Gibbon plied his lash of steel,
> Voltaire turned his wracking wheel,
> Charlemaine & his barons bold
> Stood by, and mocked in iron & gold.'

(*b*) *Sideways, in right-hand margin, at top of page :*

> 'The Wheel of Voltaire whirl'd on high,
> Gibbon aloud his lash does ply,
> Charlemaine & his Clouds of War [*& his barons bold*, 1st rdg. del.]
> Must[er around] the Polar Star.'

In printing the above, as ' Readings rejected by Blake,' EY in (*a*) 2 read 'And Voltaire ' for ' Voltaire,' (*a*) 3 ' warriors' for ' barons,' (*b*) 4 'Must now arouse the polar bear' for 'Muster around the Polar Star.' These words are partially hidden by the binding.   5 arose] armed EY.   6 wracking] racking EY.   7 The . . . roll'd] Charlemagne and his warriors bold EY. 9, 10 Thou . . . War]

> ' Seditious Monk said Charlemaine
> The Glory of War thou condemn'st in vain.'

MS. Book *1st rdg. del.*, EY reading in last line :—

> 'The glory of war thou cursedst in vain.'

18 will] shall EY.   20 sat down] sat him down EY.

His Eye was dry, no tear could flow,   21
A hollow groan first spoke his woe :
He trembled & shuddered upon the bed ;
At length with a feeble cry he said :—

'When God commanded this hand to write   25
In the studious hours of deep midnight,
He told me that all I wrote should prove
The bane of all that on Earth I love.

'My brother starved between two walls ;   29
Thy children's cry my soul appalls :
I mock'd at the wrack and griding chain ;
My bent body mocks at their torturing pain.

'Thy father drew his sword in the North ;   33
With his thousands strong he is [marchèd] forth ;
Thy brother has armed himself in steel
To revenge the wrongs thy children feel.

'But vain the sword & vain the bow,   37
They never can work war's overthrow ;
The Hermit's prayer & the widow's tear
Alone can free the world from fear.

'The hand of vengeance sought the bed   41
To which the purple tyrant fled ;
The iron hand crushed the tyrant's head,
And became a tyrant in his stead.

'Untill the Tyrant himself relent,   45
The Tyrant who first the black bow bent,
Slaughter shall heap the bloody plain :
Resistance & War is the Tyrant's gain.

21 could] would EY.   22 first spoke] bespoke EY.   22, 23 woe He] Between these is an illegible line erased.   24 At . . . said] EY *omit.* 26 studious] shadowy EY.   31 I mock'd . . . chain] I mock at the rack and the grinding pain EY.   34 marchèd] Deleted in MS. but no word substituted, EY.   36 revenge] avenge EY.   41 sought] found EY. 44 And usurped the tyrant's throne & bed MS. Book 1*st rdg. del.*   45-48 Untill . . . gain] This stanza was rewritten later. See Pref. Note.

'But the Tear of Love—& forgiveness sweet,   49
And submission to death beneath his feet—
The tear shall melt the sword of steel,
And every wound it has made shall heal.

'For the tear is an intellectual thing,   53
And a sigh is the sword of an Angel King,
And the bitter groan of the Martyr's woe
Is an arrow from the Almightie's bow.'

49-52 But . . . heal] Omitted in both the *Jerusalem* and the Pickering
MS. versions.   55 of the Martyr's] for another's MS. Book 1st *rdg.*
del.; of a martyr's EY.

xliii

Morning

To find the Western path,   1
Right thro' the Gates of Wrath
I urge my way;
Sweet Mercy leads me on   4
With soft repentant moan:
I see the break of day.

The war of swords & spears,
Melted by dewy tears,   8
Exhales on high;
The Sun is freed from fears,
And with soft grateful tears
Ascends the sky.   12

MS. Book, p. 12.   Title added later.   Printed by DGR and all later
editors with the title 'Daybreak.'

4-6 Sweet . . . day] All edd. read :—
     'Sweet morning leads me on ;
     With soft repentant moan
     I see the break of day.'

The correction of 'morning' to 'Mercy' conveys a meaning to the poem
entirely lacking in the received text. The marks of an erasure in D. G.
Rossetti's transcript of 'all that is of any value' in the MS. Book show that
he had at first written some other word—probably the right one—before
'morning.' The word 'Morning' in the title may have misled him into
supposing that the same word was repeated in l. 4 of the song, 'Morning'
and 'Mercy' being somewhat alike in Blake's handwriting.

xliv

Terror in the house does roar ;
But Pity stands before the door.

MS. Book, p. 12.   See Prefatory Note to xlii.   Here printed for the first time.

xlv

The Birds

He. Where thou dwellest, in what Grove,   1
Tell me, Fair one, tell me love ;
Where thou thy charming Nest dost build,
O thou pride of every field !

She. Yonder stands a lonely tree,   5
There I live and mourn for thee ;
Morning drinks my silent tear,
And evening winds my sorrow bear.

He. O thou summer's harmony,   9
I have liv'd and mourn'd for thee ;
Each day I mourn along the wood,
And night hath heard my sorrows loud.

She. Dost thou truly long for me ?   13
And am I thus sweet to thee ?
Sorrow now is at an end,
O my lover and my Friend !

He. Come on wings of joy we'll fly   17
To where my bower hangs on high ;
Come, and make thy calm retreat
Among green leaves and blossoms sweet.

MS. Book, p. 14.
1, 5, *sqq.* *He . . . She*] No italics in MS.   3 dost] doth EY.   11
mourn] moan EY, WBY.   18 hangs] is hung *all edd.*

xlvi

No real Style of Colouring ever appears,
But advertizing in the News Papers.
Look there—you'll see Sr Joshua's Colouring:
Look at his Pictures—All has taken Wing!

MS. Book, p. 21. Gil. i. 266. Printed by WMR among 'Epigrams and Satirical Pieces on Art and Artists' (xiv) with title 'Colour,' and by EY among 'Couplets and Fragments' (xvi) without title. The epigrams on Art which begin on this page would appear to be an overflow from those jotted down in the margins of Blake's copy of Reynolds' *Discourses.*

1 ever] now Gil., EY.   2 But ... Papers] Save thro' advertisements in the newspapers Gil., cp. Blake's *Advertisement* (MS. Book, p. 56): 'Advertisements in newspapers are no proof of popular approbation, but often the contrary.'   3 there] here EY.   4 All has taken wing] 'tis quite another thing MS. Book 1st *rdg. del.*; cp. 'Epigrams from Reynolds' Discourses,' iv :—

'When Sir Joshua Reynolds died
All Nature was degraded,
The King dropped a Tear into the Queen's Ear,
And all his Pictures Faded.'

xlvii

You don't believe—I won't attempt to make ye: 1
You are asleep—I won't attempt to wake ye.
Sleep on! Sleep on! while in your pleasant dreams
Of Reason you may drink of Life's clear streams.
Reason and Newton, they are quite two things;   5
For so the Swallow & the Sparrow sings.

MS. Book, p. 21, the two stanzas separated by a sketch. Printed among 'Couplets and Fragments' (xv) by WMR as a single, stanza with title 'Reason,' and by EY (xvii) without title.

1 You ... ye] You don't believe I would attempt to make you WMR. won't] would MS. Book 1st *rdg. del.*   2 ye] you WMR.

Reason says 'Miracle': Newton says 'Doubt.'
Aye! that's the way to make all Nature out.
'Doubt, Doubt, & don't believe without experiment': 9
That is the very thing that Jesus meant,
When he said 'Only Believe! Believe & try!
Try, Try, & never mind the Reason why!'

7–12 No quotation marks in MS. WMR omits to ll. 9 and 12. EY place around ll. 7–12 ('Doubt ... why') with enclosed single quotation marks to ll. 11, 12 ('Only ... why'). Cf. *Jerusalem*, f. 54, ll. 15–24 :—

'But the Spectre, like a hoar frost & a Mildew, rose over Albion,
Saying 'I am God, O Sons of Men! I am your Rational Power.
Am I not Bacon & Newton & Locke, who teach Humility to Man,
Who teach Doubt & Experiment, & my two Wings Voltaire Rousseau?
Where is that Friend of Sinners, that Rebel against my Laws,
Who teaches Belief to the Nations & an unknown Eternal life?
Come hither into the Desart & turn these stones to bread.
Vain Foolish Man, wilt thou believe without Experiment
And build a World of Phantasy upon my Great Abyss,
A World of Shapes, in craving lust & devouring appetite?'

xlviii

And in melodious accents I
Will sit me down, & cry 'I! I!'

MS. Book, p. 21. These lines occur in Blake's *Advertisement*, following the prose passage: ['Imagination is my World. This world of dross is beneath my notice, and beneath the notice of the Public *del*.] I demand therefore of the amateurs of art the encouragement which is my due. If they continue to refuse, theirs is the loss, not mine, and theirs is the contempt of posterity. I have enough in the approbation of fellow labourers. This is my glory, and my exceeding great reward. I go on, and nothing can hinder my course.'

xlix

And his legs carried it like a long fork,   1
Reached all the way from Chichester to York,
From York all across Scotland to the Sea ;
This was a Man of Men, as seems to me.

MS. Book, p. 22. ll. 1–14, 31–51 were first written, ll. 15–30 being added in the margin, and marked for insertion after l. 14. This fragment, of which the beginning is missing, was probably composed soon after Sept. 17, 1809,

Not only in his Mouth his own Soul lay,   5
But my soul also would he bear away.
Like as a Pedlar bears his weary Pack,
So Stewhard's Soul he buckled to his back.
But once, alas! committing a Mistake,   9
He bore the wretched Soul of William Blake
That he might turn it into Eggs of Gold ;
But neither back nor mouth those eggs could hold.
His under jaw drop'd as those Eggs he laid,   13
And Stewhard's Eggs are addled and decay'd.
The Examiner, whose very name is Hunt,
Call'd Death a Madman, trembling for the affront ;
Like trembling Hare sits on his weakly paper   17
On which he used to dance & sport & caper.
Yorkshire Jack Hemp & Quibble, blushing daw,
Clap'd Death into the corner of their jaw,
And Felpham Billy rode out every morn,   21
Horseback with Death, over the fields of corn ;
Who with iron hand cuff'd, in the afternoon,
The Ears of Billy's Lawyer & Dragoon.
And Cur my lawyer, and Dady, Jack Hemp's parson, 25
Both went to Law with Death to keep our Ears on.

when the article on 'Mr. Blake's Exhibition' appeared in Leigh Hunt's
Examiner (no. 90) and may have been part of the poem which Blake alludes
to in his *Advertisement*. See note to lxxviii. Chichester was the scene
of Blake's trial for high treason, at the instance of the 'Dragoon' (see Gilchrist, i, chap. xix) ; Yorkshire was the birthplace of Cromek, here called
'Screwmuch,' and Scotland refers to the latter's visit to that country in
search of material for his *Reliques of Burns* (1808). 'Death' is a nickname
for Blake, possibly because of his association with Blair's *Grave*, 'Yorkshire
Jack Hemp,' for Flaxman ; 'Felpham Billy,' for Hayley ; and 'Dady, Jack
Hemp's parson,' for Dr. Malkin, of the *Father's Memoirs*. 'Stewhard,' the
speaker, is of course Stothard. EY mistakenly suppose that Boydel and
Bowyer of the following piece may be the true names of the lawyers 'Cur'
and 'Quibble'; but see footnote. Only printed by EY in their 'Memoir'
(i, 78–79).

    1 carried] covered EY.   4 This] That EY.   8 So Stewhard's
Soul] He would bear my soul MS. Book 1*st rdg. del.*, EY.   10 of] and
EY.   14 Stewhard's] all my MS. Book 1*st rdg. del.*, EY.   16 trembling
. . . affront] Deadly the affront MS. Book 1*st rdg. del.*   17 weakly]
weekly EY, ignoring the play upon words.   18 sport] shout EY.
19 Yorkshire] And Yorkshire MS. Book 1*st rdg. del.*, EY.   daw] saw EY.
20 their] his EY.

For how to starve Death we had laid a plot
Against his Price—but Death was in the Pot.
He made them pay his Price, alackaday! 29
He knew both Law and Gospel better than they.
O that I ne'er had seen that William Blake,
Or could from Death Assassinette wake!
We thought—Alas, that such a thought could be!— 33
That Blake would Etch for him and draw for me.
For 'twas a kind of Bargain Screwmuch made
That Blake's designs should be by us display'd,
Because he makes designs so very cheap. 37
Then Screwmuch at Blake's soul took a long leap.
'Twas not a Mouse. 'Twas death in a disguise.
And I, alas! live to weep out my Eyes.
And Death sits laughing on their Monuments 41
On which he 's written ' Received the Contents.'
But I have writ—so sorrowful my thought is—
His epitaph ; for my tears are aquafortis.
' Come, Artists, knock your head against this stone, 45
For sorrow that our friend Bob Screwmuch 's gone.'
And now the Muses upon me smile and laugh
I'll also write my own dear epitaph,
And I'll be buried near a dyke 49
That my friends may weep as much as they like:
' Here lies Stewhard the Friend of all &c.'

27 how] now EY. 31 ne'er] never EY. that] EY *omit*. 36 designs]
design EY. 43-4 But . . . aquafortis] But I have writ with tears, as aquafortis, This Epitaph—so sorrowful my thought is MS. Book 1*st rdg. del.*
47 upon] in EY. 51 Stewhard] Stothard EY, who finish the couplet :—

   ' . . . the Friend of all Mankind
   Who has not left one enemy behind,'

explaining that ' a later page of the notebook completes the epitaph, changing
the name to John Trot.' Here again, however, they misinterpret the force
of Blake's ' &c.' which is always a reference to a passage already written.
See lxxxviii.

l

Was I angry with Hayley who us'd me so ill, 1
Or can I be angry with Felpham's old Mill?
Or angry with Flaxman, or Cromek, or Stothard,
Or poor Schiavonetti, whom they to death bother'd?
Or angry with Macklin, or Boydel, or Bowyer, 5
Because they did not say ' O what a beau ye are'?
At a Friend's Errors anger shew,
Mirth at the Errors of a Foe.

MS. Book, p. 23. Only printed by EY (i. 81), except last couplet, which
WMR and WBY print as beginning of li. As the allusion to Schiavonetti's
death shows, written after June 1810.

3 Or . . . Stothard] Or angry with Boydell, or Bowyer or Bu . . .
MS. Book 1*st rdg. del.* 5 Macklin] Malchin EY, confusing Macklin
for whom Blake engraved Stothard's ' Fall of Rosamund' (1783) with
Dr. Malkin (*Father's Memoirs of His Child*, 1806) : Boydel] *Read* 'Boydell,' for whom Blake engraved Hogarth's Scene from the *Beggar's Opera*
(1788) : Bowyer] publisher of the sumptuous illustrated edition of
Hume's *History* (1806).

li

Anger & Wrath my bosom rends: 1
I thought them the Errors of friends.
But all my limbs with warmth glow:
I find them the Errors of the foe.

MS. Book, p. 23. Written in margin of preceding piece. Printed by
WMR and WBY (' Coup. and Frag.' xvi) prefixed by l. ll. 7, 8 ; by EY
(' Coup. and Frag.' xiii) as above. WMR with title ' Friends and Foes.'
3 warmth glow] warmth do glow EY.

lii

The Sussex Men are Noted Fools,
And weak is their brain pan—
I wonder if H—— the painter
Is not a Sussex Man.

MS. Book, p. 24. Written about 1809, the date of the publication of
Hayley's *Life of Romney*, to which William Haines and Blake both contributed engravings. Cp. Gilchrist, i. 178. Only ptd. by EY i. 212.
2 is] in EY.

liii

'Madman,' I have been call'd : 'Fool,' they call thee.
I wonder which they Envy—Thee or Me?

MS. Book, p. 25.   Probably addressed to Flaxman.   Only printed by EY
i. 213.

liv

To H——

You think Fuseli is not a Great Painter.   I'm glad.
This is one of the best compliments he ever had.

MS. Book, p. 25.   Gil. i. 181, EY i. 213.   Gil. (wrongly) expands title
'To Hayley,' while EY think this and the preceding epigram are addressed
to Haines.   Both are, without doubt, 'To H[unt].'   Cp. the latter's references
to Fuseli and Blake, *Examiner*, no. 75, June 4, 1809, and no. 90, Sept. 17,
1809, also Blake's *Advertisement* (MS. Book, p. 53) : 'Many people are so
foolish to think they can wound Mr. Fuseli over my shoulder.   They will
find themselves mistaken : they could not wound even Mr. Barry so.'
1 Fuseli is] Fuseli 's EY.

lv

To F——

I mock thee not, though I by thee am Mockèd :
Thou call'st me Madman, but I call thee Blockhead.

MS. Book, p. 26.   DGR and WMR ('Coupl. and Frag.' viii, 'Epigrams,'
xvii) with title 'To the Same' [i.e. Flaxman], EY ('Coupl. and Frag.' xiv).
WBY omits.   Cf. lxxix.

lvi

Can there be anything more mean,   1
More Malice in disguise,
Than Praise a Man for doing what
That Man does most despise?   4
Reynolds lectures exactly so
When he praises Michael Angelo.

MS. Book, p. 26.   Cp. prefatory note to 'Epigrams from Blake's copy of
Sir Joshua Reynolds' *Discourses*' (1798).   Only ptd. by EY i. 213.
3 what] that MS. Book *1st rdg. del.*   4 That man] Which he *ibid.*
5 Reynolds . . . so] This Reynolds' lectures plainly shew *ibid.*

lvii

S—— in Childhood, on the nursery floor,
Was extreme Old and most extremely poor:
He has grown old & rich & what he will:
He is extreme old & extreme poor still.

MS. Book, p. 27.   EY i. 213, WBY ('Coupl. and Frag.' 19).
   1 S——] Stothard WBY.   on] upon EY.   4 & extreme] and is extreme WBY.   Cp. 'Epigrams from Reynolds' *Discourses*' (v).

lviii

To Nancy F——

How can I help thy Husband's copying Me?
Should that make difference 'twixt me and thee?

MS. Book, p. 27.   Only in EY i. 213.   Cp. *Advertisement* (MS. Book, p. 53): 'Flaxman cannot deny that one of the very first monuments he did I gratuitously designed for him, and at the same time he was blasting my character to Macklin my employer, as Macklin told me at the time. How much of his Homer and Dante he will allow to be mine I do not know, as he went far enough off to publish them, even to Italy, but the public will know.'

lix

Of H——'s birth this was the happy lot:
His Mother on his Father him begot.

MS. Book, p. 27.   Swinb. p. 38, WMR ('Coupl.' xxi. 4), EY i. 213, WBY ('Coupl.' 20).

   1 H——'s] Hayley's Swinb., WMR, WBY.   this] there EY.   2 Mother on his Father] mother or his father EY.

lx

Sir Joshua praises Michael Angelo.   1
'Tis Christian mildness when Knaves praise a foe;
But 'twould be Madness, all the world would say,
Should Michael Angelo praise Sir Joshua—
Christ us'd the Pharisees in a rougher way.   5

MS. Book, p. 28.   DGR (' Epig.' 6), WMR (' Epig.' xiii), *others omit.*   Cp.
Blake's MS. note in Reynolds' *Discourses*, p. [ii] : ' I consider Reynolds'
Discourses to the Royal Academy as the Simulations of the Hypocrite who
Smiles particularly where he means to Betray.   His Praise of Rafael is like
the Hysteric Smile of Revenge.   His Softness & Candour, the hidden trap,
& the poisoned feast.   He praises Michael Angelo for Qualities which
Michael Angelo abhorr'd : & He blames Rafael for the only Qualities which
Rafael Valued.   Whether Reynolds knew what he was doing, is nothing to
me : the Mischief is just the Same whether a Man does it Ignorantly or
Knowingly.   I always consider'd True Art & True Artists to be particularly
Insulted & Degraded by the Reputation of these Discourses.   As much as
they were Degraded by the Reputation of Reynolds' Paintings, & that
Such Artists as Reynolds are at all times Hired by the Satans for the Depres-
sion of Art.'
   2 'Tis . . . foe] And counts it outrage thus to praise his foe MS. Book *1st
rdg. del.*   mildness] meekness *all edd.*   when Knaves] thus to DGR, WMR.
3 all . . . would] that we all must MS. Book *1st rdg. del.*   5 Christ . . .
way] This line added later.

lxi

He's a Blockhead who wants a proof of what he can't
      Perceive;
And he's a fool who tries to make such a Blockhead
      believe.

MS. Book, p. 28.   DGR (' Coupl.' viii), WMR, EY (' Coupl.' x), WBY
(' Coupl.' 11).

lxii

Cr—— loves artists as he loves his Meat :
He loves the Art; but 'tis the art to cheat.

MS. Book, p. 29.   Gil. i. 208.   EY i. 214 print first line only.
            1 Cr——] Cromek Gil.   Meat] meal EY.

lxiii

A Petty Sneaking Knave I knew—
O! Mr. Cr——, how do ye do?

MS. Book, p. 29. Gil. i. 208, WMR ('Coupl.' xxII) headed 'Cromek.'
2 Cr——] Cromek Gil., WMR.   ye] you Gil.

lxiv

Sir Joshua praisèd Rubens with a smile,   1
By calling his the ornamental style ;
And yet his praise of Flaxman was the smartest,
When he called him the Ornamental Artist.
But sure such ornaments we well may spare   5
As crooked limbs and louzy heads of hair.

MS. Book, p. 29. Only in EY i. 214.
1 praisèd] praises EY.   6 As . . . hair] Like a filthy infectious head
of hair MS. Book 1*st rdg. del.*; A crooked stick & a louzy head of hair, *ibid.
2nd rdg. del.*

lxv

He is a Cock would . . . .
And would be a Cock if he could . . . .

MS. Book, p. 29. Only in EY i. 214.
1 He is] He's EY.

lxvi

He has observ'd the Golden Rule,
Till he's become the Golden Fool.

MS. Book, p. 30. Cp. lxvii. Only in EY i. 214.
2 he's] he has EY.

lxvii

To S——d

You all your Youth observ'd the Golden Rule,   1
Till you're at last become the golden fool :
I sport with Fortune, Merry, Blithe and Gay,
Like to the Lion sporting with his Prey.
Take you the hide & horns which you may wear,   5
Mine is the flesh—the bones may be your share.

MS. Book, p. 30.   Only in EY (i. 214) 'addressed to I——d (Who was
I —— d ?).'   A similar misreading of Blake's capital S for I occurs in their text
of lxxvi.   This and the preceding epigram refer of course to Stothard.   In its
original form this epigram was written in the third person, 'he' for 'you,'
'his' for 'your,' and 'He has' for 'Take you' in l. 5.
          1 Youth] life EY.   5 Take you] You have EY.

lxviii

Mr Stothard to Mr Cromek

For Fortune's favours you your riches bring,
But Fortune says she gave you no such thing.
Why should you be ungrateful to your friends,
Sneaking, & backbiting, & Odds-&-Ends ?

MS. Book, p. 31.   Swinb. p. 53, EY i. 214.
          1 favours] favour Swinb.   3 be ungrateful] prove ungrateful Swinb.;
be unfaithful EY.

lxix

Mr Cromek to Mr Stothard

Fortune favours the Brave, old proverbs say ;
But not with Money ; that is not the way.
Turn back, turn back ; you travel all in vain ;
Turn through the iron gate down sneaking lane.

MS. Book, p. 31.   Swinb. p. 53, EY i. 215, WBY ('Coupl.' 6) without
title.
          4 sneaking lane] Sneaking Lane Swinb.

lxx

I am no Homer's Hero you all know ;　　　　　　1
I profess not Generosity to a Foe.
My Generosity is to my Friends,
That for their Friendship I may make amends.
The Generous to Enemies promotes their Ends,　　5
And becomes the Enemy & Betrayer of his Friends.

MS. Book, p. 31.　Only in EY i. 215.
6 And ... Friends] Cp. ' Everlasting Gospel,' γ², l. 25 : ' He who loves his enemies betrays his friends.'

lxxi

The Angel that presided o'er my birth
Said 'Little creature, form'd of Joy and Mirth,
Go, love without the help of anything on Earth.'

MS. Book, p. 32.　Gil. i. 311, WMR (' Coupl.' xiv), EY i. 215, WBY (' Coupl.' 15).
1 that] who Gil.　　o'er] at Gil., WBY.　　2 form'd ... Mirth] thou art form'd for mirth MS. Book 1st rdg. del.　of] for EY.　3 love] live WMR.

lxxii

Florentine Ingratitude

Sir Joshua sent his own Portrait to　　　　　　1
The birth Place of Michael Angelo,
And in the hand of the simpering fool
He put a dirty paper scroll,
And on the paper, to be polite,　　　　　　　5
Did 'Sketches by Michael Angelo' write.

MS. Book, p. 32.　Title an addition.　Only in EY i. 215.　This and the other epigrams on Sir Joshua Reynolds were probably written about the same time as the marginal notes in his copy of Sir Joshua's Discourses, now in the Brit. Mus.　In 1776 Reynolds was elected a member of the Florentine Academy, and in accordance with their rule, sent his portrait painted by himself.

The Florentines said ''Tis a Dutch-English bore,
Michael Angelo's Name writ on Rembrandt's door.'
The Florentines call it an English fetch,   9
For Michael Angelo never did sketch—
Every line of his has Meaning,
And needs neither Suckling nor Weaning.
'Tis the trading English-Venetian cant   13
To speak Michael Angelo, and act Rembrandt,
It will set his Dutch friends all in a roar
To write 'Mich. Ang.' on Rembrandt's door ;
But you must not bring in your hand a Lie   17
If you mean that the Florentines should buy.
Ghiotto's Circle or Apelles' Line
Were not the Work of Sketchers drunk with Wine ;
Nor of the City Clock's running . . . fashion ;   21
Nor of Sir Isaac Newton's calculation.

7, 8 The . . . door] EY incorrectly call this a 'rejected' couplet.   10 For
Michael] EY *omit* For.   13, 14 Tis . . . Rembrandt] '*Rejected*' EY,
who insert here, after l. 14, an incorrect version of the first reading of
ll. 19-22.   18 mean that] EY *omit* that.   If . . . buy] Following this
are the lines :—

> 'These verses were written by a very envious man,
>   Who whatever likeness he may have to Michael Angelo
>   Never can have any to Sir Jehoshuan.'

19-22 Ghiotto's . . . calculation] These lines written later at foot of page.
Another reading was :—

> 'Nor of the City Clock's Idle Facilities
>   Which sprang from Sir Isaac Newton's great Abilities.'

EY omit ll. 19-22, and print this rejected couplet after l. 14, reading
'futilities' for 'facilities' and 'sprang of' for 'sprang from.'

lxxiii

A Pitiful Case

> The Villain at the Gallows tree,   1
> When he is doom'd to die,
> To assuage his misery
> In virtue's praise does cry.

MS. Book, p. 33.   Only in EY i. 216.   This epigram refers to the concluding words of the last Discourse delivered by Reynolds at the Royal

So Reynolds when he came to die,   5
To assuage his bitter woe,
Thus aloud did howl & cry :
'Michael Angelo! Michael Angelo!'

Academy, Dec. 1790 : 'I should desire that the last words which I should
pronounce in this Academy, and from this place, might be the name of
MICHAEL ANGELO.'

  3 his misery] his bitter misery EY.   7 did howl &] was heard to
MS. Book 1st *rdg. del.*

lxxiv

To the Royal Academy

A Strange Erratum in all the Editions   1
Of Sir Joshua Reynolds' Lectures
Should be corrected by the Young Gentlemen
And the Royal Academy's Directors.

Instead of 'Michael Angelo,'   5
Read 'Rembrandt'; for it is fit
To make mere common honesty
In all that he has writ.

  MS. Book, p. 33.   Only in EY i. 216.   Cp. note to lx.
  6-8 for . . . writ]

      '. . . . . & you will know
        That Sir Joshua Reynolds now wished to speak
        Of Michael Angelo.'
  MS. Book 1st *rdg. del.*   7 mere common] either sense or MS. Book
  1st *rdg. del.*   8 In] Of EY.

lxxv

If it is true, what the Prophets write,   1
That the Heathen Gods are all stocks and stones,
Shall we, for the sake of being Polite,
Feed them with the juice of our marrow-bones?

  MS. Book, p. 33.   WMR and EY with title 'Idolatry.'

And if Bezaleel and Aholiab drew   5
What the finger of God pointed to their View,
Shall we suffer the Roman and Grecian rods
To compell us to worship them as Gods?

They stole them from the Temple of the Lord   9
And worshipp'd them that they might make Inspired Art
　　abhorr'd ;

The Wood and Stone were call'd the Holy Things,   11
And their Sublime Intent given to their kings.
All the Atonements of Jehovah spurn'd,
And Criminals to Sacrifices turn'd.

9, 10 WMR and EY print as quatrain :—

> 'They stole them from
> 　The Temple of the Lord,
> And worshiped them that they might make
> 　Inspired art abhorred.'

10 that . . . make] to make MS. Book *1st rdg. del.*

lxxvi

To F—— and S——

I found them blind: I taught them how to see ;
And now they know neither themselves nor me.
'Tis excellent to turn a thorn to a pin,
A Fool to a bolt, a Knave to a glass of gin.

MS. Book, p. 34. The words ' and S—— ' are an addition. Swinb. p. 53.
WMR (' Epig.' VIII) with title ' On certain Friends,' prints first couplet only.
EY i. 217 with title ' On F —— and I——.' See note to lxvii.

　1, 2 I . . . me] Blake introduces this couplet into his *Descriptive Catalogue*
(1809).　　1 them] him MS. Book *1st rdg. del.*　　2 they know] he
knows *ibid. 1st rdg. del.*　　themselves] himself *ibid. 1st rdg. del.*

lxxvii

P—— lovèd me not as he lov'd his friends;
For he lov'd them for gain, to serve his Ends:
He lovèd me, and for no Gain at all,
But to rejoice & triumph in my fall.

MS. Book, p. 34. Only in EY i. 217. P—— is probably Thomas Phillips
the portrait painter. Cp. *Descriptive Catalogue*, p. 26: 'Those who say
that men are led by interest are knaves. A knavish character will often say,
"of what interest is it to me to do so and so?" I answer, "of none at all,
but the contrary, as you well know. It is of malice and envy that you have
done this: I am aware of you, because I know that you act, not from
interest, but from malice, even to your own destruction." '

3 and] EY *omit.*   4 in] at EY.

lxxviii

To forgive enemies H—— does pretend,
Who never in his life forgave a friend,
And when he could not act upon my wife
Hired a Villain to bereave my Life.

MS. Book, at foot of p. 34. First couplet only ptd. by DGR ('Coupl.' xi),
WMR ('Coupl.' xxi. 1), EY i. 217.

1 H——] Hayley DGR, WMR.   4 Hired . . . Life] The same line occurs
in one of the *Poetical Sketches*, cp. 'Fair Elenor,' l. 68. By the phrase
'bereave my Life' Blake here probably means, deprive me of my means of
livelihood; this is another reference to the critiques in the *Examiner* (cp.
notes to xlix, liv). Cp. *Advertisement* (MS. Book, p. 52): 'The manner in
which my character has been blasted these thirty years both as an Artist and
a Man may be seen particularly in a Sunday paper called the Examiner,
published in Beaufort's Buildings, and the manner in which I have rooted
out the nest of villains will be seen in a poem concerning my three years'
Herculean labours at Felpham, which I shall soon publish. Secret calumny
and open professions of friendship are common enough all the world over,
but have never been so good an occasion of poetic imagery. When a base
man means to be your enemy, he always begins with being your friend.
We all know that editors of newspapers trouble their heads very little about
art and science, and that they are always paid for what they put in on those
ungracious subjects.'

lxxix

To F——

You call me Mad ; 'tis folly to do so—
To seek to turn a Madman to a Foe.
If you think as you speak, you are an Ass.
If you do not, you are but what you was.

MS. Book, p. 35. DGR ('Epig.' 7), WMR ('Epig.' xvi) both with title
'To Flaxman,' EY i. 218.
    4 but what] just what MS. Book *1st rdg. del.* ; but as **EY.**

lxxx

On H——y's Friendship

When H——y finds out what you cannot do,
That is the very thing he'll set you to ;
If you break not your Neck, 'tis not his fault ;
But pecks of poison are not pecks of salt.

MS. Book, p. 35. Only in EY i. 218 (title omitted).
       3 Neck] back EY.

lxxxi

Some men, created for destruction, come
Into the World, & make the World their home.
Be they as Vile and Base as e'er they can,
They'll still be callèd 'The World's Honest Man.'

MS. Book, p. 36. Only in EY i. 218.
 2 & make] to make EY.   3, 4 Be ... Man]
    'Friend Caiaphas is one, do what he can,
     He'll still be callèd "The World's Honest Man." '
MS. Book *2nd rdg. del.* 3 Be they as] For they are EY.

lxxxii

On S——

You say reserve and modesty he has,
Whose heart is iron, his head wood, and his face brass.
The Fox, the Owl, the Beetle, and the Bat
By sweet reserve and modesty get Fat.

MS. Book, p. 36. Gil. i. 307 (last couplet only), DGR (' Coupl.' xii) without title, WMR (' Epig.' xviii) with title ' On Stothard,' EY i. 218, WBY (' Coupl.' 17) without title.

3, 4 Blake uses this couplet in his *Descriptive Catalogue* (1809). 3 Owl] mole *Descriptive Catalogue.* Beetle] spider Gil., DGR, WMR. 4 get] grow Gil., DGR, WMR.

lxxxiii

Imitation of Pope : a compliment to the Ladies

Wondrous the Gods, more wondrous are the Men,
More Wondrous, Wondrous still, the Cock and Hen,
More wondrous still the Table, Stool and Chair ;
But ah ! more wondrous still the Charming Fair.

MS. Book, p. 37. Only in EY i. 218.
Title, ' Imitation of Pope, and a Compliment,' etc., EY.

lxxxiv

To H——

Thy friendship oft has made my heart to ake :
Do be my Enemy—for Friendship's sake.

MS. Book, p. 37. Gil. i. 181, with title ' To the Same ' (i. e. Hayley), WMR (' Coupl.' xxi. 2) with general title ' On Hayley,' EY i. 218.
2 Do] *Do* Gil.

lxxxv

Cosway, Frazer, & Baldwin of Egypt's Lake   1
Fear to associate with Blake.
This Life is a Warfare against Evils ;
They heal the sick : he casts out devils.
Hayley, Flaxman, & Stothard are also in doubt   5
Lest their Virtue should be put to the rout.
One grins, t'other spits, and in corners hides,
And all the Virtuous have shewn their backsides.

MS. Book, p. 37.   EY (' Memoir' chap. vii) i. 81, with last couplet, i. 219.
6 Virtue] friendship EY.   7, 8 One . . . backsides] *A marginal*
addition.   7 t'other] other EY.   8 shewn] shaved EY.

lxxxvi

An Epitaph

Come knock your heads against this stone,
For sorrow that poor John Thompson 's gone.

MS. Book, p. 37.   This and the two following epitaphs were obviously
written before the Stothard lines (cp. xlix, ll. 45, 46).   Only in EY i. 219,
without title.

lxxxvii

Another

I was buried near this dyke,
That my Friends may weep as much as they like.

MS. Book, p. 37.   Cp. xlix, ll. 49, 50, WMR ('Coupl.' xviii), EY (1st
line only) i. 219.

lxxxviii

Another

Here lies John Trot, the Friend of all mankind :
He has not left one enemy behind.
Friends were quite hard to find, old authors say ;
But now they stand in everybody's way.

MS. Book, p. 37. Cp. xlix, l. 51. Gil. i. 181 (last couplet only), DGR, WMR, EY, WBY (' Coupl.' xiv, xvii, xv, 18). DGR entitles ' Epitaph '; the rest omit title.

lxxxix

My title as a Genius thus is prov'd :
Not prais'd by Hayley, nor by Flaxman lov'd.

MS. Book, p. 38. Gil. i. 181, WMR (' Coupl.' xxi. 3) with title ' On Hayley,' EY i. 219.
2 nor] or EY.
Cp. with this and other epigrams in the MS. Book on Flaxman and Hayley the verses written some eight years earlier : these interesting lines, which have not been previously printed, I owe to the courtesy of Mr. A. G. B. Russell.
' TO MY DEAREST FRIEND JOHN FLAXMAN THESE LINES :
I bless thee, O Father of Heaven and Earth ! that ever I saw Flax-
man's face.
Angels stand round my spirit in Heaven, the blessed of Heaven are
my friends upon Earth.
When Flaxman was taken to Italy, Fuseli was given to me for
a Season,
And now Flaxman hath given me Hayley, his friend, to be mine—
such my lot upon Earth !
Now my lot in the Heavens is this : Milton lov'd me in childhood,
and shew'd me his face ;
Ezra came with Isaiah the Prophet, but Shakespeare in riper years
gave me his hand ;
Paracelsus and Behmen appeared to me; terrors appeared in the
Heavens above ;
The American War began ; All its dark horrors passed before my face
Across the Atlantic to France ; Then the French Revolution commenc'd
in thick clouds ;
And my Angels have told me that seeing such visions, I could not
subsist on the Earth,
But by my conjunction with Flaxman, who knows to forgive nervous
fear.
                                        12 Sept., 1800.'

XC

I, Rubens, am a Statesman and a Saint.
Deceptions . . . And so I'll learn to paint.

MS. Book, p. 38.   Only in EY i. 219.
1, 2 I . . . paint]
　　　　' Rubens had been a Statesman or a Saint ;
　　　　　He mixed them both—and so he learn'd to Paint.'
MS. Book *1st rdg. del.*　1 I, Rubens, am] Rubens was EY.　2 . . .]
A word illegible in MS.

xci

To English Connoisseurs

You must agree that Rubens was a Fool,　　　　　1
And yet you make him master of your School,
And give more money for his slobberings
Than you will give for Rafael's finest things.
I understood Christ was a Carpenter　　　　　5
And not a Brewer's Servant, my good Sir.

　MS. Book, p. 38.　DGR, WMR (' Epig.' 5, xi), EY (' Coupl.' xix) without title.
　4 things] thing EY.　5, 6 I . . . Sir] *An addition*, EY *omit.*　Cp. *Advertisement* (MS. Book, p. 63) : ' He who could represent Christ uniformly like a dray-
man must have queer conceptions : consequently his execution must have
been as queer, and these must be queer fellows who give great sums for such
nonsense and think it fine art.'

xcii

Swelled limbs, with no outline that you can descry,
That stink in the nose of a stander-by.
But all the pulp-wash'd, painted, finish'd with labour,
Of an hundred journeymen's—how-d'ye do Neighbour ?

　MS. Book, p. 38.　Only in EY i. 220.　Cp. *Advertisement* (MS. Book, p. 19):
' Rubens' Luxembourg Gallery is confessed on all hands to be the work
of a blockhead.　It bears this evidence in its face.　How can its execution
be any other than the work of a blockhead ?　Bloated gods—Mercury, Juno,
Venus, and the rattle-traps of mythology, and the lumber of an awkward
French palace are thrown together, around clumsy and ricketty princes and
princesses, higledy-piggledy.'
　2 stander] passer EY.　3 But] For EY.　painted] EY *omit.*　4 an]
a EY.　journeymen's] journeymen EY.　Cp. *Advertisement* (MS. Book,
p. 18, *circa* 1810) : ' What man of sense will lay out his money upon the life's
labour of imbecility, and imbecility's journeyman . . . ? '

xciii

A Pretty Epigram for the encouragement of those Who have paid great sums in the Venetian and Flemish ooze

Nature and Art in this together suit:
What is Most Grand is always most Minute.
Rubens thinks Tables, Chairs and Stools are Grand,
But Rafael thinks a Head, a foot, a hand.

MS. Book, p. 38, where the original title (*del.*) read 'a Pretty Epigram for those who have given high Prices for Bad Pictures.' WMR prints this, xcv and xcvi, as a single poem with the title 'Raphael and Rubens' ('Epig.' xii), EY i. 220, omitting 'paid' in l. 2 of title.

xciv

These are the Idiots' chiefest arts: 1
To blend and not define the parts.
The Swallow sings, in Courts of Kings,
That Fools have their high finishings.

MS. Book, p. 38. The correct position of the lines is indicated by prefixed arabic numerals, ll. 7, 8 being a marginal addition. Only in EY i. 221, who arrange as two stanzas made up of ll. 1, 2, 7, 8, and 3, 4, 5, 6. Cp. *Descriptive Catalogue* (1809), pp. 26, 27 : 'The character and expression in this picture [Blake's 'Canterbury Pilgrims'] could never have been produced with Rubens' light and shadow, or with Rembrandt's, or any thing Venetian or Flemish. The Venetian and Flemish practice is broken lines, broken masses. and broken colours. Mr. B.'s practice is unbroken lines, unbroken masses, and unbroken colours. Their art is to lose form: his art is to find form and to keep it. His arts are opposite to theirs in all things.' Also Notes in Blake's copy of Reynolds' *Works*, p. xcviii : 'To Generalize is to be an Idiot. To Particularize is the Alone Distinction of Merit. General Knowledges are those Knowledges that Idiots possess.'

  1 the] EY *omit.*   3 The Swallow sings] Let it be told MS. Book 1st *rdg. del.* ; EY *read* 'known' *for* 'told.'   4 That . . . finishings]

And this the Princes' golden rule,   5
The Laborious Stumble of a Fool.
To make out the parts is the wise man's aim,
But to loose them the Fool makes his foolish Game.

Cp. *Advertisement* (MS. Book, p. 55) : 'I allow that there is such a thing as
high-finished ignorance, as there may be a fool or a knave in an embroidered
coat ' ; also, Blake's notes to Reynolds' Discourses, p. xlvii : 'I was once
looking over the Prints from Rafael & Michael Angelo in the Library of the
Royal Academy.   Moser came to me & said, "You should not study these
old Hard, Stiff, & Dry Unfinish'd Works of Art.   Stay a little, & I will shew
you what you should Study."   He then went and took down Le Brun's and
Rubens' Galleries.   How I did secretly rage.   I also spoke my Mind. . . .
I said to Moser, "These things that you call Finish'd are not Even Begun,
how can they then be Finish'd ?   The Man who does not know The Beginning never can know the End of Art."'   6 The . . . Fool] Cp. MS. Book
xcvi.   8 Game] aim EY.

XCV

Rafael, Sublime, Majestic, Graceful, Wise—
His Executive Power must I despise?
Rubens, Low, Vulgar, Stupid, Ignorant—
His power of Execution I must grant?

MS. Book, p. 39.   Gil. i. 265, WMR (as continuation of xciii), EY i. 220.
Cp. Blake's ms. note on flyleaf of his copy of Reynolds' Discourse no. v,
Works, vol. i, p. [114] : 'The following Discourse is written with the Same
End in View that Gainsborough had . . . Namely To Represent Vulgar Artists
as the Models of Executive Merit.'
     2, 4 Power] powers EY.   4 His . . . grant] EY obscure the whole
point of this epigram by punctuating the last line :—
           'His power of execution I must grant.'
     The following extracts, however, taken from Blake's marginal notes to
Reynolds' *Discourses*, show clearly that the last line should be read as an
indignant question involving an answer in the negative :—
     p. xxix.   'Why are we to be told that Masters who Could Think, had not
the Judgment to Perform the Inferior parts of Art, as Reynolds artfully
calls them ?   But that we are to Learn to Think from Great Masters, & to
Learn to Perform from Underlings !   Learn to Design from Rafael, and to
Execute from Rubens !'
     p. 126.   'Can any Man be Such a fool as to believe that Rafael & Michael
Angelo were Incapable of the meer Language of Art, & That Such Idiots as
Rubens, Correggio, & Titian knew how to Execute what they could not
Think or Invent.'
     p. 167.   'He who Admires Rafael, Must admire Rafael's Execution.   He
who does not admire Rafael's Execution, Cannot Admire Rafael.'

xcvi

Learn the laborious stumble of a Fool!
Go, send your Children to the Slobbering School!

MS. Book, p. 39. WMR as conclusion of xciii, xcv, interpolating between lines 1 and 2 the line, presumably his own :—

'And from an idiot's action form my rule!'

EY i. 221 invert order of the two lines.

2 Go, send] Go and send EY. Slobbering] globbering EY.

xcvii

If I e'er Grow to Man's Estate,
O! Give to me a Woman's fate.
May I govern all, both great & small,
Have the last word, and take the wall.

MS. Book, p. 39. DGR ('Coupl.' ix), WMR, EY ('Coupl.' xi), WBY ('Coupl.' 12).

1 I e'er] e'er I DGR, WMR, EY, WBY. e'en I] EY (Index, MS. Book, i. 221).

xcviii

The cripple every step drudges & labours,   1
And says : 'Come, learn to walk of me, Good Neighbours.'
Sir Joshua in astonishment cries out :
'See, what Great Labour! Pain in Modest Doubt!

MS. Book, p. 39. Gil. (first 4 ll. only) i. 265, EY i. 221, 222. Cp. *Advertisement* (MS. Book, p. 19) : 'Who that has eyes cannot see that Rubens & Corregio must have been very weak & vulgar fellows? And are we to imitate their execution? This is like what Sir Francis Bacon says :—that a healthy child should be taught & compelled to walk like a cripple, while the cripple must be taught to walk like healthy people. O, rare wisdom!'

1 drudges] smudges EY. 4 See ... Doubt] His pains are more than others, there's no doubt MS. Book 1st *rdg. del.* EY insert this after l. 4 as part of the poem. Pain in] springs from Gil.

He walks & stumbles as if he crep,   5
And how high labour'd is every step!'
Newton and Bacon cry 'Being badly Nurst,
He is all Experiments from last to first.'

5, 6 He . . . step] *A marginal addition.*   6 labour'd] finished EY.
7, 8 Newton . . . first] *An addition.*   7 cry] EY *omit.*   8 Experiments]
experiment EY.

xcix

On the great encouragement given by English Nobility & Gentry to Correggio, Rubens, Reynolds, Gainsborough, Catalani, Du Crow, and Dilbury Doodle

As the Ignorant Savage will sell his own Wife   1
For a Sword, or a Cutlass, a dagger, or Knife;
So the taught, savage Englishman, spends his whole
    Fortune
On a smear, or a squall, to destroy Picture or tune,
And I call upon Colonel Wardle   5
To give these Rascals a dose of Caudle.

MS. Book, p. 40, title an addition.   DGR ('Epig.' 3), WMR ('Epig.' ix)
prints under this title c, xcix, ci.   EY i. 222.   DGR, WMR omit 'Du Crow,'
and insert 'Rembrandt' after 'Rubens' in title ; EY insert 'The' before
'English,' omit 'and Gentry,' and read 'Catelans' for 'Catalani.'
    2 For . . . Knife] For a button, a Bauble [buckle *2nd rdg. del.*], a bead, or
a knife MS. Book *1st rdg. del.*, DGR, WMR, EY.   3 taught] wise MS.
Book *1st rdg. del.*, EY ; learned *ibid. 2nd rdg. del.*   4 On] For *ibid. 1st
rdg. del.*, EY :   to destroy] that is not MS. Book *1st rdg. del.*, EY.   5, 6
And . . . Caudle] EY print this couplet after c.   5 Wardle] Warble
EY.   For Col. Wardle see *Examiner,* 1809 *passim.*

c

Give Pensions to the Learned Pig,
Or the Hare playing on a Tabor;
Anglus can never see Perfection
But in the Journeyman's Labour.

MS. Book, p. 40. DGR, WMR (see note to xcix), EY i. 222. Cp.
Advertisement (MS. Book, p. 25) : ' In the art of painting, these impostors
sedulously propagate an opinion that great inventors cannot execute. This
opinion is as destructive of the true artist as it is false by all experience.
Even Hogarth cannot be either copied or improved. Can Anglus ever
discern perfection but in the journeyman's labour?' Cp. also *Advertisement*
(MS. Book, p. 47) : ' Englishmen have been so used to journeymen's undecided
bungling that they cannot bear the firmness of a master's touch.'
3 Anglus] Bunglers EY.

ci

All pictures that's painted with sense and with thought   1
Are painted by Madmen, as sure as a Groat;
For the Greater the Fool is the Pencil more blest,
As when they are drunk they always paint best.
They never can Rafael it, Fuseli it, nor Blake it;   5
If they can't see an outline, pray how can they make it?
When Men will draw outlines begin you to jaw them;
Madmen see outlines and therefore they draw them.

MS. Book, p. 40. DGR, WMR (see note to xcix), EY i. 222.
1 and] or DGR, WMR.   3 is the Pencil] in the art the DGR, WMR.
4 As] And DGR, WMR.   5 nor] or EY.   7 When . . . them]
All men have drawn outlines whenever they saw them DGR, WMR.

cii

On H—— the Pickthank

I write the Rascal thanks, till he and I
With Thanks and Compliments are quite drawn dry.

MS. Book, p. 41. Gil. i. 181, extending ' H——' to ' Hayley.' EY i. 223.

ciii

Cromek speaks

I always take my judgment from a Fool
Because his Judgment is so very Cool;
Not prejudiced by feelings great or small,
Amiable state! he cannot feel at all.

MS. Book, p. 41. Gil. i. 208. EY i. 223.
1 judgment] judgments Gil., EY. 2 Because . . . Cool] Because
I know he always judges cool. MS. Book 1*st rdg. del.* judgment is] judgments are EY. 3 or] and Gil. 4 Amiable state] Because we
know MS. Book 1*st rdg. del.*

civ

When you look at a picture, you always can see 1
If a Man of Sense has Painted he.
Then never flinch, but keep up a jaw
About freedom, and Jenny sink awa'.
As when it smells of the lamp, we can 5
Say all was owing to the Skilful Man ;
For the smell of water is but small:
So e'en let Ignorance do it all.

MS. Book, p. 41. Only in EY i. 223.
4 Jenny sink awa'] Blake's purposely grotesque spelling of 'Je ne sais
quoi.' Cp. 'menny wouver' in the next piece. That Blake probably read
French with ease may be inferred from his quotation of a passage from
Voltaire's *Essai sur les mœurs et l'esprit des nations*, copied with indignant
comment on p. [cxxvii] of his copy of Reynolds' *Discourses.* 5 we] all
MS. Book 1*st rdg. del.*, EY.

CV

English Encouragement of Art : Cromek's opinions put into rhyme

If you mean to Please Everybody, you will   1
Menny wouver both Bunglishness & skill ;
For a great conquest are Bunglers,
And . . . . like mad ranters !
Like displaying oil and water in a lamp,   5
'Twill hold forth a huge splutter with smoke and damp ;
For it 's all sheer loss, as it seems to me,
Of displaying up a light when we want not to see.

MS. Book, p. 41.   EY i. 223 (with 'Encouragers' for 'Encouragement'
and 'opinion' for 'opinions' in title) print the earlier and clearer version
which reads :—

> 'If you mean to please everybody you will   *1
> Set to work both ignorance and skill.
> For a great multitude are ignorant,
> And skill to them seems raving and rant.
> Like putting oil and water in a lamp,   *5
> 'Twill make a great splutter with smoke and damp.
> For there is no use as it seems to me
> Of lighting a lamp, when you don't wish to see.'

2 Menny wouver] *read* manœuvre.   See note to civ, l. 4.   4 *Obscurely
written.*   *5 in] into EY.   *8 Of] For EY.

CXVI

> You say their Pictures well Painted be,   1
> And yet they are blockheads you all agree :
> Thank God ! I never was sent to school
> To be Flog'd into following the Style of a Fool.
> The errors of a wise man make your Rule,   5
> Rather than the Perfections of a Fool.

MS. Book, p. 42.   The last couplet is separated from the two preceding
by a sketch.   DGR and WMR print the second and third couplets as
separate epigrams ; EY i. 223, ll. 1–4, and 5, 6 as distinct pieces ; WBY the
last couplet only.

3 God] heaven EY.   4 To . . . Fool] To learn to admire the works
of a Fool MS. Book 1*st rdg. del.*

cvii

The Washerwoman's Song

I wash'd them out & wash'd them in,
And they told me it was a great sin.

MS. Book, p. 42. Only in EY i. 224. Possibly a reference to Blake's manner of using water-colour. Cp. the allusion to 'water' in an epigram on the preceding page of the MS. Book, civ, l. 7.

cviii

When I see a Rubens, Rembrandt, Correggio,   1
I think of the Crippled Harry and Slobbering Joe ;
And then I question thus: Are artists' rules
To be drawn from the works of two manifest fools ?
Then God defend us from the Arts I say!   5
Send Battle, Murder, sudden death, O pray!
Rather than be such a blind Human Fool
I'd be an Ass, a Hog, a Worm, a Chair, a Stool!

MS. Book, p. 43.   DGR, WMR ('Epig.' 4 and x), EY iii. 86.
   1 When . . . Correggio] Seeing a Rembrandt or Correggio DGR, WMR ; When I see a Rembrandt or Correggio MS. Book *1st rdg. del.*, EY. 2 I . . . Joe] Of crippled Harry I think and slobbering Joe DGR, WMR ; I think of crippled Harry, or slobbering Joe EY.   3 question thus] say to myself MS. Book *1st rdg. del.*, EY.   6 Send] For DGR, WMR. O] we MS. Book *1st rdg. del.*, EY ; let's DGR, WMR.   7 blind] EY *omit.*   8 an Ass] EY *omit.* Cp. *Descriptive Catalogue*, pp. 56–59 : 'Rubens is a most outrageous demon, and by infusing the remembrances of his Pictures and style of execution, hinders all power of individual thought ; so that the man who is possessed by this demon loses all admiration of any other Artist but Rubens, and those who were his imitators and journeymen : he causes to the Florentine and Roman Artist fear to execute, and though the original conception was all fire and animation, he loads it with hellish brownness, and blocks up all its gates of light, except one, and that one he closes with iron bars, till the victim is obliged to give up the Florentine and Roman practice, and adopt the Venetian and Flemish.
   'Correggio is a soft and effeminate and consequently a most cruel demon, whose whole delight is to cause endless labour to whoever suffers him to enter his mind. The story that is told in all Lives of the Painters, about Correggio being poor and but badly paid for his Pictures, is altogether false ; he was a petty Prince, in Italy, and employed numerous Journeymen in manufacturing (as Rubens and Titian did) the Pictures that go under his name. The manual labour in these Pictures of Correggio is immense, and

was paid for originally at the immense prices that those who keep manufactories of art always charge to their employers, while they themselves pay their journeymen little enough. But, though Correggio was not poor, he will make any true artist so, who permits him to enter his mind, and take possession of his affections; he infuses a love of soft and even tints without boundaries, and of endless reflected lights, that confuse one another, and hinder all correct drawing from appearing to be correct; for if one of Rafael's or Michael Angelo's figures was to be traced, and Correggio's reflections and refractions to be added to it, there would soon be an end of proportion and strength, and it would be weak, and pappy, and lumbering, and thick-headed, like his own works; but then it would have softness and evenness, by a twelvemonth's labour, where a month would with judgment have finished it better and higher; and the poor wretch who executed it would be the Correggio that the life-writers have written of—a drudge and a miserable man, compelled to softness by poverty. I say again, O Artist! you may disbelieve all this, but it shall be at your own peril.'

cix

Great things are done when Men & Mountains meet;
This is not done by jostling in the street.

MS. Book, p. 43. DGR, WMR, WBY ('Coupl.' v, vii, and 8), EY i. 224.

2 This is] These are *all edd.*

cx

If you play a Game of Chance, Know, before you begin,
If you are benevolent You will never win.

MS. Book, p. 47. Only in EY i. 224, printed as a quatrain.

cxi

The only Man that e'er I knew
Who did not make me almost spew
Was Fuseli: he was both Turk and Jew—
And so, dear Christian Friends, how do you do?

MS. Book, p. 50. These lines are written over an erasure, with the title 'William Cowper, Esqre.' which probably belonged to the deleted passage. WMR ('Epig.' xv) with title 'Fuseli,' EY i. 225.

1 that e'er I] that ever I WMR; I ever EY.   2 make me almost] almost make me EY.   4 dear] sweet MS. Book *1st rdg. del.*   Christian Friends] Christians *ibid. 1st rdg. del.*

cxii

For this is being a Friend just in the nick,   1
Not when he 's well, but waiting till he 's sick ;
He calls you to his help ; be you not mov'd
Until, by being sick, his wants are prov'd.

You see him spend his Soul in Prophecy :   5
Do you believe it a confounded lie,
Till some Bookseller, & the Public Fame,
Prove there is truth in his extravagant claim.

For 'tis atrocious in a Friend you love   9
To tell you anything that he can't prove,
And 'tis most wicked in a Christian Nation
For any man to pretend to Inspiration.

MS. Book, p. 50.   This is probably the continuation of the erased stanza,
referred to in note to cxi, and was therefore written before the preceding
piece.   Only in WMR (' Coupl.' xix) with title ' Blake's Friends.'
    9 atrocious] most wicked MS. Book *1st rdg. del.*   12 man] one WMR.
11, 12] Cp. Notes to Reynolds' *Discourses*, p. 5 : 'Reynolds' Opinion was
That Genius May be Taught, & that all Pretence to Inspiration is a Lie &
a Deceit, to say the least of it.   For if it is a Deceit the whole Bible is
Madness.   This Opinion originates in the Greeks calling the Muse[s]
Daughters of Memory.
    'The Enquiry in England is not whether a Man has Talents & Genius !
But whether he is Passive & Polite & a Virtuous Ass, & obedient to
Noblemen's Opinions in Art & Science.   If he is, he is a Good Man.   If
Not, he must be Starved.'

cxiii

I will tell you what Joseph of Arimathea   1
Said to my Fairy : was not it very queer ?
Priestly & Bacon ! What, are you here ?
Come before Joseph of Arimathea.
Listen patient, & when Joseph has done   5
I will make a fool laugh, & a Fairy fun.

MS. Book, p. 52.   Only in EY i. 225.   For Joseph cp. Gil. i. 19 : for the
Fairy see footnote to ' Poems from *Jerusalem*,' iv.
    2 was . . . queer] was it not queer EY.   3 Priestly & Bacon] Priestly
—Bacon EY.   5 & . . . done] when Joseph is done EY.   6 I will]
Not legibly written, perhaps 'Twill; I'll EY.   & a Fairy] at a Fairy's EY.

cxiv

Grown old in Love from Seven till Seven times Seven,
I oft have wish'd for Hell, for Ease from Heaven.

MS. Book, p. 54. Apparently written in or after 1806. WMR, EY
('Coupl.' v).

CXV

Why was Cupid a Boy,   1
And why a boy was he?
He should have been a Girl,
For aught that I can see.

For he shoots with his bow,   5
And the Girl shoots with her Eye,
And they both are merry & glad,
And laugh when we do cry.

And to make Cupid a boy   9
Was the Cupid girl's mocking plan;
For a boy can't interpret the thing
Till he is become a man.

And then he's so pierc'd with cares,   13
And wounded with arrowy smarts,
That the whole business of his life
Is to pick out the heads of the darts.

MS. Book, p. 56. R¹, DGR, WMR, EY (iii. 69), WBY, all with title
'Cupid' and omission of last stanza (except R¹) which is printed separately
by Swinb. (p. 144), EY i. 225, and WBY (notes, p. 248).
    6 the] a WBY.   9-12 And . . . man] All edd. print the infinitely
preferable first draft of this stanza :—

> 'Then to make Cupid a Boy   *9
> Was surely a Woman's plan,
> For a boy ne'er learns so much
> Till he is become a man';

all reading 'never' for 'ne'er' (l. *11), all except R¹ 'has' for 'is' (l. *12)
and WBY 'And' for 'Then' (l. *9) and 'to mock' for 'so much' (l. *11).
13 he's . . . cares] he is so pierced through WBY.

'Twas the Greeks' love of war   17
Turn'd Love into a Boy,
And Woman into a Statue of Stone—
And away fled every Joy.

17-20 'Twas . . . Joy] Swinb. calls this 'the last (rejected) stanza,' but
there is no trace of deletion in the MS. Book.   17 Greeks'] Greek
Swinb.   18 Turn'd] That turned Swinb.   Love] Cupid EY, WBY.
20 And] WBY *omits*.   fled] flew EY, WBY.

cxvi

I askèd my Dear Friend Orator Prig: 1
'What's the first part of Oratory?' He said: 'A great
    wig.'
'And what is the second?' Then, dancing a jig
And bowing profoundly, he said: 'A great wig.'
'And what is the third?' Then he snored like a pig, 5
And, puffing his cheeks out, replied: 'A great wig.'
So if a Great Painter with Questions you push
'What's the first part of painting?' he'll say: 'A Paint-
    Brush.'
'And what is the second?' with most modest blush, 9
He'll smile like a cherub, and say: 'A paint-brush.'
'And what is the third?' he'll bow like a rush,
With a leer in his Eye, he'll reply: 'A Paint-brush.'
Perhaps this is all a Painter can want: 13
But, look yonder—that house is the house of Rem-
    brandt! &c.

MS. Book, p. 60.   DGR, WMR ('Epig.' 1) with title in WMR of 'Orator
Prig.'   EY ('Coupl.' xxi).   Following the '&c.' which indicates that more
of this piece was written elsewhere Blake has added the words 'to come
in *Barry: a Poem.*'
    1 my] of my DGR, WMR.   2 part of] thing in EY.   6 And . . . out]
And thrust out his cheeks and MS. Book *1st rdg. del.*, EY.   7 So . . . push]
So if to a painter the question you push DGR, WMR, EY.   8 he'll] he'd
EY.   11 he'll] He will EY.   12 he'll] and DGR, WMR, EY.   13 all
a] all that a EY.

cxvii

O dear Mother Outline! of wisdom most sage,   1
What's the First Part of Painting; she said 'Patronage.'
And what is the Second, to Please and Engage,
She frowned like a Fury, and said 'Patronage.'
And what is the Third: she put off Old Age   5
And smil'd like a Syren and said 'Patronage.'

MS. Book, p. 61.   DGR, WMR ('Epig.' 2), EY ('Coupl.' xxii).   This is perhaps the continuation of the preceding epigram (cxvi).

cxviii

To Venetian Artists

That God is Colouring Newton does shew,   1
And the devil is a black outline, all of us know.
Perhaps this little Fable may make us merry:
A dog went over the water without a wherry;
A bone which he had stolen he had in his mouth;   5
He cared not whether the wind was north or south.
As he swam he saw the reflection of the bone.
'This is quite Perfection—one Generalizing Tone!
Outline! There's no outline, there's no such thing: 9
All is Chiaroscuro, Poco-Pen—it's all Colouring!'
Snap, snap! He has lost shadow and substance too.
He had them both before. 'Now how do ye do?'
'A great deal better than I was before: 13
Those who taste colouring love it more and more.'

MS. Book, pp. 60, 61 : the first couplet with the catchwords 'Perhaps this little Fable, &c.' occurs at foot of p. 60, the rest, with the title, on p. 61. WMR ('Epig.' v), EY print first couplet ('Coupl.' xxiii) followed by the rest as a separate poem.

8 This . . . Tone] Here's two for one, what a brilliant tone MS. Book *1st rdg. del.* one] EY *omit.*   9, 10 Outline . . . Colouring] *A marginal addition* ; EY *omit.*   11 He . . . too] and lost the shadow and the substance too EY.   12 them both] both these EY.   do ye] d'ye EY.   13 A . . . before] EY *omit.*   14 taste] have tasted EY.

Cp. Blake's *Descriptive Catalogue*, pp. 63, 64, No. xv, 'Ruth a drawing' :

'If losing and obliterating the outline constitutes a Picture, Mr. B. will never be so foolish as to do one. Such art of losing the outlines is the art of Venice and Flanders ; it loses all character and leaves what some people call "expression" ; but this is a false notion of expression. . . . The great and golden rule of art as well as of life is this ;—That the more distinct, sharp, and wirey the boundary line, the more perfect the work of art,—and the less keen and sharp, The greater is the evidence of weak imitation, plagiarism, and bungling. Great inventors, in all ages, knew this.' Also *Descriptive Catalogue*, p. 54 : 'These pictures, among numerous others painted for experiment, were the result of temptations and perturbations, labouring to destroy Imaginative power, by means of that infernal machine called Chiaro Oscuro, in the hands of Venetian and Flemish Demons, whose enmity to the Painter himself, and to all Artists who study in the Florentine and Roman Schools, may be removed by an exhibition and exposure of their vile tricks.'

cxix

Great Men and Fools do often me inspire ;
But the Greater Fool, the Greater Liar.

MS. Book, p. 63 (reversed).   Only in EY ii. 384.
    1 me] we EY.   2 Fool] fools EY.

cxx

Having given great offence by writing in Prose,   1
I'll write in Verse as soft as Bartolloze.
Some blush at what others can see no crime in ;
But nobody sees any harm in Rhyming.

MS. Book, p. 65.   The rough draft of most of this piece occurs on p. 62, where the lines were composed in the following order, 5-8, 3, 4, 15-18, which Blake, interlineating ll. 1 and 2 between ll. 8 and 9 (or 4, 5 in the original draft), afterwards renumbered 1-12.   Lines 13 and 14 are also an interlineation in the first draft.   The verses were then transcribed on p. 65, with the couplet ll. 11, 12, added in a slightly changed form, from the first draft on p. 63, and the addition of ll. 19-22.   Only in EY ('Memoir' i. 76).

1] Cp. Hunt's reference to Blake's *Descriptive Catalogue, Examiner*, no. 90, September 17, 1809.   in Prose] EY *omit* in.   4 But . . . Rhyming] But Nobody at all sees harm in Rhyming MS. Book *1st rdg. del.* (p. 62).

Dryden, in rhyme, cries ' Milton only plann'd : '   5
Every Fool shook his bells throughout the land.
Tom Cooke cut Hogarth down with his clean graving :
Thousands of connoisseurs with joy ran raving.
Thus, Hayley on his Toilette seeing the sope,   9
Cries ' Homer is very much improv'd by Pope.'
Some say I've given great Provision to my foes,
And that now I lead my false friends by the nose.
Flaxman and Stothard, smelling a sweet savour,   13
Cry ' Blakefied drawing spoils painter and Engraver ; '
While I, looking up to my Umbrella,
Resolv'd to be a very contrary fellow,
Cry, looking quite from skumference to center,   17
' No one can finish so high as the original Inventor.'
Thus Poor Schiavonetti died of the Cromek—
A thing that's tied around the Examiner's neck !
This is my sweet apology to my friends,   21
That I may put them in mind of their latter ends.

5, 6] Cp. *Advertisement* (MS. Book, p. 20) : ' An example of the contrary
arts is written us in the characters of Milton and Dryden as they are
given in a poem signed with the name of Nat Lee, which perhaps he
never wrote, and perhaps he wrote in a paroxysm of insanity, in which it is
said that Milton's poem is a rough, unfinished piece, and Dryden has finished
it. Now let Dryden's Fall and Milton's Paradise be read, and I will assert
that everybody of understanding must cry out shame on such niggling and
poco-pen as Dryden has degraded Milton with. But at the same time I will
allow that stupidity will prefer Dryden, because it is rhyme, and monotonous
sing-song sing-song from beginning to end. Such are Bartolozzi, Woollett
and Strange.'   7] Cp. *Advertisement* (MS. Book, p. 57) : ' Cooke wished
to give Hogarth what he could take from Rafael, that is, outline, and mass,
and colour ; but he could not.'   8 Thousands . . . raving] How many
Thousands of Conoisseurs ran raving MS. Book *1st rdg. del.* (p. 62).
9 Thus] *An addition* ; Then EY.   10 Cries] Says MS. Book *1st rdg. del.*
11, 12 Some . . . nose]

> ' I've given great Provision to my Foes
> But now I'll lead my false Friends by the Nose.'

MS. Book *1st rdg. del.* (p. 63).   11 Some say] *A marginal addition.*
great] EY *omit.*   12 that] *A marginal addition* ; EY *omit.*   17 Cry . . .
center] Cry Tom Cooke proves from circumference to Center MS. Book
1st rdg. del. (p. 62).   19, 20 A reference to Cromek's ' Account of Mr.
Schiavonetti,' in the *Examiner*, July 1, 1810.   20 around] about EY.

cxxi

If men will act like a maid smiling over a churn,   1
They ought not, when it comes to another's turn,
To grow sour at what a friend may utter,
Knowing and feeling that we all have need of Butter.
False Friends, fie! fie! Our Friendship you shan't sever; 5
In spite we will be greater friends than ever.

MS. Book, p. 65.   Perhaps a continuation of cxx.   Printed here for the first time.
    5 fie! fie!] O no! MS. Book *1st rdg. del.*   you shan't] ne'er shall MS. Book *1st rdg. del.*   6 In spite] For now MS. Book *1st rdg. del.*

cxxii

Call that the Public Voice which is their Error?
Like as a Monkey, peeping in a Mirror,
Admires all his colours brown & warm,
And never once perceives his ugly form.

MS. Book, p. 66.   Written in continuation of a passage in Blake's *Advertisement*, in which he says that 'Rafael and Michael Angelo abhorr'd studying nature, as Vasari tells us.'   Gil. i. 266 with title 'On Colourists,' WMR ('Epig.' vi) with title 'Colour and Form,' EY i. 226.
        2 Like as] Like to EY.   3 Admires] Admireth Gil.

cxxiii

Some people admire the work of a Fool,
For it's sure to keep your judgment cool;
It does not reproach you with want of wit;
It is not like a lawyer serving a writ.

MS. Book, p. 70.   DGR, WMR, EY, WBY ('Coupl.' vii, ix, and 10).   Cp. MS. Book, ciii, ll. 1, 2.

cxxiv

To God

If you have form'd a Circle to go into,
Go into it yourself, & see how you would do.

MS. Book, p. 73.   Only in EY i. 226.
                2 how] what EY.

CXXV

Since all the Riches of this World
May be gifts from the Devil & Earthly Kings,
I should suspect that I worship'd the Devil
If I thank'd my God for worldly things.

MS. Book, p. 73 (reversed) in pencil. All edd. follow DGR in printing
as first stanza of xxx ; DGR, WMR and EY with title 'Riches,' WBY with
title 'The Two Kinds of Riches.'

4 my God] WBY *omits* my.

CXXVI

To Chloe's breast young Cupid slily stole,
But he crept in at Myra's pocket-hole.

MS. Book, p. 78. DGR, WMR, EY ('Coupl.' iv), WBY ('Coupl.' 5).
1 breast] heart R¹.

CXXVII

'Now Art has lost its mental Charms   1
France shall subdue the World in Arms.'
So spoke an Angel at my birth ;
Then said 'Descend thou upon earth
Renew the Arts on Britain's shore,   5
And France shall fall down & adore.
With works of Art their Armies meet
And War shall sink beneath thy feet.

MS. Book, p. 79. Lines 13, 14 are apparently the beginning of a second
stanza which was left unfinished. Only in EY i. 227. Cp. *Advertisement*
(MS. Book, p. 66): 'Let us teach Buonaparte and whomsoever else it
may concern that it is not Arts that follow & attend upon Empire, but
Empire that attends upon & follows The Arts.' Also Blake's notes to
Reynolds' *Works* (vol. i, p. [cxxv]), 'The Foundation of Empire is Art
& Science. Remove them, or Degrade them, & the Empire is No More.
Empire follows Art, & not Vice Versâ as Englishmen suppose.'

4 upon] on the EY.   7 their] her EY.

But if thy Nation Arts refuse, 9
And if they scorn the immortal Muse,
France shall the arts of Peace restore
And save thee from the ungrateful shore.'

Spirit who lov'st Brittannia's Isle 13
Round which the Fiends of Commerce smile—

12 And . . . shore] And save thy works from Britain's shore MS. Book
1st *rdg. del.* 13, 14 Spirit . . . smile]

'Spirit who lovest Britannia's shore
Round which the Fiends of Commerce roar.'

EY. 14 Cp. *Advertisement* (MS. Book, p. 25), 'In a commercial nation
impostors are abroad in all professions. These are the greatest enemies of
Genius.'

CXXVIII

Nail his neck to the Cross: nail it with a nail.
Nail his neck to the Cross: ye all have power over his
tail.

MS. Book, p. 79. EY ii. 57 wrongly regard this as part of *The Everlasting
Gospel,* 'for which no place can be assigned.'

CXXIX

The Caverns of the Grave I've seen, 1
And these I shew'd to England's Queen.
But now the Caves of Hell I view,
Who shall I dare to shew them to?
What mighty Soul in Beauty's form 5
Shall dauntless View the Infernal storm?

MS. Book, p. 87, on same page as part of Blake's descriptive account of
his picture of 'The Last Judgment,' headed 'For the Year 1810 : Addition
to Blake's Catalogue of Pictures, &c.' Swinb. p. 55, WMR p. 170, EY iii.
74, WBY p. 140, all except Swinb. with title 'For a Picture of the Last
Judgment : Dedication.' WMR (p. 144) seems unaware that this poem
forms part of the MS. Book.

1 Caverns] Visions MS. Book 1st *rdg. del.* 3 But] And MS. Book 1st
rdg. del. 4 Who] Whom WMR, EY, WBY. 6 dauntless] dare to
MS. Book 1st *rdg. del.*

Egremont's Countess can controll
The flames of Hell that round me roll;
If she refuse, I still go on   9
Till the Heavens & Earth are gone,
Still admir'd by Noble minds,
Follow'd by Envy on the winds,
Re-engrav'd Time after Time,   13
Ever in their Youthful prime,
My Designs unchang'd remain.
Time may rage, but rage in vain.
For above Time's troubled Fountains,   17
On the Great Atlantic Mountains,
In my Golden House on high,
There they shine Eternally.

7 can] dare MS. Book *1st rdg. del.*   8 flames] doors *ibid. 1st rdg. del.*
11 Noble] worthy *ibid. 1st rdg. del.*   15 unchang'd] shall still *ibid. 1st*
rdg. del.

CXXX

I rose up at the dawn of day—   1
'Get thee away! get thee away!
Pray'st thou for Riches? away! away!
This is the Throne of Mammon grey.'

Said I: this, sure, is very odd;   5
I took it to be the Throne of God.
For everything besides I have:
It is only for Riches that I can crave.

MS. Book, p. 89, written immediately under and partly around an entry
dated Aug. 1807. R[1] has stanzas 1, 2, 3, the first couplet of 6, then 4 and 7;
Gil. i. 309, 310, prints 1, 2, 3, a fourth stanza formed of the first couplets of
6 and 4, a fifth stanza formed of the second couplet of 4 and the first couplet
of 5, then 7; Swinb. p. 128 (with title 'Prayer') arranges stanzas in the
order 1, 2, 3, 6, 4, 5, 7; WMR follows Gilchrist with title 'Mammon'; EY
(i. 228) and WBY place stanzas in correct order, the latter with title 'The
Two Thrones.'

5 Said I] I said R[1], EY, WBY.   7 For everything] Everything R[1],
Gil., WMR; Everything else EY, WBY.   8 It . . . crave] It's only
riches that I can crave Gil., WMR; It's only riches I can crave EY, WBY.
It is] It's R[1].

I have Mental Joy, & Mental Health,   9
And Mental Friends, & Mental wealth ;
I've a Wife I love, & that loves me ;
I've all But Riches Bodily.

I am in God's presence night & day,   13
And he never turns his face away ;
The accuser of sins by my side doth stand,
And he holds my money bag in his hand.

For my worldly things God makes him pay,   17
And he'd pay for more if to him I would pray ;
And so you may do the worst you can do ;
Be assur'd, Mr Devil, I won't pray to you.

Then if for Riches I must not Pray,   21
God knows, I little of Prayers need say ;
So, as a Church is known by its Steeple,
If I pray it must be for other People.

He says, if I do not worship him for a God,   25
I shall eat coarser food, & go worse shod ;
So, as I don't value such things as these,
You must do, Mr Devil, just as God please.

9 Joy] joys R¹ *and all edd.*   10 And Mental Friends] R¹ *and all*
edd. except Swinb. *omit* 'And.'   11 Wife I love] Wife that I love R¹
and all edd. except Swinb.   13–20 I am . . . to you] Written later in
margin, and marked for insertion here.   14 And he] R¹ *and all edd.*
except Swinb. *omit* 'And.'   15, 16 Cp. 'The Laocoön' (Prophetic
Books, 21) : 'Money, which is The Great Satan or Reason the Root of Good
& Evil In the Accusation of Sin.'   15 doth] does Swinb., EY, WBY.
16 money bag] money-bags EY, WBY.   19 And so you] And you
EY, WBY.   22 God . . . say] God knows it 's little prayers I need
say R¹, Gil., WMR, EY.   25 if . . . him] if I worship not him R¹, Gil.,
WMR ; if I don't worship him EY, WBY.   27 So] But R¹, Gil.,
WMR, EY, WBY.

CXXXi

Do what you will this life 's a fiction,
And is made up of contradiction.

MS. Book, p. 98, above stanza C 4 of 'Fayette' (MS. Book, xxxvi), which
appears upside down, written from the reversed end of the book.   Printed
here for first time.

POEMS

FROM

THE ROSSETTI MS.

III
'THE EVERLASTING GOSPEL'

§ cxxxii
Written circa 1810

THE EVERLASTING GOSPEL

Prefatory Note

THIS poem—or rather rough studies for a poem which Blake never carried to completion—consists of a series of fragments scattered throughout the MS. Book. As these occur for the most part on vacant spaces of pages already partially filled with the draft of his catalogue 'for the year 1810,' it is plain that 'The Everlasting Gospel' was written not earlier (though probably not much later) than this date.

Three of these fragments (β, γ^1, and γ^2) are different treatments of the same theme, Christ's gentleness or humility; one (δ) is a mere note or suggestion; while all but the first few lines of another (η) have been lost to us through Blake's neglect to transcribe the remainder of the passage into the MS. Book. The several fragments in their present form contain repetitions of lines and overlapping of thought and expression which the author would doubtless have removed on final revision. At one stage in the evolution of the poem Blake marked the order in which he intended the parts then written to be placed, and this clue, with careful observance of the position of later marginal insertions, enables us to arrange the different sections of the poem in their proper sequence. To carry further the attempt to give unity to this unfinished piece would involve editorial omissions and transpositions contrary to the plan of the present work.

Fragment β, the 57 ll. beginning 'Was Jesus gentle,' seems to have been the first draft of the initial section of the poem. Handling the same theme again in a different manner, Blake re-wrote the entire passage in the new form

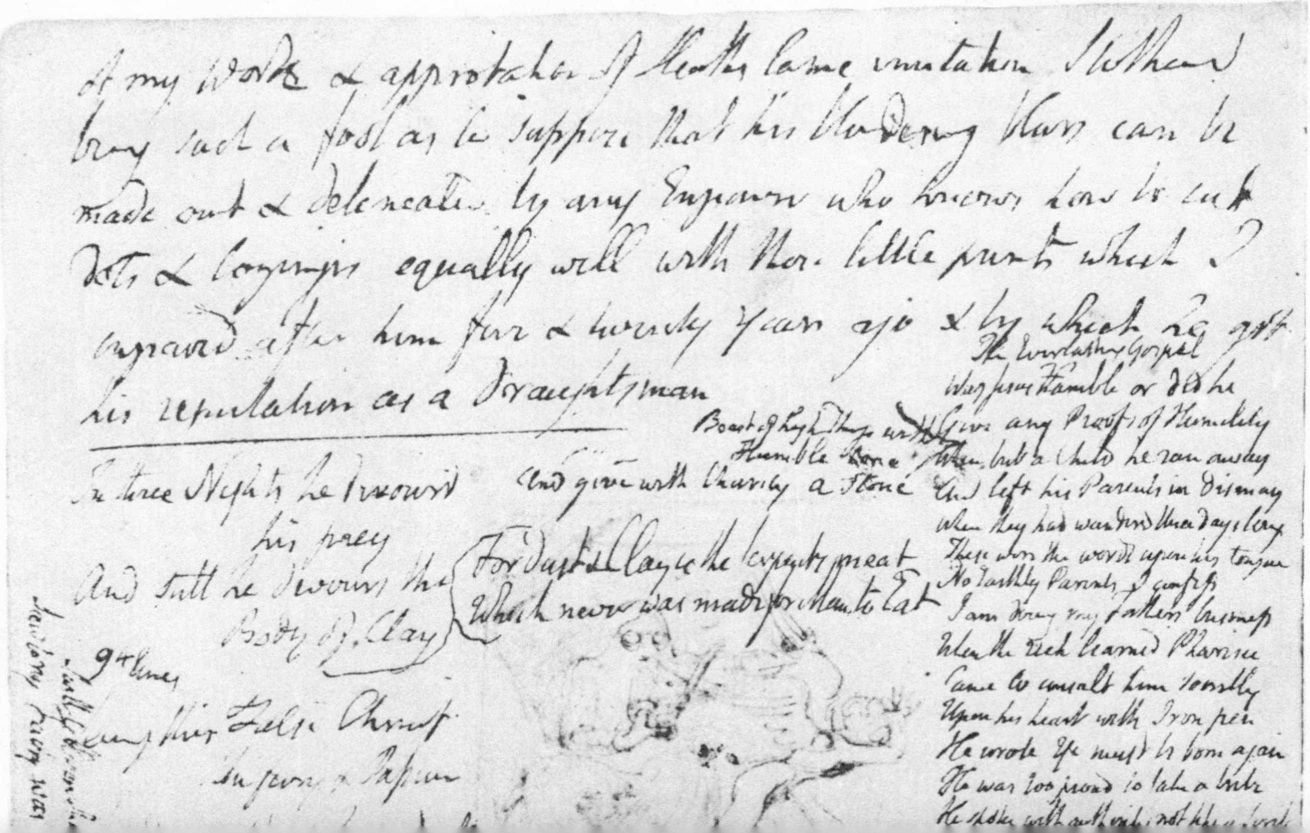
of my Works & appropriation of Another's same mistaken Stothard
being such a fool as to suppose that his blundering blurs can be
made out & delineated by any Engraver who knows how to cut
dots & lozenges equally well with those little prints which I
engraved after him five & twenty years ago & by which he got
his reputation as a Draughtsman

In three Nights he devourd
his prey
And still he devours the
Body of Clay

94 lines

Seeing this False Christ
In fury & Passion

Boast of high things with
Humble tone
And give with Charity a Stone

For Dust & Clay is the Serpents meat
Which never was made for Man to Eat

The Everlasting Gospel
Was Jesus Humble or did he
Give any Proofs of Humility
When but a Child he ran away
And left his Parents in dismay
When they had wanderd three days long
These were the words upon his tongue
No Earthly Parents I confess
I am doing my Fathers business
When the rich learned Pharisee
Came to consult him secretly
Upon his heart with Iron pen
He wrote Ye must be born again
He was too proud to take a bribe
He spoke with authority not like a Scribe

ROSSETTI MS., p. 52. In the centre of the page is the original sketch for plate 11 of *The Gates of Paradise*. At head and foot of page are portions of Blake's *Advertisement* or 'Public Address' (1810); while written still later, around centre and in left-hand margin and at foot of page, are part of 'The Everlasting Gospel', and the sestet on Joseph of Arimathea.

γ^1 (the 38 ll., or with marginal additions 46 ll., beginning 'Was Jesus humble' and ending 'And take Revenge at the last Day'), and this again was further altered and expanded into the revised version γ^2, to which the title 'The Everlasting Gospel' was prefixed for the first time. This last section contains 106 ll. which Blake, in a marginal note, reckons as 78, showing that the calculation was made before the interpolated ll. 21–24, 31–50 and 85–88 were added in the margin. At this point he indicated the connexion of γ^2 with ζ, which he then meant to be the next section, by adding the catchwords 'was Jesus chaste or did he &c.,' followed by the couplet (θ) with which the poem was apparently meant to conclude :—

> 'I am sure this Jesus will not do
> Either for Englishman or Jew.'

The fragment ζ 'Was Jesus chaste' contains 96 ll., the two last being a marginal addition, written after Blake had noted ' 94 lines ' as the length of this passage. Below l. 94, without apparent break, he added :—

> 'Seeing this false Christ in fury and passion
> I made my voice heard all over the nation.
> What are those, &c.'

followed at the side, a little lower down, by the two-line epilogue quoted above. It was Blake's practice to add '&c.' where a poem or passage had already been written elsewhere, and it seems clear that these three lines were merely catchwords marking the position of the imperfect section η. Messrs. Ellis and Yeats point out that the 7th stanza of 'To the Jews' (*Jerusalem*, 1804) begins with the words 'What are those golden builders doing?' As that poem, however, is written in quatrains with a different rime-arrangement it could not well have followed here, though Blake may have repeated this particular line.

Of the remaining portions the four-line fragment δ 'Did Jesus teach doubt' is written transversely on the page opposite the beginning of γ^2, which it was apparently meant to precede. Blake does not here add ' &c.,' and it is probable that these lines are merely suggestions of a new train of thought which he did not develop further. The 48 ll. (ϵ) beginning 'Was Jesus born of a virgin pure' are found on a scrap of different paper now bound in at the end of the MS. Book. It can hardly have been written earlier than May 1810, since it occupies the fourth page of a folded sheet, the preceding page of which contains part of the draft of Blake's Additions to his Catalogue of Pictures for the Year 1810; and it must have been written later than β as it has the amended form of l. 8, found in γ^1 and γ^2. But there are no grounds for Messrs. Ellis and Yeats' conjecture that these lines are 'an afterthought, intended to supersede much of the rest of the poems [*read* 'poem'] but rejected by the author before he made up his mind how to fix them in.' Probably all the fragments of 'The Everlasting Gospel' were first written, like ϵ, upon separate pieces of paper, which were afterwards copied into, or merely loosely inserted in, the MS. Book. The comparatively small number of corrections made in β show that it must have been copied from an earlier draft, and the loss of η (perhaps also of δ) may be attributed to the same cause. This passage has no place assigned to it, but its natural position would appear to be immediately before ζ, where I print it in the present arrangement.

The fourteen lines beginning 'The Vision of Christ that thou dost see' (α) are introductory to the whole poem, to which they are probably meant to serve as prologue. The interpolation ϵ still leaves the epilogue at the end of the poem as at first intended.

A small part only of 'The Everlasting Gospel' was included among the 'Poems hitherto Unpublished' in Gilchrist (1863); Mr. D. G. Rossetti there printing the prologue (ll. 3, 4 omitted) and 42 of 96 ll. of ζ, under the title 'The Woman taken in Adultery.' A much more comprehensive selection is given by Mr. Swinburne (*Essay*, 1868, pp. 148–175), who prints altogether 253 ll., enriched by running commentary. Here and there slight emendations are made, such as 'This life's dim windows of the soul' for 'This life's five windows of the soul'; but Blake's text is, for the most part, reverently treated. Mr. Swinburne's extracts have obviously been chosen with a view to elucidating his author's meaning, and there is consequently no attempt at strict sequence.

In the Aldine Edition (1874) Mr. W. M. Rossetti states that 'this wholly amazing and partly splendid poem is now published in full for the first time,' adding 'I have done my best to arrange the verses into some sort of order and method; with what success, the reader must judge.' The omission of γ^1, and a few odd couplets rejected for various reasons, reduce the entire number of lines in this version to 313. The poem as reconstructed by Mr. W. M.

Rossetti is divided into the following six sections, not always corresponding with those of the author—1 α (except ll. 3, 4). 2. ϵ. 3. ζ, ll. 1–80. 4. γ^2, ll. 1–20, 25–40; β, ll. 13, 57; γ^2, ll. 51–106; ζ, ll. 91, 92, 81–90; γ^2 ll. 21–24; ζ, ll. 93–96. 5. δ; γ^2, ll. 41–50. 6. θ. Mr. Rossetti has generally adopted the emendations introduced into the text by his predecessor.

Messrs. Ellis and Yeats (vol. ii, pp. 42–60) have made the only attempt up to the present to reproduce the fragments as Blake left them. They first give γ^1 and γ^2 in parallel columns, as 'final version' and 'previous version,' the latter followed by β ('Another version, apparently earlier'); then δ and ζ (treating the former as a continuation of the latter), then θ, which they think was cancelled in favour of η—'and so the MS. of "The Everlasting Gospel" terminates for us with a loose end.' Here they fail to see that the $2\frac{1}{2}$ ll. of η are merely catchwords marking the position of a complete passage, written down elsewhere, but now unfortunately lost to us. Later they print as a separate scrap γ^2, ll. 21–25, though its proper place is clearly marked in the MS., followed by ϵ, which, for no discernible reason, they regard as a cancelled passage. The numerous inaccuracies in their text are, here as elsewhere, due rather to simple blundering than to any attempt to amend their author, such as we find in Swinburne and Rossetti. Such misreadings as 'Doth read' for 'Both read' (α, l. 13), 'all day long' for 'three days long' (γ^1, l. 5), 'ten years old' for 'twelve years old' (γ^2, l. 52)—passages correctly printed by Blake's earlier editors—show the carelessness with which they transcribed their original.

Mr. W. B. Yeats gives ten lines less than WMR; but arranges the fragments with more regard for Blake's own subdivisions. His order of the passages is as follows: 1. α (except ll. 3, 4). 2. γ^2, ll. 1–20, 25–106; β, ll. 13–57. 3. ζ. 4. ϵ. 5. θ. The transposition of ζ and ϵ is scarcely happy, and the omission of η,

> 'Seeing this false Christ in fury and passion
> I made my voice heard all over the nation'—

to which the epilogue forms the natural climax—destroys the force of this concluding couplet by making it immediately follow the speech of Caiaphas (ϵ, ll. 17–48).

THE EVERLASTING GOSPEL

a

[*Prologue*]

The Vision of Christ that thou dost see
Is my Vision's Greatest Enemy.
Thine has a great hook nose like thine;
Mine has a snub nose like to mine.   4
Thine is the Friend of All Mankind;
Mine speaks in Parables to the Blind.
Thine loves the same world that mine hates;
Thy heaven doors are my Hell Gates.   8
Socrates taught what Meletus
Loath'd as a Nation's bitterest Curse,
And Caiaphas was in his own Mind
A benefactor to Mankind.   12
Both read the Bible day & night,
But thou read'st black where I read white.

MS. Book, p. 33.   On the strength of the phrase 'Friend of all Mankind'
(cp. MS. Book xlix and lxxxviii) and the reference to the 'great hook nose,'
EY suppose this prologue to be addressed to Stothard.   See also prose note
in MS. Book, p. 64 : 'I always thought that Jesus Christ was a snubby, or
I should not have worshipped him if I thought he had been one of those
long spindle-nosed rascals.'

3, 4 Thine . . . mine] This couplet omitted by all except EY.   3 great]
long EY.   4 to] EY *omit*.   5 Friend] fare DGR.   9-12 Cp.
Jerusalem, f. 93, where on the bodies of three figures with out-
stretched arms and accusing forefingers are engraved the words 'Anytus
Meletus & Lycon thought Socrates a very Pernicious Man. So Cai[a]phas
thought Jesus.'   13 Both] Doth EY, WBY.   14 read'st] readest EY,
WBY.

β

Was Jesus gentle, or did He
Give any marks of Gentility?
When twelve years old he ran away,
And left his Parents in dismay.   4
When after three days' sorrow found,
Loud as Sinai's trumpet-sound :
' No Earthly Parents I confess :
My Heavenly Father's business.   8
Ye understand not what I say,
And, angry, force me to obey.
Obedience is a duty then,
And favour gains with God & Men.'   12
John from the Wilderness loud cried ;
Satan Gloried in his Pride.
' Come,' said Satan, ' come away,
I'll soon see if you'll obey !   16
John for disobedience bled,
But you can turn the stones to bread.
God's high king & God's high Priest
Shall Plant their Glories in Your breast,   20

MS. Book, pp. 100, 101. A fair copy of an earlier draft, as appears from
the very slight alterations made after writing. First printed in full by EY,
ii. pp. 50, 51, col. 2. Swinb. pp. 168–170, quotes with commentary ll. 17–32,
35–40, 47–57, mistakenly calling these ' a later division of the poem.' WMR
inserts ll. 13–57 between γ², ll. 44 and 51. WBY places the same lines as
conclusion to γ², following l. 106.

6 trumpet-sound] trumpet's sound EY.   7, 8 No . . . business] The MS.
Book has no punctuation. In γ¹ (l. 8), γ² (l. 10), and ε (l. 34) Blake changes
the last line of this couplet to ' I am doing my Father's business.' EY make
an heroic attempt to accept the lines as they occur here, by punctuating :—

> ' No, earthly parents, I confess
> My heavenly Father's business.'

which necessitates their still weaker readings in γ¹ and γ² (abandoned
however in ε) :—

> ' No, earthly parents, I confess
> I am doing My Father's business.'

It should not be overlooked that in its present form the poem is merely
a rough draft. Cp., as another sentence of equally slovenly construction,
ll. 22, 23.   16 you'll] you EY, WBY.   18 stones] stone WBY.

If Caiaphas You will obey,
If Herod You with bloody Prey
Feed with the Sacrifice & be
Obedient; fall down, worship me.'   24
Thunders & lightnings broke around,
And Jesus' voice in thunders' sound:
'Thus I sieze the spiritual Prey.
Ye smiters with disease, make way.   28
I come your King & God to sieze,
Is God a smiter with disease?'
The God of this World raged in vain;
He bound Old Satan in His Chain,   32
And, bursting forth, his furious ire
Became a Chariot of fire.
Throughout the land he took his course,
And trac'd diseases to their source.   36
He curs'd the Scribe & Pharisee,
Trampling down Hipocrisy.
Where'er His Chariot took its way,
There Gates of death let in the Day,   40
Broke down from every Chain & Bar;
And Satan in his Spiritual War
Drag'd at His Chariot wheels: loud howl'd
The God of this World: louder roll'd   44
The Chariot Wheels, and louder still
His voice was heard from Zion's Hill,
And in his hand the Scourge shone bright;
He scourg'd the Merchant Canaanite   48
From out the Temple of his Mind,
And in his Body tight does bind
Satan & all his Hellish Crew;
And thus with wrath he did subdue   52
The Serpent Bulk of Nature's Dross,

22, 23 If Herod . . . Sacrifice] Swinb. p. 168: 'An ugly specimen of
ready-writing; meaning of course "with the sacrifice of bloody prey."'
25 Thunders] Thunder Swinb., WBY.   lightnings] lightning Swinb.,
WMR.   26 thunders'] thunder's Swinb., WMR; the thunder's EY, WBY.
28 make] give WBY.   33 And . . . ire] And, bursting forth his furious
ire, EY, WBY.   40 There] Those Swinb.; The WMR, EY, WBY.
41 &] a EY, WBY.   50 does] did WBY.

Till he had nail'd it to the Cross.
He took on Sin in the Virgin's Womb
And put it off on the Cross & Tomb   56
To be Worship'd by the Church of Rome.

55 took] put Swinb.   Womb] Followed in MS. Book by the cancelled line with which this section of the poem originally ended :—
'but on the Cross he sealed its doom.'

γ^1

Was Jesus Humble, or did He
Give any proofs of Humility?
When but a Child he ran away,
And left His Parents in dismay.   4
When they had wander'd three days long
These were the words upon His Tongue:
'No Earthly Parents I confess;
I am doing my Father's business.'   8
When the rich learnèd Pharisee
Came to consult him secretly,
He was too Proud to take a bribe;
He spoke with authority, not like a Scribe.   12
Upon his heart with Iron pen
He wrote 'Ye must be born again.'
He says, with most consummate art,
'Follow me, I am meek & lowly of heart,   16
As that is the only way to escape
The Miser's net and the Glutton's trap.'

MS. Book, p. 98. Blake's first draft of this passage. Only printed
separately by EY, ii. pp. 49, 50, col. 2.
    5 three days long] all day long EY.   7, 8 No ... business] See note
to β, ll. 7, 8.   11, 12 He ... Scribe] Marginal numbers, 1, 4, 5, 2, 3, 6,
prefixed to ll. 10–15, indicate the transposition of this and the succeeding
couplet (as found in γ^2, ll. 13–16).   16 heart] Quotation marks (wanting in
MS. Book) end here in EY.   18 trap] MS. Book has the marginal addition
marked for insertion here :—

        'He who loves his enemies hates his friends,
        This is surely not what Jesus intends:
        He must mean the mere love of civility,
        And so He must mean concerning humility.'

But he acts with triumphant, honest pride,
And this is the Reason Jesus died.   20
If, he had been Antichrist, creeping Jesus,
He'd have done anything to please us:
Gone sneaking into the synagogues
And not used the Elders & Priests like Dogs.   24
Humble toward God, Haughty toward Man,
This is the Race that Jesus ran.
But when he humbled himself to God,
Then descended the cruel rod.   28
'If thou humblest thyself, thou humblest Me;
Thou also dwelst in Eternity.
Thou art a Man. God is no more.
Thine own Humanity learn to adore,   32
And thy Revenge abroad display
In terrors at the last Judgment day.
God's Mercy & Long Suffering
Are but the sinner to Judgment to bring.   36
Thou on the Cross for them shalt pray,
And take Revenge at the last Day.'

23 the] EY *omit.*   24 Dogs] MS. Book has the marginal addition marked
for insertion here:—

> 'Not humble as a lamb or an ass,
> Obey himself to Caiaphas.
> God wants not Man to humble himself;
> This is the trick of the ancient elf.'

Omitted in EY.   29 If . . . Me] Why dost thou humble thyself to me?
MS. Book 1*st rgd. del.*   31, 32 Cp. *Natural Religion* (A.), f. **10** : 'Therefore God becomes as we are, that we may be as he is.'   35–38 EY
omit.   38 And . . . Day] Whom thou shalt torment at the last day.
MS. Book 1*st rgd. del.*

$$\gamma^2$$

The Everlasting Gospel

Was Jesus Humble? or did he
Give any Proofs of Humility?

MS. Book, pp. 52, 53, 54. The revised draft of γ^1, with title of poem
added for first time. Cp. *Descriptive Catalogue* (1809): 'All had originally
one language and one religion; this was the religion of Jesus, the everlasting Gospel.'

Swinb. pp. 159–167, quotes ll. 1–4, 11–16, 35–8, 43–54, 59–106, with

Boast of high Things with Humble tone,
And give with Charity a stone?   4
When but a Child he ran away,
And left his Parents in dismay.
When they had wander'd three days long
These were the words upon his tongue: 8
' No Earthly Parents I confess:
I am doing my Father's business.'
When the rich learnèd Pharisee
Came to consult him secretly,   12
Upon his heart with Iron pen
He wrote 'Ye must be born again.'
He was too proud to take a bribe;
He spoke with authority, not like a Scribe.   16
He says with most consummate Art
' Follow me, I am meek & lowly of heart,
As that is the only way to escape
The Miser's net & the Glutton's trap.'   20
What can be done with such desperate Fools
Who follow after the Heathen Schools?
I was standing by when Jesus died;
What I call'd Humility, they call'd Pride.   24
He who loves his Enemies betrays his Friends.
This surely is not what Jesus intends;
But the Sneaking Pride of Heroic Schools,
And the Scribes' & Pharisees' Virtuous Rules;   28
For he acts with honest, triumphant Pride,
And this is the cause that Jesus died.

He did not die with Christian Ease,
Asking Pardon of his Enemies: 32
If he had, Caiaphas would forgive;
Sneaking submission can always live.
He had only to say that God was the Devil,
And the Devil was God, like a Christian civil;   36
Mild Christian regrets to the Devil confess
For affronting him thrice in the Wilderness ;—
He had soon been bloody Caesar's Elf,
And at last he would have been Caesar himself. 40
Like d^r Priestly & Bacon & Newton
(Poor spiritual knowledge is not worth a button !)
For thus the Gospel St. Isaac confutes:
'God can only be known by His Attributes;   44
And as for the Indwelling of the Holy Ghost,
Or of Christ & His Father, it's all a boast
And pride, & vanity of the imagination,
That disdains to follow this world's fashion.'   48
To teach doubt & experiment
Certainly was not what Christ meant.
What was he doing all that time,
From twelve years old to manly prime?   52

31–50 He . . . meant] These lines are an addition, marked for insertion here, the last couplet being written still later in the margin.   37–44 Mild . . . Attributes] Thus in MS. Book, Blake's prefixed letters and figures indicating the order followed in the text :—

    (*a*) For affronting him thrice in the Wilderness   *38
          Like d^r Priestly & Bacon & Newton
    (1) Poor spiritual knowledge is not worth a button   *40
    (2) For thus the Gospel St. Isaac confutes
    (3) God can only be known by His Attributes
    (*b*) He had soon been bloody Caesar's Elf
    (*c*) And at last he would have been Caesar himself.

WMR prints ll. 41–50 as continuation of δ. EY, ignoring Blake's marginal rearrangement, print the lines as in this footnote. WBY interchanges the position of couplets *41, *42, and *43, *44.   40 he] WMR *omits*.   41 Like . . . Newton] Like Doctor Priestley, Bacon, and Newton WMR ; Like to Priestley and Bacon and Newton EY, WBY   43 For] But EY ; And WBY.   Gospel . . . Isaac] Gospel of St. Isaac EY.   44 can . . . known] is only known WBY.   45 as for] as to Swinb. WMR.   46 Or of] Or EY, WBY.   His] the Swinb., WMR.   47 And] Or EY, WBY. vanity] fallacy EY, WBY.   the] Swinb. *and* WMR. *omit*.   48 disdains] did wrong Swinb.   52 twelve] ten EY, WBY.

Was he then Idle, or the less
About his father's business?
Or was his wisdom held in scorn
Before his wrath began to burn   56
In Miracles throughout the Land,
That quite unnerved the seraph band?
If He had been Antichrist, creeping Jesus,
He'd have done anything to please us;   60
Gone sneaking into Synagogues,
And not us'd the Elders & Priests like dogs;
But Humble as a lamb or ass
Obey'd Himself to Caiaphas.   64
God wants not Man to humble himself:
That is the trick of the ancient Elf.
This is the Race that Jesus ran:
Humble to God, Haughty to man,   68
Cursing the Rulers before the People
Even to the temple's highest Steeple,
And when he Humbled himself to God
Then descended the Cruel Rod.   72
'If thou humblest thyself, thou humblest me.
Thou also dwellst in Eternity.
Thou art a Man: God is no more:
Thy own humanity learn to adore,   76
For that is my Spirit of Life.
Awake, arise to Spiritual Strife,
And thy Revenge abroad display
In terrors at the Last Judgment day.   80
God's Mercy & Long Suffering
Is but the sinner to judgment to bring.
Thou on the Cross for them shalt pray—

55–58 Or . . . band] Swinb. *omits.*   58 seraph band] Not legibly
written; seraph's hand WMR; ? seraph hand EY; seraph hand WBY.
59 Antichrist, creeping Jesus] a creeping Jesus MS. Book *1st rgd. del.*;
Antichrist aping Jesus Swinb., WMR. Cf. a passage from Blake's letter to
Cumberland, dated April 12, 1827 : 'God keep you and me from the divinity
of yes, and no too,—the yea, nay, creeping Jesus,—from supposing up and
down to be the same thing, as all experimentalists must suppose.'   76
Thy] Thine Swinb., WMR, WBY.   80 terrors] terror Swinb., WMR.
82 Is] Are *all edd.*   judgment] justice Swinb., EY, WBY.   83 shalt]
shall EY, WBY.

And take Revenge at the Last Day.'   84
Jesus replied, & thunders hurl'd :
'I never will Pray for the World.
Once I did so when I pray'd in the Garden ;
I wish'd to take with me a Bodily Pardon.'   88
Can that which was of woman born,
In the absence of the Morn,
When the soul fell into sleep,
And Archangels round it weep,   92
Shooting out against the Light
Fibres of a deadly night,
Reasoning upon its own dark Fiction,
In doubt which is Self Contradiction ?   96
Humility is only doubt,
And does the Sun & Moon blot out,
Rooting over with thorns & stems
The buried Soul & all its Gems.   100
This life's Five Windows of the Soul
Distorts the Heavens from Pole to Pole,

84] Followed in the MS. Book by the lines :—

> 'This Corporeal life's a fiction
> And is made up of contradiction.'

This couplet, which was afterwards erased in ink and retranscribed in a slightly altered form on p. 98, can hardly have been intended as part of 'The Everlasting Gospel.'   85–88 Jesus . . . Pardon] These lines are an addition. EY, WBY, perhaps rightly, carry on the quotation marks to the end of l. 106.   85 &] in EY, WBY.   89–96 Can . . . Self Contradiction] Perhaps 'Can that which was of women born, *etc.* take with it a bodily pardon ?' or possibly sentence left unfinished.   Swinb. supplies the conclusion : 'Can that reason itself into redemption ?'   89 woman] women EY.   91 When] While Swinb.   92 And Archangels] And (? heard) archangels Swinb.   it] did WBY.   95, 96 Reasoning . . . Self Contradiction] Cp. *The Gates of Paradise,* 'The Keys of the Gates,' ll. 13–15 :

> 'Two Horrid Reasoning Cloven Fiction,
> In Doubt, which is Self contradiction,
> A dark Hermaphrodite, We stood.'

97, 98 Humility . . . out] Cp. Pick. MS. 'Auguries of Innocence,' ll. 109, 110 :—

> 'If the Sun & Moon should Doubt,
> They'd immediately Go Out.'

99 Rooting] Roofing *all edd.*   Cp. *Jerusalem,* f. 43, l. 8 : 'If we are wrathful Albion will destroy Jerusalem with rooty Groves.'   101, 102 Five Windows . . . Distorts] dim window . . . Distorts Swinb. WMR ; five windows . . .

And leads you to Believe a Lie
When you see with, not through, the Eye　104
That was born in a night, to perish in a night,
When the soul slept in the beams of light.

Distort EY, WBY. Cp. the lines in the preface, on f. 3, of Mr. John Linnell's
copy of *Europe* :—
　' Five windows light the cavern'd Man ; thro' one he breathes the air ;
　Thro' one hears music of the spheres ; thro' one the eternal vine
　Flourishes that he may receive the grapes ; thro' one can look
　And see small portions of the eternal world that ever groweth;
　Thro' one himself pass out what time he please, but he will not,
　For stolen joys are sweet, & bread eaten in secret pleasant.'

103-106 And . . . light] Cp. Pick. MS. ' Auguries of Innocence,' ll. 125-128 :—
　　　　'We are led to Believe a Lie
　　　　When we see [*with del.*] not Thro' the Eye,
　　　　Which was Born in a Night, to perish in a Night,
　　　　When the Soul Slept in Beams of Light.'

103 leads] lead WBY.　　105 That] Which EY, WBY.　　106 the beams]
EY, WBY *omit* the.　　106] This line has Blake's marginal numeration
' 78 lines,' followed by the couplet :—
　　　　　　'I'm sure this Jesus will not do
　　　　　　Either for Englishman or Jew—'
and the catchword 'was Jesus Chaste or did he, &c.' a connecting line
indicating that (ζ) was then intended to follow l. 106. See Introduction to
his poem.

δ

This was spoken by my spectre to Voltaire, Bacon, &c.

　　Did Jesus teach doubt ? or did he
　　Give any lessons of Philosophy,
　　Charge Visionaries with decieving,
　　Or call Men wise for not Believing?

MS. Book, p. 48. The beginning of a new passage, apparently left
unfinished. These lines are written laterally in pencil, in margin of page
opposite the beginning of ζ. The heading is written in pencil at the top of
the same page. Blake's use of the word ' spectre' in the sense of ' reasoning power' has been already noted. Cp. *Jerusalem*, f. 10, ll. 7-16.
　Swinb. p. 164. WMR prefixes these two couplets to γ², ll. 41-50, which,
in his rearrangement, form the penultimate section of the poem. EY mis-
quote ' This was spoken by my spectre to Bacon, Newton and Locke,' and,
while pointing out that this fragment has no place assigned to it, seem
to regard it as a continuation of ζ. WBY omits.
　　　2 any] WMR *omits.*　　of] in EY.

ϵ

Was Jesus Born of a Virgin Pure
With narrow Soul & looks demure?
If He intended to take on Sin
The Mother should an Harlot been; 4
Just such a one as Magdalen,
With seven devils in her Pen.
Or were Jew virgins still more curs'd,
And more sucking devils nurs'd? 8
Or what was it which he took on,
That he might bring Salvation?
A Body subject to be Tempted,
From neither pain nor grief Exempted; 12
Or such a body as might not feel
The passions that with sinners deal?
Yes, but they say he never fell.
Ask Caiaphas; for he can tell.— 16
'He mock'd the Sabbath, and he mock'd
The Sabbath's God, and He unlock'd

Written on the fourth page of a folded scrap of paper, containing 'Blake's Chaucer,' etc., bound in at the end of the MS. Book. See prefatory note to this poem. Swinb. pp. 170-174, prints ll. 1-16, 25-38, 47, 48. WMR makes this the second section of the poem. EY and WBY also print in full, the latter placing it immediately before the epilogue.

4 The] His *all edd.* been] (have) been Swinb.; have been WMR, EY, WBY. 7, 8 Or . . . nurs'd] *Interlineated in* MS. Book. 8 more] with more EY, WBY. 9 which] that *all except* WMR. 13 might] could Swinb. 17-48 He . . . prey] *No quot. marks in* MS. Book. Cp. *Marriage of Heaven and Hell* (1790), ff. 23, 24: 'The Devil answer'd, "bray a fool in a morter with wheat, yet shall not his folly be beaten out of him": if Jesus Christ is the greatest man, you ought to love him in the greatest degree; now hear how he has given his sanction to the law of ten commandments: did he not mock at the sabbath, and so mock the sabbath's God? murder those who were murder'd because of him? turn away the law from the woman taken in adultery? steal the labor of others to support him? bear false witness when he omitted making a defence before Pilate? covet when he pray'd for his disciples, and when he bid them shake off the dust of their feet against such as refused to lodge them? I tell you no virtue can exist without breaking these ten commandments: Jesus was all virtue, and acted from impulse not from rules.'

The Evil spirits from their Shrines,
And turn'd Fishermen to Divines;   20
O'erturn'd the tent of secret sins,
And its golden cords and Pins,
In the Bloody Shrine of War
Pour'd around from star to star,—   24
Halls of justice, hating Vice,
Where the devil combs his lice.
He turn'd the devils into swine
That he might tempt the Jews to dine;   28
Since which, a Pig has got a look
That for a Jew may be mistook.
"Obey your Parents." What says he?
"Woman, what have I to do with thee?   32
No Earthly Parents I confess:
I am doing My Father's Business."
He scorn'd Earth's parents, scorn'd Earth's God,
And mock'd the one and the other's Rod;   36
His Seventy Disciples sent
Against Religion and Government—
They by the Sword of Justice fell,
And him their Cruel Murderer tell.   40
He left his Father's trade to roam,
A wand'ring vagrant without Home;
And thus he others' labour stole,
That he might live above controll.   44
The Publicans and Harlots he
Selected for his company,
And from the Adulteress turn'd away
God's righteous Law, that lost its Prey.'   48

21-24 O'erturn'd ... star] *A marginal addition.*   22 its] all its EY, WBY.
23 In] *Not plainly written;* 'Tis WMR, EY, WBY.   24 Pour'd] *Not
plainly written, perhaps* 'Pass'd.'   25, 26 Halls ... lice] *A later
marginal addition, written transversely to ll.* 21-24.   29 which] when
all edd.   33, 34 No ... Business] *See note to β,* 7, 8.   35 Earth's God]
his God MS. Book *1st rdg. del.*   36 other's] other WMR, EY, WBY.
43 labour] labours EY, WBY.

ζ

Was Jesus Chaste? or did He
Give any lessons of Chastity?
The Morning blushèd fiery red:
Mary was found in Adulterous bed;   4
Earth groan'd beneath, and Heaven above
Trembled at discovery of Love.
Jesus was sitting in Moses' Chair.
They brought the trembling woman there.   8
Moses commands she be ston'd to death.
What was the sound of Jesus' breath?
He laid His hand on Moses' Law;
The ancient heavens, in silent awe,   12
Writ with Curses from Pole to Pole,
All away began to roll.
The Earth trembling and Naked lay
In secret bed of Mortal Clay;   16
On Sinai felt the hand Divine
Pulling back the bloody shrine;
And she heard the breath of God,
As she heard by Eden's flood: 20
'Good and Evil are no more!
Sinai's trumpets cease to roar!
Cease, finger of God, to write!
The Heavens are not clean in thy sight.   24
Thou art good, and Thou alone;
Nor may the sinner cast one stone.

MS. Book, pp. 48, 49, 50, 51. Lines 7-16, 19, 20, 27-32, 39-50, 53-64,
with the Prologue, were first printed by DGR under the title 'The Woman
taken in Adultery.' Swinb., pp. 152-154, 168, 169, 261, prints ll. 1-80, 83-96.
WMR makes ll. 1-80 his third division, and places ll. 91, 92, 81-90, 93-96
among parts of β and γ² as his fourth division of the poem. EY and WBY
print in full, the latter putting this passage before ε.

 2 of] in EY, WBY.   7 was sitting] sat DGR.   8 trembling]
adulterous R¹.   17, 18 DGR *omits.*   17 felt] fell EY, WBY.
18 Pulling] Pulling [or ? Putting] Swinb.; Putting WMR, EY, WBY.
20 heard by] heard it by DGR.   21-26 Good . . . stone] DGR *omits.*

To be Good only, is to be
A God or else a Pharisee.   28
Thou Angel of the Presence Divine,
That didst create this Body of Mine,
Wherefore hast thou writ these Laws
And created Hell's dark jaws?   32
My Presence I will take from thee:
A cold Leper thou shalt be.
Though thou wast so pure and bright
That Heaven was Impure in thy sight,   36
Though thy Oath turn'd Heaven Pale,
Though thy covenant built Hell's jail,
Though thou didst all to chaos roll
With the serpent for its soul,   40
Still the breath Divine does move,
And the breath Divine is love.
Mary, Fear Not. Let me see
The Seven Devils that torment thee.   44
Hide not from my sight thy sin,
That forgiveness thou may'st win.
Has no Man condemnèd thee?'
'No Man, Lord.' 'Then what is he   48
Who shall accuse thee? Come ye forth,
Fallen fiends of Heavenly birth,
That have forgot your ancient love,
And driven away my trembling Dove.   52
You shall bow before her feet;
You shall lick the dust for Meat;
And though you cannot Love, but Hate,
Shall be beggars at Love's Gate.   56

27, 28 To be . . . Pharisee] *A marginal addition.*   27 Good only, is to
be] good only is to be WMR.   28 A God] As God EY, WBY.   31 hast]
has Swinb.   33 My] *My* Swinb.   36 Impure] not clean EY, WBY.
37 thy] thine Swinb., WMR.   38 jail] goal Swinb.   39 didst] dost
EY, WBY.   41 does] doth DGR.   43 Mary] Woman DGR.
44 torment] trouble DGR.   46 forgiveness] full forgiveness DGR.
47 Has] Hath DGR, Swinb., WMR.   50 Fallen] Ye fallen DGR.
53 You] Ye DGR.   54 You] Ye DGR.   Meat] meet EY, WBY.
55 You] Ye DGR.   56 Shall be] Ye shall be DGR; You shall be
EY, WBY.

What was thy love? Let me see it;
Was it Love or dark deceit?'
' Love too long from me has fled ;
'Twas dark deceit, to earn my bread;   60
'Twas covet, or 'twas custom, or
Some trifle not worth caring for;
That they may call a shame and sin
Love's Temple that God dwelleth in,   64
And hide in secret hidden shrine
The Naked Human form divine,
And render that a Lawless thing
On which the soul expands its wing.   68
But this, O Lord, this was my sin,
When first I let these devils in,
In dark pretence to chastity
Blaspheming Love, blaspheming Thee,   72
Thence rose secret adulteries,
And thence did covet also rise.
My sin Thou hast forgiven me ;
Canst Thou forgive my Blasphemy?   76
Canst Thou return to this dark Hell,
And in my burning bosom dwell?
And canst Thou die that I may live?
And canst Thou Pity and forgive?'   80
Then Roll'd the shadowy Man away
From the limbs of Jesus, to make them his prey,
An ever devouring appetite,
Glittering with festering Venoms bright ;   84
Crying ' Crucify this cause of distress,
Who don't keep the secrets of holiness!
The Mental Powers by Diseases we bind ;
But he heals the deaf, the dumb, & the Blind   88

---

57 see it] see't DGR, Swinb., WMR.   59 has] hath DGR.
63 That . . . call] But these would call DGR.   64 dwelleth in] DGR's
extract ends.   65–68 And . . . wing] *An addition.*   68 its] her *all edd.*
70 these] those WMR ; the EY, WBY.   84 Glittering] Glistering EY,
WBY.   85–90 Crying . . . Friends] *An addition.*   85 Crying] Saying
EY, WBY.   86 don't] does not WBY.   secrets] secret EY, WBY.
87 The] All Swinb., WMR.   by] with WMR.   Diseases] disease EY,
WBY.   88 the dumb] and the dumb Swinb., WMR.   &] EY, WBY *omit.*

Whom God has afflicted for secret ends,
He comforts and Heals and calls them Friends.'
But, when Jesus was crucified,
Then was perfected his galling pride.   92
In three Nights he devour'd his prey,
And still he devours the Body of Clay;
For Dust and Clay is the Serpent's meat,
Which never was made for Man to Eat.   96

89 has] hath EY, WBY.   91–96 But . . . eat] Swinb., p. 261.   93, 94
Cp. *Jerusalem*, f. 89, l. 13 : ' In three days he devour'd the rejected corse
of death.'   93 Nights] days Swinb., EY, WBY.   94 he] EY, WBY
omit.   the] this EY, WBY.   95, 96 For . . . Eat] *A marginal
addition*.   96 Which] That EY, WBY.   made] meant *all edd*.

η

Seeing this False Christ, in fury & Passion
I made my Voice heard all over the Nation.
What are those, &c.

MS. Book, p. 52.   These lines, catchwords marking the position of
a passage, the rest of which is lost, immediately follow ζ, l. 96.   They are
only quoted by EY, who treat them as the termination of the poem.   See
Pref. Note.

θ

[*Epilogue*]

I am sure this Jesus will not do,
Either for Englishman or Jew.

MS. Book, p. 54.   Originally meant to follow ζ.   See Prefatory Note.   In
WMR this epilogue follows γ², l. 50 ; in WBY it follows ε.
1 I am] I'm Swinb., WMR.

THE PICKERING MS.

circa 1801–1803

PREFACE

TO

THE PICKERING MS.

THE Pickering MS. is the name used throughout this edition for the smaller of the two Blake holographs from which D. G. Rossetti selected the 'poems hitherto unpublished,' printed in the second volume of Gilchrist's *Life* (pp. 76–116). In his introduction to this ' precious section ' he explains that its contents ' have been derived partly from the MS. Note Book ["the Rossetti MS."] to which frequent reference has been made in the *Life*, and partly from another small autograph collection of different matter somewhat more fairly copied.' 'The poems,' adds Rossetti, ' have been reclaimed, as regards the first-mentioned source, from as chaotic a mass as could well be imagined ; amid which it has sometimes been necessary either to omit, transpose, or combine, so as to render available what was very seldom found in a final state. And even in the pieces drawn from the second source specified above, means of the same kind have occasionally been resorted to, where they seemed to lessen obscurity or avoid redundance.'

In 1866, three years after the publication of Gilchrist's work, the MS., as we learn from Shepherd's introduction to his edition of 1874, was bought by Basil Montagu Pickering, son of the William Pickering who in 1830 had published the first letterpress edition of Blake's *Songs of Innocence and of Experience*. 'These considerations,' says Shepherd, referring to the inaccuracy of Rossetti's text, ' his father's former connexion with the *Songs of Innocence*, and the purchase eventually of a number of inedited Poems of Blake, led the Publisher to re-issue his father's volume together with the newly-acquired pieces in 1866. . . . The little volume was welcomed as satisfying a public want, and it passed into a second edition (now also exhausted) two years later (1868).'

For over thirty years nothing further was heard of the Pickering MS. It was lost sight of presumably about the date of Pickering's death in 1878, and, though occasional attempts to trace its subsequent ownership were made by the two or three students who realized that this MS. constituted the sole authority for the text of some of Blake's loveliest and most extraordinary poems, their efforts were unsuccessful. Messrs. Ellis and Yeats and later editors were thus obliged to follow the versions of these poems given by D. G. Rossetti and Shepherd, the only two editors who had made use of the original autograph. The MS. was thought to be permanently lost, and the present editor had accordingly decided to reproduce Shepherd's as the best available text. This portion of the work was indeed in proof, when the opportune reappearance of the original MS. enabled him to print this section also with the literal fidelity observed in the rest of the poems. The Pickering MS., the great importance of which would seem to have been overlooked by its last owner, had lain perdu for years in the Rowfant Library. On the purchase of the Locker Lampson collection in June, 1905, by Messrs. Dodd, Meade & Co. of New York, several Blake originals and other works were bought en bloc by Mr. W. A. White, who was surprised to find among them the long-missing Pickering MS. I owe to Mr. White's kindness the rectification of my text. as well as the following details respecting this undescribed MS.

The Pickering MS. is a foolscap quarto volume (6 x 8 inches), of 11 leaves of writing or drawing paper, without water-mark, paginated consecutively by Blake 1–22. Mr. W. M. Rossetti, who saw the MS. when in his brother's hands, describes it, in one of his letters to me, as being then, to the best of his recollection, stitched into a darkish olive-tinted cover. Traces of this simple binding may be observed in the three punctured holes, about 1½ inches apart, through which a cord had evidently once been laced. The original covers, which, it is to be presumed, bore no inscription, must have been removed when, as the binder's stamp shows, the volume was bound by F. Bedford for B. M. Pickering. The leaves were trimmed down somewhat in binding, the top and bottom lines of pages 17 and 18 being slightly grazed by the binder's knife. Inserted on the inside of the cover is the armorial book-plate of Mr. William Mitchell, into whose possession the MS. must have passed after the death of Pickering and before being acquired by Mr. Locker Lampson. There is no note of the last-named owner to indicate how it was obtained.

Differing in this respect from the larger MS. Book, where most of the poems are found in rough draft, with numerous deletions, corrections, and re-arrangements of stanzas, the Pickering MS. is obviously a fair copy of pieces already written in approved form. There is not a single alteration on the first seventeen pages, and the few corrections which occur are mostly in the use of capitals, which Blake here as elsewhere employs for the sake of emphasis. It is note-worthy that all the poems have titles, which with Blake are generally afterthoughts. As in the Rossetti MS. there is no punctuation. None of the poems are dated. There is no title-page, ascription or other indication of the cir-cumstances under which, or the person for whom, this special collection was transcribed. The pages are without illus-trations and contain no prose matter of any kind.

Unlike the Rossetti MS., the literary contents of which extend over a period of nearly twenty years, the poems of the Pickering MS. convey the impression of having been written at one time. Whether of pure lyrical loveliness like ' The Golden Net ' and ' The Land of Dreams,' uncouth and grotesque like ' Long John Brown,' obscure as ' The Mental Traveller ' and ' The Crystal Cabinet,' or outwardly simple as ' Mary '—all alike are characterized by a strain of profound mysticism which is not quite the same as that of the Prophetic Books, though each helps to explain the other. Verses such as the two couplets (ll. 67–70) in the ' Auguries of Innocence '—

> ' Every Tear from Every Eye
> Becomes a Babe in Eternity ;
> This is caught by Females bright
> And return'd to its own delight '—

or the figure in ' The Mental Traveller ' of the ' Woman Old ' who nails the babe down on a rock, and ' Catches his Shrieks in Cups of gold,' are only to be understood by reference to parallel allusions in *The Four Zoas, Milton,* or *Jerusalem.* Mere allegorical interpretations such as W. M. Rossetti's of ' The Mental Traveller,' however acceptable to readers eager for any light thrown upon Blake's darkness, are not warranted by the poet's theory or practice. The light may be there, but ' the illumination '—as Swinburne observes of a similar attempt—' is none of the author's kindling.' Blake himself disdained the use of mere allegory of this sort. ' Fable or

allegory,' he says in his account of the 'Vision of the Last
Judgment,' ' is a totally distinct and inferior kind of poetry.
Vision, or imagination, is a representation of what actually
exists, really and unchangeably. Fable, or allegory, is
formed by the daughters of Memory. Imagination is surrounded by the daughters of inspiration, who, in the aggre-
gate, are called Jerusalem.'

The poems of the Pickering MS. have a certain unity of
their own, a fact liable to be overlooked, when, as in several
editions of the poet's works, they are scattered among pieces
written at different times, and in a different manner. Among
the ' deepest' of Blake's writings—if I may use the adjective
in the sense in which English gypsies apply it to language,
meaning thereby wholly or partly unintelligible to all save
the highly initiate—they differ in their more fully developed
mysticism from the earlier prophetic writings, and from
those of later date in their avoidance of the mythological
names which crowd the pages of *Milton* and *Jerusalem*.
To the latter fact indeed part of their difficulty is due, for
these names, consistently used by Blake in a definite sense,
supply clues to the author's meaning which are absent in
these poems.

This MS. may confidently be referred to Blake's Felpham
period. 'Mary' was certainly written before August 16,
1803, when Blake in a letter to Mr. Butts introduces two of
its lines in a slightly altered form, and in a different sense.
The original drafts of two of the poems, 'The Golden Net'
and 'The Grey Monk,' which appear in a more perfected
form in this MS., are found on two leaves of the latter part
of the Rossetti MS., written probably in the same year.
There are, moreover, in several of the poems phrases repeated
in *Milton* and *Jerusalem*, both of which were engraved, in
whole or part, in 1804. In identifying the style of 'The
Mental Traveller' with that of *Tiriel*, which W. M. Rossetti
and Swinburne concur in regarding as the first of the series
of the Prophetic Books, W. B. Yeats (Notes, p. 249) would
appear to date this poem at least as early as 1789. In
so doing it will be seen that he differs from me, either in
regarding the several poems in the Pickering MS. as having
been written at widely different times, or by antedating the
whole MS. by fourteen years.

Swinburne quotes with comment two stanzas of 'The
Land of Dreams' (pp. 134, 135) and two lines of 'Mary'
(p. 177), in the latter instance using Shepherd's text instead
of Rossetti's. W. M. Rossetti prints the same pieces as his

brother, adopting some of his emendations, but rejecting others in favour of readings evidently taken from Shepherd's edition. Ellis and Yeats (ii. 31–36) print 'The Mental Traveller,' with interpretation as 'a sun-myth and a story of the Incarnation.' In the same volume (pp. 220–225), they give the MS. Book version of the 'Monk of Charlemaine,' but ignore the Pickering variant called 'The Grey Monk.' The remaining poems, including 'Long John Brown and Little Mary Bell,' they print in vol. ii, pp. 72–83. Their text generally follows that of the Aldine edition, but with some new readings of their own for which there is no authority. W. B. Yeats, under the general heading, 'Ideas of Good and Evil,' prints all the poems, with the exception of 'Long John Brown,' arbitrarily arranged among poems taken from the Rossetti MS., the *Island in the Moon,* and other late and early sources.

THE PICKERING MANUSCRIPT

The Smile

There is a Smile of Love,   1
And there is a Smile of Deceit,
And there is a Smile of Smiles
In which these two Smiles meet.

And there is a Frown of Hate,   5
And there is a Frown of Disdain,
And there is a Frown of Frowns
Which you strive to forget in vain,

For it sticks in the Heart's deep core   9
And it sticks in the deep Back-bone—
And no Smile that ever was smil'd,
But only one Smile alone,

That betwixt the Cradle & Grave   13
It only once Smil'd can be ;
And, when it once is Smil'd,
There's an end to all Misery.

Pickering MS. p. 1.   DGR and all edd. except Shep. entitle 'Smile and
Frown.'
    4 these] the DGR.   11–16 And . . . Misery] DGR, followed by
WMR and EY, evade the anacoluthon by reading :

         ' And no smile ever was smiled
           But only one smile alone

       '(And betwixt the cradle and grave
          It only once smiled can be),
        That when it once is smiled
          There's an end to all misery.'

WBY, with less violence, adopts DGR's reading of l. 11, omits the round
brackets, and retains the 'And' in l. 15.   12 Cp. 'The Crystal Cabinet,'
l. 17.

Prefatory Note to 'The Golden Net'

The original version of 'The Golden Net' is found in the Rossetti MS. Book. There Blake's first draft, without title, is written in the left-hand column of p. 14, and, except for the omission of ll. 3 and 4—

'Alas for woe! alas for woe!
They cry, and tears for ever flow— '

coincides generally with the form in which he afterwards transcribed it into the smaller autograph collection, the source of the present text.

In this early draft Blake's first attempt at emendation was to indicate by marginal numbers, 1 to 9, prefixed to ll. 5-13 (MS. Book, ll. 3-11), that the couplet,

'They bore a net of golden twine
To hang upon the branches fine,'

was now meant to follow l. 2. The initial couplet was next deleted, and the opening passage twice re-written. The first revision is found below Blake's terminal line marking the end of the poem, and runs as follows :—

'Beneath the white thorn's lovely May,
Three Virgins at the break of day.
The one was clothed in flames of fire,
The other clothed in iron wire [sweet desire (1st rdg. del.)],
The other clothed in tears & sighs,
Dazzling bright before my eyes.'

This again was erased, Blake recommencing at the head of the next column :

'Beneath the white thorn's lovely May,
"Alas for wo! alas for wo! alas for wo!"
They cry, & tears for ever flow.'

Here the first line is left rimeless, Blake evidently omitting to recopy the second line of the couplet which he had already twice written—

'Three virgins at the break of day.'

A further change consisted in the deletion of ll. 11-14 (MS. Book, ll. 9-12), opposite to which are written :

'Wings they had that soft enclose [& when they chose (1st rdg. del.)]
Round their body when they chose,
They would let them down at will
Or make translucent '

This unfinished passage is also struck out.

In transcribing this poem into the Pickering MS., Blake omitted the line with which the poem originally began :

'Beneath the white thorn's lovely May,'

without which the reference to the 'branches' in l. 10 is meaningless. Rossetti restores this line, beginning the poem with the triplet :—

'Beneath a white thorn's lovely May
Three virgins at the break of day :—
"Whither, young man, whither away?"'

This is one of Blake's 'threefold' poems. See note to 'The Crystal Cabinet.'

The Golden Net

> Three Virgins at the break of day,   1
> 'Whither, young man, whither away?
> Alas for woe! alas for woe!'
> They cry, & tears for ever flow.
> The one was cloth'd in flames of fire,   5
> The other cloth'd in iron wire,
> The other cloth'd in tears & sighs,
> Dazling bright before my Eyes.

Pickering MS. p. 2.

1, 2] R¹ begins with an amended version of Blake's second draft of the opening of the poem (MS. Book, p. 14, col. 1 *del.*)—

> 'Beneath the white thorn stood in May
> Three virgins at the break of day;'

DGR, followed by WMR and EY, begins with the triplet—

> 'Beneath a white thorn's lovely May,
> Three virgins at the break of day:—
> "Whither, young man, whither away?"'

WBY changes 'a white thorn's' to 'the white-thorn's.' For 'the white thorn's lovely May,' cp. *Milton*, f. 31, ll. 50–62 :—

> 'First e'er the morning breaks joy opens in the flowery bosoms,
> Joy even to tears, which the Sun rising dries; first the Wild-Thyme
> And Meadow-sweet downy & soft waving among the reeds,
> Light springing on the air, lead the sweet Dance; they wake
> The Honeysuckle sleeping on the Oak, the flaunting beauty
> Revels along upon the wind; the White-thorn, lovely May,
> Opens her many lovely eyes; listening, the Rose still sleeps,
> None dare to wake her; soon she bursts her crimson curtained bed
> And comes forth in the majesty of beauty; every Flower,
> The Pink, the Jessamine, the Wall-flower, the Carnation,
> The Jonquil, the mild Lilly, opes her heavens; every Tree
> And Flower & Herb soon fill the air with an innumerable Dance,
> Yet all in order sweet & lovely; Men are sick with Love.'

3, 4 Alas . . . flow] R¹ omits.   3 Alas . . . woe] Alas for wo! alas for wo! alas for wo! MS. Book.   5 one] first R¹, DGR, WMR, EY.   6 other] second R¹, DGR, WMR, EY.   cloth'd] was clothed R¹.   iron wire] sweet desire MS. Book 1st *rdg. del.*   7 other cloth'd] third was clothed R¹, DGR, WMR, EY.   tears and sighs] sighs & tears MS. Book 1st *rdg. del.*

They bore a Net of Golden twine 9
To hang upon the Branches fine.
Pitying I wept to see the woe
That Love & Beauty undergo,
To be consum'd in burning Fires 13
And in ungratified desires,
And in tears cloth'd night & day
Melted all my Soul away.
When they saw my Tears, a Smile 17
That did Heaven itself beguile,
Bore the Golden Net aloft,
As on downy Pinions soft,
Over the Morning of my Day. 21
Underneath the Net I stray,
Now intreating Burning Fire,
Now intreating Iron Wire,
Now intreating Tears & Sighs. 25
O when will the morning rise?

9 Cp. the lines in 'How sweet I roam'd from field to field' (*Poetical Sketches*) :—

'He caught me in his silken net
And shut me in his golden cage';

also the references to the 'silken net' in the *Visions of the Daughters of Albion*. In Blake's later mystical writings the simple idea of moral restrictions placed upon love, expressed by the silken net and golden cage of the earlier poems, is developed into the veil or net of Vala. Cp. *Jerusalem*, f. 20, ll. 30–32 :—

'When Albion rent thy beautiful net of gold and silver twine,
Thou hadst woven it with art, thou hadst caught me in the bands
Of love : thou refusedst to let me go.'

9, 10 They . . . fine] R¹ places after l. 2, following Blake's revised order of lines in MS. Book.   13 consum'd] clothed R¹, DGR, WMR, EY. burning Fires] flames of fire WBY.   14 ungratified desires] unsatisfied desire WBY.   16 Melted] It melted R¹ *and all edd.*   17 my Tears] me weep R¹.   18 That] which R¹.   did] might DGR, WMR, EY.   20 on] by MS. Book, R¹, WBY.   21 Over] O'er MS. Book, R¹.   23 Burning Fire] flaming fire MS. Book ; Flaming-fire R¹ *and all edd. except* Shep.   24 Iron Wire] iron wire MS. Book ; sweet desire *ibid. 1st rdg. del.* ; Iron-wire R¹ *and all edd. except* Shep.   25 Tears & sighs] Tears-and-Sighs R¹ *and all edd. except* Shep. *and* WBY.   26 O . . . rise] When, O when, will Morning rise? MS. Book *1st rdg. del.*

Prefatory Note to 'The Mental Traveller'

A passage in Blake's description of his picture of the Last Judgement (MS. Book, c. 1810) supplements the clue supplied by the author's title to the meaning of this most obscure poem. Referring to the three 'States' or 'Churches,' symbolized by the twenty-seven 'Heavens' enumerated in *Jerusalem*, f. 75—Adam to Luther, 'After which Adam begins again in endless circle'—Blake adds :—

'These states exist now. Man passes on, but states remain for ever. He passes through them like a traveller, who may well suppose that the places he has passed through exist no more ; as a man may suppose that the states he has passed through exist no more. Everything is eternal.'

The same idea is repeated in *Jerusalem*, f. 49, ll. 72–74 :—

'Learn therefore, O Sisters, to distinguish the Eternal Human,
That walks about among the stones of fire, in bliss & woe
Alternate, from those States or Worlds in which the Spirit travels.'

The poem, then, must be understood as a picture of man's spirit, passing through successive mental states, and at last returning, 'in endless circle,' to the point from which he started. In other words it is a restatement of Blake's favourite doctrine of constant generation and regeneration.

In my footnotes to 'The Mental Traveller' I give references to passages in the Prophetic Books, throwing light upon allusions otherwise unintelligible. While these, read with their context, render plain the sense of the particular lines or stanzas to which they are appended, it should be premised that the chapters quoted from will not supply the reader with a consecutive narrative of the exact myth presented in this poem. The complete picture must be pieced together from the fragments discovered and identified. The myth itself admits of no glib paraphrase, for Blake's parables, as he himself insists, are 'visions' and not 'allegories.' Such figures, moreover, as 'catching shrieks in cups of gold' are in the nature of ideograms, used invariably in the same sense and the same connexion, and must always be understood symbolically and not metaphorically. Difficult to define precisely, or to separate from their context, they serve as useful catchwords to more detailed expositions of the same myth elsewhere.

In bringing together these parallelisms from the Prophetic Books I allow Blake to be his own interpreter. Those who prefer a shorter cut to a meaning—if not to his meaning—may turn to Mr. W. M. Rossetti's ingenious exposition, first printed in Gilchrist (ii. 98) and repeated in the Aldine edition. Swinburne's commentary on this poem will be found on pp. 178–181 of his *Critical Essay*, and Messrs. Ellis and Yeats' interpretation as 'at the same time a sun-myth and a story of the Incarnation' on pp. 34–36 of the second volume of their large edition of Blake's *Works*.

The Mental Traveller

I travel'd thro' a Land of Men,   1
A Land of Men & Women too;
And heard & saw such dreadful things
As cold Earth-wanderers never knew.

For there the Babe is born in joy   5
That was begotten in dire woe;
Just as we reap in joy the fruit
Which we in bitter tears did sow.

And if the Babe is born a Boy   9
He's given to a Woman Old,
Who nails him down upon a rock,
Catches his Shrieks in Cups of gold.

Pickering MS. p. 3.

1, 2 Cp. *Jerusalem*, f. 38, ll. 31–34 :—

'My Streets are my Ideas of Imagination . . .
My Houses are Thoughts; my Inhabitants, Affections,
The children of my thoughts, walking within my blood vessels.'

3 heard & saw] saw and heard EY.   5 Cp. *Jerusalem*, f. 68, ll. 36, 37 :—
'Breeding Women walking in pride & bringing forth under green trees
With pleasure, without pain, for their food is blood of the Captive.'
5–8 Cp. 'Auguries of Innocence,' ll. 67–70 :—

'Every Tear from Every Eye
Becomes a Babe in Eternity;
This is caught by Females bright,
And return'd to its own delight';

where of course 'tear' is to be understood as the human emotion which
gives rise to it. Cp. the line in another poem ('The Grey Monk') of this
same manuscript collection :—

'For a Tear is an Intellectual Thing.'

8 Which] That EY.   9 In Blake's prophetic writings the 'spectre,' or
reasoning power in man, is always represented as masculine, in contradistinction to the 'emanation,' or affective self, which is feminine.   11 The
'rock' is the druidical altar of Albion (*Jerusalem*, f. 53, l. 17, and *passim*),
the place of torture of the victims of natural religion. See also *Jerusalem*,
f. 67, and *Four Zoas*, Night vii, l. 71 :—

'. . . my feet & hands are nail'd to the burning rock.'

12 Cp. *Milton*, f. 24, ll. 35–39 :—

'The cruel joys of Luvah's Daughters lacerating with knives
And whips their Victims, & the deadly sport of Luvah's Sons.
They dance around the dying, & they drink the howl & groan,
They catch the shrieks in cups of gold, they hand them to one another,
These are the sports of love, & these the sweet delights of amorous play.'

She binds iron thorns around his head,   13
She pierces both his hands & feet,
She cuts his heart out at his side,
To make it feel both cold & heat.

Her fingers number every Nerve,   17
Just as a Miser counts his gold ;
She lives upon his shrieks & cries,
And she grows young as he grows old.

Till he becomes a bleeding youth,   21
And she becomes a Virgin bright;
Then he rends up his Manacles,
And binds her down for his delight.

He plants himself in all her Nerves,   25
Just as a Husbandman his mould ;
And she becomes his dwelling-place
And Garden fruitful seventy-fold.

See also *Jerusalem*, f. 80, l. 81, and f. 67, l. 61.   13 iron] strong DGR. :
around] about EY. Cp. *Jerusalem*, f. 66, l. 23, where the daughters
of Albion, torturing their victim, ' bind his forehead with thorns of iron.'
17 Cp. *Four Zoas*, Night i, ll. 114–6 :—

' every nerve

She counted, every vein & lacteal, threading them among
Her woof of terror, Terrified, & drinking tears of woe.'

See also *Jerusalem*, f. 22, l. 20.   27, 28 By dwelling in a garden of delight
Blake symbolizes man in a state of unity whose ' spectre ' and ' emanation '
are not divided. Cp. *Four Zoas*, Night vii, ll. 265–71 :—

' The Spectre said, Thou lovely Vision, this delightful Tree
Is given us for a Shelter from the tempests of void & Solid,
Till once again the morn of ages shall renew upon us,
To reunite in those mild fields of happy Eternity,
Where thou & I in undivided Essence walk'd about
Imbodied,—thou my garden of Delight, & I the spirit in the garden,
Mutual there we dwelt, in one anothers joy revolving.'

See also *ibid.*, Night vii, ll. 717–719 :—

' Tharmas repli'd : " O ! Vala, once I liv'd in a garden of delight :
I watered Enion in the morning & she lived away
Among the apple trees " ' ;

and *Jerusalem*, f. 7, ll. 14, 15 :—
' thy stolen Emanation
Is his garden of pleasure.'

T 2

An Agèd Shadow, soon he fades,   29
Wand'ring round an Earthly Cot,
Full-fillèd all with gems & gold
Which he by industry had got.

And these are the gems of the Human Soul,   33
The rubies & pearls of a love-sick eye,
The countless gold of the akeing heart,
The martyr's groan & the lover's sigh.

They are his meat, they are his drink;   37
He feeds the Beggar and the Poor
And the wayfaring Traveller :
For ever open is his door.

His grief is their eternal joy;   41
They make the roofs & walls to ring.
Till from the fire on the hearth
A little Female Babe does spring ;

And she is all of solid fire   45
And gems & gold, that none his hand
Dares stretch to touch her Baby form,
Or wrap her in his swadling band.

But She comes to the Man she loves,   49
If young or old, or rich or poor ;
They soon drive out the agèd Host,
A Beggar at another's door.

He wanders weeping far away,   53
Untill some other take him in ;
Oft blind & age-bent, sore distrest,
Until he can a Maiden win.

---

31 gems] gains Shep.   32 had] has EY.   34, 35 Cp. Rossetti
MS. xxx :—

> 'The countless gold of a merry heart,
> The rubies & pearls of a loving eye,
> The idle man never can bring to the mart,
> Nor the cunning hoard up in his treasury.'

39 And] To *all edd. except* Shep.   40 For . . . door] Forever opens his
door EY.   43 on] upon *all edd. except* Shep.   44 does] doth *all edd.
except* Shep.   45, 46 Cp. the description of Jerusalem (spiritual liberty),
the emanation of Albion (*Jerusalem*, f. 86).

And to allay his freezing Age,   57
The Poor Man takes her in his arms ;
The Cottage fades before his sight,
The Garden and its lovely Charms.

The Guests are scatter'd thro' the land,   61
For the Eye altering alters all ;
The Senses roll themselves in fear,
And the flat Earth becomes a Ball ;

The Stars, Sun, Moon, all shrink away,   65
A desert vast without a bound,
And nothing left to eat or drink,
And a dark desert all around.

The honey of her Infant lips,   69
The bread & wine of her sweet smile,
The wild game of her roving Eye,
Does him to Infancy beguile ;

62 Cp. *Jerusalem*, f. 34, l. 55 :—
   'If Perceptive Organs vary, Objects of Perception seem to vary.'
64 Blake, in several passages, refers to the ' flat earth ' becoming ' a ball '
as a delusion of the modern scientific spirit. Cp. *Milton*, f. 28, ll. 4–20 :—
   'The Sky is an immortal Tent built by the Sons of Los :
   And every Space that a Man views around his dwelling-place
   Standing on his own roof, or in his garden on a mount
   Of twenty-five cubits in height, such space is his Universe :
   And on its verge the Sun rises & sets, the Clouds bow
   To meet the flat Earth & the Sea in such an order'd Space :
   The Starry heavens reach no further but here bend and set
   On all sides & the two Poles turn on their valves of gold.
   And if he move his dwelling-place his heavens also move
   Where'er he goes & all his neighbourhood bewail his loss.
   Such are the Spaces called Earth & such its dimension.
   As to that false appearance which appears to the reasoner
   As of a Globe rolling thro' Voidness, it is a delusion of Ulro.
   The Microscope knows not of this nor the Telescope, they alter
   The ratio of the Spectator's Organs but leave Objects untouch'd ;
   For every Space larger than a red Globule of Man's blood
   Is visionary.'
See also *Jerusalem*, f. 77 :—
   'By it [the wheel of religion] the Sun was roll'd into an orb,
   By it the Moon faded into a globe
   Travelling thro' the night.'
65 Cp. *Jerusalem*, f. 66, ll. 50, 51.   The . . . Moon] Stars, moon and sun
EY.   72 Does] Do *all edd. except* Shep.

For as he eats & drinks he grows   73
Younger & younger every day ;
And on the desart wild they both
Wander in terror & dismay.

Like the wild Stag she flees away,   77
Her fear plants many a thicket wild ;
While he pursues her night & day,
By various arts of love beguil'd ;

By various arts of Love & Hate,   81
Till the wide desert planted o'er
With Labyrinths of wayward Love,
Where roam the Lion, Wolf, and Boar.

Till he becomes a wayward Babe,   85
And she a weeping Woman Old.
Then many a Lover wanders here ;
The Sun & Stars are nearer roll'd ;

The trees bring forth sweet extasy   89
To all who in the desert roam ;
Till many a City there is Built,
And many a pleasant Shepherd's home.

75, 76 Cp. *Jerusalem*, f. 86, ll. 62, 63 :—
  ' Silent they wander'd hand in hand like two Infants wand'ring
    From Enion in the desarts, terrified at each others beauty.'
77 flees] flies WBY.   80 arts] art WBY.   80, 81 Cp. in *Four Zoas*,
Night i, ll. 217, 218, the description of the wanderings of Los and Enitharmon,
who ' in the Brain of Man ... live, and in his circling Nerves ' :—
  ' Alternate Love & Hate his breast, hers Scorn & Jealousy,
    In embryon passions they kiss'd not nor embrac'd for shame & fear.'
82 desart] desert 's *all edd. except* Shep.   83 wayward Love] Cp. *Jeru-
salem*, f. 16, ll. 61–64 :—
  ' All things acted on Earth are seen in the bright Sculptures of
    Los's Halls, & every Age renews its powers from these Works,
    With every pathetic story possible to happen from Hate or
    Wayward Love.'
85 Cp. *Jerusalem*, f. 82, ll. 37–39 :—
  ' Look, Hyle is become an infant Love, look, behold, see him lie
    Upon my bosom, look, here is the lovely wayward form
    That gave me sweet delight by his torments beneath my Veil.'
Also l. 50 :—
  ' The desarts tremble at his wrath, they shrink themselves in fear.'
See also ' The Crystal Cabinet,' ll. 25, 26.

But when they find the frowning Babe,⠀⠀⠀⠀⠀93
Terror strikes thro' the region wide:
They cry 'The Babe! the Babe is Born!'
And flee away on every side.

For who dare touch the frowning form,⠀⠀⠀⠀⠀97
His arm is wither'd to its root;
Lions, Boars, Wolves, all howling flee,
And every Tree does shed its fruit.

And none can touch that frowning form,⠀⠀⠀⠀⠀101
Except it be a Woman Old;
She nails him down upon the Rock,
And all is done as I have told.

94 wide] wild EY.⠀⠀⠀⠀98 its] the EY.⠀⠀⠀⠀99 Lions, Boars] Bears,
lions *all edd. except* Shep., *who reads* Lions, bears; but cp. above, l. 84.
100 does] doth *all edd.*⠀⠀⠀103 him] it DGR.⠀⠀⠀the] a EY.

The Land of Dreams

Awake, awake, my little Boy!⠀⠀⠀⠀⠀1
Thou wast thy Mother's only joy;
Why dost thou weep in thy gentle sleep?
Awake! thy Father does thee keep.

'O, what Land is the Land of Dreams?⠀⠀⠀⠀⠀5
What are its Mountains, & what are its Streams?
O Father! I saw my Mother there,
Among the Lillies by waters fair.

'Among the lambs, clothèd in white,⠀⠀⠀⠀⠀9
She walk'd with her Thomas in sweet delight.
I wept for joy, like a dove I mourn,
O! when shall I again return?'

Pickering MS. p. 7.
4 Awake] O wake DGR; Oh wake WMR, EY.⠀⠀⠀does] doth *all edd.*
except Shep.⠀⠀⠀5, 6 O... streams] I follow Shepherd in making these
two lines part of the boy's reply, instead of, as in DGR and other edd.,
part of the father's opening speech. The original MS., of course, had no
quotation marks.⠀⠀⠀10 Thomas] This name is plainly written and cannot
therefore be a misreading of 'Tharmas,' as might be conjectured from several
analogies in the story of Vala and Tharmas (*Four Zoas*, Night ix, pp. 122–
128).

Dear Child, I also by pleasant streams   13
Have wander'd all Night in the Land of Dreams;
But tho' calm & warm the waters wide,
I could not get to the other side.

' Father, O father! what do we here   17
In this Land of unbelief and fear?
The Land of Dreams is better far,
Above the light of the Morning Star.'

Mary

Sweet Mary, the first time she ever was there,   1
Came into the Ball-room among the Fair;
The young Men & Maidens around her throng,
And these are the words upon every tongue:

'An Angel is here from the heavenly Climes,   5
Or again does return the Golden times;
Her eyes outshine every brilliant ray,
She opens her lips—'tis the Month of May.'

Mary moves in soft beauty & conscious delight,   9
To augment with sweet smiles all the joys of the Night,
Nor once blushes to own to the rest of the Fair
That sweet Love and Beauty are worthy our care.

In the Morning the Villagers rose with delight,   13
And repeated with pleasure the joys of the night,
And Mary arose among Friends to be free,
But no Friend from henceforward thou, Mary, shalt see.

Pickering MS. p. 8.

According to DGR this poem ' appears to be, on one side, an allegory of the poetic or spiritual mind moving unrecognized and reviled among its fellows ; and this view of it is corroborated when we find Blake applying to himself two lines almost identically taken from it.' See note to ll. 21, 22, and Swinburne, *Essay*, p. 177.

6 again does return] *All edd. except* Shep. *omit* does.   9-12 Shep. makes this stanza part of the preceding speech.

Some said she was proud, some call'd her a whore,   17
And some, when she passèd by, shut to the door;
A damp cold came o'er her, her blushes all fled,
Her lillies & roses are blighted & shed.

'O why was I born with a different Face?   21
Why was I not born like this Envious Race?
Why did Heaven adorn me with bountiful hand,
And then set me down in an envious Land?

'To be weak as a Lamb and smooth as a Dove,   25
And not to raise Envy, is call'd Christian Love;
But if you raise Envy your Merit's to blame
For planting such spite in the weak & the tame.

'I will humble my Beauty, I will not dress fine,   29
I will keep from the Ball, and my Eyes shall not shine;
And if any Girl's Lover forsakes her for me
I'll refuse him my hand, & from Envy be free.'

She went out in Morning attir'd plain & neat;   33
'Proud Mary's gone mad,' said the Child in the Street;
She went out in Morning in plain neat attire,
And came home in Evening bespatter'd with mire.

She trembled & wept, sitting on the Bed-side,   37
She forgot it was Night, & she trembled & cried;
She forgot it was Night, she forgot it was Morn,
Her soft Memory imprinted with Faces of Scorn;

With Faces of Scorn and with Eyes of Disdain,   41
Like foul Fiends inhabiting Mary's mild Brain;
She remembers no Face like the Human Divine;
All Faces have Envy, sweet Mary, but thine;

17-20 Shepherd omits this stanza in his edition of 1866.   17 some
... whore] some reviled her still more DGR.   21, 22 O why ... Race]
Cp. the lines occurring in one of Blake's letters to Mr. Butts, dated Aug.
16, 1803 :—
> 'O why was I born with a different face?
> Why was I not born like the rest of my race?'

31 forsakes] forsake Shep., WMR, EY, WBY.   33, 35 in Morning] in
the morning *all edd. except* Shep.   36 in Evening] in the evening *all edd.
except* Shep.

And thine is a Face of sweet Love in despair,   45
And thine is a Face of mild sorrow & care,
And thine is a Face of wild terror & fear
That shall never be quiet till laid on its bier.

The Crystal Cabinet

> The Maiden caught me in the Wild,   1
> Where I was dancing merrily ;
> She put me into her Cabinet,
> And Lock'd me up with a golden Key.

Pickering MS. p. 10.

A passage in *Jerusalem*, f. 70, ll. 17–31, makes it plain that the subject of
this poem is Rahab, or moral law :—

'Imputing Sin & Righteousness to Individuals, Rahab
  Sat deep within him hid : his Feminine Power unreveal'd
  Brooding Abstract Philosophy, to destroy Imagination, the Divine-
  Humanity : A Three-fold Wonder, feminine, most beautiful, Three-fold
  Each within other.   On her white marble & even Neck, her Heart
  Inorb'd and bonified : with locks of shadowing modesty, shining
  Over her beautiful Female features, soft flourishing in beauty,
  Beams mild, all love and all perfection, that when the lips
  Recieve a kiss from Gods or Men, a threefold kiss returns
  From the press'd loveliness ; so her whole immortal form, three-fold
  Three-fold embrace returns : consuming lives of Gods & Men,
  In fires of beauty melting them as gold & silver in the furnace,
  Her Brain enlabyrinths the whole heaven of her bosom & loins
  To put in act what her Heart wills ; O who can withstand her
    power ?
  Her name is Vala in Eternity : in Time her name is Rahab.'

3 Cp. *Milton*, f. 27, ll. 1-26 :—

'Some Sons of Los surround the Passions with porches of iron &
    silver
  Creating form & beauty around the dark regions of sorrow,
  Giving to airy nothing a name and a habitation
  Delightful, with bounds to the Infinite putting off the Indefinite
  Into most holy forms of Thought (such is the power of inspiration).
  They labour incessant, with many tears and affections,
  Creating the beautiful House for the piteous sufferer.
  Others, Cabinets richly fabricate of gold & ivory
  For Doubts & fears, unform'd & wretched & melancholy
  The little weeping Spectre stands on the threshold of Death
    Eternal . . .
  Terrified the Spectre screams & rushes in fear into their Net
  Of kindness & compassion & is born a weeping terror.'

This Cabinet is form'd of Gold   5
And Pearl and Crystal shining bright,
And within it opens into a World
And a little lovely Moony Night.

Another England there I saw,   9
Another London with its Tower,
Another Thames and other Hills,
And another pleasant Surrey Bower,

Another Maiden like herself,   13
Translucent, lovely, shining clear,
Threefold each in the other clos'd,—
O what a pleasant trembling fear!

O what a smile! a threefold smile   17
Fill'd me that like a flame I burn'd;
I bent to kiss the lovely Maid,
And found a Threefold Kiss return'd.

I strove to sieze the inmost Form   21
With ardour fierce & hands of flame,
But burst the Crystal Cabinet,
And like a Weeping Babe became—

A weeping Babe upon the wild,   25
And Weeping Woman pale reclin'd,
And in the outward air again
I fill'd with woes the passing Wind.

14 For Blake's definitions and comparison of ' Translucence ' and ' Opake-
ness,' see *Jerusalem*, f. 42, l. 29 sqq.   25, 26 Cp. ' The Mental Traveller,'
ll. 85, 86 :—

> ' Till he becomes a wayward Babe,
> And she a weeping Woman Old.'

Prefatory Note to 'The Grey Monk'

The original draft of 'The Grey Monk' is found on p. 12 of the Rossetti
MS., where it forms part of xlii. The MS. Book version consisted of fourteen
stanzas, which Blake afterwards separated into two poems—transcribing
eight stanzas into the Pickering MS., under the title 'The Grey Monk,' and
engraving seven as the untitled lines at the end of his 'Address to the

Deists' (*Jerusalem*, f. 52). The latter includes two stanzas which occur in 'The Grey Monk' version also. The greater part of *Jerusalem*, as we gather from one of Blake's letters to Mr. Butts, had been written before April 25, 1803, though its actual completion in engraved form was probably later than the date on the title-page, 1804. This dates 'The Grey Monk' as belonging to the earlier part of the Felpham period.

Mr. D. G. Rossetti's first version of this poem is based solely on the draft in the MS. Book, in his early transcript of which he gives stanzas 5-10, with a few verbal changes of his own. In his second version, printed in Gilchrist (ii. 206), he adds the two final stanzas, taking these from the Pickering MS. and not from the MS. Book, and still omitting the second stanza—

'The blood red ran from the grey monk's side.'

Mr. W. M. Rossetti follows Shepherd in the number and arrangement of verses, and generally as to text, adopting two out of the three important changes from the MS. Book version—'I die' *for* 'I see' (l. 1), and 'found' *for* 'sought' (l. 33). He makes six changes on the authority of the MS. Book, one from the engraved version in *Jerusalem*, and adopts four of his brother's emendations. Messrs. Ellis and Yeats, here as elsewhere, seem ignorant of the fact that Shepherd's edition preserved for us the text of the Pickering MS., and omit 'The Grey Monk' as a separate poem. Mr. W. B. Yeats falls into the same error, when, in his note to this poem (p. 247), he says, 'The arrangement of the verses in the Aldine edition is quite arbitrary.' It is, on the other hand, his own text which is entirely unauthorized, as under the title 'The Grey Monk' he prints stanzas 5-14 of the MS. Book version, with readings sometimes adopted from the Aldine, and sometimes made on his own responsibility—among the most meaningless of which are his transposition and misreadings of ll. 11, 12.

In the footnotes to the present poem I give only the final readings of the MS. Book version. For deleted words and passages see MS. Book xlii.

The Grey Monk

'I die, I die!' the Mother said,   1
'My Children die for lack of Bread.
What more has the merciless Tyrant said?'
The Monk sat down on the Stony Bed.

The blood red ran from the grey Monk's side,   5
His hands & feet were wounded wide,
His Body bent, his arms & knees
Like to the roots of ancient trees.

Pickering MS. p. 12.

1 I die, I die] I see, I see MS. Book, DGR, WBY.   2 die] will die MS. Book, DGR ; shall die WBY.   3 has] hath R¹.   4 sat down] sat him down DGR, WMR.   the] her MS. Book, DGR, WMR, WBY. 5-8 The ... trees] R¹, DGR, *and* WBY *omit*.

His eye was dry; no tear could flow: 9
A hollow groan first spoke his woe.
He trembled & shudder'd upon the Bed ;
At length with a feeble cry he said:

'When God commanded this hand to write   13
In the studious hours of deep midnight,
He told me the writing I wrote should prove
The Bane of all that on Earth I love.

'My brother starv'd between two Walls,   17
His Children's Cry my soul appalls ;
I mock'd at the wrack and griding chain,
My bent body mocks their torturing pain.

'Thy Father drew his Sword in the North,   21
With his thousands strong he marchèd forth ;
Thy Brother has arm'd himself in Steel,
To avenge the wrongs thy Children feel.

'But vain the Sword and vain the Bow,   25
They never can work War's overthrow.
The Hermit's Prayer and the Widow's Tear
Alone can free the World from fear.

---

9 tear] tears WBY.   10 first spoke] bespoke R[1], DGR, WMR, WBY.
11, 12 He . . . said] WBY inverts the order of these two lines.   12 with]
WBY *omits.*   14 studious] shadowy DGR, WMR, WBY.   15 the
writing] that all MS. Book, DGR, WMR, WBY.   13–16 In a letter to
Mr. Butts, dated July 6, 1803, Blake speaks of Hayley's aversion and
contempt for his prophetic writings. Cp. also the lines in an earlier letter
to the same friend :—

> 'Must Flaxman look upon me as wild ?
> And all my friends be with doubts beguil'd ?
> Must my Wife live in my Sister's bane ?
> Or my sister survive on my Love's pain ? '

18 His] Thy R[1], DGR, WBY.   Cry] crying DGR.   19 griding] grinding
Shep. ; the grinding WMR, WBY.   20 mocks their] mocks at their
MS. Book, DGR, WMR, WBY.   21 See note to version in MS.
Book xlii.   22 With his thousands strong] By his strong courage R[1].
marchèd] is marched MS. Book, DGR, WMR, WBY.   23 has] hath
DGR, WMR.   24 avenge] revenge MS. Book, DGR, WMR.   wrongs]
wrongs that R[1].

'For a Tear is an Intellectual Thing,   29
And a Sigh is the Sword of an Angel King,
And the bitter groan of the Martyr's woe
Is an Arrow from the Almightie's Bow.

'The hand of Vengeance found the Bed   33
To which the Purple Tyrant fled;
The iron hand crush'd the Tyrant's head,
And became a Tyrant in his Stead.'

29-36 For . . . Stead] R¹ *omits.* Following the MS. Book version WBY inverts the order of stanzas 8 and 9, and inserts between them the two stanzas :—

'Until the tyrant himself relent,
The tyrant who the first [MS. Book *first the*] black bow bent,
Slaughter shall heap the bloody plain :
Resistance and war is the tyrant's gain.

'But the tear of love—and forgiveness sweet,
And submission to death beneath his feet—
The tear shall melt the sword of steel,
And every wound it has made shall heal.'

29 a Tear] the tear MS. Book, WBY.   31 the Martyr's] a martyr's DGR, WMR, WBY.   33 found] sought MS. Book, WBY.

Prefatory Note to 'Auguries of Innocence'

Pickering MS. p. 13. Written in a single column, without marginal additions, marks of transposition, or numerical rearrangement of lines. The couplets are not divided into sections, nor is there a terminal line or other mark of separation between the opening stanza and the proverb-couplets which follow. The conjecture, therefore, that Blake intended the title to refer to the initial quatrain only is not supported by the evidence of the MS.

It will be seen that the poem consists of an opening quatrain, followed by sixty-four couplets. Turning to the latter, it may be noticed in the first place that the couplets are almost always arranged together in pairs, as if forming quatrains with the rime-arrangement *aabb* or sometimes *aaaa*. The few exceptions to this rule have the appearance of being marginal interpolations. The first five stanzas (ll. 5–24) deal with cruelty or kindness to animals, its penalty or reward—a theme which may have been suggested to Blake's mind while engraving the plates for Hayley's

Ballads. In the sixth stanza (ll. 25-28) Blake wanders off into a different aspect of animal life, obscene or noxious animals symbolizing human faults or vices. This theme is continued later in the couplets following l. 44.

Stanzas 9, 10 and 11, 12 (ll. 37-44 and 45-52) are continuations respectively of these two themes. The couplet which follows (ll. 53, 54)—

> 'A Truth that's told with bad intent
> Beats all the Lies you can invent'—

is not very closely bound to the preceding lines. It has the appearance of being an afterthought, perhaps in the nature of a personal reflection on one of the chief modes by which 'slander,' 'envy,' and 'jealousy' work for evil.

At l. 55 the return to the quatrain unit is clearly marked by the rime-arrangement of the next three stanzas, all, as in the last stanza of 'The Grey Monk,' having four identical rimes. Stanzas 13 and 14 (ll. 55-88 and 59-62) appear to have been mistakenly copied down in inverted order. This paragraph discusses a new topic, alternate pleasure and grief in human life, a theme entirely different from the darker one of predestined misery or delight (ll. 119-132) with which Rossetti links it in his rearrangement.

The subjects of the remaining stanzas are strongly reminiscent of those of the *Songs of Experience*, and often compress within the narrow limit of a couplet the strength and tenderness of some of the most familiar of the songs. In stanzas 15-17 (ll. 63-74) we have 'Infant Sorrow,' and in stanzas 18, 19 (ll. 75-84) 'marks of weakness, marks of woe' in beggar, soldier, and pauper. Stanzas 20-22 (ll. 85-96) pass on from reverence of infant faith to denunciation of doubt, a theme returned to (after a short digression contrasting war and peace) in stanzas 24, 25 (ll. 108-110). Stanzas 26, 27 recall 'London,' and may be regarded as a continuation of stanzas 18, 19, and 23. Three more stanzas (ll. 119-132) expressing, with exquisite compassion, pity for those whose lot is cast in the land of 'eternal winter,' conclude this truly great poem.

The foregoing analysis reveals the curious fact that Blake would seem to have treated two different themes alternately, interweaving one with another like the rimes in a canto of terza rima. It appears probable that he either wrote down the couplets in the order of composition or transcribed them from loose jottings, deferring rearrangement for future consideration. Continuity may be given the poem by following each theme separately to its conclusion. It would then form seven sections, divided as follows:—

    (*a*) ll. 1-4.
    (*b*) ll. 5-24, 29-44.
    (*c*) ll. 25-28, 45-50, 53, 54.
    (*d*) ll. 59-62, 55-58.
    (*e*) ll. 63-74, 85-96, 103-110.
    (*f*) ll. 51, 52, 75, 76, 79-84, 77, 78, 97-102, 111-118.
    (*g*) ll. 119-132.

I print the text as in the original MS., followed in smaller type by my own revised version for those who may prefer to read the poem as a whole, instead of as a number of disconnected proverb-couplets.

With this may be compared Rossetti's rearrangement :—

   (*a*) ll. 1-4.
   (*b*) ll. 5-10, 17, 18, 11-12, 19, 20, 13-16.
   (*c*) ll. 29-32, 41, 42, 33-38, 21-24, 39, 40, 43, 44, 67, 68, 71, 72.
   (*d*) ll. 25-28, 45-50, 97, 98.
   (*e*) ll. 99, 100, 77, 78, 101, 102, 75, 76, 51, 52, 81-84, 79, 80, 113-118.
   (*f*) ll. 85-90, 63-66, 93-96, 103, 104, 91, 92, 105, 106, 53, 54, 107-110.
   (*g*) ll. 119-124, 59-62, 55-58.
   (*h*) 125-132.

The latter arrangement (which has been adopted by all later editors except Shepherd), readable as it appears on first glance, seems to me to do great violence to the author's meaning. Passages are torn from their context and given an entirely different sense, by being placed in an artificial position. An example of this may be seen in Rossetti's penultimate section, where, by the juxtaposition of two separate passages, Blake is made to argue that a correct apprehension of the fact that some are born to misery and endless night will enable us to go through life with safety.

Auguries of Innocence

To see a World in a Grain of Sand,   1
And a Heaven in a Wild Flower,
Hold Infinity in the palm of your hand,
And Eternity in an hour.
A Robin Redbreast in a Cage   5
Puts all Heaven in a Rage.
A dove-house fill'd with Doves & Pigeons
Shudders Hell thro' all its regions.
A dog starv'd at his Master's Gate   9
Predicts the ruin of the State.
A Horse misused upon the Road
Calls to Heaven for Human blood.
Each outcry of the hunted Hare   13
A fibre from the Brain does tear.
A Skylark wounded in the wing ;
A Cherubim does cease to sing.
The Game Cock clipt and arm'd for fight   17
Does the Rising Sun affright.

Pickering MS. p. 13.
1 a] the Shep., WMR.   14 does] doth DGR, WMR, EY.   15 in]
on *all edd. except* Shep.   16 A . . . sing] Doth make a cherub cease to
sing *all edd. except* Shep.   17 The] A *all edd. except* Shep.   18 Does]
Doth *all edd. except* Shep.

Every Wolf's & Lion's howl
Raises from Hell a Human Soul.
The wild Deer, wand'ring here & there,   21
Keeps the Human Soul from Care.
The Lamb misus'd breeds Public Strife,
And yet forgives the Butcher's knife.
The Bat that flits at close of Eve   25
Has left the Brain that won't Believe.
The Owl that calls upon the Night
Speaks the Unbeliever's fright.
He who shall hurt the little Wren   29
Shall never be belov'd by Men.
He who the Ox to wrath has mov'd
Shall never be by Woman lov'd.
The wanton Boy that kills the Fly   33
Shall feel the Spider's enmity.
He who torments the Chafer's Sprite
Weaves a Bower in endless Night.
The Catterpiller on the Leaf   37
Repeats to thee thy Mother's grief.
Kill not the Moth nor Butterfly,
For the Last Judgment draweth nigh.
He who shall train the Horse to war   41
Shall never pass the Polar Bar.
The Beggar's Dog & Widow's Cat,
Feed them & thou wilt grow fat.
The Gnat that sings his Summer's Song   45
Poison gets from Slander's tongue.
The poison of the Snake & Newt
Is the sweat of Envy's Foot.
The poison of the Honey Bee   49
Is the Artist's Jealousy.
The Prince's Robes & Beggar's Rags
Are Toadstools on the Miser's Bags.

---

22 Keeps] Keep *all edd. except* Shep.   24 Cp. footnote to 'The Fly'
in the *Songs of Experience.*   37, 38 The . . . grief] Cp. *The Gates of
Paradise,* 'Keys of the Gates,' ll. 1, 2 :—

> 'The Catterpiller on the Leaf
>   Reminds thee of thy Mother's Grief.'

44 wilt] shalt *all edd. except* Shep.

A Truth that's told with bad intent   53
Beats all the Lies you can invent.
It is right it should be so;
Man was made for Joy & Woe;
And when this we rightly know,   57
Thro' the World we safely go.
Joy & Woe are woven fine,
A Clothing for the soul divine.
Under every grief & pine   61
Runs a joy with silken twine.
The Babe is more than Swadling Bands;
Throughout all these Human Lands
Tools were made, & Born were hands,   65
Every Farmer understands.
Every Tear from Every Eye
Becomes a Babe in Eternity;
This is caught by Females bright,   69
And return'd to its own delight.
The Bleat, the Bark, Bellow, & Roar,
Are Waves that Beat on Heaven's Shore.
The Babe that weeps the Rod beneath   73
Writes Revenge in realms of Death.
The Beggar's Rags, fluttering in Air,
Does to Rags the Heavens tear.
The Soldier, arm'd with Sword & Gun,   77
Palsied strikes the Summer's Sun.
The poor Man's Farthing is worth more
Than all the Gold on Afric's Shore.
One Mite wrung from the Lab'rer's hands   81
Shall buy & sell the Miser's Lands;
Or, if protected from on high,
Does that whole Nation sell & buy.
He who mocks the Infant's Faith   85
Shall be mock'd in Age & Death.

58 Thro' . . . go] Safely through the world we go *all edd. except* Shep.
63, 64 *All edd. except* Shep. *omit semicolon after* 'Bands' *and punctuate with
semicolon after* 'lands.'   69, 70 This . . . delight] DGR, WMR, *and*
EY *omit*; WBY *prints in* Notes.   69 bright] aright WBY.   73, 74
The Babe . . . Death] DGR, WMR, *and* EY *omit*; WBY *prints in* Notes.
76 Does] Do *all edd. except* Shep.   48 Does] Shall *all edd. except* Shep.

He who shall teach the Child to Doubt
The rotting Grave shall ne'er get out.
He who respects the Infant's faith 89
Triumphs over Hell & Death.
The Child's Toys and the Old Man's Reasons
Are the Fruits of the Two Seasons.
The Questioner, who sits so sly, 93
Shall never know how to Reply.
He who replies to words of Doubt
Doth put the Light of Knowledge out.
The Strongest Poison ever known 97
Came from Caesar's Laurel Crown.
Nought can Deform the Human Race
Like to the Armour's iron brace.
When Gold and Gems adorn the Plow 101
To peaceful Arts shall Envy Bow.
A Riddle, or the Cricket's Cry,
Is to Doubt a fit Reply.
The Emmet's Inch & Eagle's Mile 105
Make Lame Philosophy to smile.
He who Doubts from what he sees
Will ne'er Believe, do what you Please.
If the Sun & Moon should Doubt, 109
They'd immediately Go Out.
To be in a Passion you Good may do,
But no Good if a Passion is in you.
The Whore & Gambler, by the State 113
Licensed, build that Nation's Fate.
The Harlot's cry from Street to Street
Shall weave Old England's winding-Sheet.

---

92 Cp. *Milton*, f. 43, ll. 12–17 :—

'To cast off the idiot Questioner who is always questioning
But never capable of answering : who sits, with a sly grin,
Silent, plotting when to question, like a thief in a cave,
Who publishes doubt & calls it knowledge, whose Science is Despair,
Whose pretence to knowledge is Envy, whose whole Science is
To destroy the wisdom of ages to gratify ravenous Envy.'

100 Armour's] armourer's *all edd. except* Shep. 102 Arts] hearts EY.
103 Riddle] puddle DGR, WMR, EY.   111–112 To . . . you] DGR,
WMR, EY *omit*; WBY *prints in* Notes.

The Winner's shout, the Loser's Curse,   117
Dance before dead England's Hearse.
Every Night and every Morn
Some to Misery are Born.
Every Morn and every Night   121
Some are Born to Sweet Delight.
Some are Born to Sweet Delight,
Some are Born to Endless Night.
We are led to Believe a Lie   125
When we see not Thro' the Eye,
Which was Born in a Night to perish in a Night,
When the Soul Slept in Beams of Light.
God appears, & God is light,   129
To those poor souls who dwell in Night;
But does a Human Form Display
To those who Dwell in Realms of Day.

118 Dance] Shall dance *all edd. except* Shep.   125-128 We . . . Light]
Cp. 'Everlasting Gospel' γ^2, ll. 103-106 :—

> 'And leads you to believe a lie
> When you see with, not through, the eye;
> That was born in a night, to perish in a night,
> When the soul slept in the beams of light.'

126 When . . . Eye] When we see with, not through, the eye, Pickering MS.
1*st rdg. del. and all edd. except* Shep.   131 does] doth *all edd. except* Shep.

Auguries of Innocence

(*Revised Arrangement*)

To see a World in a Grain of Sand,
And a Heaven in a Wild Flower,
Hold Infinity in the palm of your hand,
And Eternity in an hour.

A Robin Redbreast in a Cage
Puts all Heaven in a Rage.
A dove-house fill'd with Doves & Pigeons
Shudders Hell thro' all its regions.
A dog starv'd at his Master's Gate
Predicts the ruin of the State.
A Horse misused upon the Road
Calls to Heaven for Human blood.

Each outcry of the hunted Hare
A fibre from the Brain does tear.
A Skylark wounded in the wing,
A Cherubim does cease to sing.
The Game-Cock clipt and arm'd for fight
Does the Rising Sun affright.
Every Wolf's & Lion's howl
Raises from Hell a Human Soul.
The wild Deer, wand'ring here & there,
Keeps the Human Soul from Care.
The Lamb misus'd breeds Public Strife,
And yet forgives the Butcher's knife.
He who shall hurt the little Wren
Shall never be belov'd by Men.
He who the Ox to wrath has mov'd
Shall never be by Woman lov'd.
The wanton Boy that kills the Fly
Shall feel the Spider's enmity.
He who torments the Chafer's Sprite
Weaves a Bower in endless Night.
The Catterpiller on the Leaf
Repeats to thee thy Mother's grief.
Kill not the Moth nor Butterfly,
For the Last Judgment draweth nigh.
He who shall train the Horse to war
Shall never pass the Polar Bar.
The Beggar's Dog & Widow's Cat,
Feed them & thou wilt grow fat.

The Bat that flits at close of Eve
Has left the Brain that won't Believe.
The Owl that calls upon the Night
Speaks the Unbeliever's fright.
The Gnat that sings his Summer's Song
Poison gets from Slander's tongue.
The poison of the Snake & Newt
Is the sweat of Envy's Foot.
The poison of the Honey-Bee
Is the Artist's Jealousy.
A Truth that's told with bad intent
Beats all the Lies you can invent.

Joy & Woe are woven fine,
A Clothing for the soul divine ;
Under every grief & pine
Runs a joy with silken twine.
It is right it should be so ;
Man was made for Joy & Woe ;
And, when this we rightly know,
Thro' the World we safely go.

The Babe is more than Swadling Bands;
Throughout all these Human Lands
Tools were made, & Born were hands,
Every Farmer understands.
Every Tear from Every Eye
Becomes a Babe in Eternity;
This is caught by Females bright,
And return'd to its own delight.
The Bleat, the Bark, Bellow, & Roar,
Are Waves that Beat on Heaven's Shore.
The Babe that weeps the Rod beneath
Writes Revenge in realms of Death.
He who mocks the Infant's Faith
Shall be mock'd in Age & Death.
He who shall teach the Child to Doubt
The rotting Grave shall ne'er get out.
He who respects the Infant's faith
Triumphs over Hell & Death.
The Child's Toys and the Old Man's Reasons
Are the Fruits of the Two Seasons.
The Questioner, who sits so sly,
Shall never know how to Reply.
He who replies to words of Doubt
Doth put the Light of Knowledge out.
A Riddle, or the Cricket's Cry,
Is to Doubt a fit Reply.
The Emmet's Inch & Eagle's Mile
Make Lame Philosophy to smile.
He who Doubts from what he sees
Will ne'er Believe, do what you Please.
If the Sun & Moon should Doubt,
They'd immediately Go Out.

The Prince's Robes & Beggar's Rags
Are Toadstools on the Miser's Bags.
The Beggar's Rags, fluttering in Air,
Does to Rags the Heavens tear.
The poor Man's Farthing is worth more
Than all the Gold on Afric's Shore.
One Mite wrung from the Lab'rer's hands
Shall buy & sell the Miser's Lands;
Or, if protected from on high,
Does that whole Nation sell & buy.
The Soldier, arm'd with Sword & Gun,
Palsied strikes the Summer's Sun.
The Strongest Poison ever known
Came from Caesar's Laurel Crown.
Nought can Deform the human Race
Like to the Armour's iron brace.

When Gold and Gems adorn the Plow
To peaceful Arts shall Envy Bow.
To be in a Passion you Good may do,
But no Good if a Passion is in you.
The Whore & Gambler, by the State
Licensed, build that Nation's Fate.
The Harlot's cry from Street to Street
Shall weave Old England's winding Sheet.
The Winner's shout, the Loser's Curse,
Dance before dead England's Hearse.

Every Night and every Morn
Some to Misery are Born.
Every Morn and every Night
Some are Born to Sweet Delight.
Some are Born to Sweet Delight,
Some are Born to Endless Night.
We are led to Believe a Lie
When we see not Thro' the Eye,
Which was Born in a Night to perish in a Night,
When the Soul Slept in Beams of Light.
God appears, & God is light,
To those poor souls who dwell in Night,
But does a Human Form Display
To those who Dwell in Realms of Day.

Long John Brown & Little Mary Bell

Little Mary Bell had a Fairy in a Nut, 1
Long John Brown had the Devil in his Gut ;
Long John Brown lov'd little Mary Bell,
And the Fairy drew the Devil into the Nutshell.

Pickering MS. p. 19.
  In *Jerusalem*, f. 36, ll. 35-37, fairies are described as one of ' Four ravening deathlike Forms. . . . States Permanently Fixed by the Divine Power.'
Cp. from the ' Motto to the *Songs of Innocence and of Experience*,' in the MS.
Book (xxxi) :—
    ' The Good are attracted by Men's perceptions,
      And think not for themselves ;
    Till Experience teaches them to catch
      And to cage the Fairies & Elves' :
lines perhaps explained by the quatrain which almost immediately precedes
them in the MS. Book (xxvii) :—
      ' If you trap the moment before it 's ripe,
        The tears of repentance you'll certainly wipe ;
      But if once you let the ripe moment go
        You can never wipe off the tears of woe.'

Her Fairy skip'd out, & her Fairy skip'd in ;   5
He laugh'd at the Devil saying, 'Love is a Sin.'
The Devil he raged, & the Devil he was wroth,
And the Devil enter'd into the Young Man's broth.

He was soon in the Gut of the loving Young Swain,   9
For John eat & drank to drive away Love's pain ;
But all he could do he grew thinner and thinner,
Though he eat & drank as much as ten Men for his
        dinner.

Some said he had a Wolf in his stomach day & night,   13
Some said he had the Devil, & they guess'd right ;
The fairy skip'd about in his Glory, Joy, and Pride,
And he laugh'd at the Devil till poor John Brown Died.

Then the Fairy skip'd out of the old Nutshell,   17
And woe & alack ! for Pretty Mary Bell ;
For the Devil crept in when the Fairy skip'd out,
And there goes Miss Bell with her fusty old Nut.

Title] At first ' John Brown & Mary Bell,' the adjectives being an addition.
1, 3 Little] Pretty Pickering MS. *1st rdg. del.*   2, 3 Long] Young
Pickering MS. *1st rdg. del.*   5 & her] EY *omits* &.   15 Joy] love
EY.

William Bond

I wonder whether the Girls are mad,   1
And I wonder whether they mean to kill,
And I wonder if William Bond will die,
For assuredly he is very ill.

He went to Church in a May morning,   5
Attended by Fairies, one, two, and three ;
But the Angels of Providence drove them away,
And he return'd home in Misery.

Pickering MS. p. 20.
    5 in] on *all edd. except* Shep.

He went not out to the Field nor Fold,   9
He went not out to the Village nor Town,
But he came home in a black black cloud,
And took to his Bed, and there lay down.

And an Angel of Providence at his Feet,   13
And an Angel of Providence at his Head,
And in the midst a Black Black Cloud,
And in the midst the Sick Man on his Bed.

And on his Right hand was Mary Green,   17
And on his Left hand was his Sister Jane,
And their tears fell thro' the black black Cloud
To drive away the sick man's pain.

'O William, if thou dost another Love,   21
Dost another Love better than poor Mary,
Go & take that other to be thy Wife,
And Mary Green shall her Servant be.'

'Yes, Mary, I do another Love,   25
Another I Love far better than thee,
And Another I will have for my Wife;
Then what have I to do with thee?

'For thou art Melancholy Pale,   29
And on thy Head is the cold Moon's Shine,
But she is ruddy & bright as day,
And the sunbeams dazzle from her eyne.'

Mary trembled & Mary chill'd,   33
And Mary fell down on the right hand floor,
That William Bond & his Sister Jane
Scarce could recover Mary more.

When Mary woke & found her laid   37
On the Right hand of her William dear,
On the Right hand of his loved Bed,
And saw her William Bond so near,

21 **O William**] Shep. *omits* O.   28 **Then . . . thee**] Cp. in *Songs of Experience* 'To Tirzah,' l. 4.

The Fairies that fled from William Bond 41
Dancèd around her Shining Head ;
They dancèd over the Pillow white,
And the Angels of Providence left the Bed.

I thought Love lived in the hot sunshine, 45
But O, he lives in the Moony light !
I thought to find Love in the heat of Day,
But sweet Love is the Comforter of Night.

Seek Love in the Pity of others' Woe, 49
In the gentle relief of another's care,
In the darkness of night & the Winter's Snow,
In the naked & outcast, seek Love there !

45-52 All edd. place in inverted commas as if the speech were William
Bond's. I treat it rather as that of the narrator of the story, who begins
the poem in the first person.   52 In] With DGR, WMR, EY, WBY.

POEMS

FROM

LETTERS

1800–1803

PREFACE

POEMS FROM LETTERS

FIVE of the six poems in this section are taken from letters written by Blake or his wife. The earliest of these are the stanzas enclosed in a letter from Mrs. Blake to Mrs. Flaxman, dated September 14, 1800, i.e. immediately before the Blakes' removal to Felpham. Four of the pieces are contained in letters to Mr. Butts written from Felpham, 1800–1803. I place here also a little fairy poem which seems to belong to the same period. It was first printed by Swinburne (*Essay*, pp. 143, 144) from an autograph of Blake's on the back of a small pencil-sketch.

My text of the poems in the letters to Mr. Butts is taken from the originals, kindly lent me by Capt. Butts, the grandson of Blake's friend. I follow Gilchrist for the lines to Mrs. Anna Flaxman, being unable to trace the present whereabouts of the original; and for the same reason take my text of 'A fairy leapt upon my knee' from Swinburne's *Essay*.

The first five poems are printed by all editors except Shepherd : the last by Swinburne and Ellis and Yeats only.

POEMS FROM LETTERS

i

To my dear Friend, Mrs. Anna Flaxman

This song to the flower of Flaxman's joy,   1
To the blossom of hope for a sweet decoy;
Do all that you can, or all that you may,
To entice him to Felpham and far away.

Away to sweet Felpham, for Heaven is there; 5
The Ladder of Angels descends through the air;
On the turret its spiral does softly descend,
Through the village then winds, at my cot it does end.

You stand in the village and look up to heaven; 9
The precious stones glitter on flight seventy-seven;
And my brother is there, and *my* friend and thine
Descend and ascend with the bread and the wine.

The bread of sweet thought and the wine of delight 13
Feed the village of Felpham by day and by night,
And at his own door the bless'd hermit does stand,
Dispensing unceasing to all the wide land.

Gilchrist, i. 149, 150, from a copy supplied to the biographer by Miss Den-
man, Mrs. Flaxman's sister. The poem, signed 'W. Blake,' is in a letter
dated 'H[ercules] B[uildings], Lambeth, 14 Sept. 1800,' and signed
'Catherine Blake,' though obviously Blake's own composition.

 7 turret] the turret of Hayley's house : see note to l. 15. 11 *my*] The
italics are probably Gilchrist's, other edd. print in roman. 15 William
Hayley, Blake's patron, constantly refers to himself as the 'Hermit of
Eartham' or the 'Hermit of the Turret' in his letters to his friends.

ii

To my Friend Butts I write   1
My first Vision of Light,
On the yellow sands sitting.
The Sun was Emitting
His Glorious beams   5
From Heaven's high Streams.
Over Sea, over Land,
My Eyes did Expand
Into regions of air,
Away from all Care;   10
Into regions of fire,
Remote from Desire ;
The Light of the Morning
Heaven's Mountains adorning :
In particles bright,   15
The jewels of Light
Distinct shone & clear.
Amaz'd & in fear
I each particle gazèd,
Astonish'd, Amazèd;   20

Written in two columns on the first and second pages of a letter dated 'Felpham, Oct'. 2ᵈ, 1800,' addressed to 'Mr. Butts, Great Marlborough Street.' (See Gilchrist, ii. 180, 181.) These verses are prefaced by the lines : 'Recieve from me a return of verses such as Felpham produces by me, tho' not such as she produces by her Eldest Son ; however, such as they are, I cannot resist the temptation to send them to you.'   WMR, EY, and WBY entitle 'To Mr. Butts.'

13-17 Cp. the stanzas in the verses beginning 'Mock on, Mock on, Voltaire, Rousseau' (MS. Book xli) :—

> 'And every sand becomes a Gem
> Reflected in the beams divine ;
> Blown back they blind the mocking eye,
> But still in Israel's paths they shine.

> 'The Atoms of Democritus
> And Newton's Particles of Light
> Are sands upon the Red sea shore
> Where Israel's tents do shine so bright.'

19, 20 gazèd . . . Amazèd] *All edd. read* gazed . . . amazed, ignoring Blake's precise use of the spelling 'èd' when he intends the final syllable to be pronounced.

For each was a Man
Human-form'd. Swift I ran,
For they beckon'd to me,
Remote by the Sea,
Saying: 'Each grain of Sand,   25
Every Stone on the Land,
Each rock & each hill,
Each fountain & rill,
Each herb & each tree,
Mountain, hill, earth, & sea,   30
Cloud, Meteor, & Star,
Are Men Seen Afar.'
I stood in the Streams
Of Heaven's bright beams,
And Saw Felpham sweet   35
Beneath my bright feet,
In soft Female charms;
And in her fair arms
My Shadow I knew,
And my wife's shadow too,   40
And My Sister, & Friend.
We like Infants descend
In our Shadows on Earth,
Like a weak mortal birth.
My Eyes, more & more,   45
Like a Sea without shore,
Continue Expanding,
The Heavens commanding;
Till the Jewels of Light,
Heavenly Men beaming bright,   50
Appear'd as One Man,
Who Complacent began
My limbs to infold
In his beams of bright gold;
Like dross purg'd away   55
All my mire & my clay.
Soft consum'd in delight,
In his bosom Sun-bright
I remain'd. Soft he smil'd,

And I heard his voice Mild,   60
Saying: 'This is My Fold,
O thou Ram horn'd with gold,
Who awakest from Sleep
On the Sides of the Deep.
On the Mountains around   65
The roarings resound
Of the lion & wolf,
The loud Sea, & deep gulph.
These are guards of My Fold,
O thou Ram horn'd with gold!'   70
And the voice faded mild:
I remain'd as a Child;
All I ever had known
Before me bright Shone:
I saw you & your wife   75
By the fountains of life.
Such the Vision to me
Appear'd on the Sea.

iii

To Mrs. Butts

Wife of the Friend of those I most revere,   1
Recieve this tribute from a Harp sincere;
Go on in Virtuous Seed sowing on Mold
Of Human Vegetation, & Behold
Your Harvest Springing to Eternal Life,   5
Parent of Youthful Minds, & happy Wife!

These lines, signed 'W. B.,' which the author hopes Mrs. Butts 'will excuse,' conclude the letter from which the preceding poem is taken. 4 Human Vegetation] Cp. the passage in Blake's introduction to *Jerusalem*, chap. iv, 'To the Christians':—'Imagination, the real & eternal World of which this Vegetable Universe is but a faint shadow, & in which we shall live in our Eternal or Imaginative Bodies when these Vegetable Mortal Bodies are no more.'

iv

With happiness stretch'd across the hills   1
In a cloud that dewy sweetness distills;
With a blue sky spread over with wings,
And a mild Sun that mounts & sings;
With trees & fields full of Fairy elves,   5
And little devils who fight for themselves—
Rememb'ring the Verses that Hayley sung
When my heart knock'd against the root of my tongue—
With Angels planted in Hawthorn bowers,
And God himself in the passing hours;   10
With Silver Angels across my way,
And Golden demons that none can stay;
With my Father hovering upon the wind,
And my Brother Robert just behind,
And my Brother John, the evil one,   15
In a black cloud making his mone,—
Tho' dead, they appear upon my path,
Notwithstanding my terrible wrath;
They beg, they intreat, they drop their tears,
Fill'd full of hopes, fill'd full of fears—   20
With a thousand Angels upon the Wind,
Pouring disconsolate from behind
To drive them off, & before my way
A frowning Thistle implores my stay.
What to others a trifle appears   25
Fills me full of smiles or tears;

These verses, written in two columns in a postscript to a letter dated 'Felpham, Novr 22, 1802,' Blake says 'were Composed above a twelve-month ago while Walking from Felpham to Lavant to meet my Sister.' Printed by all editors except Shepherd. WMR and EY entitle 'Verses,' WBY, 'Los the Terrible.'

    3, 4 Cp. *Jerusalem*, f. 19, ll. 43, 44 :—

        'In a sweet moony night & silence that they had created,
        With a blue sky spread over with wings and a mild moon.'

7, 8 These two lines are written sideways in the margin, with the note :— 'These 2 lines were omitted when transcribing & ought to come in at x' (i.e. after line 6, the position being also indicated by Blake's catchword 'Rememb'ring').   16 See note to 'Mad Song' (*Poetical Sketches*), l. 17.

For double the vision my Eyes do see,
And a double vision is always with me.
With my inward Eye, 'tis an old Man grey,
With my outward, a Thistle across my way.   30
'If thou goest back,' the thistle said,
'Thou art to endless woe betray'd ;
For here does Theotormon lower,
And here is Enitharmon's bower ;
And Los the terrible thus hath sworn,   35
Because thou backward dost return,
Poverty, Envy, old age, & fear,
Shall bring thy Wife upon a bier ;
And Butts shall give what Fuseli gave,
A dark black Rock & a gloomy Cave.'   40

27 See note to l. 87.   33 Theotormon, first mentioned in *Visions of the Daughters of Albion* (1793), is the third of the 'Four Sons of Jerusalem that never were Generated' (*Jerusalem*, f. 71, l. 50), elsewhere referred to as the sons of Los. He is described as 'fill'd with care' (*Milton*, f. 23, l. 12) and associated with storms and weeping (*Jerusalem*, f. 16, l. 8, and *Visions of the Daughters of Albion*, *passim*).   34 'lovely Enitharmon' (*Jerusalem*, f. 10, l. 42), the emanation of Los' (*ibid.*, f. 30, ll. 3, 4) and one of the daughters of Albion (*ibid.* f. 42, l. 15), symbolizes space ; see *Milton*, f. 23, l. 68 :—

'Los is by mortals nam'd Time, Enitharmon is nam'd Space.'

35 'Los . . . the Vehicular Form of strong Urthona' (*Jerusalem*, f. 53, l. 1), one of the Four Zoas (*ibid.* f. 47, l. 4), is depicted as a blacksmith working at his furnace. Los is Time (see note to l. 34), the spirit of prophecy and inspiration (*Jerusalem*, f. 8, l. 17, and f. 90, l. 39). In Blake's reference to his own 'terrible wrath' (l. 18) he appears to identify himself with Los in his capacity of prophet and seer. The name Los, as Mr. Oliver Madox-Brown conjectured, is probably a transposition of Sol (cp. ll. 55-57, and the passage from *Milton* quoted in the footnote).   39, 40 This allusion is only to be understood by a knowledge of one of the chief articles of Blake's faith in ethics and art, as to the supreme importance of cultivating and recognizing what he terms 'Minute Particulars,' meaning thereby those personal characteristics which constitute the identity of the individual. See *Jerusalem*, f. 69, l. 42 :—'Every Minute Particular is Holy'; *ibid.* f. 31, ll. 44-46 :—

'. . . thine own Minute Particulars
Belong to God alone, and all thy little ones are holy.
They are of Faith, & not of Demonstration ';

ibid. f. 43, ll. 16-23 :—

'. . . Heavens over Hells
Brooding in holy hypocritic lust, drinking the cries of pain
From howling victims of Law ; building Heavens Twenty-seven-fold,

I struck the Thistle with my foot,
And broke him up from his delving root.
'Must the duties of life each other cross?
Must every joy be dung & dross?
Must my dear Butts feel cold neglect   45
Because I give Hayley his due respect?
Must Flaxman look upon me as wild,
And all my friends be with doubts beguil'd?
Must my Wife live in my Sister's bane,
Or my sister survive on my Love's pain?   50
The curses of Los, the terrible shade,
And his dismal terrors make me afraid.'

So I spoke, & struck in my wrath
The old man weltering upon my path.
Then Los appear'd in all his power: 55
In the Sun he appear'd, descending before

Swell'd & bloated General Forms repugnant to the Divine
Humanity, who is the Only General and Universal Form,
To which all Lineaments tend, & seek with love & sympathy.
All broad & general principles belong to benevolence
Who protects minute particulars, every one in their own identity' :

ibid. f. 55, ll. 60–64 :—

' He who would do good to another must do it in Minute Particulars.
General Good is the plea of the scoundrel, hypocrite, & flatterer ;
For Art & Science cannot exist but in minutely organized Particulars,
And not in generalizing Demonstrations of the Rational Power.
The Infinite alone resides in Definite & Determinate Identity.'

The Rock and the Cave, constantly recurring figures in Blake's later
Prophetic Books, are invariably used as symbols of the state opposed
to Jerusalem (or the life of spiritual liberty and imagination), in which
'Minute Particulars' of personal identity are crushed under the weight
of reason and natural religion. This is rendered clear by the passage
in *Jerusalem*, f. 43, ll. 56–62 :—

' It is easy to acknowledge a man to be great & good, while we
Derogate from him in the trifles & small articles of that goodness.
Those alone are his friends who admire his minutest powers.
Instead of Albion's lovely mountains, & the curtains of Jerusalem,
I see a Cave, a Rock, a Tree deadly and poisonous, unimaginative :
Instead of the Mutual Forgivenesses, the Minute Particulars, I see
Pits of bitumen ever burning.'

47 Cp. MS. Book liii and lv.   49 Cp. note to ' The Grey Monk,' l. 16.
Pickering MS.

X 2

My face in fierce flames; in my double sight
'Twas outward a Sun, inward Los in his might.
' My hands are labour'd day & night,
And Ease comes never in my sight.   60
My Wife has no indulgence given
Except what comes to her from heaven.
We eat little, we drink less,
This Earth breeds not our happiness.
Another Sun feeds our life's streams,   65
We are not warmèd with thy beams;
Thou measurest not the Time to me,
Nor yet the Space that I do see;
My Mind is not with thy light array'd,
Thy terrors shall not make me afraid.'   70

When I had my Defiance given,
The Sun stood trembling in heaven;
The Moon, that glow'd remote below,
Became leprous & white as snow;
And every Soul of men on the Earth   75
Felt affliction, & sorrow, & sickness, & dearth.
Los flam'd in my path, & the Sun was hot
With the bows of my Mind & the Arrows of Thought.

55–58 Cp. *Milton*, f. 20, ll. 6–25 :—

' And Los behind me stood, a terrible flaming Sun, just close
Behind my back. I turned round in terror, and behold,
Los stood in that fierce glowing fire . . .
And I became One Man with him arising in my strength.
'Twas too late now to recede. Los had entered into my soul :
His terrors now posses'd me whole : I arose in fury & strength.

' I am that Shadowy Prophet who, Six Thousand Years ago,
Fell from my station in the Eternal bosom. Six Thousand Years
Are finish'd. I return : both Time & Space obey my will.
I, in Six Thousand Years, walk up and down; for not one Moment
Of Time is lost, nor one Event of Space unpermanent ;
But all remain : every fabric of Six Thousand Years
Remains permanent, tho' on the Earth, where Satan
Fell and was cut off, all things vanish & are seen no more.
They vanish not from me & mine : we guard them first & last :
The generations of men run on in the tide of Time,
But leave their destin'd lineaments permanent for ever & ever.'

60 Ease] rest Swinb.   75 men] man *all edd.*   78 the Arrows] with
arrows Swinb.

My bowstring fierce with Ardour breathes;
My arrows glow in their golden sheaves;   80
My brothers & father march before;
The heavens drop with human gore.

Now I a fourfold vision see,
And a fourfold vision is given to me;
'Tis fourfold in my supreme delight,   85
And threefold in soft Beulah's night,

81 brothers] brother *all edd.*   85 Fourfold—the basic idea of Blake's
symbolic system, which abounds in fourfold correspondences—always conveys
the idea of perfection and harmony. Cp. *Jerusalem*, f. 98, and the later Pro-
phetic Books, *passim.*   86 Beulah] In Blake's mythology the four states
of man are Beulah, Alla, Al-Ulro, and Or-Ulro. Cp. *Milton*, f. 34, ll. 8-11 :—
'And the Four States of Humanity in its Repose
Were shewed them. First of Beulah a most pleasant Sleep
On Couches soft with mild music tended by Flowers of Beulah,
Sweet Female forms winged or floating in the air spontaneous.'
See also *The Four Zoas*, Night i, ll. 197-203 :—
'There is from Great Eternity a mild & pleasant rest
Nam'd Beulah, a Soft Moony Universe, feminine, lovely,
Pure, mild & Gentle, given in Mercy to those who sleep,
Eternally Created by the Lamb of God around
On all sides, within & without the Universal Man.
The Daughters of Beulah follow Sleepers in all their Dreams,
Creating Spaces, lest they fall into Eternal Death.'
See also the opening lines of the second book of *Milton* :—
'There is a place where Contrarieties are equally True.
This place is called Beulah: It is a pleasant lovely Shadow
Where no dispute can come, Because of those who Sleep.
Into this place the Sons & Daughters of Ololon descended
With solemn mourning into Beulah's moony shades & hills,
Weeping for Milton : mute wonder held the Daughters of Beulah,
Enraptur'd with affection sweet and mild benevolence.
Beulah is evermore Created around Eternity : appearing
To the Inhabitants of Eden around them on all sides.
But Beulah to its Inhabitants appears, within each district,
As the belovèd infant in his mother's bosom, round incircled
With arms of love & pity & sweet compassion. But to
The Sons of Eden, the moony habitations of Beulah
Are from Great Eternity a mild & pleasant Rest.
And it is thus Created. Lo! the Eternal Great Humanity,
To whom be Glory & Dominion, Evermore, Amen!
Walks among all his awful Family, seen in every face,
As the breath of the Almighty : such are the words of man to man,
In the great Wars of Eternity, in fury of Poetic Inspiration,
To build the Universe stupendous, Mental forms Creating.

And twofold Always.   May God us keep
From Single vision, & Newton's sleep!

87 twofold] By 'twofold' is meant man's reason and imagination in a state
of harmony, or, in Blake's own language, not 'divided' into 'spectre' and
'emanation.'   Cp. ll. 27-30, where the 'inward eye' of imagination is
contrasted with the 'outward eye' of reason, a comparison repeated and
emphasized in a couplet of 'The Everlasting Gospel,' γ^2, ll. 103, 104 :—

> 'And leads you to believe a lie
> When you see with, not through, the eye':

for 'spectre' and 'emanation' see introductory note to MS. Book xxxvii.
88 Cp. *Jerusalem*, f. 53, ll. 10, 11 :—

> 'incomprehensible
> To the Vegetated Mortal Eye's perverted & single vision

[i. e. to reason separated from imagination].

V

O why was I born with a different face?   1
Why was I not born like the rest of my race?
When I look, each one starts; when I speak, I offend;
Then I'm silent & passive, & lose every Friend.

Then my verse I dishonour, My pictures despise;   5
My person degrade, & my temper chastise;
And the pen is my terror, the pencil my shame;
All my Talents I bury, and dead is my Fame.

I am either too low, or too highly priz'd;   9
When Elate I'm Envy'd, When Meek I'm despis'd.

In a letter addressed to 'M^r. Butts Gr. Marlborough St London' dated
'Felpham, August 16, 1803,' in which Blake describes the circumstances
which led to his trial for high treason (see Gilchrist's *Life*, i, chap. xix), prefaced by 'Give me your advice in my perilous adventure : burn what I have
peevishly written about my friend. I have been very much degraded
& injuriously treated; but, if it all arise from my own fault, I ought to
blame myself.'   Printed by DGR, EY, and WMR, the latter with the
title 'Verses.'

1, 2 See note to 'Mary,' ll. 21, 22, Pickering MS.   3 When] If EY.
10 I'm Envy'd] I am envied WMR, EY.

vi

A fairy leapt upon my knee   1
Singing and dancing merrily ;
I said, 'Thou thing of patches, rings,
Pins, necklaces, and such-like things,
Disgracer of the female form,   5
Thou paltry, gilded, poisonous worm !'
Weeping, he fell upon my thigh,
And thus in tears did soft reply :
'Knowest thou not, O fairies' lord !   9
How much by us contemned, abhorred,
Whatever hides the female form
That cannot bear the mortal storm ?
Therefore in pity still we give   13
Our lives to make the female live ;
And what would turn into disease
We turn to what will joy and please.'

Swinburne's text (pp. 143, 144, *note*), 'copied from a loose scrap of paper, on the back of which is a pencilled sketch of Hercules throttling the serpents, whose twisted limbs make a sort of spiral cradle around and above the child's triumphant figure : an attendant, naked, falls back in terror with sharp recoil of drawn-up limbs ; Alcmene and Amphitryon watch the struggle in silence, he grasping her hand.'

6 paltry] pretty EY.   9 O] EY *omit*.

DEDICATION

OF

BLAKE'S ILLUSTRATIONS

OF

BLAIR'S 'GRAVE'

Published May 1st, 1808

Written circa 1806–1807

PREFACE

BLAKE'S *Illustrations of Blair's Grave* is the only work which, during his lifetime, achieved any degree of popularity, or brought his name prominently before the public. The edition, widely advertised by its publisher, R. H. Cromek, appeared with the recommendations of West, Flaxman, Fuseli, and others, and the list of subscribers alone considerably exceeded five hundred. Blake's twelve designs or 'inventions' were purchased by Cromek for the sum of twenty guineas, on the understanding that the engraving of the plates was also to be entrusted to the artist. Cromek, however, violating this unwritten agreement, employed instead a talented pupil of Bartolozzi's, Louis Schiavonetti—an action resented by Blake, whose strong feeling with regard to this transaction is evidenced in several of the epigrams in the Rossetti MS.

The dedication of this work to Queen Charlotte, which is printed in ordinary type on the recto of the leaf following the title-page, was to have formed an additional engraved plate with a vignette of Blake's invention. The design was actually prepared, and submitted by the artist to Cromek, but was returned by the latter upon grounds sufficiently clearly stated in his letter dated May, 1807. This letter, which was first printed in the *Gentleman's Magazine*, February, 1852, and reprinted by Gilchrist (i. 205–207), begins: 'Sir, I rec'd, not with^t great surprise, your letter demanding four guineas for the *sketched* vignette ded^n to the Queen. I have returned the drawing with this note, and I will briefly state my reasons for so doing. In the first place, I do not think it merits the price you affix to it, *under any circumstances*. In the next place, I never had the remotest suspicion that you^d for a moment entertain the idea of writing *me* to supply money to create an honour in w^h I cannot possibly participate. The Queen allowed *you*, not *me*, to dedicate the work to *her*! The honour w^d have been yours exclus^y ; but that you might not be deprived of any advantage likely to contribute to your reputation, I was willing to pay Mr. Schiavonetti *ten* guineas for etching a plate from the drawing in question.'

The original design, preserved in the British Museum, is thus described by Mr. W. M. Rossetti in his ' Annotated Lists of Blake's Paintings, Drawings, and Engravings,' List I, no. 70 (Gilchrist, ii. 209) : ' Executed with most special care and completeness in pale semi-neutral tints ; a very beautiful work. The subject is the deliverance of the Human Soul from Death, and the Ascension of the Just. Above, are two angels, one sheathing the sword, another holding the unequally-poised balance and a sealed roll ; a third descends with a key to unlock the fetters of the grave. A mother with her adolescent and infant family rises to the left ; a man and children to the right, their chains riven, clasp their upraised hands in thankfulness for the great deliverance. Between the upper angels a space is left for the inscription.'

To the Queen

The Door of Death is made of Gold,　　　　1
That Mortal Eyes cannot behold ;
But, when the Mortal Eyes are clos'd,
And cold and pale the Limbs repos'd,
The Soul awakes ; and, wond'ring, sees　　5
In her mild Hand the golden Keys :
The Grave is Heaven's golden Gate,
And rich and poor around it wait ;
O Shepherdess of England's Fold,
Behold this Gate of Pearl and Gold!　　　10

　　To dedicate to England's Queen
The Visions that my Soul has seen,
And, by Her kind permission, bring
What I have borne on solemn Wing,
From the vast regions of the Grave,　　　15
Before Her Throne my Wings I wave ;
Bowing before my Sov'reign's Feet,
' The Grave produc'd these Blossoms sweet
In mild repose from Earthly strife ;
The Blossoms of Eternal Life!'　　　　　20

Blair's *Grave*, 1808.　The Dedication is signed 'William Blake.'
14 solemn] silken Wilk., Shep.　　15 regions] region Wilk., Shep.

EPIGRAMS

FROM

BLAKE'S ANNOTATED COPY OF REYNOLDS' WORKS

circa 1808

PREFACE TO THE EPIGRAMS

THE nine epigrams which follow are found interspersed among a number of prose annotations to Sir Joshua Reynolds' 'Discourses,' written in Blake's autograph on the margins of the first volume of his copy of Reynolds' *Works* (2nd edition, 1798).

These marginal notes were made at first in pencil, and afterwards copied over and supplemented in ink. According to Ellis and Yeats (ii. 315) there 'can be no doubt that at the time Blake was writing extracts from the 'Discourses' to Butts, and reconsidering, as he says, all his thoughts on art, he was looking over his pencilled notes and adding to them.' His only reference, however, to Reynolds is in a letter to Mr. Butts dated Felpham, November 2, 1802, in which he quotes with approval a passage from the 'Discourses,' adding, 'So says Sir Joshua, and So say I.' Blake's later and more prejudiced view of the President of the Academy is forcibly expressed in his note on the title-page : 'This Man was Hired to Depress Art. This is the Opinion of Will. Blake : my Proofs of this Opinion are given in the following Notes.' These epigrams, moreover, are precisely of the same order as those scattered through the pages of the later part of the Rossetti MS. The annotations in Blake's Reynolds all refer to the first eight 'Discourses' contained in the first volume of the *Works*, while those on the following 'Discourses' are jotted down in the MS. Book. As the latter are mixed with verses referring to his quarrel with Cromek and Stothard the whole of the epigrams may be dated circa 1808, those written in the copy of Reynolds being probably rather the earlier of the two.

Gilchrist, on 'intrinsic evidence,' attributes the annotations and epigrams in the 'Discourses' to the year 1820. This is obviously a conclusion from the words 'Aged Sixty-three' in the lines beginning, 'When Nations grow Old.' Whatever Blake may have meant by this cryptic saying, it certainly cannot refer to his own age at the time of writing. A very similar reference to being born old occurs in one of his epigrams in the MS. Book written about the same period:—

> ' S[tothard] in childhood, upon the nursery floor,
> Was extreme old and most extremely poor:
> He has grown old and rich and what he will:
> He is extreme old and extreme poor still.'

My text is taken from Blake's annotated copy of Reynolds. which is now preserved in the British Museum.

EPIGRAMS

i

Advice of the Popes who succeeded the Age of Rafael

Degrade first the Arts if you'd Mankind Degrade,
Hire Idiots to Paint with cold light & hot shade,
Give high Price for the worst, leave the best in disgrace,
And with Labours of Ignorance fill every place.

Reynolds, vol. i, written at foot of title-page.
Gil. i. 257, EY ii. 318 (*reading* ' to the popes who succeeded to the age of Rafail ').
1 you'd] you would Gil. 2 hot] not EY. 4 Labours of Ignorance] labour of idleness Gil.

ii

Some look to see the sweet Outlines,
And beauteous Forms that Love does wear ;
Some look to find out Patches, Paint,
Bracelets & Stays & Powder'd Hair.

Reynolds, vol. i, p. xv. Blake's comment on Sir Joshua Reynolds' account of his disappointment at his first impressions of Raphael. The prose passage preceding these lines runs :—' Men who have been Educated with Works of Venetian Artists under their Eyes Cannot see Rafael, unless they are born with Determinate Organs. I am happy I cannot say that Rafael Ever was from my Earliest Childhood hidden from Me. I saw & I knew immediately the difference between Rafael & Rubens.' Gil. i. 259, WMR (' Epig.' III), EY ii. 320.

iii

When France got free, Europe, 'twixt fools & Knaves,
Were Savage first to France, & after—Slaves.

Reynolds, vol. i, p. ciii. Suggested by the following footnote in Malone's memoir of Reynolds prefixed to the *Discourses* :—'How justly may we apply the immediately following lines of the same great Poet to those demagogues among us, who since the era above mentioned, have not only on all occasions gratuitously pleaded the cause of the enemies of their country with the zeal of fee'd advocates, but by every other mode incessantly endeavoured to debase and assimilate this *free* and *happy* country to the model of the *ferocious* and *enslaved* Republick of France !—

> "These Adam-wits, too fortunately free,
> Began to dream they wanted liberty ;
> And when no rule, no precedent was found
> Of MEN, by laws less circumscribed and bound,
> They led their wild desires to woods and caves,
> And thought that all but SAVAGES were slaves." '

This couplet is printed only by EY ii. 323.

iv

When Sʳ Joshua Reynolds died
All Nature was degraded ;
The King drop'd a tear into the Queen's Ear,
And all his Pictures Faded.

Reynolds, vol. i, p. cix, below the account of Reynolds' death. Only in Gil. i. 259 and EY ii. 323. Cf. MS. Book xlvi.
3 The . . . Ear] Gil. prints as two lines.

v

When Nations grow Old, the Arts grow Cold,
And Commerce settles on every Tree;
And the Poor & the Old can live upon Gold,
For all are Born Poor, Aged Sixty-three.

Reynolds, vol. i, p. [iv], beneath Reynolds' dedicatory letter to the Members of the Royal Academy and following Blake's prose comment :—
' The Rich Men of England form themselves into a society to Sell & Not to

Buy Pictures. The Artist who does not throw his Contempt on such Trading Exhibitions, does not know either his own Interest or his Duty.' Gil. i. 258, 259, WMR ('Epig. xix'), EY ii. 324.

1 When . . . Cold] Gil. and WMR print as two lines.   3 And . . . Gold] Gil. and WMR print as two lines.   4 Aged Sixty-three] Gil. and WMR print as a separate line, in italics.   See Introduction.

vi

On the Venetian Painter

He makes the Lame to walk, we all agree,
But then he Strives to blind all who can see.

Reynolds, vol. i, p. 98.   Suggested by the following passage in the fourth *Discourse* :—' By this it appears that the principal attention of the Venetian painters, in the opinion of Michael Angelo, seemed to be engrossed by the study of colours, to the neglect of the *ideal beauty of form*, or propriety of expression.   But if general censure was given to that school from the sight of a picture of Titian, how much more heavily and more justly would the censure fall on Paolo Veronese, and more especially on Tintoret?' Blake prefaces his couplet by the note :—' Venetian attention is to a Contempt & Neglect of Form Itself, & to the Destruction of all Form or Outline, Purposely & Intentionally.   As if Mich. Ang. had seen but One Picture of Titian !   Mich. Ang. knew & despised all that Titian could do.'
Gil. i. 264, WMR ('Epig.' iv), EY ii.

vii

A pair of Stays to mend the Shape
Of crooked Humpy Woman,
Put on, O Venus; now thou art
Quite a Venetian Roman.

Reynolds, vol. i, p. 99.   Following Blake's prose note :—' If the Venetian's Outline was Right, his Shadows would destroy it & deform its appearance.'
Printed only by EY ii. 333.

viii

Venetian! all thy Colouring is no more
Than Boulster'd Plasters on a Crooked Whore.

Reynolds, vol. i, p. 100. Suggested by the following passage in the fourth *Discourse* :—' For my own part, when I speak of the Venetian painters, I wish to be understood to mean Paolo Veronese and Tintoret, to the exclusion of Titian ; for though his style is not so pure as that of many other of the Italian school, yet there is a sort of senatorial dignity about him, which, however awkward in his imitators, seems to become him exceedingly.' Blake's note on this is :—' Titian, as well as the other Venetians, so far from Senatorial Dignity appear to me to give always the Characters of Vulgar Stupidity. Why should Titian and the Venetians be Named in a Discourse on Art ? Such Idiots are not Artists '—followed by the present couplet.
Printed only by EY ii. 333.

ix

O Reader, behold the Philosopher's grave!
He was born quite a Fool, but he died quite a Knave.

Reynolds, vol. i, p. 147. Suggested by the passage in the sixth *Discourse* :—' Those who have undertaken to write on our art and have represented it as a kind of *inspiration*, as a *gift* bestowed upon peculiar favourites at their birth, seem to insure a much more favourable disposition from their readers, and have a much more captivating and liberal air, than he who attempts to examine, coldly, whether there are any means by which this art may be acquired.' This couplet follows Blake's prose note :—
' Bacon's philosophy has Destroy'd true Art & Science. The Man who says that the Genius is not Born but Taught, is a Knave.'
Printed only by EY ii. 337.

POEMS

FROM

THE 'PROPHETIC BOOKS'

1789–180–

BIBLIOGRAPHICAL PREFACE

TO

POEMS FROM THE 'PROPHETIC BOOKS'

IN the present section I group together the lyrical poems from the works commonly known as the ' Prophetic Books.' This name, first employed by Gilchrist to describe Blake's Visionary Writings, is nowhere used by the poet himself, though he refers to them as ' inspired ' or ' dictated,' and prefixes to two of the number the sub-title ' A Prophecy.'

The Prophetic Books fall under a category of their own. Either more or less than literature according to the point of view of the reader, it is impossible to subject them to any ordinary standard of criticism without ignoring the primary intention of the author. Broadly epic in character, they are in content a verbal and pictorial rendering of Blake's visions, a storehouse of his mythology, and a fervent exposition of his mystical gospel. In the earlier of these writings symbolism is wholly, or almost wholly, absent; in the later books nearly every phrase, name, and epithet must be interpreted symbolically.

The greater number of the Prophetic Books are written in a variety of forms of free verse. One book, *The Marriage of Heaven and Hell*, is almost entirely in prose ; the others are composed in different measures, varying from the semi-rhythmic Ossianic verses of *Tiriel* to the short irregular metre of *Ahania* or the pseudo-hexameters of *Jerusalem*. The latter may possibly have been suggested to Blake's ear by the passages from Klopstock's *Messiah* which Hayley read and translated to him during his stay at Felpham. In Blake's ' Address to the Public ' which serves as Introduction to the first chapter of *Jerusalem*, he furnishes, in imitation of Milton, the following account of the measure in which the poem is written :—

' We who dwell on Earth can do nothing of ourselves : every thing is conducted by Spirits, no less than Digestion or Sleep.

'When this verse was first dictated to me, I consider'd a Monotonous Cadence, like that used by Milton & Shakspeare & all writers of English Blank Verse derived from the modern bondage of Rhyming, to be a necessary and indispensible part of Verse. But I soon found that, in the mouth of a true Orator, such monotony was not only awkward, but as much a bondage as rhyme itself. I therefore have produced a variety in every line, both of cadences & number of syllables. Every word and every letter is studied and put into its fit place: the terrific numbers are reserved for the terrific parts, the mild & gentle for the mild & gentle parts, and the prosaic for inferior parts: all are necessary to each other. Poetry Fetter'd Fetters the Human Race! Nations are Destroy'd or Flourish in proportion as Their Poetry, Painting, and Music are Destroy'd or Flourish! The Primeval State of Man was Wisdom, Art, and Science!'

The greater number of the Prophetic Books were produced by the method of relief engraving which Blake first employed in the *Songs of Innocence*. The labour of this must have been very great, and probably for this reason in two works, *The Book of Los* and *Ahania*, both published in 1795, the artist appears to have resorted to the simpler process of ordinary etching. The effect, however, is less grand, and in Blake's next books, *Milton* and *Jerusalem*, he reverted to his original method. In the works engraved in relief, pictorial design plays an increasingly prominent part, ceasing to be mere illustration as in the *Songs of Innocence*, and developing into a species of secondary symbolism, complementary to and scarcely less important than the text itself.

A few of these engraved Prophetic Books are known to us by two or three examples only, while one at least would appear to have been lost or destroyed. This is the 'work called *Outhoon*,' included in a list of books by Blake, offered for sale by his widow to a Mr. Ferguson (Gil. ii. 262). No copy is known to exist.

Other of the Visionary Writings were never engraved. Two of these, *Tiriel* and *The Four Zoas*, survive in MS.; but by far the greater number were destroyed, on religious grounds, by Frederick Tatham, an 'Angel' of the Irvingite church, into whose hands they passed after the death of Mrs. Blake. A MS. attributed to Blake, forming part of the Lakelands Library of Mr. W. H. Crawford, was sold at Sotheby's in March, 1891. This MS., which was

purchased by Mr. Quaritch, was catalogued—'Blake (W.)
Angels and Devils, autograph manuscript, containing poems,
inscriptions to the 7 sections, and 34 original drawings by
this celebrated artist, neatly mounted on cartridge paper,
cf. 4to.' I am informed by Mr. Quaritch that the MS. was
proved to be not by Blake; it was put up again at Sotheby's,
and resold for a small sum.

Few of Blake's editors have endeavoured to grapple with
the difficulties of the Prophetic Books. In the absence,
indeed, of any adequate apparatus for the study of his text,
notably through the want of legible and properly indexed
reprints, and of a concordance displaying in chronological
sequence the names, words, and phrases symbolically used,
any attempt at interpretation must necessarily be of a somewhat tentative character. An initial step towards supplying
the former want has been taken by Messrs. Russell and
Maclagan, who print *Jerusalem* with a brief introduction,
and an index which, however, is too incomplete to be of any
real utility. In the exegetical field the only important
names are those of Swinburne and Messrs. Ellis and Yeats.
Swinburne's *Critical Essay* (1868) still remains the greatest
and most readable introduction to the Prophetic Books.
The latter editors, in their three-volume edition of Blake,
devote much space to their theory of his symbolic system,
and paraphrased commentaries of the different books.
The value of their work, in many ways helpful and sugges-
tive, is somewhat lessened by the omission of references to
the passages upon which their conclusions are based, and
by the introduction of private opinions not drawn from
Blake's writings.

In the following list of the Prophetic Books the term is
interpreted in its broader sense to include some of the
earlier writings in which the mythological element is not
very prominent. I append also, under the heading Dog-
matic Writings, descriptions of two small early works, both
entitled *There is no Natural Religion*, and two of the so-
called 'Sibylline Leaves.' The former consist of a series
of propositions couched in purely abstract terms, the latter
being small leaflets treating of art and classic poetry.
Strictly speaking, as my introduction and footnotes to that
poem show, 'The Keys of the Gates,' a sequel to *The Gates
of Paradise*, should also be accounted one of the Prophetic
Books.

I

EARLIER WORKS

(Characterized by little or no symbolism, but anticipatory to some extent of the Prophetic Books proper)

1. Seven-Page MS., *circa* 1777–1783.

This extremely early autograph MS. evidently belongs to the same period as 'Contemplation,' 'The Couch of Death,' and a few other of the last pieces in Blake's *Poetical Sketches*. I have therefore dated it as falling between the year 1777 (when, according to Mathew's 'Advertisement,' the last pieces in that volume were written) and 1783, the year in which the book was printed. The MS., which is incomplete, consists of four leaves of crown 8vo paper, 7½ × 5 inches, the verso of the last leaf being blank. There is no dated watermark. These leaves are now mounted upon rather larger paper, on the outer cover of which is written '7 (seven) Pages MS.: The handwriting of William Blake.' The MS. is plainly written in ink, with a few deletions, and ink and pencil corrections and additions. It contains two pieces, the first of which begins imperfectly in the middle of a poem. Both are written straightforwardly as prose, the division into metrical lines being marked in red ink by Mr. W. M. Rossetti, its former owner. There is also a red ink note of Mr. Rossetti's, indicating where two of Blake's afterthoughts should be inserted.

The First Piece begins (*imperfectly*) (p. [1]): 'then She bore Pale desire, father of Curiosity, | a Virgin ever young. And after Leaden Sloth, | from whom came Ignorance, who brought forth | wonder. These are the Gods which came from | fear—[*interpolated* for Gods like these nor male nor female are, | but Single Pregnate; or, if they list, together ming | ling bring forth mighty powers—] She knew them not; yet they all war with | Shame, and Strengthen her weak arm.'

The First Piece ends (p. [5]): 'Go! see the City— | friends Join'd Hand in Hand: Go! see the Natu | ral tie of flesh & blood: Go! see, more strong, | the ties of marriage love; thou Scarce Shalt | find but Self love Stands Between.'

The Second Piece begins (p. [6]): '"Woe," cried the muse, tears started at the Sound, Grief perch'd | upon my brow, and thought Embrac'd Her. "What does this | mean," I cried, "when all around Summer hath spred her | Plumes, and tunes her Notes? When Buxom Joy | doth fan his wings, & Golden Pleasures Beam around my | head, why, Grief, dost thou accost me?"'

The Second Piece ends (p. [6], l. 22): '"O'er yonder lake | the winds their

Sad Complainings bear for Conrade lost, | untimely lost, thy Conrade once, When living, thee I | lov'd even unto Death ; now Dead, I'll guard thee from | approaching ill. farewell, my time is gone." it Said | no more, but vanished ever from my Sight.'

On p. [7] are two passages belonging to the first piece, marked for insertion on p. [4].

The whole of the first fragment has been printed by Mr. W. M. Rossetti in the *Monthly Review* (August, 1903, vol. xii, pp. 123–129), divided into metrical lines by the editor, who entitles the poem 'The Passions.' On grounds of the character of the handwriting Mr. Rossetti ascribes this piece to a ' rather early date in [Blake's] career—say 1785, when he was twenty-eight years of age, or even before that.'

I owe the above description to the courtesy of Signora Rossetti Angeli, who has been kind enough to lend me the original MS.

2. Tiriel. *Autograph MS., circa* 1788–1789.

Neatly written, though with several deletions, corrections, and additions, in Blake's earlier hand, upon eight leaves of foolscap quarto paper 8¼ × 6½ inches. Written upon both sides of the leaf, the verso of f. 8 blank. Each section of the poem, headed by arabic numerals 1–8, begins at the top of a new page. There is no date on the watermark of the paper. In the original blue-grey paper cover bearing the inscription in Blake's autograph, ' Tiriel | M. S. by Mr. Blake.'

This MS., formerly the property of Mrs. Gilchrist, and now in the possession of Mr. B. Quaritch, was first printed by Mr. W. M. Rossetti in his ' Aldine edition ' (1874). Its correct place, he conceives, would ' have seen just before or just after *Thel*.' It is evidently just before, for an erased passage on the verso of f. 7 contains the line : ' Can wisdom be put in a silver rod, or love in a golden bowl ?' which Blake afterwards engraved as part of the ' Motto ' to *The Book of Thel*. (See footnote to that poem where the erased passage is quoted in full.) Another line on the same page, ' Why is one law given for the lion & the patient Ox ?' is obviously the source of the last line of *The Marriage of Heaven and Hell* (1790), ' One Law for the Lion & Ox is Oppression,' as well as of another line in the *Visions of the Daughters of Albion* (1793, f. 6, l. 22) : ' And is there not one law for both the lion and the ox ?'

An additional proof that *Tiriel* was written before *Thel* is found in the opening line of the latter book : ' The daughters of Mne Seraphim led round their sunny flocks.' Here, as Mr. W. B. Yeats conjectures, it seems probable that Blake at first intended to write ' The daughters of Mnetha ' (one of the personages first introduced in *Tiriel*), and afterwards altered this to ' The daughters of the Seraphim ' without erasing the meaningless ' Mne ' from the plate. Mr. Yeats' statement that ' the letters " Mne " are scratched out in the Bodleian copy ' is incorrect.

Referring to the handwriting of *Tiriel*, Mr. W. M. Rossetti says the MS. is 'neatly executed, and is evidently not the rough first draft : the hand-writing appears to me to belong to no late period in his life. This character of handwriting prevails up to near the close of the poem. With the words (in section 8) " I am Tiriel, King of the West," a new and less precise kind of handwriting begins ; clearly indicating, I think, that Blake, after an interval of some years, took up the poem and finished it, perhaps in much more summary fashion than he had at first intended.' In the opinion of the present editor, the quality of the handwriting is the same throughout, and the slight difference perceptible between that of the last page and a half and the earlier portion is merely such as may be attributed to the sharpening of a quill pen which had grown somewhat coarse. Moreover, the erased line referred to repeated in *Thel* proves that this page could not have been written later than 1789. The point is worthy of notice since it appears to have misled one at least of Blake's commentators. Referring to Mr. Rossetti's remarks on the two handwritings Mr. W. B. Yeats says : ' The style of the poem, which resembles rather that of " The Mental Traveller " than the more vehement and broken style of the later prophetic poems, makes it clear that " Tiriel " belongs to an earlier period than any other of the prophetic books. It was probably followed by " The Ghost of Abel." . . . The style of the later lines seems to the present writer to be much later than the style of the rest of the poem. It is more directly mystical, more of a direct appeal from the soul of Blake to the soul of the reader, and much more wholly dependent upon mystical knowledge for its interest. The rest of the poem has a certain interest and meaning as a story, but this latter page is as purely mystical as " Europe," or "America," or " Jerusalem." It is symbolical rather than allegorical.'

Begins (f. 1 recto, l. 1) :—

' I.

' And Aged Tiriel stood before the Gates of his beautiful palace,
[*But dark were his once piercing eyes* del.]
With Myratana, once the Queen of all the western plains ;
But now his eyes were darkenèd, & his wife fading in death :
They stood before their once delightful palace, and thus the Voice
Of aged Tiriel arose, that his sons might hear in their gates.

' " Accursèd race of Tiriel ! behold your [*agèd* del.] father ;
Come forth & look on her that bore you. Come, you accursèd sons.
In my weak [*agèd* del.] arms I here have borne your dying mother ;
Come forth, sons of the Curse, come forth, see the death of Myratana." '

Ends (f. 7 verso, l. 31 ; f. 8 recto, ll. 1–7) :—

' Such was Tiriel—
[*Hypocrisy the ideot's wisdom & the wise man's folly* del.] (f. 7 *ends*)
Compell'd to pray repugnant & to humble the immortal spirit,
Till I am subtil as a serpent in a paradise,
Consuming all, both flowers & fruits, insects & warbling birds,
And now my paradise is fall'n, & a drear sandy plain
Returns my thirsty hissings in a curse on thee, O Har,
Mistaken father of a lawless race ! my voice is past.

' He ceast, outstretch'd at Har & Heva's feet in awful death.'

Typ. Reprints : WMR, EY iii, WBY.

3. The | Book | of | Thel | The Author & Printer Willm Blake 1789.

Collation : ' Thel's Motto' 1 plate, title-page 1 plate, 'Thel' 6 plates ; 8 plates, relief engraving, about 6 × 4½ inches.

Begins (f. 3, l. 3) : ' The daughters of Mne (*sic*, read 'the') Seraphim led round their sunny flocks,

All but the youngest : she in paleness sought the secret air,

To fade away like morning beauty from her mortal day.

Down by the river of Adona her soft voice is heard,

And thus her gentle lamentation falls like morning dew.'

Ends (f. 8, ll. 16–22) : ' Why a Tongue impress'd with honey from every wind ?

Why an Ear, a whirlpool fierce to draw creations in ?

Why a Nostril wide, inhaling terror, trembling & affright ?

Why a tender curb upon the youthful burning boy ?

Why a little curtain of flesh on the bed of our desire ?

' The Virgin started from her seat, & with a shriek

Fled back unhinder'd till she came into the vales of Har.'

Facsimile Reproductions : B. M. 1876, W. Muir (coloured), EY iii.

Typ. Reprints : DGR (Gil. ii. 71–5), WMR, WBY, L. H.   *Extracts* : Gil. i. 76.

4. The | Marriage | of | Heaven | and Hell.   *Without date, but written and probably engraved in* 1790.

Collation : title-page 1 plate, ' The Argument ' 1 plate, text 25 plates ; 27 plates, relief engraving, about 6 × 4 inches. The last three plates, containing ' A Song of Liberty,' would seem to have been wanting in the copy described by Gilchrist (*Life*, i. 79–89) and may have been an addition to the book as originally conceived. This 'Song' also occurs separately.

The Argument *begins* (f. 2, l. 2) :—

' Rintrah roars, & shakes his fires in the burden'd air :

Hungry clouds swag on the deep.'

Text *begins* (f. 3) : ' As a new heaven is begun, and it is now thir | ty-three years since its advent, the Eternal Hell | revives. And lo ! Swedenborg is the Angel, sitting | at the tomb ; his writings are the linen clothes folded | up. Now is the dominion of Edom, & the return of | Adam into Paradise ; see Isaiah XXXIV & XXXV Chap. | Without Contraries is no progression. Attraction | and Repulsion, Reason and Energy, Love and | Hate, are necessary to Human existence. | From these contraries spring what the religious call | Good & Evil. Good is the passive that obeys Reason : | Evil is the active springing from Energy. | Good is Heaven. Evil is Hell.'

Text *ends* (f. 24, ll. 2–10) : ' When he had so spoken, I beheld the Angel, who | stretched out his arms, embracing the flame of fire, | & he was consumed, and arose as Elijah. | Note ! This Angel, who is now become a Devil, is | my particular friend : we often read the Bible to- | gether in its infernal or diabolical sense, which | the world shall have if they behave well. | I have also The Bible of Hell, which the world | shall have whether they will or no. [*half-page picture of Nebuchadnezzar.*] One Law for the Lion & Ox is Oppression.'

'A Song of Liberty' *begins* (f. 25, l. 2) : ' 1. The Eternal Female groan'd : it was | heard over all the Earth ' ; *ends* (f. 27, ll. 14–21) : ' Let the Priests of the Raven of dawn | no longer, in deadly black, with hoarse note, | curse the sons of joy ! Nor his accepted | brethren, whom tyrant he calls free, lay the | bound, or build the roof ! Nor pale religion's | letchery call that virginity that wishes | but acts not ! | For every thing that lives is Holy ! '

Facsimile Reproductions : W. Muir (coloured), Camden Hotten (coloured), EY iii.

Typ. Reprints : WBY, L. H. *Extracts*, Gil. i. 78–86, Swinb. 208–224.

5. The French Revolution : a Poem in Seven Books. Book the First, One Shilling. 1791.

According to Gilchrist, from whom the above title is transcribed, this work of Blake's, which, like the *Poetical Sketches* and *Descriptive Catalogue*, was printed in ordinary typography, was published anonymously, without illustrations, in quarto format, by J. Johnson. Contrary to his usual practice, Gilchrist gives no description or extracts from this book. In a letter to Mr. W. M. Rossetti, dated July 19, 1863 (*Rossetti Papers*, p. 27), Mrs. Gilchrist refers to her MS. copy of the poem, adding : 'Mr. Linnell is the only possessor I know of an original copy.' In a later letter to Mr. Rossetti, dated November 18 of the same year, Mrs. Gilchrist writes : 'I send by this post . . . *The French Revolution*, minus, I am grieved to say, the best passage in it, which must have been among the residuum your brother destroyed. I thought I had (and still believe I have, though I cannot, after a long hunt, find it) a copy of this piece about the prisoners in the Bastille, in Mr. Palmer's handwriting.' Swinburne also would appear to have seen either this transcript or the original, since in his *Essay* (p. 15) he says that this 'poem or apology for a poem, called *The French Revolution* (the first of seven projected books), is, as far as I know, the only original work of its author worth little or even nothing ; consisting mainly of mere wind and splutter. The six other books, if extant, ought nevertheless to be looked up, as they can hardly be without some personal interest or empirical value, even if no better in workmanship than this first book.' In a letter to the present editor dated June 21, 1905, Mr. W. M. Rossetti writes : 'I myself have actually seen & read B.'s *French Revolution*, Book I. This was at the time, say 1862, when I was lending some help to Mrs. Gilchrist in relation to the *Life*. . . . That *French Revolution* is an ordinary piece of typography, unillustrated, & not in the tone of the Prophetic Books. Severely realistic it of course is not, being Blake's work, but it comes much nearer than any Prophetic Book to dealing with historical facts as such. Its interest is necessarily great in a certain way, but I did not think it at all a striking or memorable performance in itself. My Brother, who also looked into it, held it in no esteem, & (if I remember right) Swinburne also read that copy about the same time, & concurred with my Brother.'

Neither original nor transcript can now be traced. The statement that Mr. Linnell is or was the possessor of an original copy is incorrect.

II

THE PROPHETIC BOOKS

6. Visions | of | the Daughters of | Albion | The Eye
sees more than the Heart knows | Printed by Willm Blake :
1793.

Collation : title-page and 'The Argument' 1 plate each, 'Visions' 8 plates,
full-page design, sometimes placed last and sometimes as frontispiece,
1 plate ; 11 plates, relief engraving, about 6¾ × 4⅝ inches.

Begins (f. 3, l. 2) :—

' Enslav'd, the Daughters of Albion weep ; a trembling lamentation
Upon their mountains ; in their valleys, sighs towards America.
For the soft soul of America, Oothoon wander'd in woe,
Along the vales of Leutha seeking flowers to comfort her ;
And thus she spoke to the bright Marygold of Leutha's vale.

  " Art thou a flower ? art thou a nymph ? I see thee now a flower,
    Now a nymph ! I dare not pluck thee from thy dewy bed ! " '

Ends (f. 10, ll. 6–13) :—

' " The sea fowl takes the wintry blast for a cov'ring to her limbs ;
  And the wild snake, the pestilence to adorn him with gems & gold ;
  And trees, & birds, & beasts, & men behold their eternal joy.
  Arise, you little glancing wings, and sing your infant joy !
  Arise, and drink your bliss ; for every thing that lives is holy."

' Thus every morning wails Oothoon ; but Theotormon sits
  Upon the margin'd ocean, conversing with shadows dire.

' The Daughters of Albion hear her woes, & echo back her sighs.'

Facsimile Reproductions : B. M. 1876, EY iii (reduced), W. Muir (coloured).
Typ. Reprint : WBY 179–187. *Extracts* : Gil. i. 105–108, Swinb. 229–234,
L. H. 179–183.

7. America | a | Prophecy | Lambeth | Printed by
William Blake in the year 1793.

Collation : frontispiece and title-page 1 plate each, 'Preludium' 2 plates,
'A Prophecy' 14 plates ; 18 plates, relief engraving, about 9¼ × 6⅝ inches.

Begins (f. 3, l. 2) :—

' The shadowy daughter of Urthona stood before red Orc,
  When fourteen suns had faintly journey'd o'er his dark abode :
  His food she brought in iron baskets, his drink in cups of iron ;
  Crown'd with a helmet & dark hair the nameless female stood,
  A quiver with its burning stores, a bow like that of night.'

Ends (f. 18, ll. 16–23) :—

'Stiff shudderings shook the heav'nly thrones. France, Spain & Italy
In terror view'd the bands of Albion, and the ancient Guardians,
Fainting upon the elements, smitten with their own plagues.
They slow advance to shut the five gates of their law-built heaven,
Filled with blasting fancies, and with mildews of despair,
With fierce disease and lust, unable to stem the fires of Orc.
But the five gates were consum'd, & their bolts and hinges melted,
And the fierce flames burnt round the heavens, & round the abodes of
        men.'

Facsimile Reproductions : B. M. 1876, W. Muir, EY iii (reduced).
Typ. Reprints (*Extracts*), Gil. i. 109–112, Swinb. 235–237.

8. Europe | a | Prophecy | Lambeth | Printed By Willm
Blake 1794.

Collation : frontispiece and title-page 1 plate each, 'Preludium' 2 plates,
'A Prophecy' 11 plates, two full-page illustrations without text 2 plates ;
17 plates, relief engraving, about 9¼ × 6⅝ inches. The arrangement of the
plates varies somewhat in different copies.

Begins (f. 3, l. 2) :—

'The nameless shadowy female rose from out the breast of Orc,
Her snaky hair brandishing on the winds of Enitharmon,
And thus her voice arose :

'"O mother Enitharmon, wilt thou bring forth other sons,
To cause my name to vanish, that my place may not be found ?
For I am faint with travel,
Like the dark cloud disburden'd in the day of dismal thunder."'

Ends (f. 17, ll. 3–11):—'The sun glow'd fiery red,
The furious terrors flew around
On golden chariots, raging with red wheels dropping with blood ;
The Lions lash their wrathful tails,
The Tygers couch upon the prey, & suck the ruddy tide,
And Enitharmon groans & cries in anguish and dismay.

'Then Los arose : his head he rear'd, in snaky thunders clad,
And, with a cry that shook all nature to the utmost pole,
Call'd all his sons to the strife of blood.'

Facsimile Reproductions : B. M. 1797, W. Muir (coloured), EY iii (reduced).
Typ. Reprints (*Extracts*) : Gil. i. 129, 130, Swinb. 242–245.

9. The | [First] Book | of | Urizen | Lambeth Printed
by Wm Blake 1794. *Colophon* : The End of the | first book
of Urizen.

Collation : title-page and 'Preludium' 1 plate each, chapters i–ix 15 plates,
ten full-page illustrations without text variously arranged in different copies
10 plates ; 27 plates, relief engraving, about 6 × 4 inches. The word 'First'

in the title-page, which was probably purposely erased from Blake's stereo-type, is wanting in most copies.

Begins (f. 2, l. 6) :—'Of the primeval Priest's assum'd power,
When Eternals spurn'd back his religion,
And gave him a place in the north,
Obscure, shadowy, void, solitary!

'Eternals, I hear your call gladly,
Dictate swift wingèd words, & fear not
To unfold your dark visions of torment.'

Ends (f. 27, col. 2, ll. 5–9) :—'8. So Fuzon call'd all together
The remaining children of Urizen,
And they left the pendulous earth :
They called it Egypt & left it.

'9. And the salt ocean rolled englob'd.'

Facsimile Reproductions : B. M. 1876, EY iii (reduced).
Typ. Reprint (*Extracts*) : Gil. i. 131.

10. The | Song of | Los | Lambeth Printed by W. Blake 1795. *Colophon* : The Song of Los is Ended | Urizen Wept.

Collation : title-page 1 plate, 'Africa' 2 plates, 'Asia' 2 plates, three full-page illustrations variously arranged in different copies ; 8 plates, relief engraving, about 9 × 6⅛ inches.

Begins (f. 2, l. 2) :—'I will sing you a song of Los, the Eternal Prophet.
He sung it to four harps, at the tables of Eternity,
In heart-formed Africa.
Urizen faded, Ariston shudder'd,
And thus the Song began.'

Ends (f. 6, ll. 35–40) :—'The Grave shrieks with delight, & shakes
Her hollow womb, & clasps the solid stem.
Her bosom swells with wild desire,
And milk, & blood, & glandous wine
In rivers rush, & shout, & dance
On mountain, dale, and plain.'

Facsimile Reproductions : B. M. 1876, EY iii (reduced), W. Muir (coloured).
Typ. Reprints (*Extracts*) : Gil. i. 132–134, Swinb. 255–257.

11. The | Book of | Los | Lambeth | Printed by W. Blake 1795. *Colophon* : The End of the | Book of Los.

Collation : frontispiece and title-page 1 plate each, 'Los' 3 plates ; 5 plates, etched text.

Begins (f. 3, col. 1, l. 2) : '1. Eno, Agèd Mother,
Who the chariot of Leutha guides
Since the day of thunders in old time,

'2. Sitting beneath the eternal Oak,
Trembled, and shook the steadfast Earth,
And thus her speech broke forth.'

Ends (f. 5, col. 2, ll. 21-26) : ‘9. Till his Brain in a rock, & his Heart
 In a fleshy slough, formed four rivers,
 Obscuring the immense Orb of fire,
 Flowing down into night; till a Form
 Was completed, a Human Illusion
 In darkness and deep clouds involv'd.’

Facsimile Reproduction : EY iii.

12. The | Book of | Ahania | Lambeth | Printed by W. Blake 1795.

Collation : frontispiece and title-page 1 plate each, ‘Ahania’ 4 plates ;
6 plates, etched text, about 5⅜ x 3⅞ inches. According to Swinburne *The
Book of Ahania* may have been originally intended as the second book
of *Urizen*.

Begins (f. 3, col. 1, l. 2) : ‘ 1. Fuzon on a chariot iron-wing'd,
 On spikèd flames rose : his hot visage
 Flam'd furious ; sparkles his hair & beard,
 Shot down his wide bosom and shoulders ;
 On clouds of smoke rages his chariot,
 And his right hand burns red in its cloud,
 Moulding into a vast globe his wrath,
 As the thunder-stone is moulded,
 Son of Urizen's silent burnings.’

Ends (f. 6, col. 2, ll. 13-21) : ‘ 14. But now alone over rocks, mountains,
 Cast out from thy lovely bosom
 Cruel jealousy, selfish fear,
 Self-destroying ; how can delight
 Renew in these chains of darkness,
 Where bones of beasts are strown
 On the bleak and snowy mountains,
 Where bones from the birth are buried
 Before they see the light ? ’

Facsimile Reproduction : EY iii.
Typ. Reprint : WBY. *Extracts* : Gil. i. 135, 136 ; Swinb. 252, 253.

13. The Four Zoas | The Torments of Love & Jealousy in | The Death and | Judgement | of Albion the | Ancient Man | by William Blake 1797.

Description : I owe to the kindness of Mr. John Linnell, Jun., the following admirably clear and exact account of this autograph MS.

‘The MS. consists of 70 separate leaves or sheets of paper (not 70 pp.,
as stated by Mr. Ellis), size 16¼ by 12¾ in., together with 4 small fragments.
These 70 loose sheets are made up as follows :—drawing paper, blank, with
watermark ‘J. Whatman 1794,’ 21 sheets ; working proofs of Blake's
illustrations to Young's “ *Night Thoughts* ” (published 1797), the paper same
size and date where marked, 47 sheets ; old engraving by Blake cut in two

and written upon on one side only (back) 2 sheets = 70 sheets. The 68 sheets, with 7 exceptions (where one side only is written on)—i. e. 61 sheets—have the text of the poem written upon both sides of the paper ; with regard to the 47 sheets with the engravings to *Night Thoughts* printed upon one side of each sheet, the only available space on the printed side was the blank rectangular space in the middle of each sheet, left for the text of Young's poem ; and here Blake has written.

'The title is written on one side of the first sheet of paper. In its first form, as written in ink, it read : "VALA | or | The Death and | Judgement | of the | Ancient Man | A DREAM | of Nine Nights | by William Blake 1797." This was afterwards altered in pencil to the final form given above. At the head of the second sheet, the page upon which the poem begins, is· the motto from Ephesians vi. 12, written in Greek characters, without accents, followed in bold script capitals by the heading "VALA," which is not here, as in the title-page, erased in favour of "The Four Zoas."

'The date of the MS. is specified on the title-page, " 1797," and this date was not altered by subsequent revision. There is no other evidence as to when the MS. was written except that afforded by the date of the paper, 1794 ; Mr. Ellis considers it was in progress for some years, but it cannot of course have been begun before 1794.

'The poem is written in ink throughout, afterwards some alterations and additions were made upon the text or upon the margins. According to Messrs. Ellis and Yeats' description of it, this MS. is in an unfinished condition, parts written fairly, and a large part a first draft of the poem, "many erasures" and corrections are made, "the MS. was never properly looked over by the author or finally sorted into Nights," "it is only possible to conjecture the sequence," "it was unpaged and unsorted," "the arrangement of the loose sheets occupied us during several long days." (See vol. ii, pp. 295-300.) Now besides the beginning and the ending of each Night which are marked by Blake, only the first 14 pages were numbered by himself ; consequently the position of many of the sheets as determined by Messrs. Ellis and Yeats must be in a degree conjectural. Had they marked in their printed copy where the beginning and the end of each sheet of paper of the MS. occur, critics would have been enabled to judge for themselves as to whether the arrangement or order of the sheets as printed has been correctly made or not.

' In vol. ii, p. 298, Ellis and Yeats say that Blake in the ninth Night quotes "Ephes. xiv. 10," and add "by what slip Blake gave the Epistle 14 chapters is incomprehensible." This, however, must be Mr. Ellis' own error in transcription, for Blake himself has written plainly in ink (in his usual form) " Ephesians III c. 10 v." (i.e. 3rd chap. 10th verse).

' I do not, on the grounds of fairness, hold that this "Vala" poem should be placed in the same category with those poems or "Prophecies" that Blake wrote, finished for publication, and himself printed and published. The text of *The Four Zoas* appears to be in an unsettled condition, and not put in order. I consider this work more as a private study that Blake executed for himself, wherein he registered and expressed his ideas without any restriction, and that he never once intended this MS. with its pencil illustrations for publication, nor even as a whole for any public inspection ; there are good and substantial reasons why he never did or could have done this. Therefore he kept this study in an unfinished state by h'm during his life with his other papers that were never made public, and at last made a private gift of it, just as he had left it, to my father.'

The Four Zoas exhibits in a less condensed and consequently more intelligible form the same set of ideas that characterize *Milton* and *Jerusalem*, the three books constituting a group in which one may trace the highest development of Blake's mysticism. Detached lines and lengthy passages of *The Four Zoas* were engraved by Blake as part of *Jerusalem*.

Only printed by EY (iii, *end*), in a somewhat incorrect text, with facsimiles of a few pages of the original. Following Mr. W. M. Rossetti, EY entitle the poem 'Vala,' which title, however, as Mr. Linnell's note shows, was afterwards rejected in favour of *The Four Zoas*. Short extracts are printed by WBY 196, 197.

Night the First *begins* :—

'The Song of the Aged Mother, which shook the heavens with wrath,
Hearing the march of long resounding strong heroic Verse,
Marshalled in order for the day of Intellectual Battle.
The heavens quake, the earth was moved & shudder'd, & the mountains,
With all their woods, the streams & valleys, wail'd in dismal fear.'

Night the Ninth *ends* :—

'Urthona is arisen in his strength ; no longer now
Divided from Enitharmon, no longer the Spectre Los.
Where is the Spectre of Prophecy ? where the delusive Phantom ?
Departed ! & Urthona rises from the ruinous walls,
In all his ancient strength, to form the golden armour of science
For intellectual War, The war of swords departed now,
The Dark Religions are departed, & sweet Science reigns.'

14. Mil|ton a Poem | in 12 Books | The Author | & Printer W. Blake | 1804 | To Justify the Ways of God to Men.

Collation : title-page and 'Preface' 1 plate each, 'Book the First' 26 plates, ff. 3–28 (ff. 8, 13, 15 and 21 being full-page illustrations), 'Book the Second' 17 plates, ff. 29–45 (ff. 29, 33, 38, 41 and 45 being full-page illustrations) ; 45 plates, relief engraving, about 6¼ × 4¼ inches. The Beckford copy from the Hamilton Palace Library, now in the Lenox Library, New York, lacks the Preface and has five additional plates of text numbered 3, 5, 8*, 17, 32*. The order of the plates in this copy differs somewhat from that of the example in the Print Room of the British Museum, which is also identical in arrangement with the copy described in the catalogue of the Blake Exhibition held at the Grolier Club of New York in 1905. In quoting from *Milton* in my footnotes the folio references are to the Print Room copy.

The date on the title-page probably represents the year in which the engraving of the First Book was begun or finished, rather than that which saw the completion of the entire work.

Book the First *begins* (f. 3, l. 3) :—

' Daughters of Beulah, Muses who inspire the Poet's Song,
  Record the journey of immortal Milton thro' your Realms
  Of terror, & mild moony lustre, in soft sexual delusions
  Of varied beauty, to delight the wanderer and repose
  His burning thirst & freezing hunger ! Come into my hand,
  By your mild power descending down the Nerves of my right arm,
  From out the Portals of my Brain, where by your ministry
  The Eternal Great Humanity Divine planted his Paradise,
  And in it caus'd the Spectres of the Dead to take sweet form
  In likeness of himself. Tell also of the False Tongue, vegetated
  Beneath your land of shadows, of its sacrifices and
  Its offerings, even till Jesus, the image of the Invisible God,
  Became its prey, a curse, an offering and an atonement
  For Death Eternal, in the heavens of Albion, & before the Gates
  Of Jerusalem, his Emanation, in the heavens beneath Beulah.'

Book the Second *ends* (f. 44, ll. 36–39 ; f. 45, l. 1) :—

' Rintrah & Palamabron view the Human Harvest ; beneath
  Their Wine-presses & Barns stand open ; the Ovens are prepar'd,
  The Waggons ready ; terrific Lions & Tygers sport & play ;
  All Animals upon the Earth are prepar'd, in all their strength,
  To go forth to the Great Harvest & Vintage of the Nations.'

Facsimile Reproductions : W. Muir (coloured), EY iii.
  Typ. Reprints (*Extracts*) : Gil. i. 195–198, Swinb. 259–274, WBY 207–209,
L. H. 184–195.

15. Jerusalem | The | Emanation of | The Giant |
Albion | 1804 | Printed by W. Blake Sᵗʰ Molton St.
Colophon: The End of The Song | of Jerusalem.

Collation : frontispiece, title-page, 'To the Public' 1 plate each (ff. 1–3) ;
' Chap. 1 ' 22 plates (ff. 4–25), frontispiece to Chap. 2 (f. 26), 'To the Jews '
(f. 27) ; 'Chap. 2' 23 plates (ff. 28–50), frontispiece to Chap. 3 (f. 51), ' To the
Deists ' (f. 52); 'Chap. 3' 23 plates (ff. 53–75), frontispiece to Chap. 4 (f. 76),
' To the Christians ' (f. 77) ; 'Chap. 4' 22 plates (ff. 78–99), full-page end-
piece (f. 100) ; 100 plates, relief engraving, about 9 × 6½ inches. For introductions to chapters 1–4, see ' Poems from *Jerusalem*.'

The engraving of *Jerusalem* was apparently begun about the same time as
that of *Milton*, the former and longer work being probably the last to be
completed. As in the case of *Milton* the date on the title-page, 1804, must
be understood to represent the year in which the first chapter was begun
or finished, and not that of the completion of the whole work.

'Chap. 1 ' *begins* (f. 4, l. 4) :—

' Of the Sleep of Ulro ! and of the passage through
  Eternal Death ! and of the awaking to Eternal Life !

'This theme calls me in sleep, night after night, & ev'ry morn
Awakes me at sun-rise : then I see the Saviour over me,
Spreading his beams of Love, & dictating the words of this mild song.

' "Awake ! awake ! O sleeper of the land of shadows, wake ! expand !
I am in you, and you in me, mutual in love divine :
Fibres of love from man to man thro' Albion's pleasant land." '

' Chap. 4 ' *ends* (f. 98, ll. 54-56 ; f. 99, ll. 1-5) :—

' Such is the Cry from all the Earth, from the Living Creatures of the Earth,
And from the great City of Golgonooza in the Shadowy Generation,
And from the Thirty-two Nations of the Earth among the Living
    Creatures.

' All Human **Forms** identified ; even Tree, Metal, Earth & Stone, all
Human Forms identified ; living, going forth, & returning wearied
Into the Planetary lives of Years, Months, Days & Hours ; reposing,
And then Awaking into his Bosom in the Life of Immortality.
And I heard the Name of their Emanations : they are named Jerusalem.'

Facsimile Reproductions : Pearson, EY iii (reduced).
Typ. Reprint : Russell and Maclagan, 1904. *Extracts* : Gil. i. 183-194,
Swinb. 276-292, WBY 198-207.

16. The Ghost of Abel | A Revelation In the Visions
of Jehovah | Seen by William Blake. *Colophon* : 1822,
W. Blake's Original Stereotype was 1788.

The reference to Blake's first stereotype probably refers to his earliest use
of this process in the *Songs of Innocence*, and not, as has been commonly
supposed, to an earlier issue of *The Ghost of Abel*.

Collation : 2 plates, relief engraving, about $4\frac{7}{8} \times 6\frac{9}{16}$ inches.
Begins (f. 1, l. 4, *after title as above*) :—

' To Lord Byron in the Wilderness.
What doest thou here, Elijah ? | Can a Poet doubt the Visions of
Jehovah ? Nature has no Outline, | but Imagination has. Nature has no
Time, but Imagination has. | Nature has no Supernatural & dissolves.
Imagination is Eternity.'

Ends (f. 2, ll. 26-31) :—

' On each side a Chorus of Angels entering Sing the following :
The Elohim of the Heathen Swore Vengeance for Sin ! Then Thou
    stood'st
Forth, O Elohim Jehovah, in the midst of the darkness of the Oath,
    All Clothèd
In thy Covenant of the Forgiveness of Sins, Death, O Holy ! Is this
    Brotherhood ?

The Elohim saw their Oath Eternal Fire ; they rolled apart trembling
over The

Mercy Seat, each in his station fixt in the Firmament, by Peace,
Brotherhood, and Love.'

Facsimile Reproductions : W. Muir (coloured), EY iii.
Typ. Reprint : Swinb. 295-297.

17. Outhoon.   ? *Relief engraving.   Date unknown.*

All that is known of this book is the entry among a number of works by
Blake offered for sale by his widow to Mr. Ferguson (Gil. ii. 262) : ' A work
called Outhoon.   12 plates, 6 inches more or less.   Price £2. 2s. 0d.'
WMR adds : ' I have never seen a copy of this, nor been able to find any one
who has.   Even Mr. Linnell has never heard of it.   But the above must be
taken, I think, as indisputable evidence that such a book does or did exist.
An ingenious friend suggested that " Outhoon" might be another title for the
Visions of the Daughters of Albion, in which one Oothoon plays a prominent
part.   But the number of plates in the two not corresponding decisively
negatives such a supposition.'

III

DOGMATIC WRITINGS

18. There | is No | Natural | Religion [a].   *Without date, but probably circa* 1790.

Collation : frontispiece, title-page, ' The Argument' 1 plate each, pro-
positions I-VI, 6 plates ; ' Therefore | God becomes as | we are, that we | may
be as he | is' 1 plate ; propositions I, II 2 plates ; 12 plates, relief engraving,
with small pictorial designs, about 2 x 1½ inches.   On the frontispiece,
in reversed writing, is the imprint ' The Author & Printer W. Blake.'

Begins (f. 3) : ' The Argument | Man has no notion of moral | fitness
but from Education. | Naturally he is only a natu|ral organ subject to
Sense.'

Ends (f. 12) : II | ' Reason or the ra-|tio of all we have | already known
is | not the same that | it shall be when | we know more.'

Facsimile Reproductions : W. Muir (coloured), EY iii.

Typ. Reprint : L. H. 175, 176.   *Extracts* : WBY 229, 230.

19. There | is No | Natural | Religion [*b*]. *Without date, but probably circa* 1790.

Collation : title-page, frontispiece ('The Voice of one crying in the Wilderness'), 'The Argument' 1 plate each, 'Principle 1st '— 'Principle 7th,' 7 plates ; 10 plates, relief engraving, with surrounding designs, about 2 x 1½ inches.

Begins (f. 3) : 'The Argument. As the true method of knowledge is experiment, the true faculty of knowing must be the faculty which experiences. This faculty I treat of.'

Ends (f. 10) : 'PRINCIPLE 7th. As all men are alike (tho' infinitely various) So all Religions, & as all similars have one source The true Man.'

Typ. Reprint : EY iii.

20. On Homer's Poetry. (On Virgil.) *Without date, but circa* 1816–1820.

Small Broadside, relief engraving, 4½ × 3⅞ inches.

'On Homer's Poetry' *begins* (l. 2) : 'Every Poem must necessarily be a perfect Unity, but why | Homer's is peculiarly so I cannot tell.'

Ends (ll. 22–24) : 'The Classics, it is, the Classics, | & not Goths nor Monks, that | Desolate Europe with Wars.'

'On Virgil' *begins* (l. 26) : 'Sacred Truth has pronounced that Greece & Rome, as | Babylon & Egypt, so far from being parents of Arts & Sci-| ences as they pretend, were destroyers of all Art.'

Ends (l. 37) : . . . 'Grecian is Mathematic Form : (ll. 38, 39 *at right*) Gothic is Living | Form. (ll. 38–40 *at left*) Mathematic Form is Eternal in | the Reasoning Memory : Living Form | is Eternal Existence.'

Facsimile Reproduction : EY iii.

Typ. Reprint : Gil. ii. 159, 160. *Extract* : L. H. 232–233.

21. [The Laocoon.] *Imprint* : Drawn & Engraved by William Blake. *Without date, but circa* 1816–1820.

Small print, line engraving, 5⅜ × 4⅔ inches.

A drawing of the Laocoon occupies the centre of the plate, while the whole of the surrounding space is filled with disconnected aphorisms on art and the conditions under which it is fostered.

At head of leaf : 'Where any view of Money exists, Art cannot be carried on but War only. Read Matthew c. x, 9, 10, v.'

At foot of leaf : 'Art Degraded, Imagination Denied, War Governed the Nations.'

Facsimile Reproduction : EY iii.

POEMS FROM THE PROPHETIC BOOKS

From

THE BOOK OF THEL

Thel's Motto

Does the Eagle know what is in the pit;
Or wilt thou go ask the Mole?
Can Wisdom be put in a silver rod,
Or Love in a golden bowl?

Thel, f. 1. DGR and WMR omit title.

3, 4. These lines occur in a passage in *Tiriel* of which all but ll. 1, 2 and 4 were deleted by Blake.

'He said, "O weak, mistaken, father of a lawless race!
Thy laws, O Har! & Tiriel's wisdom, end together in a curse.
Thy God of Love, thy heaven of joy!
Why is one law given to the lion & the [Ox *del.*] patient Ox?
Dost thou not see that men cannot be formèd all alike;
Some nostril'd wide, breathing out blood; Some close shut up
In silent deceit, poisons inhaling from the morning rose,
With daggers hid beneath their lips, & poison in their tongue;
Or eyed with little sparks of Hell, or with infernal brands
Flinging flames of discontent & plagues of dark despair;
Or those whose mouths are graves, whose teeth the gates of eternal death?
Can wisdom be put in a silver rod, or love in a golden bowl?
Is the sun a king warmèd without wool, or does he cry with a voice
Of thunder; does he look upon the sun & laugh, or stretch
His little hands unto the depths of the sea to bring forth
The deadly cunning of the scaly tribe [*word above illegible*] & spread it to the morning?"'

4 Cp. note to song from *An Island in the Moon*, iii, l. 27, and to 'The Golden Net' (Pickering MS.), l. 9.

From

THE MARRIAGE OF HEAVEN AND HELL

Prayers plow not: Praises reap not.
Joys laugh not: Sorrows weep not.

Marriage of Heaven and Hell, f. 9, two last lines. Among the 'Proverbs of Hell,' the rest being in prose. Cp. one of the preceding proverbs, 'As the plow follows words, so God rewards prayers.'

From

VISIONS OF THE DAUGHTERS OF ALBION

The Argument

I lovèd Theotormon, 1
And I was not ashamèd;
I trembled in my virgin fears,
And I hid in Leutha's vale!

I pluckèd Leutha's Flower, 5
And I rose up from the vale;
But the terrible thunders tore
My virgin mantle in twain.

Visions, f. 2, above an illustration of a nude kneeling female figure, kissing a sprite who springs upwards from the petals of a flower.

The speaker here is Oothoon, a daughter of Los, whose story—references to which occur in several of the Prophetic Books—probably formed the subject of the lost engraved work *Outhoon*. See list of Prophetic Books, no. 17.

1 See note to 'Poems from Letters,' iv, l. 33. 4 Leutha, one of the daughters of Beulah (cp. *Milton*, f. 9, l. 28), is depicted as a bird of paradise in a vale of flowers : see *Europe*, f. 12, ll. 9-14, and the Prophetic Books, *passim*.

From

THE FOUR ZOAS

i

At the first Sound the Golden Sun arises from the Deep, 1
And shakes his awful hair,
The Eccho wakes the moon to unbind her silver locks,
The golden Sun bears on my song,
And nine bright spheres of harmony rise round the fiery
king.

Four Zoas, Night ii. The song which Enitharmon 'sang O'er Los, reviving him to Life.'

3 to unbind] again to unbind EY, WBY.

The joy of woman is the Death of her most best belovèd 6
Who dies for Love of her
In torments of fierce jealousy & pangs of adoration.
The Lovers' night bears on my song
And the nine Spheres rejoice beneath my powerful
    controll.

They sing unceasing to the notes of my immortal hand. 11
The solemn silent moon
Reverberates the long harmony upon my limbs,
The birds & beasts rejoice & play,
And every one seeks for his mate to prove his inmost joy.

Furious & terrible they sport & rend the nether
    deep;   16
The deep lifts up his rugged head
And, lost in infinite hovering wings, vanishes with a cry.
The fading cry is ever dying,
The living voice is ever living in its inmost joy.

Arise, you little glancing wings & sing your infant joy, 21
Arise & drink your bliss!
For every thing that lives is holy; for the source of life
Descends to be a weeping babe;
For the Earthworm renews the moisture of the sandy plain.

Now my left hand I stretch to Earth beneath,   26
And strike the terrible string.
I wake sweet joy in dens of sorrow, & I plant a smile
In forests of affliction,
And wake the bubbling springs of life in regions of dark
    death.

6 is] in WBY.   of her most best] even of her most EY; of her most
WBY.   11 unceasing] unwearied EY, WBY; this word is not distinctly
written in the MS., and may be 'unweary.'   13 upon] sounding upon
EY, WBY.   23 For . . . holy] The same words end the chorus of the
'Song of Liberty,' *Marriage of Heaven and Hell*, f. 27.   26 stretch to]
stretch abroad, even to EY, WBY.   28 dens] dews EY, WBY.
30 regions] region WBY.

O, I am weary ! lay thine hand upon me, or I faint.   31
I faint beneath these beams of thine,
For thou hast touchèd my five senses & they answer'd thee.
Now I am nothing, & I sink
And on the bed of solemn sleep till thou awakest me.

31-35 WBY *omits.*   31 thine] thy EY.   33 five] fine EY.
35 And on] And fall on EY.   awakest me] The poem continues :—
'Thus sang this Lovely one, in Rapturous delusive trance.
Los heard reviving : he Siez'd her in his arms, delusive hopes
Kindling. She led him into Shadows & thence fled, outstretch'd
Upon the immense, like a bright rainbow, weeping, & smiling, & fading.'

ii

Ah ! how shall Urizen the King submit to this dark
  mansion ?   1
Ah ! how is this ? Once on the heights I stretch'd my
  throne sublime.
The mountains of Urizen, once of silver, where the sons
  of wisdom dwelt,
And on whose tops the Virgins sang, are rocks of
  Desolation.

My fountains, once the haunt of Swans, now breed the
  scaly tortoise,   5
The houses of my harpers are become a haunt of crows,
The gardens of wisdom are become a field of horrid graves,
And on the bones I drop my tears, & water them in vain.

Once how I walkèd from my palace in gardens of delight, 9
The sons of wisdom stood around, the harpers follow'd
  with harps,
Nine virgins cloth'd in light compos'd the song to their
  immortal voices,
And at my banquets of new wine my head was crown'd
  with joy.

Four Zoas, Night v, *end*, 'The Woes of Urizen shut up in the deep dens
of Urthona.'
3 of Urizen] EY *omit.*   9 Once . . . delight] Once how I from my
palace walked in gardens of delight, EY.   10 follow'd] came EY.
11 compos'd the song] made songs EY.   12 banquets] banquet EY.

Then in my ivory pavilions I slumber'd in the noon, 13
And walkèd in the silent night among sweet smelling
flowers,
Till on my silver bed I slept, & sweet dreams round me
hover'd;
But now my land is darken'd & my wise men are
departed.

My songs are turnèd into cries of Lamentation 17
Heard on my Mountains, & deep sighs under my palace
roofs;
Because the Steeds of Urizen, once swifter than the
light,
Were kept back from my Lord & from his chariot of
mercies.

O! did I keep the horses of the day in silver pastures? 21
O! I refused the lord of day the horses of his prince.
O! did I close my treasuries with roofs of solid stone,
And darken all my Palace walls with envyings & hate?

O Fool! to think that I could hide from his all piercing
eyes 25
The gold & silver & costly stones, his holy workmanship.
O Fool! could I forget the light that fillèd my bright
spheres
Was a reflection of his face who call'd me from the deep.

I well remember, for I heard the mild & holy voice 29
Saying, 'O Light spring up & shine,' & I sprang up
from the Deep.
He gave to me a silver scepter, & crown'd me with a
golden crown,
And said, 'Go forth & guide my Son who wanders on
the ocean.'

13 pavilions] palaces EY.   15 round me hover'd] hovered round EY.
24 darken] darkened EY.   envyings] envying EY.   25 eyes] eye EY.
30 Saying . . . Deep] Saying, Light spring up and shine, and lo, I sprang
up from the deep EY.   31 & crown'd me] crowned EY.

I went not forth : I hid myself on black clouds of my
    wrath :   33
I call'd the stars around my feet in the night of councils dark,
The stars threw down their spears & fled naked away.
We fell. I siez'd thee, dark Urthona, In my left hand falling.

I siez'd thee, beauteous Luvah; thou art faded like a flower, 37
And like a lilly is thy wife Vala, wither'd by winds.
When thou didst bear the golden cup at the immortal tables
Thy children smote their fiery wings, crown'd with the
    gold of heaven.

Thy pure feet step'd on the steps divine, too pure for
    other feet,   41
And thy fair locks shadow'd thine eyes from the divine
    effulgence,
Then thou didst keep with Strong Urthona the living
    gates of heaven;
But now thou art bow'd down with him, even to the
    gates of hell.

Because thou gavest Urizen the wine of the Almighty 45
For steeds of Light, that they might run in thy golden
    chariot of pride,
I gave to thee the Steeds. I pour'd the stolen wine,
And, drunken with the immortal draught, fell from my
    throne sublime.

I will arise, Explore these dens, & find that deep
    pulsation   49
That shakes my caverns with strong Shudders; perhaps
    this is the night
Of Prophecy, & Luvah hath burst his way from Enitharmon.
When Thought is clos'd in Caves, Then love shall shew its
    root in deepest Hell.

34 councils] council EY.   35 spears] spears of light EY.   38 is
thy wife] EY *omit* is.   by winds] by the winds EY.   41 on the steps]
on steps EY.   42 the] this EY.   46 steeds of Light] EY *omit* of
Light   thy] the EY.   47 Steeds] steeds of light EY.   50 That
. . . night] That shakes my cavern with strong shudders. This may be the
night EY.   52 When . . . Hell] When thought is closed in caverns,
love shows roots in deepest hell EY.

iii

Till thou dost [conquer] the distrest,
Thou shalt never have peace within thy breast.

Four Zoas. Written in pencil on the right-hand margin of the verso of the
third sheet of Night vi.

1 conquer] With regard to this word EY comment: 'One word,
illegible in the original, looks like nothing but an impossible term, and
causes the couplet to read as follows :—

> "Till thou dost (?) injure the distrest
> Thou shalt never have peace within thy breast."

After fruitless efforts, we reluctantly leave the deciphering of the word that
cannot be *injure* to future editors. It would have biographical interest.'
In the opinion of Mr. John Linnell, Jun., the doubtful word might be
intended for 'compose,' 'conquer,' 'inspire,' or 'improve.' From a photo-
graph of this passage, kindly supplied to me by Mr. Linnell, I read the word
as 'conquer,' but was unable to see how this could make good sense.
Since then I have come to the conclusion that this is the right reading,
connecting the couplet with a passage in *The Four Zoas.* The lines are
worthy of quotation, not only as a specimen of Blake's shrewd satire, but
as an interesting illustration of the note of Elizabethan imitation surviving in
his prophetic writings as late as 1797, or nearly twenty years after the date
of his boyish effort 'King Edward the Third.' The argument of this
passage seems to me explanatory of that of the couplet. Both are contemptuous advice, addressed to the worldly-wise man, as to the attitude to
be cultivated towards the poor and oppressed—in fact the antithesis of
Blake's own sentiment :—

> 'Can I see another's woe,
> And not be in sorrow too?'

This passage, which occurs in Night vii, runs :—

'Compell the poor to live upon a Crust of bread by soft mild arts ;
So shall we gove[r]n over all: let Moral duty tune your tongue ;
But be your hearts harder than the nether millstone.
Smile when they frown, frown when they smile; and when a man
    looks pale
With labour & abstinence say he looks healthy & happy.
And, when his children sicken, let them die ; there are enough
Born, even too many, & our Earth will be overrun
Without these arts. If you would make the poor live with temper,
With pomp give every crust of bread you give, with gracious cunning
Magnify small gifts : reduce the man to want a gift, & then give with
    pomp.
Say he smiles if you hear him sigh. If pale, say he is ruddy.
Preach temperance. Say he is overgorg'd, & drowns his wit
In strong drink ; tho' you know that bread & water are all

He can afford. Flatter his wife : pity his children ; till we can
Reduce all to our will, as spaniels are taught with art.'

For the context see Ellis and Yeats (iii. 70, 71), where, however, this passage
is printed with such extraordinary inaccuracy as to suggest that the whole
poem has been practically rewritten by Mr. Ellis.

From

MILTON

And did those feet in ancient time   1
Walk upon England's mountains green ?
And was the holy Lamb of God
On England's pleasant pastures seen ?

And did the Countenance Divine   5
Shine forth upon our clouded hills ?
And was Jerusalem builded here
Among these dark Satanic Mills ?

Milton, f. 2. These lines occur as part of the ' Preface' following the prose
passage : 'The Stolen and Perverted Writings of Homer & Ovid, of Plato
& Cicero, which all Men ought to contemn, are set up by artifice against the
Sublime of the Bible, but when the New Age is at leisure to Pronounce, all
will be set right, & those Grand Works of the more ancient & consciously
& professedly Inspired Men will hold their proper rank, & the Daughters of
Memory shall become the Daughters of Inspiration. Shakspeare & Milton
were both curb'd by the general malady & infection from the silly Greek &
Latin slaves of the Sword. Rouze up, O Young Men of the New Age ! set
your foreheads against the ignorant Hirelings. For we have Hirelings
in the Camp, the Court & the University, who would, if they could, for ever
depress Mental & prolong Corporeal War. Painters ! on you I call,
Sculptors ! Architects ! Suffer not the fash[i]onable Fools to depress your
powers by the prices they pretend to give for contemptible works, or the
expensive advertizing boasts that they make of such works : believe Christ
& his Apostles that there is a Class of Men whose whole delight is in
Destroying. We do not want either Greek or Roman Models if we are but
just & true to our own Imaginations, those Worlds of Eternity in which we
shall live for ever, in Jesus our Lord.'

    2 upon] over Swinb.   mountains] mountain Gil., WMR, WBY.
8 Mills] hills Gil. In Blake's mythological world the mills of Satan are
situated eastward of Golgonooza (or Law), on the strand of a lake 'not
of waters but of spaces, Perturbed black and deadly,' which is formed of the
'tears and sighs and death-sweat of the victims of Urizen's laws.' Beside
them is rooted the tree of Mystery. All these, in different aspects, symbolize
Blake's conception of natural religion. See *Four Zoas*, Night viii, and the
Prophetic Books, *passim*.

Bring me my Bow of burning gold!   9
Bring me my Arrows of desire!
Bring me my Spear! O clouds, unfold!
Bring me my Chariot of fire!

I will not cease from Mental Fight,   13
Nor shall my Sword sleep in my hand,
Till we have built Jerusalem
In England's green & pleasant Land.

From

JERUSALEM

i

[To the Public]

Reader . . . . . . of books . . . . . . of heaven   1
And of that God from whom . . . .

Jerusalem, f. 3, forming part of Blake's introduction to Chap. 1. This
address, which is headed 'To the Public' (flanked on either side by the
words 'Sheep' and 'Goats'), begins: 'After my three years slumber
on the banks of the Ocean, I again display my Giant forms to the Public.
My former Giants & Fairies having reciev'd the highest reward possible, the
. . . and . . . of those with whom to be connected is to be . . . I cannot doubt
that this more consolidated & extended Work will be as kindly recieved.
The Enthusiasm of the following Poem, the Author hopes . . . I also hope
the Reader will be with me, wholly One in Jesus our Lord, who is the God
. . . and Lord . . . to whom the Ancients look'd and saw his day afar off,
with trembling & amazement. The Spirit of Jesus is continual forgiveness
of Sin; he who waits to be righteous before he enters into the Saviour's
kingdom, the Divine Body, will never enter there. I am perhaps the most
sinful of men! I pretend not to holiness! yet I pretend to love, to see,
to converse with daily as man with man, & the more to have an interest in
the Friend of Sinners. Therefore . . . Reader, . . . what you do not
approve, & . . . me for this energetic exertion of my talent.'
    After this come the lines above, followed by Blake's account 'Of the
Measure in which the . . . Poem is written.' Printed only by Swinb.,
WMR, and WBY.
    1, 2 The gaps here and in the preceding prose passage are the result
of flaws in Blake's stereotype, the missing words having been chipped out
either by accident or design. It may have been Blake's intention to insert
them by hand, but I know of no copy in which this has been done. Swin-

Who in mysterious Sinai's awful cave
To Man the wondrous art of writing gave,
Again he speaks in thunder and in fire,   5
Thunder of Thought, & flames of fierce desire.
Even from the depths of Hell his voice I hear
Within the unfathom'd caverns of my Ear.
Therefore I print: nor vain my types shall be.   9
Heaven, Earth, & Hell, henceforth shall live in harmony.

burne, *Essay*, p. 284, thus supplies the lacunae, though not, in my opinion,
very happily :—
    ' Reader ! lover of books ! lover of heaven
    And of that God from whom all things are given.'
The continuity of the passage might be better preserved by some such
reading as :—
    ' Reader ! [lover] of books !—[best boon] of heaven—
    And of that God from whom [they first were given].'
          9 types] type WBY.

ii

Such visions have appear'd to me
As I my order'd race have run:
Jerusalem is named Liberty,
Among the Sons of Albion.

Jerusalem, f. 26. Engraved in capital letters, white on a black ground, on
a plate containing a full-page illustration of the figure of Jerusalem watching
Hand in flames. Cp. *Jerusalem*, f. 54, ll. 1–5 :—
' In great Eternity, every particular Form gives forth or Emanates
  Its own peculiar Light, & the form is the Divine Vision,
  And the Light is his Garment. This is Jerusalem in every Man,
  A Tent & Tabernacle of Mutual Forgiveness, Male & Female Clothings.
  And Jerusalem is called Liberty among the Children of Albion.'
        2 race] course Russell and Maclagan.

iii

[To the Jews]

The fields from Islington to Marybone,   1
To Primrose Hill and Saint John's Wood,
Were builded over with pillars of gold ;
And there Jerusalem's pillars stood.

Jerusalem, f. 27, forming part of Blake's introduction to Chap. 2. This
preface, which is headed ' To the Jews,' begins :—

Her Little-ones ran on the fields,   5
The Lamb of God among them seen,
And fair Jerusalem, his Bride,
Among the little meadows green.

Pancrass & Kentish-town repose   9
Among her golden pillars high,
Among her golden arches which
Shine upon the starry sky.

'Jerusalem, the Emanation of the Giant Albion! Can it be? Is it a Truth
that the Learned have explored? Was Britain the Primitive Seat of the
Patriarchal Religion? If it is true, my title-page is also True, that Jerusalem
was, & is, the Emanation of the Giant Albion. It is True and cannot
be controverted. Ye are united, O ye Inhabitants of Earth, in One Religion.
The Religion of Jesus, the most Ancient, the Eternal, & the Everlasting
Gospel. The Wicked will turn it to Wickedness, the Righteous to Righteousness. Amen! Huzza! Selah!

'"All things Begin & End in Albion's Ancient Druid Rocky Shore."

'Your Ancestors derived their origin from Abraham, Heber, Shem, and
Noah, who were Druids, as the Druid Temples (which are the Patriarchal
Pillars & Oak Groves) over the whole Earth witness to this day.

'You have a tradition that Man anciently contain'd in his mighty limbs all
things in Heaven & Earth, this you received from the Druids.

'"But now the Starry Heavens are fled from the mighty limbs of
    Albion."

'Albion was the Parent of the Druids, & in his Chaotic State of Sleep
Satan & Adam & the whole World was Created by the Elohim.'

After this come the lines above, followed by the paragraph :—

'If Humility is Christianity you, O Jews, are the true Christians :
If your tradition that Man contained in his Limbs all Animals is True, & they
were separated from him by cruel Sacrifices ; and when compulsory cruel
Sacrifices had brought Humanity into a Feminine Tabernacle, in the loins of
Abraham & David, the Lamb of God, the Saviour, became apparent on Earth,
as the Prophets had foretold. The Return of Israel is a Return to Mental
Sacrifice & War. Take up the Cross, O Israel, & follow Jesus.'

This poem summarizes the principal myth told in more detailed form in
Chap. 2. The geographical symbolism under which Blake typifies mental
states by London districts, divided under his fourfold system into four
quarters, is explained by a passage in the same chapter, f. 38, ll. 42, 43 :—

'I write in South Molton Street, what I both see and hear
In regions of Humanity, in London's opening streets.'

It will be unnecessary to explain to any student of Blake that 'Jews' here
as little mean the Hebrew race as 'Jerusalem' means the city so named.
The former signifies merely the dwellers in 'Jerusalem' or state of spiritual
liberty. Paraphrases of this poem may be referred to in Ellis and Yeats

The Jew's-harp-house & the Green Man,   13
The Ponds where Boys to bathe delight,
The fields of Cows by William's farm,
Shine in Jerusalem's pleasant sight.

She walks upon our meadows green;   17
The Lamb of God walks by her side;
And every English Child is seen,
Children of Jesus & his Bride.

Forgiving trespasses and sins   21
Lest Babylon, with cruel Og,
With Moral & Self-righteous Law,
Should Crucify in Satan's Synagogue.

What are those golden Builders doing   25
Near mournful ever-weeping Paddington,
Standing above that mighty Ruin,
Where Satan the first victory won: '

(ii. 196–198) and in the Introduction to the reprint of *Jerusalem* edited by
Russell and Maclagan.

  1 Marybone] Marylebone WBY.   15 William's] This name is obscurely
written in the original stereotype; Willan's Shep.; Welling's Gil., WMR,
WBY.   17 our] her Shep.   25 Cp. *Jerusalem*, f. 12, ll. 25–44 :—

'What are those golden builders doing? where was the burying-place
Of soft Ethinthus? near Tyburn's fatal Tree? is that
Mild Zion's hills, most ancient promontory, near mournful
Ever weeping Paddington? is that Calvary and Golgotha
Becoming a building of pity and compassion? Lo!
The stones are pity, and the bricks, well wrought affections:
Enamel'd with love & kindness, & the tiles engraven gold,
Labour of merciful hands: the beams & rafters are forgiveness:
The mortar & cement of the work, tears of honesty: the nails
And the screws & iron braces are well wrought blandishments,
And well contrived words, firm fixing, never forgotten,
Always comforting the remembrance; the floors, humility:
The cielings, devotion: the hearths, thanksgiving:
Prepare the furniture, O Lambeth, in thy pitying looms;
The curtains, woven tears & sighs, wrought into lovely forms
For comfort: there the secret furniture of Jerusalem's chamber
Is wrought: Lambeth! the Bride, the Lamb's Wife, loveth thee:
Thou art one with her & knowest not of self in thy supreme joy.
Go on, builders in hope: tho' Jerusalem wanders far away,
Without the gate of Los: among the dark Satanic wheels.'

See also the conclusion of prose note to vi.

Where Albion slept beneath the fatal Tree,   29
And the Druid's golden Knife
Rioted in human gore
In Offerings of Human Life?

They groan'd aloud on London Stone,   33
They groan'd aloud on Tyburn's Brook:
Albion gave his deadly groan,
And all the Atlantic Mountains shook.

Albion's Spectre from his Loins   37
Tore forth in all the pomp of War;
Satan his name; in flames of fire
He stretch'd his Druid Pillars far.

Jerusalem fell from Lambeth's Vale,   41
Down thro' Poplar & Old Bow,
Thro' Malden, & acros the Sea,
In War & howling, death & woe.

The Rhine was red with human blood;   45
The Danube roll'd a purple tide;
On the Euphrates Satan stood,
And over Asia stretch'd his pride.

He wither'd up sweet Zion's Hill   49
From every Nation of the Earth;
He wither'd up Jerusalem's Gates,
And in a dark Land gave her birth.

He wither'd up the Human Form   53
By laws of sacrifice for sin,
Till it became a Mortal Worm,
But O! translucent all within.

53 Cp. *Jerusalem*, f. 49, ll. 24–31 :—
'O Polypus of Death, O Spectre over Europe and Asia,
Withering the Human Form by Laws of Sacrifice for Sin,
By Laws of Chastity & Abhorrence I am wither'd up,
Striving to Create a Heaven in which all shall be pure & holy
In their Own Selfhoods, in Natural Selfish Chastity: to banish Pity
And dear Mutual Forgiveness: & to become One Great Satan
Inslav'd to the most powerful Selfhood: to murder the Divine Humanity
In whose sight all are as the dust, & who chargeth his Angels with folly!'

The Divine Vision still was seen,   57
Still was the Human Form Divine;
Weeping, in weak & mortal clay,
O Jesus! still the Form was thine!

And thine the Human Face; & thine   61
The Human Hands, & Feet, & Breath,
Entering thro' the Gates of Birth,
And passing thro' the Gates of Death.

And O thou Lamb of God! whom I   65
Slew in my dark self-righteous pride,
Art thou return'd to Albion's Land,
And is Jerusalem thy Bride?

Come to my arms: & never more   69
Depart; but dwell for ever here;
Create my Spirit to thy Love;
Subdue my Spectre to thy Fear.

Spectre of Albion! warlike Fiend!   73
In clouds of blood & ruin roll'd,
I here reclaim thee as my own,
My Selfhood—Satan arm'd in gold!

Is this thy soft Family-Love,   77
Thy cruel Patriarchal pride;
Planting thy Family alone,
Destroying all the World beside?

A man's worst enemies are those   81
Of his own house & family;
And he who makes his law a curse,
By his own law shall surely die.

76 Cp. *Jerusalem*, f. 33, ll. 17, 18 :—
'So spoke the Spectre to Albion; he is the Great Selfhood
Satan, Worship'd as God by the Mighty Ones of the Earth.'
79 alone] above Shep.   81 Cp. *Jerusalem*, f. 46, ll. 25-28 :—
'Alas!—The time will come, when a man's worst enemies
Shall be those of his own house and family; in a Religion
Of Generation, to destroy by Sin and Atonement happy Jerusalem,
The Bride and Wife of the Lamb. O God, thou art Not an Avenger!'
84 law] hand Russell and Maclagan.

In my Exchanges every Land   85
Shall walk ; & mine, in every Land,
Mutual shall build Jerusalem,
Both heart in heart & hand in hand.

85 Cp. *Jerusalem*, f. 24, ll. 42, 43 :—

' In the Exchanges of London every Nation walk'd,
  And London walk'd in every Nation, mutual in love & harmony.'

iv

Each Man is in his Spectre's power
Untill the arrival of that hour
When his Humanity awake,
And cast his Spectre into the Lake.

Jerusalem, f. 41, written in reversed characters on a scroll to the left of a large bowed figure.   Seated on the scroll is a sprite holding a pen in his hand.

The original draft of these lines is found on p. 12 of the MS. Book, written immediately below one of the stanzas of 'The Monk of Charlemaine' ('When Satan first the black bow bent').

1 Each Man] This world MS. Book 1*st rdg. del.*   his] the MS. Book.
3 When his] Untill MS. Book 1*st rdg. del.*   4 his] his own MS. Book ; the MS. Book 1*st rdg. del.*   At some time Blake numbered these four lines in the MS., 4, 3, 1, 2, afterwards deleted, intending the stanzas to read :—

          'When his Humanity awake,
           And cast his own Spectre into the Lake—
           Untill the arrival of that hour,
           Each Man is in his Spectre's power.'

In the margin of the MS. opposite these lines is an unfinished stanza, here printed for the first time, apparently intended as a continuation of the preceding :—

          'And there to Eternity aspire
           The selfhood in a flame of fire,
           Till then the Lamb of God——'

4 Cp. *Milton*, f. 40, ll. 10–12 :—

' Awake, Albion, awake ! reclaim thy Reasoning Spectre. Subdue
  Him to the Divine Mercy. Cast him down into the Lake
  Of Los, that ever burneth with fire, ever & ever, Amen.'

V

[To the Deists] .

I saw a Monk of Charlemaine   I
Arise before my sight:
I talk'd with the Grey Monk as we stood
In beams of infernal light.

Jerusalem, f. 52, following the conclusion of Blake's preface to Chap. 3.
On either side of the title 'To the Deists' are the bracketed sentences
'Rahab is an Eternal State,' and 'The Spiritual States of the Soul are all
Eternal. Distinguish between the Man, & his present State.' The address
runs :—
    'He never can be a Friend to the Human Race who is the Preacher of
Natural Morality, or Natural Religion ; he is a flatterer who means to betray,
to perpetuate Tyrant Pride, & the Laws of that Babylon which he foresees
shall shortly be destroyed with the Spiritual and not the Natural Sword.
He is in the State named Rahab ; which State must be put off before he can
be the Friend of Man.
    'You, O Deists! profess yourselves the Enemies of Christianity and you
are so : you are also the Enemies of the Human Race & of Universal
Nature. Man is born a Spectre or Satan, & is altogether an Evil, & requires
a New Selfhood continually & must continually be changed into his direct
Contrary. But your Greek Philosophy (which is a remnant of Druidism)
teaches that Man is Righteous in his Vegetated Spectre—an Opinion of fatal
& accursed consequence to Man, as the Ancients saw plainly by Revelation,
to the intire abrogation of Experimental Theory, and many believed what
they saw, and Prophecied of Jesus.
    'Man must & will have Some Religion : if he has not the Religion of Jesus
he will have the Religion of Satan, & will erect the Synagogue of Satan,
calling the Prince of this World "God," and destroying all who do not
worship Satan under the Name of God. Will any one say "Where are
those who worship Satan under the Name of God?" Where are they?
Listen! Every Religion that Preaches Vengeance for Sin is the Religion of
the Enemy & Avenger, and not of the Forgiver of Sin ; and their God
is Satan Named by the Divine Name. Your Religion, O Deists!—Deism
is the Worship of the God of this World, by the means of what you call
Natural Religion and Natural Philosophy, and of Natural Morality or Self-
Righteousness, the Selfish Virtues of the Natural Heart. This was the
Religion of the Pharisees who murder'd Jesus. Deism is the same, & ends
in the same.
    'Voltaire, Rousseau, Gibbon, Hume, charge the Spiritually Religious with
Hypocrisy ; but how a Monk, or a Methodist either, can be a Hypocrite
I cannot concieve. We are Men of like passions with others, & pretend not
to be holier than others ; therefore, when a Religious Man falls into Sin, he

Gibbon arose with a lash of steel, 5
And Voltaire with a wracking wheel ;
The Schools, in clouds of learning roll'd,
Arose with War in iron & gold.

'Thou lazy Monk!' they sound afar, 9
'In vain condemning glorious War ;
And, in your Cell, you shall ever dwell :
Rise, War, & bind him in his Cell !'

ought not to be call'd a Hypocrite ; this title is more properly to be given to
a Player who falls into Sin, whose profession is Virtue & Morality & the
making Men Self-Righteous. Foote in calling Whitefield Hypocrite was
himself one, for Whitefield pretended not to be holier than others but confessed his Sins before all the World. Voltaire! Rousseau! You cannot
escape my charge that you are Pharisees & Hypocrites, for you are constantly talking of the Virtues of the Human Heart, and particularly of your
own, that you may accuse others, & especially the Religious whose errors
you by this display of pretended Virtue chiefly design to expose. Rousseau
thought Men Good by Nature, he found them Evil, & found no friend.
Friendship cannot exist without Forgiveness of sins continually. The Book
written by Rousseau, call'd his Confessions, is an apology & cloke for
his sin, & not a confession.

'But you also charge the poor Monks & Religious with being the causes of
War, while you acquit & flatter the Alexanders & Caesars, the Lewis's
& Fredericks, who alone are its causes & its actors. But the Religion
of Jesus, Forgiveness of Sin, can never be the cause of a War nor of a single
Martyrdom.

'Those who Martyr others or who cause War are Deists, but never can be
Forgivers of Sin. The Glory of Christianity is To Conquer by Forgiveness.
All the Destruction therefore in Christian Europe has arisen from Deism,
which is Natural Religion.'

The original version forms part of a larger poem found in first draft
on p. 12 of the MS. Book. This Blake afterwards separated into two
distinct poems, engraving seven stanzas here as part of *Jerusalem*, and transcribing others, under the title 'The Grey Monk,' into the Pickering MS.
(see MS. Book xlii, and 'The Grey Monk' in the Pickering MS.). The first
four stanzas are practically the same as those of the version in the MS. Book ;
stanza 5, 'When Satan first the black bow bent,' is a revised version of the
original stanza 12 ; stanza 7 is also the final version of the original draft ; and
stanza 6 is a marginal addition, probably added by Blake when about to
engrave this poem. Stanzas 4 and 6 occur also as stanzas 2 and 8 of the
version in the Pickering MS. In my footnotes I give here the final readings
of the MS. Book version. For deleted readings see MS. Book xlii.

3 as we] where he MS. Book ; as he WBY.   4 In beams] In the
beams WBY.   9 sound] said MS. Book.   11 your] thy MS. Book.
you] thou MS. Book.

The blood red ran from the Grey Monk's side,   13
His hands & feet were wounded wide,
His body bent, his arms & knees
Like to the roots of ancient trees.

When Satan first the black bow bent   17
And the Moral Law from the Gospel rent,
He forg'd the Law into a Sword,
And spill'd the blood of mercy's Lord.

Titus! Constantine! Charlemaine!   21
O Voltaire! Rousseau! Gibbon! Vain
Your Grecian Mocks & Roman Sword
Against this image of his Lord;

For a Tear is an Intellectual thing;   25
And a Sigh is the Sword of an Angel King;
And the bitter groan of a Martyr's woe
Is an Arrow from the Almightie's Bow.

13 red ran] ran red WBY.   17 Cp. *Four Zoas*, Night vii (EY,
ll. 642-644):—

'Again the black bow draw:
Again the elemental strings to your right breasts draw,
And let the shadowy drum speed on the arrows black.'

These lines occur as continuation of a passage which in its reference to the
battle and the northern drum are reminiscent of the stanza 'Thy father drew
his sword in the north,' which is found both in the MS. Book and in the
Pickering MS. version.   18 And the Moral] WBY *omits* the.   24 this]
the WMR, WBY.   25 a Tear] the tear MS. Book.   27 a Martyr's]
the Martyr's MS. Book.

vi

[To the Christians]

I give you the end of a golden string,
Only wind it into a ball,
It will lead you in at Heaven's gate
Built in Jerusalem's wall.

Jerusalem, f. 77, engraved from the first draft on p. 46 (*reversed*) of
the MS. Book, the only difference in the MS. version being the first deleted

reading 'have given' for 'give' in l. 1. This stanza forms the opening lines of Blake's preface to Chap. 3, addressed 'To the Christians.' The preface, which has the two mottos in the left margin 'Devils are False Religions' and 'Saul, Saul, Why persecutest thou me?' runs :—

'We are told to abstain from fleshly desires that we may lose no time from the Work of the Lord. Every moment lost is a moment that cannot be redeemed ; every pleasure that intermingles with the duty of our station is a folly unredeemable, & is planted like the seed of a wild flower among our wheat. All the tortures of repentance are tortures of self-reproach on account of our leaving the Divine Harvest to the Enemy, the struggles of intanglement with incoherent roots. I know of no other Christianity, and of no other Gospel, than the liberty both of body & mind to exercise the Divine Arts of Imagination. Imagination, the real & eternal World, of which this Vegetable Universe is but a faint shadow, & in which we shall live in our Eternal or Imaginative Bodies when these Vegetable Mortal Bodies are no more. The Apostles knew of no other Gospel. What were all their spiritual gifts? What is the Divine Spirit? is the Holy Ghost any other than an Intellectual Fountain? What is the Harvest of the Gospel & its Labours? What is that Talent which it is a curse to hide? What are the Treasures of Heaven which we are to lay up for ourselves, are they any other than Mental Studies & Performances? What are all the Gifts of the Gospel, are they not all Mental Gifts? Is God a Spirit who must be wor-shipped in Spirit & in Truth, and are not the Gifts of the Spirit Every-thing to Man? O ye Religious, discountenance every one among you who shall pretend to despise Art & Science! I call upon you in the Name of Jesus! What is the Life of Man but Art & Science? is it Meat & Drink? is not the Body more than Raiment? What is Mortality but the things relating to the Body, which Dies? What is Immortality but the things relating to the Spirit, which Lives Eternally? What is the Joy of Heaven but Improvement in the things of the Spirit? What are the Pains of Hell but Ignorance, Bodily Lust, Idleness, & devastation of the things of the Spirit? Answer this to yourselves, & expel from among you those who pretend to despise the labours of Art & Science, which alone are the labours of the Gospel. Is not this plain & manifest to the thought? Can you think at all & not pronounce heartily, That to Labour in Knowledge is to build up Jerusalem : and to Despise Knowledge is to Despise Jerusalem & her Builders? And remember! He who despises & mocks a Mental Gift in another, calling it pride & selfishness & sin, mocks Jesus, the giver of every Mental Gift, which always appear to the ignorance-loving Hypocrite as Sins, but that which is a Sin in the sight of cruel Man, is not so in the sight of our kind God. Let every Christian as much as in him lies engage himself openly & publicly, before all the World, in some Mental pursuit for the Building up of Jerusalem.

> ' I stood among my valleys of the south ;
> And saw a flame of fire, even as a Wheel
> Of fire surrounding all the heavens : it went
> From west to east against the current of
> Creation, and devour'd all things in its loud
> Fury, & thundering course round heaven & earth.

By it the Sun was roll'd into an orb;
By it the Moon faded into a globe
Travelling thro' the night; for, from its dire
And restless fury Man himself shrunk up
Into a little root a fathom long.
And I asked a Watcher & a Holy-One
Its Name : he answer'd, "It is the Wheel of Religion."
I wept, & said, "Is this the law of Jesus,
This terrible devouring sword turning every way?"
He answered : "Jesus died because he strove
Against the current of this Wheel; its Name
Is Caiaphas, the dark Preacher of Death,
Of sin, of sorrow, & of punishment,
Opposing Nature. It is Natural Religion.
But Jesus is the bright Preacher of Life,
Creating Nature from this fiery Law
By self-denial & forgiveness of Sin.
Go therefore, cast out devils in Christ's name,
Heal thou the sick of spiritual disease,
Pity the evil; for thou art not sent
To smite with terror & with punishments
Those that are sick, like to the Pharisees
Crucifying & encompasing sea & land
For proselytes to tyranny & wrath.
But to the Publicans & Harlots go :
Teach them True Happiness, but let no curse
Go forth out of thy mouth 'to blight their peace :
For Hell is open'd to Heaven : thine eyes beheld
The dungeons burst, & the Prisoners set free."'

vii

[To the Christians]

England! awake! awake! awake!   1
Jerusalem thy Sister calls!
Why wilt thou sleep the sleep of death,
And close her from thy ancient walls?

Jerusalem, at foot of f. 77, forming the conclusion of the address 'To the
Christians,' and immediately following the long passage quoted in the footnote to the preceding poem. Not in the MS. Book. Shepherd prints
vi and vii as a single poem with the title ' To the Christians.'

4 close] chase Swinb.

Thy hills & valleys felt her feet   5
Gently upon their bosoms move :
Thy Gates beheld sweet Zion's ways ;
Then was a time of joy and love.

And now the time returns again :   9
Our souls exult, & London's towers
Recieve the Lamb of God to dwell
In England's green & pleasant bowers.

viii

[Especially to the Female]

In Heaven the only Art of Living
Is Forgetting & Forgiving ;
But if you on Earth Forgive
You shall not find where to Live.

Jerusalem, f. 81, where this stanza is engraved in reversed characters in the left margin of a three-quarter-page illustration. Below the two couplets, also written in reversed writing, are the words ' Especially to the Female,' which seem intended as title to the lines above. Russell and Maclagan misread ' especially the Female,' and place between ll. 2 and 3.

VERSES

from

FOR THE SEXES

THE GATES OF PARADISE

Written between 1805 and 1810, and revised at some
later date

BIBLIOGRAPHICAL PREFACE

TO

THE GATES OF PARADISE

BLAKE'S *Gates of Paradise*, as first issued, was a small foolscap octavo picture-book with the title : *For Children* | [*a flying figure*] | *The* | *Gates* | *of* | *Paradise* | [*rule*] | 1793 | *Published by W. Blake—No.* 13 | *Hercules Buildings Lambeth* | *and* | *J. Johnson St. Paul's Church Yard.* The book in this form consisted of a frontispiece, title-page, and sixteen numbered plates of emblematic designs, the original pencil sketches for which are found in the Rossetti MS. The plates, which vary in size from $2\frac{5}{8} \times 1\frac{5}{8}$ to $4\frac{1}{8} \times 2\frac{5}{8}$ inches, are executed, not by the artist's usual cameo etching process, but by ordinary line engraving. At the foot of each is a short inscription or legend, with Blake's imprint as publisher, dated [Lambeth] May 17, 1793. The British Museum Print Room copy is an example of this first issue, or edition, of *The Gates of Paradise*. The Beckford copy, sold at the Hamilton Palace sale, in 1882, has the engravings in their earliest state, before the date and imprint on title and publishers' imprint on plates were added.

The book is advertised in Blake's prospectus of October 10, 1793, where it is described as ' The Gates of Paradise, a small book of Engravings. Price, 3*s*.' The preceding entry, ' The History of England, a small book of Engravings. Price, 3*s*.,' would seem to refer to a companion volume of which no copy is known to exist. It appears to me probable that the rough draft of subjects for a history of England written on the outer page of Blake's Manuscript- and Sketch-book supplies a clue to the contents of this missing work[1]. Blake may also have intended to

---

[1] This entry reads : 1. Giants ancient inhabitants of England. 2. The Landing of Brutus. 3. Corineus throws Gogmagog the Giant into the sea. 4. King Lear. 5. (*del.*) The Ancient Britons according to Caesar. *The frontispiece* (*del.*). 6. The Druids. 7. The Landing of Julius Caesar. 8. Boadicea inspiring the Britons against the Romans. The Britons' distress & depopulation. Women fleeing from War. Women in a Siege (*these three unnumbered subjects are a marginal addition*). 9. Alfred in the countryman's

engrave and issue, as the contrary to 'For Children,' *The Gates of Paradise*—a book which is known to us only from its title-page—'For Children, the Gates of Hell.' (See W. M. Rossetti's 'Annotated Lists of Blake's Paintings, Drawings, and Engravings,' Gil. i. 250.)

The Gates of Paradise also appeared with the new *undated* title-page : For the Sexes | The | Gates | of | Paradise | [*prologue of ten lines*]. This is in reality a second and considerably changed edition, printed several years later ; though Blake has left unaltered the original imprints, dated 1793, at the foot of the frontispiece and sixteen plates of emblems. The lines on the new title-page beginning 'Mutual Forgiveness of each Vice,' and some part of the legends, are additions. The three supplementary plates containing the 'Keys of the Gates' and 'To the Accuser' appear also for the first time.

Gilchrist (i. 102) regards the *Keys*, 'themselves a little obscure,' merely as versified explanations of the artist's original motives. This, however, is an error into which the poet's biographer could not have fallen had he made any serious attempt to trace the gradual evolution of Blake's symbolic system. These lines, as my footnotes to the *Keys* amply demonstrate, belong to the same period as *Milton* and *Jerusalem*, reading into what were at first simple allegorical pictures for children the later developed elaborate symbolism in which Blake clothed his full-fledged mystical gospel. Thus we find 'Water,' represented in the earlier issue by the figure of a survivor of the Deluge, interpreted 'for the sexes,' as 'Doubt self-jealous, watry folly,' while the 'dark hermaphrodite' (or humanity divided against itself)— a favourite figure in *Jerusalem*—is somewhat violently offered as the interpretation of the picture illustrating 'Fire.' The original plates have been worked over and elaborated in this second issue, the figure of 'Fire' being now represented as blind in order that it may agree with the descriptive text.

house. 10. Edwin & Morcar stirring up the Londoners to resist W. the Conq^r. 11. W. the Con^q crown'd. 12. King John & Mag. Charta. A Famine occasioned by the Popish interdict (*a marginal addition*). 13. Edward at Calais. 14. Edward the Black Prince brings his Captives to his father. 15. The Penance of Jane Shore. 17. The Reformation by H. VIII. 18. Ch. I beheaded (*subjects 17, 18 are a marginal addition, subsequently deleted*). 19 (*16, 17 del.*). The Plague. 20 (*17, 18 del.*). The fire of London. 16 (*18 del.*). The Cruelties used by Kings & Priests. 21 (*19 del.*). A prospect of Liberty. 22 (*20 del.*). A Cloud.

My authority for the text of *The Gates of Paradise* in this second form is the copy in the possession of Mr. John Linnell, junior, formerly belonging to his father, Blake's friend and patron. The twenty-one plates are printed upon separate sheets of paper measuring about $6\frac{1}{4} \times 4\frac{3}{8}$ inches. There is no dated watermark. One of the two copies from the Rowfant Library is an example of the first issue, with imprints, but without the legends to the plates, and with the second title-page and the 'Keys of the Gates' inserted from the later impression, probably by Mr. Frederick Tatham, to whom it formerly belonged. The plate 'To the Accuser who is the God of this World' is lacking.

At a still later date Blake retouched the plates and made some further alterations in the text. These last revisions occur in the prologue on the title-page, and in the change of 'I' to 'We' in the 'Keys of the Gates.' In the present edition I follow Blake's final version, taking my text from a copy in the possession of Mr. W. A. White, of Brooklyn, New York. This copy, which must have been one of the last printed, bears the dated watermark 1825. There are two other examples of this book in its final form—one a copy in the possession of Mr. James T. Linnell, and the other a duplicate from the Rowfant Library since acquired by Mr. W. A. White.

Gilchrist, misled perhaps by Blake's retention in the later issues of the original dated imprints, appears to regard the two forms of *The Gates of Paradise* 'For Children' and 'For the Sexes' as contemporaneous issues of the same work with different title-pages. He also ignores the fact (first, so far as I am aware, suggested by Mr. W. A. White in a letter to the present writer) that the 'Keys of the Gates' must have been written long after the first appearance of the little book in 1793.

A comparison of the metaphorical figures found in the 'Keys of the Gates' with those used by Blake in his earlier and later prophetic books has convinced me that the verses in the two issues 'for the sexes' could only have been written about the same time as *Jerusalem* or *Milton*. Blake, it is true, not infrequently in certain earlier writings anticipates the complex mystical formulae found in those written several years later, or repeats, after long intervals, thoughts or expressions adumbrated in his simpler poems. But in the 'Keys of the Gates' we find no such confusion of earlier and later symbolism. The whole is a harmonious composition, repeating in an extremely condensed form, often in identical words, the full evangel of *Jerusalem*.

A further clue to the date of the 'Keys' of *The Gates of Paradise* 'for the sexes' may be found in the repetition in 'The Everlasting Gospel' (γ^2, l. 96) of the line 'In doubt which is self-contradiction.' 'The Everlasting Gospel,' which was written about 1810, itself contains a considerable number of striking parallelisms with passages in *Jerusalem* which I have given in the footnotes to that poem. *Jerusalem* bears on its title-page the date 1804, but this represents the year its engraving was begun rather than finished, and its completion may well have been the work of several years. The first issue of *The Gates of Paradise* in its altered form 'for the sexes' may thus be assigned with some certainty to the last half of the decade ending 1810 [1].

Mr. W. M. Rossetti, followed by all later editors, dates the 'Keys of the Gates' 1793, with the remark that it should, strictly speaking, be placed chronologically between the *Songs of Innocence* and the *Songs of Experience*. Messrs. Ellis and Yeats stumble at the threshold of the truth in curiously stating it in its converse form : '*The Gates of Paradise* soon after "Lafayette" are of incalculable value as interpreting the Prophetic Books. Their "keys" will open the meaning of all the myth, though they will not, of course, explain its story.'

All editors follow Gilchrist's text (based apparently upon B[1]), but omit the numbers referring to the engraved plates. A facsimile by Mary Hughes and William Muir reproduces

---

[1] Ellis and Yeats (ii. 260), on the strength of a passage in Blake's *Advertisement* or 'Public Address,' which refers to the *Examiner's* attack upon him, place the first appearance of *Jerusalem* at some time later than August, 1808. This passage, which is found on p. 52 of the MS. Book, runs : 'The manner in which my character has been blasted these thirty years, both as an Artist and as a Man, may be seen particularly in a Sunday paper called the *Examiner*, published in Beaufort's Buildings ; the manner in which I have rooted out the nest of villains will be seen in a poem concerning my three years' Herculean labours at Felpham, which I shall soon publish.' This, however, can hardly refer to *Jerusalem*, though Blake's allusion to his 'three years' Herculean labours at Felpham' are reminiscent of the opening words of the 'Address to the Public' with which that poem commences. But *Jerusalem*, though part of it may be the result of his three years' labours at Felpham, is certainly not a poem *concerning* them ; and only a very esoteric school indeed could interpret it as an allegory of his quarrel with Hayley and Hunt.

the frontispiece, plates 1–6, 8–16, and the plate 'To the Accuser,' apparently from B¹ or B², with the title-page of A, 'For Children.' Plate 7, as the legend shows, also belongs to A. Prefixed in ordinary letterpress is the prologue from the title-page of B¹, and in a somewhat corrupt version 'The Keys of the Gates,' which would seem to have been wanting in the copy facsimilied.

Appended is a list of the plates of *The Gates of Paradise* with their several legends, in the first issue 'For Children' (A), and in the first and second issue 'For the Sexes' (B¹ and B²).

[i] Frontispiece. [A caterpillar on a leaf. On a second leaf a human chrysalis like a babe in swaddling-clothes.] A. What is Man! B¹ and B². What is Man! | The Sun's Light when he unfolds it | Depends on the Organ that beholds it.

[ii] [*Title-page.*] A. For Children *etc.* B¹. For the Sexes *etc.* B². For the Sexes *etc.* (with changes in text of prologue, for which see footnotes).

1. [A woman under a weeping-willow, holding a babe in her left arm, and pulling a mandrake out of the ground by its hair.] A, B¹, and B². I found him beneath a Tree.

2. [Old man, resting his hands on his knees, sits upon a rock beneath a leafless tree in a deluge of rain. The encroaching flood rises to his feet.] A. Water. B¹ and B². Water | Thou Waterest him with Tears.

3. [Crouching figure of a man emerging from a crevice in a rock.] A. Earth. B¹ and B². Earth | He struggles into Life.

4. [Man seated upon a white cloud clasps his forehead with both hands and gazes steadfastly before him. Behind him the sky studded with stars.] A. Air. B¹ and B². Air | On Cloudy Doubts and Reasoning Cares.

5. [Fiend, blind in B¹ and B², but not in A, standing in flames, armed with spear and shield.] A. Fire. B¹ and B². Fire. That end in endless Strife.

6. [Cherub issuing from an egg.] A, B¹, and B². At length for hatching ripe | he breaks the shell.

7. [Boy in garden, hat in hand, chases flying fairy. A second fairy lies face downwards crushed at his feet.] A. Alas! B¹ and B². Alas! [the original inscription written in centre of page with the addition of the words on either side and below] What are these? . . . the Female Martyr | Is She also the Divine Image?

8. [Seated old man, with sword in right hand, leans

sorrowfully on his elbow, averting his head from the figure of a joyfully departing youth.] A, B¹, and B². My son! my son!

9. [Man standing on edge of world prepares to mount ladder reared against the crescent moon. Two lovers watch him.] A, B¹, and B². I want! I want!

10. [Man drowning in sea. One arm upthrust, and head just disappearing beneath the waves.] A, B¹, and B². Help! Help!

11. [Seated under a tree, an old man with spectacles clips the wings of a boy who struggles to escape. Before him the setting sun. *See facsimile.*] A. Aged Ignorance. B¹ and B². Aged Ignorance | Perceptive Organs closed, their Objects close.

12. [Old man and four sons and daughters in dungeon cell.] A, B¹, and B². Does thy God, O Priest, take such vengeance | as this?

13. [Man, woman, and two children, beside bed on which lies a corpse, watch the ascending spirit of an old man who points upward.] A, B¹, and B². Fear and Hope are— Vision.

14. [Man with walking-stick striding along country lane.] A, B¹ and B². The Traveller hasteth in the | Evening.

15. [Old man, leaning on crutch, passes through gateway of tomb.] A, B¹, and B². Death's Door.

16. [Woman in white grave cerements, seated on the ground in burial crypt. A huge worm crawls around her feet.] A, B¹, and B². I have said to the worm ; Thou | art my mother and my sister.

[17, 18]. Keys of the Gates. *See text.*

[19]. To the Accuser who is the God of this world. *See text.*

FOR THE SEXES. THE GATES OF PARADISE

[*Prologue*]

Mutual Forgiveness of each Vice,   1
Such are the Gates of Paradise,
Against the Accuser's chief desire,
Who walk'd among the Stones of Fire.

Not in the first issue of *The Gates of Paradise*, 'for Children' (1793). Engraved, in slightly different form, on the title-page of the undated first issue of the *Gates* ' for the Sexes' (B¹), and, as above, on the later issue of the same (B²). Printed by Gilchrist (i. 102), WMR, EY (iii. 62), and WBY, the three latter with the title 'Introduction,' and by W. Muir with title ' Prologue.'

1 Cp. *Jerusalem*, f. 49, ll. 25-29 :—

' Withering the Human Form by Laws of Sacrifice for Sin,
By Laws of Chastity & Abhorrence I am wither'd up,
Striving to Create a Heaven in which all shall be pure & holy
In their Own Selfhoods, in Natural Selfish Chastity : to banish Pity
And dear Mutual Forgiveness ';
also f. 92, ll. 15-20 :—

' When all their Crimes, their Punishments, their Accusations of Sin,
All their Jealousies, Revenges, Murders, hidings of Cruelty in Deceit,
Appear only in the Outward Spheres of Visionary Space and Time,
In the Shadows of Possibility by Mutual Forgiveness for evermore,
And in the Vision & in the Prophecy, that we may Forsee & Avoid
The terrors of Creation & Redemption & Judgment.'

See also *Jerusalem*, f. 7, l. 66, and f. 43, l. 61. Here also may be added Blake's daring and beautiful perversion of the *Agnus Dei*, which forms the concluding lines of the second chapter of *Jerusalem* :—

' Come, O thou Lamb of God, and take away the remembrance of Sin.
To Sin & to hide the Sin in sweet deceit is lovely !
To Sin in the open face of day is cruel & pitiless ! But
To record the Sin for a reproach, to let the Sun go down
In a remembrance of the Sin is a Woe & a Horror,
A brooder of an Evil Day, and a Sun rising in blood !
Come then, O Lamb of God, and take away the remembrance of Sin.'

3 See note to ' Epilogue.'   4, 5 Cp. *Jerusalem* 'To the Public,' f. 3, ll. 18-27.   4 Cp. *Jerusalem*, f. 49, ll. 72-74 :—

' Learn therefore, O Sisters, to distinguish the Eternal Human
That walks about among the stones of fire in bliss & woe
Alternate.'

Jehovah's Finger Wrote The Law;   5
Then Wept; then rose in Zeal and Awe,
And the Dead Corpse, from Sinai's heat,
Buried beneath his Mercy Seat.
O Christians! Christians! tell me Why   9
You rear it on your Altars high?

5 Finger] fingers B¹ *and all edd.*   6 Then] He *all edd.*   7, 8 And
... Seat]

> 'And in the midst of Sinai's heat
> Hid it beneath His Mercy Seat.'

B¹, Gil., WMR, EY, WBY.

> 'And in the midst of Sinai's heat
> Hid it beneath the Mercy Seat.'

W. Muir.

The Keys

The Catterpiller on the Leaf   1
Reminds thee of thy Mother's Grief.

of the Gates

1. My Eternal Man set in Repose,
   The Female from his darkness rose;

Engraved upon two plates of 23 and 29 lines respectively, which are
printed to follow plate 16 in both issues of *Gates of Paradise* 'for the
Sexes.'

1, 2 Cp. 'Auguries of Innocence' (*Pickering MS.*), ll. 37, 38 :—

> 'The Caterpillar on the leaf
> Repeats to thee thy mother's grief.'

3 The 'Eternal Man,' or 'Fourfold Man' (called by the name of 'Albion'
when fallen into mortality) is Blake's term for Universal Humanity. For the
'Four states of Humanity in its Repose' see *Milton*, f. 34, l. 8, also l. 46 :—

> 'And the Eternal Man, even Albion upon the Rock of Ages.'

4 This refers to the 'division' of Man into his 'Male and Female Contrarieties,' 'Spectre' (reasoning power) and 'Emanation' (imagination)—the
chief theme of *Jerusalem.* Cp. f. 90, ll. 52, 53 :—

> 'When the Individual appropriates Universality
> He divides into Male & Female.'

And She found me beneath a Tree,   5
A Mandrake, and in her Veil hid me.
Serpent Reasonings us entice
Of Good and Evil, Virtue & Vice,
2. Doubt Self Jealous, Watry folly.   9
3. Struggling thro' Earth's Melancholy,
4. Naked in Air, in Shame and Fear,
5. Blind in Fire, with shield and spear,
Two Horrid Reasoning Cloven Fiction,   13
In Doubt, which is Self contradiction,

6 Cp. *Jerusalem*, f. 11, l. 22 :—

> 'He is like a mandrake in the earth.'

For the 'Veil' see note to l. 19.   7 'Serpent' is one of Blake's names
for Nature, this and the lines immediately following referring to his *bête noir*
' Natural Religion.' Cp. *Jerusalem*, f. 29, l. 76 :—

> 'And the vast form of Nature like a serpent play'd before them.'

Also ' The Everlasting Gospel ' (*Rossetti MS.* cxxxii), *β*, l. 53 :—

> 'The Serpent Bulk of Nature's Dross.'

8 &] *all edd. omit.* Cp. *Jerusalem*, f. 91, ll. 54, 55 :—

> ' I care not whether a Man is Good or Evil : all that I care
> Is whether he is a Wise Man or a Fool.'

For definition of ' Good and Evil ' see *Jerusalem*, f. 10, ll. 7–16.   9 Cp. the
description of the Shadow from Albion's ' wearied intellect,' *Jerusalem*,
f. 29, ll. 39, 40 :—

> 'A sweet entrancing self-delusion, a wat'ry vision of Albion,
> Soft exulting in existence ; all the Man absorbing.'

It is interesting to note (a fact hitherto, I believe, overlooked) that the whole
of the page of *Jerusalem* in which these lines are found occurs also, with
a few trifling differences such as the substitution of ' Man ' or ' Ancient Man '
for ' Albion,' in *The Four Zoas* (Night iii).   *The Four Zoas* was written or
begun about 1797, the date on the title-page, though its completion may
perhaps be some years later.   Forty-seven out of the seventy leaves of which
the manuscript is composed are proofs of Blake's illustrations to Young's
Night Thoughts, published in the same year.

11, 12 Cp. *Jerusalem*, f. 7, ll. 38, 39 :—

> 'Vala comes from the Furnace in a cloud, but wretched Luvah
> Is howling in the Furnaces, in flames among Albion's Spectres.'

13 Fiction] fictions *all edd.*   13–15 Cp. *Jerusalem*, f. 64, ll. 27-31 :—

> ' in self contradicting agony
> . . . A dark Hermaphrodite they stood.'

Cp. also ' The Everlasting Gospel,' *γ²*, ll. 95, 96 :—

> ' Reasoning on its own dark Fiction,
> In doubt, which is Self Contradiction.'

A dark Hermaphrodite We stood,—
Rational Truth, Root of Evil and Good.
Round me flew the Flaming Sword;　　　17
Round her snowy Whirlwinds roar'd,
Freezing her Veil, the Mundane Shell.
6. I rent the Veil where the Dead dwell:
When weary Man enters his Cave,　　　21
He meets his Saviour in the Grave.
Some find a Female Garment there,
And some a Male, woven with care;
Lest the Sexual Garments sweet　　　25
Should grow a devouring Winding sheet.
7. One Dies! Alas! the Living and Dead!
One is slain! and One is fled!

15 We] I B¹ *and all edd.*　　　17 Cp. *Jerusalem*, f. 77, ll. 56-62:—
　　'I wept & said : "Is this the law of Jesus,
　　This terrible devouring sword turning every way?
　　He answer'd . . .　　　It is Natural Religion.'
18 Cp. *Jerusalem*, f. 7, l. 73:—
　　'. . . indignant self-righteousness like whirlwinds of the north.'
19 Freezing] Freeing W. Muir. Cp. *Jerusalem*, f. 63, l. 44; f. 64, l. 1 :—
　　　　　　　　　　'among the Caverns
　Of the Mundane Shell, which froze on all sides';
also f. 59, ll. 2-9 :—
　'For the Veil of Vala, which Albion cast into the Atlantic Deep
　To catch the Souls of the Dead, began to Vegetate & Petrify . . .
　Thus, in process of time, it became the beautiful Mundane Shell,
　The Habitation of the Spectres of the Dead & the Place
　Of Redemption & of awaking again into Eternity.'
23, 24 Cp. *Jerusalem*, f. 54, ll. 3, 4 :—
　　　　　　　　　　'This is Jerusalem in every Man,
　A Tent & Tabernacle of Mutual Forgiveness, Male and Female
　　Clothings';
also f. 61, l. 51 :—
　'Man in the Resurrection changes his Sexual Garments at Will.'
25 Cp. *Jerusalem*, f. 90, l. 37 :—
　　'Lest the Sexual Generation swallow up Regeneration';
and *Milton*, f. 43, ll. 25-28 :—
　'These are the Sexual Garments, the Abomination of Desolation,
　Hiding the Human Lineaments, as with an Ark & Curtains
　Which Jesus rent; & now shall wholly purge away with Fire
　Till Generation is swallow'd up in Regeneration.'
27 Dead] the dead W. Muir. In the later Prophetic Books Blake uses

8. In Vain-glory hatcht and nurst,   29
   By double Spectres, Self Accurst.
   My Son! my Son! thou treatest me
   But as I have instructed thee.

9. On the shadows of the Moon,   33
   Climbing thro' Night's highest noon:

10. In Time's Ocean falling, drown'd:

11. In Aged Ignorance profound,
    Holy and cold, I clip'd the Wings   37
    Of all Sublunary Things,

12. And in depths of my Dungeons
    Closed the Father and the Sons.

13. But when once I did descry   41
    The Immortal Man that cannot Die,

14. Thro' evening shades I haste away
    To close the Labours of my Day.

15. The Door of Death I open found,   45
    And the Worm Weaving in the Ground:

16. Thou'rt my Mother, from the Womb;
    Wife, Sister, Daughter, to the Tomb:
    Weaving to Dreams the Sexual strife,   49
    And weeping over the Web of Life.

'death' as the equivalent of bodily or 'vegetative' life. Cp. *Jerusalem*, f. 90, ll. 53-55 :—

> '. . . & when the Male & Female
> Appropriate Individuality, they become an Eternal Death,
> Hermaphroditic worshippers of a God of cruelty & law.'

See also *Jerusalem, Milton*, and *The Four Zoas, passim*.   30 Spectres] speeches **W. Muir.** For references to the divided spectre ('Reasoning Power in every Man,' *Jerusalem*, f. 54, l. 7, and ' Pride & Self-righteousness,' *ibid*. f. 8, l. 30) see *Jerusalem*, f. 6, l. 3 ; f. 17, l. 1, and *passim*. 31, 32 See description of plate 8 ; also *Jerusalem*, f. 18, ll. 20, 21 :—

> 'War and deadly contention, Between
> Father and Son, and light and love.'

39 my] icy *all edd.*   42 Cp. *Jerusalem*, f. 96, l. 4-6 :—

> '. . . Albion knew that it
> Was the Lord, the Universal Humanity, & Albion saw his Form,
> A Man, & they conversed as Man with Man, in Ages of Eternity.'

43 shades] shadows W. Muir.   45 Cp. Blake's illustration to Blair's *Grave*, f. 31, ' Death's Door.'   49, 50 Cp. description, too long for quotation, of the Daughters of Los weaving the Web of Life with tears and lamentations, *Jerusalem*, f. 59, ll. 26-55.

[*Epilogue*]

To the Accuser who is The God of This World

Truly, My Satan, thou art but a Dunce,　　　　1
And dost not know the Garment from the Man ;
Every Harlot was a Virgin once,
Nor canst thou ever change Kate into Nan.

Tho' thou art Worshippèd by the Names Divine　5
Of Jesus and Jehovah, thou art still
The Son of Morn in weary Night's decline,
The lost Traveller's Dream under the Hill.

Engraved on a single plate printed as the last leaf of the issue ' for the
Sexes.'　All edd. print as a single stanza.

Title] Cp. *Jerusalem*, f. 98, ll. 48, 49 :—

　　　　　　　' where are all his Human Sacrifice
　For Sin, in War, & in the Druid Temples of the Accuser of Sin.'

In the untitled poem in the Rossetti MS. which Rossetti calls ' Mammon '
and Swinburne 'Prayer' (MS. Book, cxxx), the ' accuser of sins ' stands
for Satan or ' Mr. Devil.'　　　3 Cp. *Jerusalem*, f. 61, l. 52 :—

' Every Harlot was once a Virgin : every Criminal an Infant Love.'

5–8 Cp. Blake's ' Address to the Deists ' at the beginning of the third
chapter of *Jerusalem* (f. 52, ll. 18–25) :—

' Man must & will have Some Religion : if he has not the Religion of
Jesus, he will have the Religion of Satan, & will erect the Synagogue
of Satan, calling the Prince of this World, God ; and destroying all who do
not worship Satan under the Name of God.　Will any one say, Where are
those who worship Satan under the Name of God?　Where are they?
Listen ! Every Religion that Preaches Vengeance for Sin is the Religion of
the Enemy & Avenger : and not of the Forgiver of Sin : and their God
is Satan, Named by the Divine Name.'　See also *Jerusalem*, f. 33, l. 18 :—

' Satan, Worship'd as God by the Mighty Ones of the Earth ' ;
and *Milton*, f. 9, ll. 10–14 :—

' Where Satan, making to himself Laws from his own identity,
　Compell'd others to serve him in moral gratitude & submission,
　Being call'd God, setting himself above all that is called God ;
　And all the Spectres of the Dead, calling themselves Sons of God,
　In his Synagogues worship Satan under the Unutterable Name.'

[*From the Legends to the Plates*]

i

The Sun's Light, when he unfolds it,
Depends on the Organ that beholds it.

Not in A.   Legend to Frontispiece of *The Gates* 'for the Sexes' (B^1 and
B^2) *all edd. omit.*   Cp. *Jerusalem*, f. 98, ll. 37, 38 :—
            'such was the variation of Time & Space,
        Which vary according as the Organs of Perception vary.'
See also *ibid.*, f. 34, ll. 55, 56 :—
    'If Perceptive Organs vary : Objects of Perception seem to vary :
    If the Perceptive Organs close : their Objects seem to close also' :
note also the repetition of the latter line, slightly changed, in the addition
to the legend of plate 11 in B^1 and B^2.

ii

Thou waterest him with Tears :
He struggles into Life,
On cloudy Doubts and Reasoning Cares,
That end in endless Strife.

Not in A.   In B^1 and B^2 these four lines, which seem intended to be read
consecutively, forming a quatrain, occur as legends to plates 2, 3, 4, and 5,
respectively illustrating Water, Earth, Air and Fire.   *All edd. omit.*

INDEX OF FIRST LINES

Oxford : Printed at the Clarendon Press by Horace Hart, M.A.